This is a classic soldier's chronicle, told in unvarnished candor, about the author's experiences as a volunteer with the Walloon Legion of the German Army and later the *5th SS Volunteer Assault Brigade Wallonien* and *28th SS Volunteer Grenadier Division Wallonien*. However, it also ventures far beyond the usual soldier's story and approaches a travelogue of the Eastern Front campaign, seldom attained by the memoirs of the period.

His self-published book in French is highly regarded by Belgian historian and expert on these volunteers Eddy de Bruyne, and *Battle of Cherkassy* author Douglas Nash. This book merits attention as the *SS* volunteer equivalent of Guy Sajer's *The Forgotten Soldier*, a bestseller in the USA and in Europe. By comparison, Kaisergruber's story has the advantage of being completely verifiable by documents and serious historical narratives already published, such as Eddy de Bruyne's *For Rex and for Belgium* (Helion, 2004) and Kenneth W. Estes' *A European Anabasis* (Helion, 2015).

Until recent years, very little was known of the tens of thousands of foreign nationals from Norway, Denmark, Holland, Belgium, France and Spain who served voluntarily in the military formations of the German Army and the German *Waffen-SS*. In Kaisergruber's book, the reader discovers important issues of collaboration, the apparent contributions of the volunteers to the German war effort, their varied experiences, their motives, the attitude of the German High Command and bureaucracy, and the reaction to these in the occupied countries. The combat experiences of the Walloons echoed those of the very best volunteer units of the *Waffen-SS*, although they shared equally in the collapse of the Third Reich in May 1945.

Although unapologetic for his service, Kaisergruber makes no special claims for the German cause and writes not from any post-war apologia and dogma, but instead from his first-hand observations as a young man experiencing war for the first time, extending far beyond what had been imaginable at the time. His observations of fellow soldiers, commanders, Russian civilians and the battlefields prove poignant and telling. They remain as fresh as when he first wrote some of them down in his travel diary *Pensées fugitives et Souvenirs (1941-46)*. Fernand Kaisergruber draws upon his contemporary diaries, those of his comrades and his later work with them while secretary of their post-war veterans' league to present a thoroughly engaging epic.

Fernand Kaisergruber was born in 1923 into the family of an administrative officer in the Belgian Colonial Office. While still in school, he fell in with Leon Degrelle's Rex Party before the coming of the Second World War. Amid the turmoil of the German conquests of 1940-41, his interesting wanderings led to his returning from the factory job he had taken in Germany and enlisting in the Walloon Legion that had formed in 1941 with the German Army. He finished the war in *SS-Sturmbrigade Wallonien* as a sergeant, or *SS-Unterscharführer*, having fought as an infantryman in the Caucasus, the Battle of Korsun/Tcherkassy and the defense of the Oder River, all against the Red Army.

After the war, while working in sales and as an insurance inspector, he served as the secretary and archivist of the veterans' league of the Walloon volunteers. He has participated and given interviews in documentaries on film and television, and assisted researchers and scholars for several decades in their work. Numerous scholars have read and endorsed the French edition of his war experiences as authentic and revealing, with unique insights into the campaigning and military experiences of foreign volunteers in the German forces during the Second World War.

WE WILL NOT GO TO TUAPSE

From the Donets to the Oder with the *Légion Wallonie* and *5th SS Volunteer Assault Brigade 'Wallonien'* 1942-45

Fernand Kaisergruber

Translated by Frederick P. Steinhardt PhD
Edited by Kenneth W. Estes PhD

Helion & Company

Helion & Company Limited
26 Willow Road
Solihull
West Midlands
B91 1UE
England
Tel. 0121 705 3393
Fax 0121 711 4075
Email: info@helion.co.uk
Website: www.helion.co.uk
Twitter: @helionbooks
Visit our blog http://blog.helion.co.uk/

Published by Helion & Company 2016
Designed and typeset by Mach 3 Solutions Ltd, Bussage, Gloucestershire
Cover designed by Paul Hewitt, Battlefield Design (www.battlefield-design.co.uk)
Printed by Gutenberg Press Limited, Tarxien, Malta

ISBN 978-1-910777-24-4

British Library Cataloguing-in-Publication Data.
A catalogue record for this book is available from the British Library.

For details of other military history titles published by Helion & Company Limited contact
the above address, or visit our website: http://www.helion.co.uk

We always welcome receiving book proposals from prospective authors.

For my comrades,

To the memory of all those who have passed and who remained there,
killed in combat or captured,
of those who have been murdered,
of those whom we have since forsaken.

To the memory of my friend "Fritz"!

We will remain united and maintain our solidarity to the end.

I have used the names of those whom I was able to contact and who gave me permission, as I have done with the names of those who are well enough known, and also the names of those who are dead. For the others, out of tact, I have only used initials.

Contents

List of Illustrations

List of Maps

Author's Notes[1]

I wrote this volume of recollections in a few months in 1991 without stopping, while I was immersed in my past. Since then I reread several passages on a number of occasions in the hope of retrieving details that I no longer remembered.

Even during the first rereading I asked myself if it would be good to rewrite it – to put it in a little more 'classic' style – for I recognized a certain lack of classicism on my part in its composition. The truth is that I committed to paper all of the memories that returned to me in a flood, in the spirit and as they came to me.

After my last rereading I told myself that it would be better to change nothing because the first draft was what came to me naturally – and I think that it is better thus! I hope that the readers will agree.

Translator's Notes

I kept this author's note in mind as I translated. At first I was tempted to render his account into smooth, flowing English, with perfect syntax and grammar… but it lost too much of the freshness and vivacity. After all, a translator is rather like an actor. His job is to get inside the author, as an actor gets inside his character.

When I started the translating, I was still thinking of the work I usually do, where my job is to translate military history, usually written by military professionals, into professional military language for other military professionals to read. Before I read Fernand's note that he wanted inserted, I started doing that – and it just did not feel right! Then I read his note and realized what he was saying. I remembered that translating, as I understand it, is not just rendering equivalent words in perfect grammar and syntax, but getting inside the author's head, or rather, letting him get inside mine, so that he can use me to express his thoughts, his feelings in his words, but in another language.

So, if there are incomplete sentences, and at times it is almost stream of consciousness, that is the nature of this young man's account – and that is the captivating beauty and intensity that inspires it. The choice of words also required careful thought, for in the original French, the author does not always employ 'the usual words' and sometimes his language is fanciful, different, with a hint of the romance of youth; the author delights in plays on words. Where possible, I tried to carry that over to the English. There were, however, a few instances where that was impossible. In some cases, it would have made no sense at all, so I had to drop the wordplay in the translation.

Ranks in *La Légion Wallonien* are Belgian Army ranks – hence *Commandeur, Capitaine, Lieutenant, Adjudant* [warrant officer], *Sergent* etc. rather than German ranks such as *Kommandant, Hauptmann, Leutnant, Feldwebel, Unteroffizier* etc.

All of the footnotes are mine, except the few noted as 'Author's footnote'.

---

1 Added in May 2013.

Editor's Notes

I first met Fernand Kaisergruber in June of 1982, while researching my doctoral dissertation on the Western European Volunteers in the German Army and *Waffen-SS*. We had corresponded briefly before my trip to Europe, and without hesitation he opened his home to me on two separate occasions, and made introductions to facilitate interviews with some of the volunteers. He has, since then, assisted a host of scholars and writers and given film and video interviews on several occasions to recount his experiences – and above all to enhance the understanding of himself and his cohorts during World War II. It has been my privilege to participate in this publication of his chronicle for the first time in English.

The unique ending of World War II influenced greatly its aftermath, as well as our remembrance of many related factors. Today, with the collapse of the USSR and the end of the division of Europe between East and West on ideological, economic and military lines, the ongoing post-war history now has to be rethought. This also means that the recovery of memory can take place. Already under way in the 1960's, the younger generations have asked not only about the war, but also what happened after the war?

What was the holocaust about, what was collaboration, who participated; the same for the resistance? Then there is the question of justice, and how it has operated since liberation and war's end. These and more debates began in earnest in post-1989 Europe. 'Who did what to whom – and with whose help?' served as a valid question not only for the war, but also its aftermath – extending well into the 1950's. We now must consider matters of political justice, collective memory, the differences between resistance and collaboration, and the long-term social and political consequences of the war.

No clear lines existed between collaboration and resistance, and various shades of gray remained. Although collaboration's usage today owes from this period, some other terms become more useful in explaining the experiences of the occupied countries: co-operation, collusion, compliance and complicity (if we just stick to the 'c' range).

The punishments doled out to those found guilty also varied – from lynchings committed during the last months of the war to post-war sentences of death, imprisonment or hard labor. In addition, there were penalties of national disgrace, loss of civil rights, government employment, pensions and the imposition of travel restrictions, fines and other administrative strictures. Not only a wide array of individuals received punishment, but also groups were held collectively responsible for what had taken place. Some ethnic groups were charged with crimes and treason and largely killed or expelled in the months immediately after the German surrender. Then there are the military tribunals held post-war, where the accused had to prove their innocence instead of the court proving their guilt.

These purges and expulsions came in the aftermath of over five years of wartime mass movements and exterminations of other ethnic minorities. How the surviving societies processed the occupation and the return of their pre-war governments reflected various shocks with an acceleration of social changes wrought by the war *and* by pre-war conditions. Numerous states had experienced social upheaval before the war. Then came the war and either alliances with the major warring powers, occupation or armed neutrality. Some countries were dismembered in the process, others expanded their territories.

By using middle terms between collaboration and resistance, we can deal retroactively with the experience of war and occupation in Europe. The previous measure of post-war judicial actions we must recast as political justice. The resulting narratives of wartime stress and destruction were used post-war to justify the post-war states, as if those problems taking place before the war no longer existed. We can now see the 1989 collapse of Europe's walls – and in the aftermath, the USSR

WE WILL NOT GO TO TUAPSE

itself can only be explained if we remember pre-war, wartime and post-war periods as a continuing process; a struggle toward an end not yet defined for us in 2015.

Kenneth W. Estes

Recommended Reading for English Language Readers

de Bruyne, Eddy and Rikmenspoel, Marc, *For Rex and for Belgium, Léon Degrelle and Walloon Political & Military Collaboration 1940–45* (Solihull: Helion, 2004).

Conway, Martin, *Collaboration in Belgium, Léon Degrelle and the Rexist Movement* (New York: Yale University Press, 1993).

Estes, Kenneth W., *A European Anabasis: Western European Volunteers in the German Army and SS, 1940–1945* (Solihull: Helion, 2015).

Lukacs, John A., *The Last European War* (Garden City, NY: Anchor, 1976).

Nash, Douglas E., *Hell's Gate, The Battle of the Cherkassy Pocket, January – February 1944* (Southbury, CT: RZM Imports, 2002).

Wegner, Bernd, *The Waffen-SS: Organization, Ideology and Function* (Oxford: Basil Blackwell, 1990).

de Wever, Bruno, "Military Collaboration in Belgium" in Benz, Wolfgang; Houwink ten Cate, Johannes; and Otto, Gerhard (ed.), *Die Bürocratie der Okkupation. Strukturen der Herrschaft und Verwaltung im besetzten Europe.* Vol. 4 of *Nationsozialisische Besatzungspolitik in Europa 1939-1945* (Berlin: Metropol, 1998).

Preface

I am not writing my "memoirs". I consider that word to be pompous. After those of Chateaubriand, Beaumarchais and others, I would feel quite ridiculous! I might, more modestly, speak of "chronicles", but there too, more illustrious personages have preceded me. Rather, I shall relate my memories simply and without the least literary pretension; without embellishment – adding nothing, but concealing nothing. It is not in my nature, and it would be totally ridiculous to "lay it on" – having lived all those years through events of such dramatic or exalting intensity (sometimes both at the same time).

I believe that I lived intensely, as if each day was to be my last, and I think that it was very good to have done so. In any case, I have always been at the very limit of what seemed important to me in the end. Several times I told myself that, one day, I would recount the most interesting years of my life – in any case, the most captivating (for me) of the years one cannot forget… how could we? Of the years of which, above all, I have no regrets. How could I?

Neither the years of the war, nor the five years of imprisonment in the penal colonies and concentration camps in Belgium, have beaten me down – no more than they have broken the majority of us. God knows, however, what the conditions were at times – and the crowding of those years of the penal colonies! For me, all of that was subject to reflection and a lesson of experience, but the fruits of this lesson certainly have no resemblance to those imagined by the "authorities" of the time, judicial and otherwise, who were responsible for our convictions.

A few months of detention – a year, or possibly two – would have largely sufficed for my experience, but, too bad; it is the past – neither regrets nor bitterness! Not that (you may believe me) I have been able to accept the legitimacy of this conviction, based (and do not forget this) upon retroactive laws – thus a denial of justice, pure and simple – but, quite simply, because it has then given me the strength to overcome all the pitfalls that life spread in my path, or yet more traps that these same "authorities" set for us after our liberation, such as after having served our prison terms, preventing us from being able to find work and thereby forcing us to become criminals – and yet, I have never known of any of us being later condemned as a "common criminal". It is worth remembering that there never was such an example (or, in any case, very few), for the press would not have missed the opportunity to make much of such a case (but I shall talk of all this later).

Unconsciously, I saved all the notes that I made right after the events with the intention of, one day, telling the story. Obviously, those concerning the last months of the war were lost in the torment of those final days and when I was arrested.

Five years of imprisonment provided me with sufficient leisure to recreate these notes to a large degree, and I had, around me, a number of my comrades who were able to help me when my memory of dates or of certain locations was less than exact. Moreover, during my imprisonment in the different jails of the realm, I was able to see again most of the survivors of our common epic.

I finally made the decision to write because Roland D. asked me to relate the circumstances of the period of instruction in 1942. He then requested that I relate my memories of the other events of those years, and thus it is entirely logical that I maintained the momentum. The reader must excuse a certain lack of uniformity between this period of instruction and what ensues, but I have preferred to change nothing, or very little, in this initial part of my life in the *Légion* for fear of altering the first impression.

I must speak briefly of the last years before the war to make clear the course of my thoughts and the decisions that my reasoning led me, in all logic, to take. I was never a timid soul, and am no more so 75 years later!

As I start this narrative, I tell myself that, one day in the future, my children (perhaps other people too, a little more concerned with informing themselves than the others) may find something of interest here and will better understand the whys and the hows.

Bitterness? It is true that I have, at times, encountered it, but I have not succumbed to it – and it will never overwhelm me! It is what I decided a long time ago – back when I could only see the sky through the bars of my various jails. I have acquired this equanimity (not without difficulty) at the cost of effort, of blood, and, above all, through the will to surmount all – for at the risk of insanity, of self-destruction, there was no other choice! You must remember that we emerged from five years of war – three-and-a-half of which (and more than four years for some of our comrades who survived) were under arms and we then passed without transition from these last (and extremely trying) months at the front to the shadow of years in prisons… and we were only 20 years old! This is not an outcry, let alone a complaint. Others have suffered, I know, but the fact that we were vanquished does not, necessarily, make us wrong. It was necessary, at any price, to shut us up and to hide the truth to the end of time!

'The German breakthrough was led by the *SS-Wiking Division* and the *Brigade Motorisée Wallonie*. The Walloons fought fiercely alongside the *SS* of the *Wiking Division*, doing everything to prove themselves worthy of the uniform they wore'. This appreciation is taken from the work *L'URSS dans la seconde guerre mondiale* (*The USSR in the Second World War* – published in five volumes in French) in Volume 4 – describing the Battle of Korsun/Tcherkassy.

> It was one of the units encircled at Tcherkassy in January 1944, and in February played a major part in the successful break-out; the brigade was given the task of holding the escape corridor open, which it performed with considerable distinction, although suffering appalling casualties in the process. It is believed that the brigade was reduced from 2,000 to 632 men in this action…. The Walloon volunteers earned a very high fighting reputation during their service with the German Army and *Waffen-SS*.

This other opinion or judgment is taken from *The Waffen-SS* by Martin Windrow (Oxford, 1992).

These eulogies, which we have never sought – nor solicited, allow us to freely ignore the opinions or commentaries of a certain number of our own country's "historians". There are also honest men to be found here, but the media have an irritating tendency to avoid or ignore them!

Foreword

At least the girls were beautiful...

For F. Kaisergruber and his "comrades" I was, at that time, a terrorist. To the *La Légia* newspaper, I was a bandit. I have always been proud of that. If, in 1943 or 1944 (before December), my commander had ordered me to "knock off" Kaisergruber, I would have done it without moodiness, without hate, with no pangs of conscience, without remorse. "*Befehl*" [an order] was always "*Befehl*" on all sides. All too often that is forgotten.

My conception of life, my political or philosophical ideas (such as I took the time or trouble to have) were often the opposite of the author's.

Always resisting in my soul, I nevertheless read this book and agreed to write these lines, not out of admiration for the author, nor for his "*Bourguignons*" [Burgundians] nor for their "*Chanson de Geste*", but out of curiosity about our past history and out of respect for all that is human. The considerations, the digressions, the inopportune positions taken by F. Kaisergruber frequently irritated me. His blind and naive admiration for everything German, his suspicion, his contempt, his sarcasm toward the things and the beings that are precious to me have often tempted me to open a second front (with the pen). I regret that his memory is more alert to the mistakes of the allies than for those of the others, but I applaud his enthusiasm, his loyalty to his pledged word and to his comrades.

When, in the depths of his narrative, he sings of the heroism, the suffering and the battles of the "*Bourguignons*" of *la Légion Wallonne*, I often say, "That's fine for you, you only had to f... around in that s...." His book has aroused in me sympathy for the Russians that I had never possessed before reading this.

I have now known F. Kaisergruber for years as an upright man, honest, decent, cultivated, and I discover his attractive personality in his book as simple, honest and straightforward. He bears witness for his friends and for "the others", the (sincere) opponents of long ago to a certain mentality, a very genuine ideal, romanticism, a camaraderie that is often unknown, despised or unrecognized, but moving beyond compare.

A devoted Flamand, ever devoted to an unforgettable Belgian Resistance in Wallonia, I feel that, now that the war is over, the combatants of all sides, especially those that have truly known the fire, the hand-hand fighting, the fear and the death, those who did not await the evolution of events to enlist in one or the other camp, those that risked all, ought to get together if only to be able to hear, to understand, and to understand beyond the dissension, the quarrels, the hostilities of half a century ago. This book by F. Kaisergruber is valuable because, without embellishments, it invites the entire world to examine its conscience, because he recounts events that are inadequately known, or entirely unknown, that are too quickly forgotten or hastily hidden, because it is yet one more proof that all the flags, all the soldiers and all the ideals are worthy of the highest respect, for young men have fallen under all the flags and for all the ideals, each of them dreaming on their side of a better world and a more beautiful future. This book proves that if, to our eyes, the *légionnaires* of the East were wrong, they were not, therefore, traitors, and that, in every way, they had the courage to live and to risk their lives for their ideals.

I believe that though they were adversaries, they were not enemies. I believe that true democracy need not fear the ideas, the beliefs, the dreams, the regrets or the nostalgia of the veterans. All that belongs, like us, to history. My companions fell (and we were beaten) for liberty and freedom, wherever it comes from. Faithful to this ideal, I believe that F. Kaisergruber also has the liberty to speak and to write, that his book has the right to exist and that it is of interest as a credo that is, at times, moving, and also pertinent, insolent and impertinent, as a witness that is certainly extremely personal and subjective, but vibrant with the ideals, the loves, the combats, the adventures, the suffering, the disillusionment, the hopes and despair of our generation that were in their twenties during the forties.

I love to read that, for the "*Bourguignons*", "*les autres*" [the "others"], and, for us – the "*terroristes*" – that the girls everywhere were pretty and desirable and that, with or without uniform, "black" or "white", we have all at least approached a subject with the same eyes and the same ideas: the girls of our youth and the courage of our mothers.

As a believer, I believe that we must reconcile with our brothers before leaving for the House of our Father. The Christ did not say that we must make exceptions for the brothers of the left or of the right. "*Gott mit Uns*", is well over with. God does not allow himself to be wrapped in a uniform, even if one calls him Allah.

And, as I have already had the pleasure to say before the cameras, as a believer or not, it is time for our generation to understand that the hour of departure (not to arms, but from life) is approaching and that it is still laughable even more than it is futile to arrive on the other side with our flags and our submachine guns.

Louis De Lentdecker
Former editor of *De Standaard – Het Kieuwsblad*
Former *Président de la Presse Bruxelloise*
Member of the *Armée Secrète*
Croix de Guerre avec palmes
"for acts of courage under fire before the enemy".
Unabridged text – 5 August, 1991.

Acknowledgments and Sources

I cannot fail to thank Duncan Rogers of Helion & Company, Kenneth Estes – a long-time friend – and "Ted" Frederick Steinhardt, the translator of my book. Without all of these people, this book could not have appeared in English. I do this not for what it may bring me, but so that a large number of readers will learn the true facts of our epic! All the more because it is translated perfectly in accord with my feelings and not in poetic style.

Sources

Photos: Alexis, J. Gillet, P.K. Weber and the author.

Glossary

Chenillette   Full-track cargo carrier – probably referring here to the *RSO*, or *Raupenschlepper Ost*, a small, full-track cargo carrier originally developed by Styr – Daimler – Puch for service on the Eastern Front

List of French exclamations

Ma Foi!	(literally) My Faith! – usually translated as Well!
Mon Dieu!	My God!
Bon Dieu!	Good God!
Tiens!	Well! Really!
Voici!	Here! or Well!
Voilà!	That's it! There is… Well…

Ranks

Caporal	*Gefreiter, Obergefreiter = Rottenführer, Sturmmann* = Corporal
Sergent	*Unteroffizier = Unterscharführer* = Sergeant
	Scharführer = Unterfeldwebel = Staff Sergeant
Adjudant	*Feldwebel = Oberscharführer* = Technical Sergeant
sous – Officier	non-commissioned officer
Capitaine	*Hauptmann = Hauptsturmführer* = Captain

1

From Peace to War

My early childhood and my youth were happy and carefree, even privileged. There was nothing to excite me to go and see something different. I had no extenuating circumstances, as the military interrogators delight to say, nor have I ever claimed such! What I have laid claim to, precisely and jealously, is complete responsibility for my commitment! Even if the environment in which I lived could undoubtedly explain the course of this evolution, I would disavow that, or at least a good part of it, since even though the choices of my older brothers were similar to mine, my parents and my sister did not espouse them at all!

Ever since I was 13 or 14 my friends were mostly older than myself. I hung out with my brothers' friends and embraced the politics of one of them. I did not miss a political gathering – whether it was at the local REX in the *Rue Mercelis*, at the "*Zonneke*", on the move, in the *chaussée de Wavre* at Auderghem or at the Sports Palace. I was at Lombeek Ste. – Marie and also at Place Keym – at Watermael – to receive the defrocked *Abbé* Moreau. The *soirées*, the "weekends", were well attended.

My youthful age did not prevent me from recognizing connections between the conduct of certain authorities, notably religious. This developed according to circumstances and, more precisely, regarding the conduct of our parish priest, for whom, despite everything, I had a certain respect, at least until the day when I was able to confirm, with a certain irony, his incoherence; his duplicity.

We lived 200 to 300 meters from a worker's housing estate, a staunchly Red housing estate, where *JGS* (*Jeunes gardes socialiste*) [Socialist young guards] and *Faucons Rouges*[1] [Red Falcon youth movement] were more numerous than the "good parishioners" – that is self-evident – and the Catholic scouts, which I belonged to until the day when, very paradoxically, they decided that I had ideas that were, on the whole, not at all orthodox!

Due to proximity and the force of circumstances, I also had friends among the "Reds". How could it have been otherwise? The more so since I did not have the same prejudices as certain priests and other "adults". I did indeed say "certain", but, in all truth, a large number – and, among these "Reds", there were certainly men of good faith (honest men, as one puts it) – very good fellows. But our parish priest had an entirely different opinion. He believed that there were respectable people and that there were others who were not at all so – thus, one good day he went to find my father to tell him that "one" had seen me talking or playing with those people. No less than that!

My father, who was, nevertheless, very close to the parish priest when he was a member and even president of different congregations and other parish associations, replied very politely and also diplomatically that I was, doubtless, in the process of developing my judgment and also my perspective. When the parish priest, with such good intentions, then departed, my father nevertheless advised me to keep an eye on my relationships and to sort them out, if necessary.

---

1   The *Faucons Rouges*, or Red Falcon youth movement, was founded in 1928 and particularly served youths of the working class. It continues today.

When, a little later, the 1937 elections began – where Léon Degrelle was face to face with Van Zeeland and the right-thinking people were, little by little, separated from me – I asked myself under what influences, for I could not imagine that it was due to the advice of our parish priest. I asked myself if I had not dreamed all this, for from the first collections of election posters that I saw, and all the world could see them, this Catholic, right-thinking youth was now united as a good family ought to be with all those that I had been exhorted to shun, denying me even the right to talk to them. [Tr. Note: Liberals, Socialists and Catholics united for Van Zeeland as a coalition candidate against Degrelle.] Together they put up posters vaunting the merits and fundamental honesty of Van Zeeland. They drank the glass of friendship in the local bistros and quickly united to beat us in an apparently pre-ecumenical spirit, against which we had not the slightest ally!

If I had been as naive as our parish priest thought, I would have been quite astonished, but I was not so at all, alas. On the contrary, it caused me to reflect on the constancy and inconstancy of the … "Moral Authorities"!

During the Van Zeeland[2] scandal I remember approaching Van Zeeland along with some of my comrades as he was leaving the church in the quarter and shouting, "We want REX, the Van Zeeland scandal!" while thrusting the newspaper at him.

I also remember a long wait at the top of a tall telephone pylon of the sort that existed at that time. It was on the *boulevard du Souverain*, at the foot of *l'avenue Chaudron*, at the moment of the elections. We had stretched a big white sheet with one or another electoral slogan on it around the crown of the pylon. When we were going to descend, two policemen – holding their bicycles with their hands – passed and stopped at the foot of our high perch. We thought that they had seen us and were waiting for us. In actual fact, it was not that at all, but pure chance. They chatted away for nearly an hour. All the same, we remained stuck up there, exposed to the four winds, waiting until they left!

The *soirées* at the local Rex meeting room on the *rue des Charteux* did not lack for animation or, at times, anxious waiting when we hoped for the miracle to finance the publication of the next day's paper. The euphoria of the elections of 1936, the consternation after those of 1937, but never discouragement! I don't believe that I have ever seen such political fervor, met such fervid devotion, later, in any other party.

It was often very late when we returned in the evening, after the meetings or after we had put up the election posters, and it was rare that we returned alone. We then made chips or *crêpes* and ate in gay company until late in the night, while my parents slept upstairs, or, at least, gave the impression of so doing. The crazy *ambiance* of these meetings thus continued in a small group of friends. It is necessary to have known this fervent and dynamic atmosphere to better understand the later repercussions.

There was the war in Spain and the prayers for Franco. There was the campaign in Abyssinia. I felt more sympathy for the *"Duce"* than for the *"Caudillo"*. Thus we passed through all these political developments to arrive at the international Munich accords, the German-Soviet Pact, the *Anschluss* and the "phony war" to the actual war! My brothers were mobilized, one stationed at the Albert Canal, the other in the Hautes – Fagnes.

On the evening of 9 May, 1940, I go to bed as usual, without any apprehension other than the latent anxiety of my circle of acquaintances since the declaration of war by the "Allies" on 3 September, 1939. When I open my eyes the next day, waking from sleep, I rapidly have a feeling of something strange. It is a feeling that something unusual has awakened me. I hear what sounds

---

2   Paul Van Zeeland (1893–1973) was a Belgian lawyer, economist, Catholic politician and statesman. In March 1935, he became Prime Minister of a government of national unity or the three major parties: Catholics, Liberals and Socialists. His government resigned in the spring of 1936 in the face of Rexist agitation.

like fireworks exploding, and it is broad daylight. The sun shines on the drapes, a few rays penetrate into the room and cut through the shadow. Intrigued, I spring to my feet and tear open the drapes. The sun immediately floods my room. Little white clouds suddenly appear here and there in the sky, followed immediately by the sound of explosions. I think of anti-aircraft practice firing at aircraft, but do not see any [planes] at first. It is only a little later that I see first one, then another, then – shortly thereafter – a third, flying off, barely clearing the hedges.

The sky is marvelously blue and clear, without the least clouds other than the few little puffs from the anti-aircraft fire. I am now certain that it really is anti-aircraft fire. The temperature is exceptionally mild, despite the hour of the morning, for I feel that it is still very early. A glance at my watch tells me that it is barely six o'clock.

I am puzzled for a moment, not knowing what to think. But soon the thought of the war occurs, which, at first, I reject, but which returns and will not let go of me. It is almost a certainty! It is all taking place over the Etterbeek barracks and the parade ground. Other than that, everything is strangely calm. There is no traffic yet. It is still too early, it is true. The household now begins to stir. Certainly my father and my sister are also waking up. A moment later they are in my room and talking with me about the spectacle taking place before us. We then go downstairs and turn on the radio. The radio confirms that it is, indeed, the war! *Communiquées* alternate with a message from the king, then military march music.

Washing up is quickly taken care of. All this time the anti-aircraft fire continues and other sounds of aircraft mix in the din. Whistling and sharp cracks, much closer, shake the air and one's nerves. We go down to the cellar, dragging along the mattresses of the vacant bedrooms. We place them in front of the windows of the food cellar and the laundry, which is only half underground.

The noise becomes a bit more distant; we go into the street to see what is happening. The neighbors also come out and engage in conversation. Thick clouds of smoke immediately appear a hundred meters from here in the *avenue des Princes*, and we head that way. When we get there we find that it is the house of a certain V.T. – an insurance agent, I believe – that is burning, or the one beside it. I do not know exactly which of the two he lives in. The roof is on fire. An incendiary bomb has pierced it. Another bomb is sitting on the tracks of the streetcar line, just in the groove of a rail. It seems to me that it is a hexagonal cylinder, six or seven centimeters diameter, 35 to 40 centimeters long. It is made of two parts and has a sort of little nipple on one of the faces. One of the parts seems to me to be aluminum, the other of a different metal.

Here I meet a friend, Freddy A., the son of a neighbor. On the fringe of the group of adults, we talk about what is going on, in our fashion, and our thoughts crystallize into certainty: we will not go to school today, nor, doubtless, in ensuing days. The war is really on. Other preoccupations quickly vanish, to put it frankly, before this agreeable perspective.

While the adults worry most particularly about the incendiary as they wait for the firemen, and while some attempt to extinguish it, Freddy and I are more interested in the incendiary bomb that is on the rail, and we approach it. We conclude that if it has not caught fire, it is because it has not been armed, and we pick it up, holding it in our hands, passing it back and forth, to examine it. Curious! The little nipple moves and goes down into the body of the cylinder when it is pressed! Now that it has been pressed, I do not dare to let go of it after Freddy remarks that he thinks that the bomb will be triggered when I release it. A bit worried, I do not dare release my pressure.

Now the adults notice what we are doing and pull back, saying that we are crazy. All of a sudden our confidence returns. I ask Freddy to bring me bit of wood, which he pulls off a lilac bush in a little garden. We place it on the nipple and I tie the whole thing up tightly with a handkerchief. People call us all sorts of names and want us to put the thing back where we found it. Someone brings over a stepladder and places it on the tracks near the little bomb. Another person puts some red cloth on top of [the stepladder] to attract attention so that, he says, a streetcar will not run over it without noticing it. That makes us think of a bullfight, but already Freddy and I are looking for other games, thinking of other projects and going elsewhere. The fire is already extinguished. Only the attic is burned.

The days that follow are not lacking in excitement. I see at least two priests arrested, flanked by civilians. Already the civilians are substituting for the judicial authorities. It is decidedly a Belgian mania. It is a hint of what is to come in 1944 and 1945! The adults affirm in all seriousness that there are a number of parachutists among us! It also seems that the enameled metal signs vaunting the virtues of a chicory *"qui a bu boira"* have messages on their back directed to the fifth column! So, in derision, we follow the example of the adults, tearing down certain signs, assured that no one will dare say anything to us! And if someone were to tell us that we were rascals, we are only following the example of the adults!

Many people are running around with their noses in the air, hoping to discover a paratrooper coming down on them from the sky, preferably unarmed, no doubt! A unit of the Belgian Army arrives, I believe on 11 May, and takes position on the level ground above the quarry 200 meters from our house, rising to the street. *Lieutenant* Yvon M., the officer of this unit, stays at our house. The next morning English soldiers arrive, equipped with heavy anti-aircraft guns. One or two of the officers also stay with us. Thus I will see lots of people come to our house to bring information to these various military men, assured, no doubt, that each one of these will be able to tip them off to all the secrets of the *E.M.*[3]

Freddy and I are bewildered, and we also have a good laugh, not knowing which of these two sentiments takes precedence, for we are dumbfounded at the *naïveté* of these adults. I may be lying when I say that we are simply amused, without ever seeing the tragedy of the situation, but I think I can say without too much presumption that Freddy and I, who are barely 17, keep our *sang froid* better than many of these adults around us, whom, up till then, we more or less respected – my parents excepted, whom I secretly venerated, without ever telling them so. Perhaps, and I say it all the same, it was because of our young age, but the febricity of these people surprises us, alarms us!

We sleep a night or two in the cellar, in the shelter of the mattresses, conceding the bedrooms to the military. During those days Freddy and I make many friends among the Belgian and English soldiers, but we choose our friends among the troops, leaving the officers to my parents and the other adults. We invite them to join us for coffee, sometimes in the garden. During the night more than during the day, the anti-aircraft near the house keep us in suspense, interrupting our sleep.

On 13 May, the one of my two brothers who is in the *1st Lancers* arrived, totally unexpected and to our great joy, coming from the *Hautes – Fagnes*.[4] He and a comrade arrive in a "Marmon",[5] a sort of armored reconnaissance vehicle with rubber tires. Their unit is to reform at Meise, where they report immediately, returning in the evening to stay at the house.

Up till then I had a little admiration for Hitler as the result of certain writings vaunting his social and political achievements and, indirectly, as a result of my sympathy with Fascist Italy and Franco Spain. At the moment, for sure, my convictions were shaken, like those of others. Furthermore, the environment and the wild democratic propaganda bored us. For the sake of the cause they called on all the *image d'Épinal*,[6] all the bedtime stories that the naive and children

---

3   *État Major*, General Staff.
4   *Les Hautes – Fagnes* is an upland area consisting mainly of moorland, raised bogs and low, grass- or wood-covered hill and forest – a plateau region east of Liège in the east of Belgium and adjoining parts of Germany, between the Ardennes and the Eifel highlands.
5   Probably a Marmon-Herrington armored car.
6   The expression '*image d'Épinal*' has become proverbial in French for a traditionalist, one-sided depiction of something. Épinal prints were popular, bright-colored prints produced by the *Imagerie d'Épinal* in the 19th

swallow without batting an eyelid, of children with their hands cut off, of couples tied back-to-back and thrown into the Meuse…

Our political leaders had, in the meantime, made it clear that every Rexist was to do his duty in the ranks of the army or at other posts. Thus it was with all the more astonishment that we then learned of the arrest of the *Chef*[7] and of his ignominious deportation along with Joris Van Severen, the leader of the *Verdinaso*,[8] and other sympathizers, but also people of all sorts of different political views. Among these deportees were militant communists, Jews and a great number of other people who had come from central Europe for all sorts of reasons. The "Authorities" of our country thus were guilty of the first deportations, well before the question of deportations by the enemy of the moment became a question. Worse yet, they were turned over to a country foreign to their own nationalities. I cannot find an example of another country that did this!

On 14 May, at 2200 hours, we leave our house intending to go to Portugal and, from there, perhaps, to the Congo, with a mattress on the roof of the automobile. I find, furthermore, that in time of war, this seems standard for all makes of automobiles, all models, including the bottom of the line! There are eight of us in the automobile: six adults, a little girl and myself. With some difficulty we find petrol and spend the night at Assche in a *café* where a great many refugees are already sleeping.

On the 15th we depart toward Ninove, then Tournai and Froidmont, where we spend the night at a farm. The roads are filled with all sorts of vehicles, as much civilian as military, blocking normal traffic and forcing endless detours. Once or twice German aircraft fly low over us, but without strafing. However, we hear dull explosions in the distance. People peremptorily assert that it is the bombing of Boulogne, Calais and Dunkirk, but I ask myself how they can know that.

On 16 May, at 1400 hours, we cross the French frontier, aided in this by some judiciously distributed banknotes. With a man in uniform on each running board in the uniform of the military or the French customs service, I do not know which, we pass with no problems through a compact hostile crowd. The firm's money provides this advantage, buys everything; pays for everything. Corruption, even in such circumstances! We stand around for maybe an hour or two; the others have already been here since yesterday evening!

The roads are as jammed here on this side of the frontier as on the other. The line extends as far as one can see. Automobiles, carts, pedestrians, all loaded with more than one can imagine. I even see hearses and carts drawn by dogs. The stops are numerous and often long. On the shoulders are broken-down automobiles, carts with broken wheels or axles, too dilapidated or too overloaded, and pedestrians who can go no further.

During one stop that is a bit longer than the others we witness an incredible scene, a horrible spectacle! Twenty or 30 meters in front of us a man gets out of his automobile to cross the fields toward a farm. He is dressed in a sort of gray raincoat, apparently at least 40 years old and quite corpulent. A voice, then other cries, arise from the column. I cannot understand what these people are shouting as they run toward the man who just left the column. Then I understand: "Parachutist!"

When I realize the situation, along with other people I say, I cry, I shout that this man just got out of his automobile, right in front of us! The wife of the man in the raincoat tries by every means to make the people understand that this man is her husband and that he is going to the farm to

---

century.

7   *Le Chef de Rex*, Léon Degrelle – the founder and leader of the Rexist Party.
8   The *Verdinaso* (*Verbond van Dietsche Nationaal-Solidaristen* – Union of German National Solidarists) was an authoritarian and fascist-inspired political party in Belgium and the Netherlands founded by Joris Van Severen in the 1930's.

find milk for the infants. Nothing works! A dozen people pounce on the man and beat him. The kids shout, the wife weeps and struggles. The aged parents in the automobile are beside themselves. A harridan cries that she saw the man fall from the sky, that he is a parachutist! She is the one who triggered the drama, who first cried out.

Nobody is struck by the absurdity of it all. If he really had been a paratrooper, hundreds, maybe thousands, would have seen him descend and the parachute would have to be there, for we are in open country! The man falls under the blows of the people who constantly beat him, but nobody intervenes, not even with words.

The column moves on, the automobile of the victim is bypassed, pushed aside with the kids and the old parents inside. The woman is beside her husband on the ground, the thugs get back in their vehicles. Everybody goes on their way as if nothing had happened!

Whose fault is it that all these people are on the road, these frenzied disoriented people, all these dramas, for I would be astonished if this is an isolated case? The war and the invasion are a good excuse. The majority of the government at the time, the responsible people of the country, those who wanted to run everything, have panicked. They ended up believing their own lies, making themselves afraid. They lied, sparked the panic, sending all these people out on the roads. They, themselves, have fled in the literal sense at the same time that they fled from their responsibilities, but in more comfort than all these poor folk!

A few months later these same people will realize that they all need to return to their homes, without fear! To reconstruct the country – and it is true that the Germans fed them on their way home, even gave them petrol!

After this episode we arrive at Douai where we find something to eat and then continue our journey to Arras. We dine and find lodging there after a good bath at the house of some charming people. During the night the city is bombed by German aircraft, but it is an English anti-aircraft gun positioned at the back of the garden that wakes me up. Every time it fires it makes me jump and shakes the house. In the morning we fraternize and have breakfast with the gun crew. We exchange addresses. The guys are nice. On our way to the railroad station we see the *Banque du France*, warehouses and a block of destroyed houses that are ablaze.

We have, indeed, decided to continue our journey by rail. Despite the dimensions and comfort of the Packard of the firm's *président–directeur général*, it is no longer bearable to go on in these conditions. On the platform of the railroad station, swarming with an ill-assorted crowd cluttered with luggage, with packages of all sorts, a woman nurses here baby as if she was the only one there. The trains are also packed. Instead of those trains we prefer a passenger train and its very relative comfort which we have just been told about. This train leaves for Paris. We will travel with a group of students.

In Paris we spend a few hours at the *Hôtel Altona*, in the *rue Faubourg Poissonnière*, where there is no longer any room for the night. My father and his colleague set out searching for lodging. Paris is in a fever. We spend the first part of the night at the bar of the hotel, along with some American journalists. The sirens sound the alarm two or three times for air-raid alerts, but nobody tries to find shelter. We finish the night, some in a disreputable bar, my sister and I in a brothel. That is all that we can find for lodging!

On the 19th, after a short night, a taxi drops us off at the Austerlitz railway station and, at 0630 hours, our express train carries us to Bordeaux, where we have arranged to meet the *chauffeur* with car and the secretary. Arriving at Bordeaux in the evening we have a hard time finding lodging. The women on one side, we are, again, in a brothel where the fleas rule in the depths of an infamous alley.

On 20 May we are at the *Maison de Brésil* for breakfast. One group sets out once more, looking for lodging, while the other goes in quest for the automobile. We find them both and thus lodge at the home of *la Baronne X.*, whose vineyards supply wine for my father's firm. We then take quarters in the *rue St. Séverin*, not far from the St. Seurin church. We have learned that it will not be possible for us to cross the Spanish frontier with the company archives and, therefore, decide to remain in Bordeaux, at least for the time being.

On 22 May I go to the *gare St. Jean* to volunteer for the Belgian Army. To my great stupefaction, the Belgian and French military commanders whom I meet there send me back home saying, "Do you want to prolong the war?" Not me, all alone, in any case! There is a young Belgian boy scout there who works in the office, but whom I no longer remember. However, it turns out that I will meet this fellow by chance on the Eastern Front in 1942, in an entirely different uniform! It is our friend, Freddy J.

In one of the ensuing days I go to the employment office, hoping to find work, to do something useful, but in vain. It will be the same at the *Société nationale de constructions aéronautiques de Bacalan (SNCAB)* and in other firms that are advertising to hire people. They tell me that they do not trust the "*boches du Nord*!" And yet, they "are hiring!"

Henceforth, and to the end of my sojourn in Bordeaux, I spend my time strolling, to the *Quinconces*, to the *parc de Caudéran*, along the port where there is a passenger ship of the *Compagnie Maritime Belge*, the *cours du Chapeau rouge* and other public places.[9] Also I often go the house of a French aunt whom we met here, a female cousin and a male cousin who are often my companions on these jaunts. I have not seen them since I was very young. During our stay in Bordeaux there is also a bombing and several bombs fall in the *quartier de St. Seurin* where we are living. Three or four dead and, if I remember correctly, several wounded.

I could easily go on citing many details, but they are of no importance, except for one that struck me. At the moment of the armistice, on 22 June, or a day very close to that, I see German troops, especially tanks, on the other bank of the Garonne. The men drive the tanks to the bank of the river to wash them. They wash themselves and shave, their mirrors placed on the tanks. From this bank I can see very well all that is happening on the other. On this occasion I learn that the German troops will enter the city the next day, if I remember correctly.

That day there is a crowd in the center of the city to watch the troops enter. I must say that they look good and make a good impression on all the people of Bordeaux. Well dressed and very well equipped. What a contrast with the "Allied" troops that I have seen up to then – with the possible exception of the English, who were less sloppy, no doubt, but whose helmets and uniforms seemed rather ridiculous to me. Obviously, I do not dare to say all this out loud, but my Bordeaux neighbors do not hesitate to express their admiration out loud.

With a band leading, tanks, motorcycles, horsemen and infantry march past in perfect order such as I have never seen any army do, except, perhaps, the Russians, but that is much later. The crowd around me cannot believe it. It is impressive beyond belief.

During the ensuing days one can see the men strolling around the city, visiting the monuments and sites and checking out the stores. With no relaxation in dress or comportment, everything perfectly correct, they circulate in small groups of two or three, with discipline that surpasses anything we are accustomed to. These are my first contacts with the German troops and my first reflections.

At the beginning of September my father decides to return to Belgium. The Germans spontaneously provide petrol for the automobile, but we will return home by railroad. We arrive in Brussels on 8 or 9 September, and it is the German Red Cross that feeds us *en route*. My brothers have returned from the army and the one who is still unmarried is at the house.

---

9 The *Place des Quinconces* – the central square in Bordeaux – is one of the largest city squares in Europe.

During the ensuing days I have several reasons to be surprised. In the street I meet a neighbor who is wearing my neckties and shirts! Several other objects or clothes have also disappeared. The effect of the surprise passes quickly, and my father does not want me to bring up the subject with this neighbor. When we left for France, my father entrusted the keys of the house to one of the neighbors, in case my brother returned. Before he departed, this neighbor left the keys with another neighbor, and that is the one who found himself a new wardrobe at my expense. I later learned that this man joined the resistance and was decorated thereby, but in 1940 there was not yet any question that I was a "collaborator". I thereby conclude that he acted for the resistance before it was created and, doubtless, as a preventive measure.

All this does nothing to prevent a return to a more or less normal life. A few days later I return to my studies of agronomy, but quickly realize that my heart is no longer in it. I left the school four months ago. I have lived four months of total freedom! I am now approaching the beginning of March 1941.

During this period I rediscover my friends, my relationships, some of my habitual activities and, finally, the movement, which has resumed its activities. Very logically, I resume mine. The *Formations de Combat* have been created. I thus pass from the *Cadre actif de Propagande* (*CAP*) to the *FC*. There are exercises at the *ferme St. Eloi*, property of *Lieutenant* Rouleay, where the *procureur du Roi* [the Royal Prosecutor] shows up one day wanting to forbid these gatherings. We meet at the "*Métropole St. Josse*", in the *chaussée de Louvain*, and are introduced to the martial arts, in the *rue Mercelils* and at the "*Zonneke*" at Auderghem with our first boxing lessons. I have no problem resuming the trend of my political ideas.

The hesitations, the cowardice, the pirouettes and the about-turns of those responsible for our country during this period of the hostilities, extensions of their pre-war attitudes, and I refer most definitely to our ministers who were distinguished for such behavior in France, and those, too, whom one never heard speak since then! Everything goes on in the same state of mind.

We, too, have to resume or pursue our action. Otherwise, the great majority of the population is behind the King and only has contempt for these politicians who had scoffed at them and had plunged the Belgians into shame by their wrongdoings on French soil. On the other hand, the population does not recognize in these disciplined, friendly German troops the scoundrels that had so often been depicted to them. Everyone agrees that, for "occupation troops" they behave quite well, often much better than what they had seen among the "Allied" troops that had been called in as reinforcements. I have no intention of incriminating here all the Allied or Belgian soldiers, who may have lacked supervision, but especially discipline. I am only expressing here what I felt at the time, what I heard around me, using the same words and nothing more. And nobody is contradicting me today! This is how the Belgian people reacted at that time.

Since, aside from the fact of the invasion, we had no reason to hate the occupiers, it was necessary to create a certain climate, to provoke this hate, and that would be an easy thing. Thus, as time passed, appeals came from London, appeals for murder, for sabotage, for general terrorism. Victor De Laveleye played a major part among these *provocateurs*. It is hardly remarkable that the terrorism then engendered today's terrorism! Why would all that was permitted yesterday, all that was good, even recommended at that time, suddenly come to an end? The infernal process was begun, nothing would be able to halt it! These acts, contrary to the Hague and Geneva Conventions, would necessarily lead to reactions, warnings at first, and then result in reprisals. That, then, was the endless sequence that was never desired by the population, nor the occupiers, but which the "inciters to crime" in London provoked. Alone, in safety in England or elsewhere, these jackals delighted in it.

I took another path. Curious about the world, I was even more so about Germany when circumstances led me there. The idea of going to see it gradually seeped into me; then took hold. And it was only a small step from that to the decision. Fate may well arrange things, but I still ask myself today if I may not have solicited it. An opportune dismissal from school would have facilitated it all, except for a stormy confrontation I then had with my father. It is evident that he wanted to prevent me from carrying out my projects, but that he understood my determination. Without doing anything to facilitate my departure, neither did he do anything more to hinder it. We are now at the end of the month of March 1941.

On this last day of the month I leave home, early in the morning, to report to the recruiting office (*Werbestelle*) for voluntary work in Germany to sign a contract. I want to see Germany and what is happening there. I want to learn how the Germans live. I want to breathe, to forget all the depressed faces that filled my exodus in France and that I found in Belgium upon my return. I have just turned 18, but I feel like I am no more than 16 at most, I feel so young. Two years at that age is a lot! Yet I feel that I understand everything and know nothing. A little later I will discover to my great astonishment that most of the fellows my age who surrounded me before my departure seemed to know everything, but, it reality, understood nothing!

During the streetcar ride that takes me to the *rue des Chaertreux*, I realize that, all at once, I am going from my childhood or adolescence to enter, with a crash and a twinge of sorrow, the unknown world of the adults! In a confused way I feel in the very depths of my being that the ensuing days, months, maybe years, are going to mark my life, doubtless turn it topsy-turvy. I already know, I well understand that, alone at the present moment, I will have to surmount all my difficulties, my fears, my timidity. As for the fears, I am already accustomed to dealing with them. I must succeed alone in assuming all the responsibilities that I, myself, created. I must succeed in this great leap and attempt to control where I land. That is how I see things. At that age one feels so strong, and believes that one is hardened, but it is not as simple as that. Nevertheless, I must find the strength inside me to overcome everything, and do it entirely on my own, without showing doubt or the slightest weakness. I decide, once and for all to build myself a shell and to pull in my head at every stroke of fate, just in time to find a defense. I said it!

As I said above, my father did not agree with me, far from it, but, even though we may have shouted at times, I loved him. Did he know it? At 18 years, modesty regarding feelings is such that one is afraid to say, "Papa, Mama, I love you", for one is so afraid of being vulnerable! However, they would have been so pleased to hear it! I lost my mother in 1939. If only there had not been the obstacle of this reserve that was the custom in our family, there would have been more opportunities for mutual understanding so that the difference in political opinions and philosophical convictions would have been unable to complicate our reciprocal feelings. I never actually had problems with my mother, in fact, nor with my father, but I believed that they were less accessible, as, in fact, I understood much later. It would have been easier than I would ever have believed at that time. My youth prevented me from seeing it. It was not easy for me to break these inhibitions. Always this modesty, the feeling of stripping naked, of disarming myself, but I determined to pass this test. So many other comrades and even all youngsters have had to go through this. Doubtless some find themselves there.

The streetcar does not complete its run, and I am afraid that I will miss my *rendezvous* with destiny. The romanticism of my age dictates words filled with emotion, which, on reflection, seem ridiculous to me, but the reality of the months, of the years to come are going to disabuse me, for there will not be words strong enough, then, to describe these things. If, however, I do choose words, my sentiments were, at the time, those that I record here. Standing on the rear platform I tell myself that this journey seems much too short. This monster of a streetcar, object of so much of our student pleasantries, does not move forward, and I would happily have taken the place of the driver, eager and curious to know the future, but too excited to be disturbed.

A few minutes later, however, I pass through the *porte – cochère* that gives access to the employment office where I am directed to the first story. I establish my identity, am given forms to fill out and sign. I have a choice, I go to Cologne. At the end of the morning I return to my house to gather my clothes, a few objects, my camera. I suddenly remember that one day I told my friend, Paul Van Brusselen, that someday, I would go to Germany. He made me promise that I would not go without him. Therefore I immediately go to his house to tell him of my upcoming departure. His mother is upset. His father and she go off to talk together. I tell Paul to be at my house at 1400 hours if he decides to go. At 1439 hours we are *en route* for the *"Werbestelle"* and, at the end of the afternoon, we each return to our homes to prepare our few suitcases.

On 3 April at about 0600 hours we leave the house. A little after 0700 hours the train pulls out, taking the hundreds of volunteers who, just like me, are turning a new page in their destiny toward a new life. We disembark at Aachen where we are fed bread, butter, sausage and coffee – *Ersatz*,[10] of course. We are also served a very thick soup (*Eintopf*[11]), which we consume on the spot. There we meet French men and women, including two young women from Nice. I ask myself how they got there. Not that it matters, we will travel together as far as Cologne, where they will go on to Düsseldorf. If I had only known! After all, nobody is waiting for us at Cologne. It is too late to change our destination. Too bad. We would have enjoyed the accent of the *midi* and, in other respects, the girls were not bad at all – indeed, rather better than that.

We are now at Cologne, and at about 1700 hours we enter our lodgings, consisting of wooden barracks, but not at all bad, quite clean and with numerous flowerbeds. These barracks, or pavilions, are built on a little triangular 'square' behind the Humboldt factory, at Köln – Kalk. A number of volunteers have already preceded us there, and more will join us, in all, a little more than 200 Flemish, Walloons or people from Brussels. Workers, students from two or three universities, all classes mixed, but generally very suitable except for a dozen fellows who seem less respectable to me.

Thus a new experience commences for me, that of communal life, with dormitories and a canteen. This form of life causes me no problems. I learn to live and get along with people of all sorts, mostly young, between 16 and 30 years old. I am extremely surprised to meet here several old buddies from my quarter, Roger Schr. and Edgar S., with whom I renew my friendship and make other friends according to my affinities. I can remember at least 30 names. I will meet a good number of them later in the *Légion* and others will join the Flemish *Légion "Flandern"*, including that excellent comrade, Theo B., whom I shall see again during a convalescent leave, promoted to an officer and with an amputated forearm – a tremendous chap of whom I shall always have the best memories, as have all those who knew him.

In brief, here we study in the school of the Humboldt factory. All the students are Belgian, except for two Germans, already wounded in the war, who are being recycled. The professors are Germans, considerably older, and very friendly with us, even endowed with a sense of humor! When something doesn't go well or one of us does something stupid, one of the professors vanishes and returns shortly, with a severe air, wearing his pointed helmet from the 1914–18 war and armed with his ceremonial saber! The gag is repeated two or three times but never loses its effect; the professor's mimicry is hilarious.

From the very start relations are cordial, even if there were a few small problems before my arrival. It is explained to me that our camp had available an athletic field and a swimming pool, but that a certain number of our compatriots caused so much damage to the installations, principally graffiti carved with a knife into the glossy white paint of the doors and seats that, after numerous vain warnings, we are no longer granted access to the swimming pool. It was, doubtless,

---

10 Wartime substitute, *Ersatz* – literally 'replacement' – is also used with regard to military replacements.
11 Literally 'one-pot' – a whole meal cooked together as a single dish, standard for the German military field kitchens.

the work of a minority, but since, in the autonomy of our camp, the Belgians were unable to establish self-discipline among themselves, there could be no reproach directed at the German authorities. We still have use of the athletic field, which I do not hesitate to use, along with a minority of the comrades in the camp.

I have heard much talk in Belgium of religious persecution by Hitler's regime. However, I can affirm that the churches are full for the services, that many of the people who enter the churches wear party insignia, that the Winter Relief (*Winterhilfswerk, WHW*), created by the same party, has enormous sales of badges and insignia of all sorts at the church exits, especially from the Protestant churches. The only assertion that I heard, among other slogans, before the war that I found undeniably true, is the qualification that it is an "orderly country". Yes, Germany has without doubt a strong regime, and order rules there, but I do not see how this is a disadvantage. No bold headlines in the newspapers about outrageous thefts, spectacular murders, bank robberies, attacks by citizens or rapes.

Doubtless there are crimes. How could the country escape them? Whatever the regime, people are people. But, punished, as I suppose they were, the crimes did not increase disproportionately and there were not many recidivists on the loose. It is also true that the press never magnified, even insidiously, certain crimes and I willingly believe that the thieves, the rapists and other criminals are not supporters of the regime. Is it wrong for me to discover these things and see them such as they are? Yes, I discover Germany, which pleases me as it is, just as I see it with my own eyes, and not through the lenses of certain journalists. I say what I have seen, why shouldn't I? One detail of small importance nevertheless struck me at this time, that in the Germany of 50 years ago [from the first writing of this book] they already separated categories of waste collection.

At the camp the food is absolutely sufficient and rich, I do not say costly. I am 18 years old with a good appetite, like all who are my age. Furthermore, if one wants a bit more, we have no trouble getting little loaves of bread (*Brötchen*), white bread or brown, raisin bread or other pastries in the numerous bakeries of the *Kalker – Hauptstraße*, with no ration stamps and despite our status as foreigners. We have no problems with obtaining food, but it is more difficult with textiles. There are many synthetic fabrics, but everyone is well dressed.

In the camp the few fellows that are less desirable, some I spoke of earlier, play cards and, at times, for substantial sums. One day there is a complaint about theft of money. This results in a police raid on the barracks. They confiscate my camera. A few days later I am called to the "*Kriminal – Polilzei*". Since the weather is good and I have time, I walk there. The bad weather seems to have ceased, for a moment, for it is beautiful and calm. I am in front of the building of the *Völkishcer Beobachter* newspaper, a marvelous and immense clump of broom [flowers], all in flower. It is beautiful, truly beautiful! All around are well cared for green lawns and, above, a blue springtime sky, very clear.

In the offices of the "*Kri-Po*" I do not have to wait. I am immediately invited into an office. I am questioned on my identity, my reasons for voluntary enlistment, etc. My questioner is already prejudiced in my favor, because I manage to make my way pretty well in German. He asks about the Rex insignia that I wear in my buttonhole. The police officer pulls some negatives and photos from a folder. They are from the film in my camera, ones I took *en route*. There is a photo of the railroad station at Aix – la – Chapelle, and two others of factories at Stolberg. He tells me that it is imprudent on my part, that, in the future, I should avoid these types of photos, but he returns all of them to me. My photos are thus developed and printed for free. The policeman shakes my hand, it is over, I can return to the camp.

Then there are one or two air-raid alerts at night, and we are led into the shelter of the basements of the Humboldt factory. Some play cards, others chat, others sleep. Among those is Roger Schr., who does not leave [the shelter] until 0600 hours, for he does not realize that the alert ended at about 0200 hours and everybody went back to the barracks. We laugh about that for a long time.

One day I have a slight misadventure when we are eating at the canteen. I am sitting with Paul Van Brusselen, and there are a dozen other fellows at the other tables. Charles Gr., assistant to the chief of the camp, is present and Edmond Q., too, I think. He must remember it! There is a little gang in the camp that I think I have already mentioned. One of them, I don't remember just why, suddenly appears about five or six meters from me with a knife in his hand. Pointed at me. With an evil glare he curses me out. I think that it is because of some remarks I made regarding his conduct. In fact, he did not seem to me to be a hooligan by nature, it seemed more that he wanted to give the impression that he was tough, or that he wanted to become so, to establish his place in his little gang. I think that he reproached me for not taking him seriously enough.

He seems sturdier than me, without being any taller, and, does not want to lose face, I do not want to leave the initiative in his hands any longer. Doubtless he is waiting for me to back down, or, at least, is hoping for that and is surprised by my riposte. I myself am surprised at how easy it is to shove him into the porcelain or stoneware bowls that are piled on a table behind him. I inwardly thank Serlet, Jean Maroy and the barber who taught us several rudiments of wrestling and boxing at the *Métropole à St. Josse*. Out of bravado I throw his knife, which had fallen on the ground, back to him, and I awaited his next move. He hesitates an instant but does not insist. Regaining his weapon, he leaves, growling through his teeth that he will get me later. If I remember correctly, the fellows had to pay for between 40 and 60 bowls! The witnesses of the scene and the friends who later learn of it cannot understand why I returned his weapon to him. Me, I know full well, that a bit of *panache* was well worth the risk!

One day I am called to the engineer who is the director of the school. He offers me the opportunity to go work at Köln – Mülheim, at Felten and Guilleaume, Carlswerk- Neptun. At the same time I will be more or less an interpreter and, with three other Belgians, we will have an apartment at the factory, a private apartment. All right! Immediately, all right!

Two days later I am working at Mülheim. My team member and foreman is Franz Hochscherf. We work together at a press which shapes aluminum aircraft wing sections. Franz is in his forties. I am the press operator. We immediately get along well and form an excellent team, even after he lets me know that he was formerly communist, and I tell him that I am resolutely of the new order. That changes absolutely nothing in our relations of trust and friendship. His confidence is such that he introduces me to other friends of his, including Fritz Lucas, whom I have never forgotten. This trust was never betrayed. We had profound respect for each other, certain of the purity of our feelings and of our reciprocal political convictions.

The work is not hard, not hard at all, and, with the bonuses and extra bonuses, I earn 30 *RM* a week, I no longer remember exactly. My private lodging is paid for by the factory, which is not bad at all. We manage to accumulate work pieces in reserve, which is to say that, without difficulty, we are able to shape more pieces than are expected of us. We set them aside, hidden by other pieces, and we bring them back out when we have the night shift, some Sunday or other. Then we are alone in the great hall and, on these nights, Franz and I sleep part of the night in the cab of an overhead bridge-crane in the adjoining shop, 30 meters above the ground. In the morning we bring out our reserve pieces before the new team arrives.

If I remember correctly I was paying 2 *RM* 50 a week for hot meals, consisting of soup and dessert, in the canteen, and then, for, I believe, a dozen *RM*, one had claim on the attention of a pretty girl in the *Nägelgasse* or *Kammacher – Gasse* – the red-light district of Cologne. The fellows in Cologne pronounced them "*Nächelgasse*" or "*Kammaché*"!

Since I am speaking of it, let me tell a little story. As usual, we were wandering around the city one Saturday evening, Paul and I, along with a buddy, Charly Delh. Charly is a very kind fellow with an absolute terror of bombings, but no girlfriend. So this night he wants to meet one girl or another. His problem is not in the choice of a girl, there are enough for all tastes. What preoccupies him is, above all, to choose the favorable moment, not with regard to a physiologically favorable state, as you might believe, but in relation to the probability of an air-raid alert. That would, in any case, "put him at a disadvantage" because of his fear of bombs. We could see Charly hesitate, equivocate, take one step forward, two back, and then rush forward as if he was going to dive in the water!

Paul and I then see the half-open door open all the way to swallow Charly and the girl at the same time and shut again. At this very moment the sirens start to howl, sounding the alert and the very moment when the door hides Charly from our view. Paul and I laugh uncontrollably when we see Charly's pale face appear for an instant as the door opens suddenly, only to disappear anew and quickly, his silhouette snatched by the arms of the girl, the door slams and is closed with a key from the inside.

Homeric! Charly kidnapped! We wait. We want to know what comes next. Besides, we are shaking so hard with laughter that we cannot move anyway. We slap our thighs and slap each other on the back, trying, at the same time, to stifle the laughter and all that it engenders.

Ten minutes later, the door suddenly opens, as if blown open by a hurricane. We have just time to recognize Charly, who dashes out and immediately disappears around a bend in the road. He has not even seen us. We try to catch up with him, but in vain. He vanishes from our sight toward the river. We, in turn, reach the bank of the Rhine, which we slowly follow toward the north, leaving the city and heading toward the Müllheim bridge. This is what we do every time an alert surprises us in the city at night. We lean against a tree every time the fragments of the anti-aircraft rounds ("*Flak*") fall heavily or too close to us. When the danger clears we sit on a bench at the edge of the river to admire the reflection of the flashes produced by the firing. I enjoy speaking of these special moments that we succeeded in enjoying in this war that seemed, at once, so far from us, since it did not yet concern us, and yet so close, for we were plunged into it up to our necks in spite of ourselves.

The period of seven months I spent in Cologne was already a fantastic experience. My memories of it are marvelous, despite everything. There is also a tender memory for the romanticism of our first steps as adolescents on the roads of an adult world. They were the ones who declared war, but it is us who will end up by fighting it, and finishing it, right up to the last day!

At this point there were not yet violent bombings of Cologne, and so far it was only, or primarily, private homes that were damaged. The factories or their shelters were the safest places! Not one of the factories that I knew had been hit yet. Neither Humboldt, nor Klöckner, nor Deutz – Magirus, nor Carlswerk – Neptun had suffered the slightest damage.

The falling fragments of the "*Flak*" thin out at the same time that the firing dies away. A few "ploufs" in the water of the river, a few torn branches in the trees and the snapping sound of fragments hitting ground as the last fragments fall, then it is calm again. We return to our lodgings. It is Sunday, we can sleep. At about 1300 hours we go to eat in an "*Imbiss – Stube*" [literally, 'snack-room' in German] near our house. Today one would say "snack". That is what one might call a change of regime, even if one still eats practically the same thing. We see Charly again Monday evening, but he does not know how he got home! We are never bored. We always keep up our morale, even in the most difficult moments. Especially in these moments like this!

I find a way to lengthen my "weekends". Whenever I can, I ask for the night shift. Often I thus replace married men who prefer day shifts. This way I make many friends. Thus I finish one week Saturday morning at 0600 hours to start the next week on Monday at 2200 hours. Since the air-raid alarms come mainly at night, I also serve as fire-watch (*Brandwache*) on the very top of the immense shelter-towers, shaped like mushrooms. Air-raid alerts, seen from up there, are a truly sensational spectacle. The anti-aircraft searchlights, whose beams cross each other high in the sky, often catch an enemy airplane that attempts to escape them. The "*Flak*" bursts, the explosion, the bombs or the fires ignited by the incendiary bombs, all that combines to produce scenes I have never seen the like of. On-the-spot news! The damage caused, when I go see it, always seems less important than I would have supposed during the night action, at least in this first part of 1941! Soon that will not be true. Like everyone else, I learn in June of the invasion of Russia by German troops. At that moment I felt a sensation of a sort of relief, I don't know why, but that is what I felt, and many other people along with me, as I was able to confirm. Thus ended a sort of unnatural alliance. At least that is how I reacted at the moment that the German-Soviet Pact was signed, though I told myself at the moment that there must have been a reason for it that we, of course, did not know.

I see two comrades of the Kalk camp, two Flemish, De Wit and De Vadder, join the *Waffen-SS* and leave Cologne for the Eastern Front, via a training camp. I want to go too. I tell this to an engineer at the factory, who is amazed, but advises me to inquire in an office in the city. Done. I obtain 10 days' holiday to return to Belgium. I am told that a *Légion* of Belgian volunteers is in the process of being formed and I am given the opportunity to go for information. When, a few days later, I arrive in Belgium I learn that a contingent has just left for the East. It is what we will later call the contingent of 8 August, 1941. But they tell me that a second contingent is going to be formed. What should I do? Wait and take the risk of arriving too late?[12] Return to Germany and enlist directly in the *Waffen-SS*?

When I return to Germany on the 22nd or 24th of August, I still hesitate. Paul Van Brusselen tells me that he would also like to enlist, but that he prefers the Belgian *Légion*, since he does not speak a word of German. I believe that the essential thing is to fight in the East, but I opt for enlistment in the Belgian *Légion*. I announce my choice at the factory. I inform the engineer, my German friends, my Belgian friends and also my girlfriend, Leni Fl., who lives at Clevischer Ring. My friend Franz, my kind Red friend, congratulates me for my courage. What will be left of my modesty? It seems to me that he is proud of me!

September passes and October is nearly done. It is now the 26th of that month, the night before my return to Belgium. My comrade, Franz, asks me to accompany him in the other shops to make my farewells, introducing me to some whom I do not know. He wants to explain my gesture to everyone. It is genuine homage that he pays to me. He who has told me that he is Red, is not, obviously, a member of the National Socialist Party (*NSDAP, Nazi*) but he has often told me that he has a great deal of sympathy or admiration for Hitler, for he has accomplished great things for his country. If, someday, he might be an adversary, Franz will never be an enemy. He is sincere, an upright man. Wherever they may be found, I deeply respect this sort of person.

Why have I never been able to find him again? If he is still alive today, and I believe that he is, he must be well into his nineties! The next day he takes time off to accompany me to the railroad station. His eyes are brimming with tears! I do not turn back. All the same, I cannot wait for the moment when it will take all my courage to leave! It is 1100 hours when we arrive at the "*Hauptbahnhof*" [main railroad station] and, by mutual agreement, Franz leaves before I go to the train platform to shorten the farewells. By about 1800 hours I arrive in Brussels.

The next day I am off to enlist. I am told that a *Garde Walonne*[13] is being formed and that I will have the best chance for a speedy departure for the *Légion* from there. Accordingly I sign up and

---

12 At the time, the campaign in Russia was expected to be so brief that eager youngsters like Fernand were afraid it would all be over before they got to the front.

13 The *Garde Wallone*, created at the same time as the *Légion Wallone*, was a Rexist military formation. It was not intended for frontline service, but would guard places of strategic importance such as airfields, bridges and

find myself at the Brasschaat firing range on 3 November, 1941. My friend Paul Van Brusselen, who was unable to leave Cologne at the same time that I did, was able to get back to Brussels shortly after I did and I find him here.

I can say of the *Garde Wallone* that I have very good memories of it. With the exception of the uniform, which seemed rather basic to me, a bit ridiculous. It was, I believe, soon modified, when I was no longer there. The morale, the atmosphere, suits me. But everything is new for me, starting with the discipline, and I have to adapt to it. My first, and also my only punishment, aroused a moment of revolt in me. Happily, I was surrounded by friends who calmed me down. My brother, first; the company clerk, Maréchal; the *adjudant-chef,* Ernest C.; and other friends made me listen to reason and helped me to accept this punishment, restriction to base for the weekend. The *sergent de jour* [duty sergeant], Léopold L., coming to whistle *Reveille*, entered the room and found me lying on my bed while my comrades were already at the feet of their own. Then seconds too late for me. *Crac, dedans!* I got the impression that L. was very happy to have caught me. It was this impression that provoked this spirit of revolt in me. I used the 24 hours to calm myself down. It is done, I shall never again be punished. In fact, I shall be punished once more, two years later in the *Légion*.

Contrary to what one might believe who was not there, the formation was very serious, even severe, without concessions, neither for the close order drill nor for the exercises out on the terrain. Of course, I preferred the latter by far. I had a sort of romantic predilection for exercises in the field, for this sandy land, covered with heather and pine or silver birch woods seemed truly beautiful to me in the heart of this autumn. It was truly beautiful, this *Campine*,[14] even when bathed in fog or in dreary weather. But it glows in the light of the autumn sun. This land of the *Campine* literally shines and then the hoarfrost covers it with a veil lighter than tulle,[15] when the dew clings to the slightest blade of grass or has condensed on the delicate webs of the little spiders.

I enjoy a certain satisfaction in this kind of life, the hours filled, but scheduled, a hard life, clean and close to nature. The brisk chill of the first frosts numb my fingers and hands without chilling my ardor for exercise, far to the contrary. The cold encourages the effort. I rapidly find numerous comrades, a very close little group immediately forms. We are four young men between 17 and 19 years old, overflowing with life and enthusiasm, and these same feelings unite us: Emile M., Raymond P., Alfred D. and myself. This little cell would come together, separate, then rejoin at the mercy of events of which we were not the masters, for the entire time of the war. The understanding was perfect among this little group, and with our non-commissioned instructors, as it was with our captain.

Among the instructors, the one I remember best is certainly the one we nicknamed "Zag-Zag". Not very tall, stocky, one might even say stout, but incredibly agile considering his corpulence. Severely wounded in the 1914–18 war, his skull marked with a large and deep scar in the form of a cross, evidence of a trepanation. That is why some also nicknamed him "*Croix de Bourgogne*" [Cross of Burgundy]. Always in a good humor, with no nastiness, tough at exercises, but no less so on himself than on us. He never required more than what he himself could do, but, since he could do everything… "Zag-Zag" was his way of explaining the speed, the vigor and the conciseness of movements on exercises. Even today I hold a warm feeling for him. He was my first instructor, the first German soldier with whom we had relations of friendship as much as of service, conversations

---

railway lines within the jurisdiction of the *Militärverwaltung* (Belgium and the Nord and Pas de Calais in France).

14 The *Campine*, chiefly situated in north-eastern Belgium and parts of the south-eastern Netherlands, formerly consisted largely of extensive moors, tracts of sandy heath and wetlands.

15 Tulle is a very fine fabric netting, often starched, which is used for wedding gowns and veils.

as equal to equal, in spite of his rank as a non-commissioned officer, but that was outside of service hours, for *Dienst ist Dienst* [service is service], *Schnaps ist Schnaps*!

The German *Capitaine* [*Hauptmann*] Lambrichts also left me with an equally good memory, just a bit more distant. Fifty years old, cheerful, a little moustache like Hitler's, graying and distinguished. A gold-capped tooth accentuated his smile, for the man was courteous, affable and not miserly with his smiles, but with no weakness. A pre-eminent cavalier, he looked good and had a fine presence on his horse when he led our company *en route* to the exercise or on the training marches.

At the higher echelon there was *Major* Wolff, who commanded all of this little world in the *cadre de l'école de cavalerie du polygone* [cavalry school staff of the firing range]. Tall, lean, bald, his back very arched, and with reason. He seemed as if he wore a corset. He also wore a monocle, quite naturally, the very model of a Prussian officer, distant, but without the slightest arrogance. Every morning, even when there was a hard freeze or snow, he was out there practicing his gymnastics in gym clothes, with great dexterity and much conviction. His age? Much older, in his sixties, I am sure. All the other instructors were Belgian, many veteran officers or other non-commissioned officers of the Belgian Army.

We had a frequent series of shots against all the usual maladies, and moving picture sessions which inevitably ended those days. We also had our evening or weekend leaves to Brasschaat or Anvers, generally in small groups. All in all, a quite orderly life, well organized, all oriented toward exercise, toward physical conditioning. One small recollection remains enduring in my memory, a little memory of no real importance. One morning we were leaving for exercise at the hour when children go to school. We were singing one of the marching songs, translated into French, but to a German melody, well-chanted, well-articulated. A little 12-year-old girl was marching on the sidewalk, level with me, accompanied by a little boy, a little younger, her brother, no doubt. The two of them tried to march to the same rhythm as us, smiling quite nicely at us, without restraint. When the song was done they spoke to us while marching, asking us to keep on singing, since they liked what we were singing. They spoke French, doubtless children of the Belgian soldiers who were barracked there before us. Perhaps this memory remains with me because the children were so close to us and this brief dialogue seemed so natural to me, so spontaneous. It is this sort of thing that stands out. I wonder why, when so many other events took place at the same time that affected the course of the world, the orientation of entire generations, and which, at the time, passed by in the background. Such are the vagaries of the human mind, the labyrinth of the sentiments.

One day in December, during a special assembly, our *adjudant-chef* (*Spieß*[16]) reads a communication to us. The *Légion* has an immediate need for horse-drivers. Paul and I exchange glances, a wink suffices. The *Spieß*, who knows of our desire to join our comrades in the *Légion* as soon as possible, derisively asks us where we learned this skill? He must know full well that the closest we have come to riding is the merry-go-round at the fairgrounds. He tells us to return to our place in the ranks. Then comes an appeal for cooks, which the *Légion* also seems to be lacking. Paul and I once more step out in front of the troop to again be sent back like the first time. We will be neither cooks nor drivers of horses!

A few days later, however, we are able to apply for subsequent departure. On this occasion we are before a little committee composed of a German recruiter, assisted by our *Spieß* and the company clerk. The clerk asks us if we have already been employed. "Yes, most certainly, in Germany."

"You have two alternatives to set your pay rate in the army: 80 percent of your final salary or the general pay of one *RM* per day."

---

16 In the German Army, the *Spieß* – or 'top sergeant' – is the 'mother of the company'.

"The pay of one *RM* per day." The recruiter looks at me incredulously! "Yes, the pay of one *RM*."
The *Spieß* and Maréchal tell me that I am crazy, which is also what I believe I also understood the recruiter to mutter between his teeth, and they translate for me, forgetting that I understand German, or pretending not to know it. I do not go back on what I said. I would have blushed if I chose the alternative. Don't talk of selflessness, let's call it bravado! But I am enlisted. Now we only have to wait.

The activity is such that it is already Christmas, and it seems that it was only yesterday that I started my life as a soldier. The army offers us the Christmas packages and has invited our families to join with us this for this evening. My family is not there, you already know why. It does not espouse my ideas, I understand their absence. I have one of my brothers here, and I also have the families of the others. Nothing can darken the joy of this family evening for us, no matter what. It is our first big "*Kameradshaft*" [friendly get-together]. New Year's Day is celebrated soon after and, in the course of the month all the companies leave the *polygone* for their respective barracks. Ours will be Namur. Shortly after embarkation I and my other comrades receive leave slips. I will leave the train at Brussels for a few days' relaxation. At the end of my leave I get to Namur during the night. The next day I get acquainted with my new barracks. It is the cadet school that is in the city.

Life here differs from what it was in Brasschaat, when the period of special instruction is ended, which is not to say that there are no more exercises! The missions are uniquely, essentially, guard duty. There are numerous bridges in the city and the vicinity to guard. We also stand guard at the *Hôpital de Salzinnes*, at the *Hôtel de Ville* [city hall], at the *Place d'Armes* [military exercise grounds] and at the *Citadelle*. For my part, I stand guard at the *Salzinnes*, at the *Place d'Armes* and at certain bridges, and it is precisely at the *pont de Sambre* [Sambre bridge] that I have my first taste of Russia. This night the temperature drops to –18° or –20° (0 – +2°F), and the bridge, which was wooden, moans all night because of the temperature, to a degree such that one would have believed that someone was trying to break it up, and this kept up for the entire term of my guard duty there. Each time it was two long hours of suffering for feet, hands and ears. One of our chaps, a certain Fondu, a man of a good 30 years, was surprised on guard duty with his boots stuffed with straw. He then had the straw of the dungeons to allow him to meditate on proper uniform for a soldier in the field, 24 hours, just time for reflection. In this same period there was a little comical episode that I remember. A few male and female students wanted to play "wise-guys". I do not know what the circumstances were, since I was not present. To provide them with opportunity for reflection the commander of the post had them spend an entire afternoon or evening in the delicate mission of cleaning the guardroom and the corridors with a toothbrush. The girls earned the privilege of darning the socks of the men on guard.

In the course of the month of February, during a company assembly, *Capitaine* H., veteran officer of the Belgian Army, announces the formation of the second contingent for the Eastern Front. After first having those who have already placed their request step forward from the ranks, he exhorts the others to do the same. He does this with such vigor and conviction that I have no doubt that he is going to join us. Some men join our group and thereby signify their enlistment. We are assembled facing the ones who are remaining at home, and the *capitaine* so eulogizes us for the benefit of those who are not going that we are embarrassed. I am not really embarrassed for myself, but more for the sake of those who are not going with us. I do not at all appreciate what the *capitaine* is doing to incite others to depart, to influence them! There are 30 of us facing the company. Not the *capitaine*, who, assuredly, will discreetly fulfill the formalities of enlistment later. Spellbound, we discover that, for the time being, the *capitaine* has never had the slightest intention of going! The *capitaine* will remain at Namur.

Later, in the *Légion*, I will, however, get to know the son of this *capitaine*, Jean, who enlisted on 8 August, 1941, and this friend will make me forget that his father did not have as much courage as him. It was strictly within his rights not to go, but … after his harangue! What shocked me was not so much the fact that he did not enlist, for that I will not reproach anyone, but instead the way he behaved to push others to do so!

One evening in the last days of February it is announced that the volunteers for the Eastern Front will depart on leave the next afternoon. From that moment we are all naturally feverish with excitement, but, alas, at *Reveille* the next morning I have a very real fever. I caught cold during guard duty the previous night. When I inform my comrades it rapidly becomes clear to me that, if I recognize it and request to see the doctor, I run the risk of compromising my departure on leave. I say no more of it and go along with the company which reports to the *Hauteurs de Jambes* [heights of Jambes] for a field exercise. The plateau is covered with a thick layer of snow, which makes the exercise quite difficult, but which should prevent me from getting cold. But, once more, alas! For the first time I regret that there is a pause, for it would be better for me if there were not. When the exercise resumes, I am short of breath, my cheeks burning. Happily, the first part of the exercise does not last long and we reform ranks to return to our barracks. Without taking time to gulp down the meal, for which I have little desire, I prepare my affairs. At about 1300 hours we are at the railroad station, Paul Van Brusselen, Arthur V.E., Maurice V. and I, along with several others, are going in the same direction. I do not like to parade my ills, and I do my best to control myself but I can certainly feel that my temperature must be quite high. Perhaps the calm of traveling after the feverish activity of the recent days has been too brusque a contrast. I have time to think and, perhaps, it is good that there is no shortage of time.

Miraculously, the train slows almost to a stop just before the Boitsfort railroad station. We seize the opportunity as well as our luggage and jump off the moving train. Here, too, there is snow. We then go our separate ways to our own homes. As soon as I enter my home, I collapse into an armchair. When I wake up I see Dr K., our family doctor, leaning over me, listening to my chest. Doubtless that is what woke me up. My father is at his side with a troubled expression. Diagnosis, pleurisy! I am permitted to smoke, which is curious. That pleases me. Injection of camphor oil, thick, pretty painful. What is essential is to quickly be back on my feet. I slept all night, like a log. Breathless, I have the impression that I am constantly somewhere between waking and sleeping. I am, however, conscious enough to make it known that my unit must be informed of my condition.

The next day I receive a visit from a German doctor delegated by the military hospital on the *avenue de la Couronne*, accompanied by a medical orderly. The military ambulance is before the door. The doctor converses with us for a good bit of time. He speaks French. Before departing he informs us that he will come back tomorrow and asks to be informed if there are any problems or if he can be of service. The doctor considers that I am not transportable. My father, who had stayed home on purpose, will later tell me that he found the doctor to be extremely friendly and that he was astonished at such great courtesy. Intensive care continues and my pleurisy quickly develops most favorably! A few days later Dr K. forbids me to continue smoking! That beats everything! When I felt worst, I could smoke, now that everything is going better, I can't. I later learn that the doctor allowed me to smoke because he did not think much of my chances to survive.

Shortly thereafter, one morning at about 1100 hours, a military ambulance comes for me and takes me to the military hospital on the *avenue de la Couronne*. I am given a single room on the isolation pavilion which adjoins the rear of the hospital, on the *rue J. Paquot*. I remember that this detail made me think that, perhaps, they were not telling me something about my condition. In actual fact, there was nothing to it. After two or three days I receive a visit from a German soldier who speaks French, Flemish and Brussels! It is the Belgian nurse who brings him to me. He lived 15 years in Etterbeek. He is in his forties, quite bald, no taller than a good meter 60 centimeters tall (five feet two inches). He is courting my nurse, who is easily one meter 80 centimeters (five feet

11 inches) and must weigh close to 85 kilograms (187 lbs). The three of us get on very well and we have a good laugh every time we get together.

I get up too soon, for I start to feel better quickly, and I walk around in the corridors of the pavilion. The result: I wake up the next day with a sore throat and a new fever! Stupid imprudence. Happily, my nurse gives me something and insists that I not talk to anyone, especially to the doctor or the other nurses. I gargle with hydrogen peroxide mixed with water, repeating this every two or three hours. Miracle! In two days it is gone. We have here a little hairdresser from Brussels who is very resourceful. He gathers all the little bits of soap that he can find and then sells them back to us after melting them and recasting them into normal bars of soap.

A few days later the doctors decide that I am ready and, on about 20 March, I go on sick leave to the *Château d'Ardennes*. An error directs me first to a *Hôtel de Poix – St-Hubert*, in the company of a German comrade. New departure by train to Houyet, where we finally arrive at our *château*. A perspective of three weeks of the real *château* life! My room is as big as a dormitory, but I am alone. But it has only the dimensions of a dormitory. Extreme luxury, of course, all in pale blue, cozy bed, stylish furniture. What great people of this world have preceded me in this bed, and me a poor soldier? Boots and belt are already polished when I get up. Breakfast and other meals served in style, as is all the service here. The *château*, which was part of the chain of European *Grand Hôtels*, is in the grand style of the start of the century. The German authorities have merely modified its decoration a bit, with grand mural frescoes painted in the places where the tapestries or paintings formerly hung. It is winter now, but the weather does not prevent promenades in the forest nor excursions. With the others, my friend Carl and I go to see the *château de Ciergnon*, without, in fact, visiting it. I do not know if that is possible. I discover several wagons of the former royal train and the stopping place planned for this train, another *château* where the ex-King of Rumania, Carol, lived. In brief, we see everything of interest in the immediate surroundings.

On 6 April I am informed of the imminent departure of a small contingent that is going to rejoin the group which left on 10 March. I immediately request termination of my convalescence and return in all haste to the military hospital to obtain my discharge papers stating that I am fit for the front (*KF-Entlassunsschein*[17]). The doctor declares me fit for duty and gives me the requested authorization, but only after telling me of a conversation that he had with my father, who came to demand my demobilization. The doctor promised him that he would talk to me and would demobilize me if I agreed. The good man did what he thought to be his humanitarian duty, and I what I think to be mine, to respect my enlistment. Thus we were all able to have clean consciences, but my father, doubtless, would not have a peaceful soul, and I well understand then. Better today than then.

In the evening of 9 April, 1942, I stay at the St. Jean barracks, *boulevard Botanique*, and on 10 June, the train carries us toward Meseritz. Today begins my life as a *légionnaire*!

---

17 *Kriegsverwendungsfahig* – fit for active service (actually abbreviated to *k.v.*).

2

Instruction (in Brandenburg)

I have no chronological notes from the time of my instruction, so I shall share those memories that bring it alive to me. After leaving Brussels by train on 10 April, 1942 to rejoin my comrades, who had left on 10 March, I believe that I arrived at Meseritz on 11 April or 12, and then at the *Regenwurmlager*.[1] After all these years I recollect these things, some with great clarity; others more vaguely. The camp was quite distant from the city of Meseritz in an area of birch and fir woods, on dry, sandy soil, moderately hilly. The terrain seemed quite broken and very difficult for drill. Be that as it may, the camp was quite agreeable and the site quite the same. The two-story buildings had all the comforts necessary for rationally constructed barracks, the surroundings well landscaped with lawns and gardens of flowers and shrubs, as well as big trees.

The weather, still cool when we arrived, quickly changes to spring and soon we enjoy days of delightful temperatures and lots of sun. We have excellent instructors, tough during the exercises but friendly when off duty. More than once they take me into their confidence and show me pictures of their families. One of them is a landscape gardener with a wife and two daughters. He is, I believe, 32 years old. These conversations are usually during a "cigarette break", stretched out on the grass or on the sand, or leaning against the trees near the stacked rifles.

Reveille is early, followed by a quick shave, then assembly in athletic uniform in front of the building. Then we immediately set out at a jog-trot to an athletic area outside the camp enclosure. We trot through woods and juniper bushes and other thorny plants – that is no accident – that scratch us despite our precautions. We then scale the barricade that surrounds the camp, made of tree-trunks arranged diagonally, about three meters high. Jumping from the far side, always on the run, we head for the flat ground. There we can choose to jump off into thin air from the top of the sandpit, throw the shot (shot put), play ball, high-jump, long-jump or play leapfrog. In short, it does not matter what we do, so long as it is always on the run and without a single minute of inactivity. After an hour, and always at a jog-trot, we return to the barracks area, sometimes by the lake for a short swim. Then we wash up, have breakfast and assemble for exercises. In the afternoon we have instruction in theory, clean weapons and clothes, followed by inspection. Sometimes there are also night exercises and long marches, all trying, but all that is good for me and makes me healthy and fit after my pleurisy.

The instruction is hard, very hard, but it prepares us to better face all that we will undergo in Russia. All of us look radiant and, no doubt, put on pounds of muscle and centimeters of height, just as I do. Those, however, who were overweight certainly lose superfluous kilos of fat and gain endurance. In fact, I have excellent memories of the *Regenwurmlager*. Physically, I feel that I have become a man, and the war will take care of my morale. The 6th Company, that of the

---

1   The *Regenwurmlager* (literally, Earthworm camp) – an extensive underground fortified area, a system of underground bunkers interconnected by tunnels and corridors with a total length of over 100 km. It was constructed by Germany in the 1920's to 1940's near the city of Meseritz (now Międzyrcecz, in what is now western Poland) and served as a military training camp.

"youngsters", always drinks more than us! Yes! Since I am 19 years old I am placed in the 7th, the company of the "Old Men"! How many times, in the evening, after our duty is done, do I take pity on those youngsters who it is thought need to be toughened up more than the others, who are punished "as a group", and more than us, and who assemble, at the run, for inspections, for sessions of "sleeping on their feet", assemblies in canvas uniform, assemblies in woolen uniform. Assemblies with knapsack, then without knapsack, with gas mask, then without, and I am leaving out a lot, believe me!

Even so, we find time and inclination on Sundays to take long walks in the country in little groups, to make "raids" on the pastry shops of Meseritz, at least 12 kilometers from the camp to stuff ourselves with cakes. I never suffered from hunger during my time at the *Regenwurmlager*. I remember that, but others were hungry. Still, I never left anything on my plate or in my mess tin. That is for certain. However, there was a little stealing of one sort or another: a cigarette, a ration of jam or a slice of bread. Then there was a commotion! The perpetrator needed to learn the sense of solidarity and the heinousness of that deed. Locking the wardrobes was forbidden. So, once known, uncovered or self-confessed, he learned to know the "snake-bite of the centurion". Stretched out on the table, with bare torso, held firmly by several of the comrades of the barrack room, the others filed by, flogging him without mercy. But then, afterwards, everything was forgotten, absolutely everything. Doubtless that was the reason why, when at all possible, a "*Bourguignon*" was never left in difficulty without help from his comrades. It was our solidarity, our friendship, such as it was, such as it is and such as it will ever remain!

In our *Regenwurmlager* camp there is also a small battalion or two of Hindus, who excite our astonishment. Clothed in the "*Feldgrau*" [field-gray] uniform, but wearing their multi-colored turbans (according to their caste, if I remember), they make an impression. Many of them have fingers covered with rings, which are not paste, and the officers have particularly beautiful hair. Oftentimes we watch with curiosity when they wash their long hair or coil their heavy black tresses before putting on their turbans. The "*Bourguignons*",[2] with ultra-short hair, had to feel truly deprived in the face of this unusual spectacle! What thoughts must have haunted their spirits at moments like that?

Other memories of the instruction at the *Regenwurmlager* return pell-mell to me from thin air. The memory of the young German women (*BDM*)[3] of the camp on the far side of the lake, who, it seemed, watched us from the shelter of the bushes on the other shore when we bathed. Of course, we did not have swim-trunks. At the barbers, the "*Bourguignons*" always talked bitterly about the official regulations on the cut and length of hair, making undisguised allusions to the "Hindus".

Forty meters from our block, on a little hillock, there is a gas chamber where we test the effectiveness of our gas masks and accustom ourselves to the usage of this barbarous accessory, which most of us rapidly discarded, replacing it in its tin by other *impedimenta*, or *impedimenti*[4] that seemed more useful in our eyes!

We also have a dog that we make our mascot, a very beautiful sheepdog, German, by chance, but who could blame us for it? This companion would be seriously wounded, later, by a shell

---

2 Léon Degrelle, the leader of the Rexist movement, propounded 'a fanciful dream of a Greater Belgium based on the former Burgundian Empire of the 15th and 16th centuries. This vision of a reconstituted empire, incorporating large areas of both the Netherlands and northern France, was to become a consistent feature of Degrelle's wartime rhetoric'. (Conway, p. 33). At Degrelle's insistence, the cross of the old Burgundian Empire appeared on the *Légion's* flag. This Burgundian theme became a constant part of Degrelle's recruitment rhetoric – thus it is that the author romantically refers to himself and his comrades of the *Légion Wallonie* as '*Bourguignons*', or 'Burgundians', as was universal among members of the *Légion Wallonie*.

3 *Bund Deutscher Mädel* – Nazi girl's organization.

4 Latin for baggage (in the sense of military baggage).

fragment. Cared for, he recovered. Was he finally killed at the Donetz? We named him *PAK*, the name for our anti-tank guns, and I still have a photo where he is beside me.

There is also boxing. R. Marchal against Jean Maroy, who was killed in an auto accident after the war, the same Jean who, when our company crossed paths with the "youth" company, would sing out, "*Maman, les p'tit bateaux*"[5], and the *prévot* [leader] of the youngsters, with his charges would reply, "It is us, *gagas*[6] of the 7th…" There are several memories that are still with me from that period, up to 23 May!

On that day we make our grand departure. As I remember, we learned of it the day before. All of those youths or adolescents that we were, prematurely matured, live in a paroxysm of excitement. The great day, "*Jour J*",[7] finally arrives. We are ready to face anything, to suffer anything, but, above all, to overcome anything, to conquer everything, starting with ourselves.

All ready, as if for a parade, everything buckled: knapsack, bread bag, cartridge pouches, spade, gas mask and anti-mustard gas cloth, arms, tent canvas. We are preparing to leave on a great voyage that will provide marvelous memories of unknown horizons to all those who return, for we do know that not everyone will return. In the freight wagons: eight horses or 40 men, we each arrange our own little corner on the straw. Sleeping bags and equipment lined up or piled against the wall. These few square meters will be our only home for 16 days. The horses, their bedding and fodder on board, everything, including a field kitchen, the armourer's stowage and our rations, we are moving on to a new stage.

The sight of all this enthusiastic, voluble youth gathering before the sliding doors of the wagons, mostly open, cannot but bring a smile of sympathy to the faces of all those, civilian or military, who watch us depart. And then … a wave of farewell from all the people whose paths we have, at some time, no doubt, crossed in the fields or in the city. These people, who are by no means effusive by nature, no longer hide their emotions. They cannot help but communicate with us there and I would thank them, here, for their encouragement. Unconsciously, they help us to surmount all of our uncertainties.

Insensibly, if not without a few jolts, our train picks up speed and the railroad station fades away. Even so, we can still make out the people whose gaze is certainly still following us. What are they thinking? Of a son, a spouse, a *fiancé* who is departing with us? Or of those who would, undoubtedly, depart one day?

The plains of Mecklenburg now pass by, monotonous, but brightened by the sunlight. Our journey takes us past several small stations, grade crossings and, in the background, peasants who wave amicably, sitting on their carts, their wives or their daughters behind, their hair in scarfs. Surprised by the badges on our sleeves, they must have been left with questions. It is true that by that time, it was not usual to see foreign volunteers. Soon the landscape will change every day and we will develop new habits, but despite everything, as the days and opportunities go by, the "*Bourguignons*" will improvise and often to the limit of what is conceivable or possible in an army – especially in the German Army.

---

5   A counting-rhyme song for little children. '*Maman les p'tits bateaux qui vont sur l'eau ont – ils des jambes? Mais oui, mon gros bêta. S'ils n'en avaient pas. Ils ne march'raient pas… .*' – 'Mama, The little boats that go on the water , do they have legs? Why yes, my little silly. If they did not have them, they would not move…'

6   Doddering old senile fools.

7   French equivalent to D-Day.

The young men of 10 March on the move.
[Tr. Note: the second contingent of volunteers
for *La Légion Wallonie*, to which the author
belonged, departed on 10 March.]

Me in 1942.

On the way to exercise, May 1942.

The field kitchen also comes
to the exercises.

PAK and me: we get along very well.

A map of north Germany/Poland showing locations of interest, such as the encampments of the *Légion*, *Sturmbrigade* and *Division Wallonien*. (George Anderson)

3

En Route to the East:
16 Days on Straw

Leaving Meseritz, our train proceeds toward Schwiebus, through Lissa, Glogau, Brno, Vienna, Sopron, Budapest, then Debrecen, Pascali and Iasi, before entering the USSR. We see the Carpathians and the rich plains of Bessarabia, and rivers and streams beyond count. On 28 May, 1942 we pass through Tiraspol, to move yet onward, but always to the east. The weather is glorious and remains so for this entire marvelous journey. Endless sun and truly quite hot. That quickly leads us and a few comrades to arrange summertime billets. Perched on the wagons of straw that is supposed to be bedding for horses, we remove a certain number of bales from the center. We make a sort of living space in the open air. We spend most of the days and nearly all of the nights there. It is far more agreeable and far less hot than in the wagons. It is also far softer for sleeping or lounging on than on the planks of the wagons. We have suntan lotion that we bought at the *Regenwurmlager* canteen shortly before our departure and we cover ourselves well with it while accustoming ourselves to the sun. We come to regret this, for as we look at each other, a little bit later, we burst out in paroxysms of insane laughter. The two locomotives that pull the train are for sure not electric and the falling soot rapidly transforms us into chimney sweeps. Wiping only homogenizes our complexions by making a mixture of soot and suntan lotion. Ever resourceful, we quickly find the best showers, the towers that provide water for the locomotives. But the water falls from on high in a great stream. We have to use extreme caution while a comrade operates the chain.

A detail, trivial but comical, also comes to mind. It is the way one relieves oneself, *en route*, while the train does not stop moving and when you can no longer wait. Squatting on the running board, face turned toward the wagon and firmly grasped by two buddies, the officiate cries out, as a joke, to the occupants of the wagons behind who lean out a bit too much, that they should watch out. There are always those who, in turn, remain sitting at the doors, legs to the outside. This method was passed on to us, explained, even demonstrated, by way of instruction, with explanatory gestures, by a German captain, quite corpulent but extremely agile. The captain never lost his prestige, for it all seemed so natural. A few laughs, including those of the captain himself, and it was noted, no more needed.

However, during this voyage, there were so many events, so many humorous episodes, that I can no longer place them chronologically or geographically. I present them as they come back to me. First, there was a half-starved wretch, who, on a wager, in less time than it takes to write, swallowed 40 hard-boiled eggs that the young girls sold alongside the cars every time the train stopped near a village, a town or even in the open fields. Who knew where they came from? I have to tell you that the champion of the eggs had to be evacuated that afternoon, suffering from horrible cramps and that he was never seen again in the *Légion*! Far into the Ukraine there are such young girls, women or children, at every station or other stop. They rush from every direction offering, depending on the region, to sell us chocolate, pastries, sometimes quite good ones, or bacon, in

Rumania and Hungary. Then, corn pancakes, hard-boiled eggs nearly everywhere, or fruits. As we go farther to the east, the commodities offered become less rich, less elaborate, less appetizing, but our young constitutions digest everything with no problems, the more easily since it has been a long time since we had been accustomed to such opulence!

The field kitchen, secured on a flatcar, feeds us when the train stops for any length of time, and the quartermaster sergeant does the same, distributing bread and canteen-goods.[1] There is also, certainly, much cleaning of arms and many inspections along the right-of-way, in front of the wagons. There are also more precisely oriented inspections to make sure that nobody has broken into his iron rations, at the end of which, it must be stated, several are punished.

The stops of the train, especially in Russia, are sometimes quite long, since the railroad track is only a single track, rarely more. There is in such cases a siding and we have to wait for trains going in the opposite direction to pass, or others loaded with *matériel* or ammunition, or with men returning from leave. These trains, well protected against pillagers or possible partisans, are less safe from certain astute *"Bourguignons"*, for there are also trains loaded with provisions! At that time there were few partisans, even less in the Ukraine. However, the fortuitous encounter between these trains loaded with edibles and certain famished and insatiable *"Bourguignons"* challenges the consciences of some of these. Judging by the menu of certain *"Bourguignons"*, I think that some cargoes of foodstuffs failed to arrive intact at their destinations and, thereby, presented problems for the quartermaster sergeant consignees. I have seen at least one of the tank wagons of a train, pissing wine the entire length of the railroad ballast. An accidental shot? In every case well aimed and at the right height. At that time there were a number of helmets and mess kits that still smelled like wine eight days later. What a waste!

It was in Rumania, at Iasi, I believe, that the little park across from the railroad station bore witness to the *élan* of certain amorous *"Bourguignons"*. It must be said that at that time we did not yet speak Russian there, but on the contrary, much French. Idiotically, I talk to the station master, happy to speak French, and also to a couple of uncertain age in *bourgeois* clothes while my companions, at least some of them, prefer more intimate and more advanced conversations in that little park with the local beauties, who are of an age less certain than that of the woman I am talking with. To be quite honest I must say that I only learned all this later. Too late, alas! Our train starts to depart. And, perhaps that is why it is a virgin who listens, too late to the impassioned narratives of the prowess of his mates. Nevertheless, I suspect there are some exaggerations and embellishments, since they are still talking about it for the next 15 days.

On the other hand, something that is quite exact since I was present and invited, is this wedding, also in Rumania. This is right out in the country. There is, indeed, a little shelter, a small house for the railroad guard, but, far away, a noise, more precisely, the sound of violins, and of other musical instruments! We are stopped, once more, and already for a good length of time, with no signs of imminent departure. But that is something we never know ahead of time. The music grows louder and soon a long procession appears, preceded by a Gypsy orchestra. The people are dressed as if they are in some bizarre postcard, in peculiar trousers, like long underwear, with black jackets and beautifully embroidered white shirts. The women are in white dresses, even more richly embroidered in all colors. We are there, watching, and, along with some others, I approach. Very politely we are immediately invited to follow, and we require no urging. Thus it is that some of the *"Bourguignons"* find themselves part of the wedding, behind the violins, and are soon at the village that was a kilometer from the railroad and their train. There is dancing before the village hall of the little village, and I see a *"Bourguignon"* dancing with the young bride, very pretty and

---

1   Condiments, dried vegetables, toiletries, tobacco etc.

much younger than his own wife. I prefer to abstain, since I have only danced once or twice in my whole life and the nails of my new clodhoppers present too great a risk for the feet of my potential partners. However, I accept the glasses that I am offered and also the beautiful smiles that are aimed our way. But I do not dare to respond to the insistent looks, the provocative smiles, since it is necessary to maintain my courage to be able to leave at any moment! We stay there quite a spell, as if we are cousins who have not been seen for a long time. Two hours, maybe three, can I say for sure? But the memory of that reception, of that jubilation will long haunt the hours of our nightly vigils, our hours of solitude. Yes, all of those who were there still remember, even today, with the heart of a 17- or 18-year-old. It was a moment of rest, a moment of cheerfulness in the inexorable destiny that we had voluntarily taken upon ourselves. We have to tear ourselves away from the spectacle and think of rejoining our train, for the locomotive is always smoking in the distance. With regrets, with a heavy heart and a catch in my throat I say my farewells, as do my friends. A few kisses, very chaste, to my great regret, kisses of friendship from those we barely know, hence another memory. It is better that way, less bitterness, and a more precious memory!

Now it is necessary to show a good pair of heels and get back to the train on the double. For fear of too much suffering, for the heart is easily inflamed at that age, I cannot help returning two or three times to make gestures of friendship, to respond to the signs of farewell from those friends of a few hours. We are no more than a hundred meters from our wagons when the train blows its whistle and repeats its call several times. We start to run and I see those on the train waving their arms toward the village that is already so distant. Looking back, I see two *"Bourguignons"* who lingered longer than we and who are paying for the blessed time they had gained at that wedding by running after the train. Two small silhouettes in the distance, panting in the dust of the road. Already the train pulls away and they have just time to take a running leap on board, with the help of their comrades. A last look back, heavy with nostalgia, on that marvelous plain where the corn and the wheat are already well grown. A tranquil countryside, drenched with sun where the dust stirred by our dash gently settles and which returns to the bucolic charm that ignores the war. What serenity, what a vision of spring! Soon all of that is blurred by other countrysides, other horizons. Another memory, but I cannot forget that every turn of the wheel carries us closer to the front! At times all of us think of that, envision it, but each keeps that thought in his secret garden so as not to disturb the dream of a friend that lingers in the soul. Our youth has this modesty that diminishes with age.

There is also another type of misadventure which several *"Bourguignons"* nonchalantly survive. During unexpected halts or stops, these *"Bourguignons"* develop the habit of leaving the train, without paying too much attention to the others, in search of some sort of adventure or to do some domestic shopping, without concern for the length of the stop, losing sight of the train. There are those who, to satisfy a need, without even going that far, are surprised to see the train depart, immediately and without waiting, since it has just stopped. Thus it was that, at times, here or there, one or another *"Bourguignon"* wanders along the tracks in shirt and trousers, or, at times, with only the latter. Sometimes, that same day or, perhaps, two or three days later, we would see them reappear, wearing the jacket of a station master or something totally different, received *en route* from some compassionate soul, or, quite simply, from someone who desired to safeguard the prestige and preserve the respect of the civil population. These insouciant comrades would wait for us on the platform of a railroad station where they had been left by a trainload of men returning from leave or a high-priority train that we had allowed to pass us in the hours just past as we waited on a siding. That is what happened to our comrade, Ernst, killed a few months later in the Caucasus. We did not recognize him, and for good reason! He was awaiting us, two days after his disappearance, on the platform of a railroad station, dressed like a railway man in dark blue with red piping, without the field-gray trousers he was wearing when he left the train.

It is a Sunday morning when we pass through Czechoslovakia. It must be 8:00 or 8:30. The sky is uniform blue, the weather as glorious as ever. The train makes its way through open country with small farms of a few little houses scattered here and there. The small gardens, surrounded by little wooden fences, already abounding with all the flowers of spring and summer, delicately color the scene. In the distance, seen through the mist of the hot morning, I can make out a suburb, a city. I see groups of bicyclists, sometimes side by side, sometimes in tandem, on a road leading to the city alongside the railroad. A great many young people going into the country from the city, and others going the opposite direction, toward the city. The shorts and light dresses of the young girls stir up a fresh little whiff of romanticism. Again a few dreams. Groups going to mass, or returning, others going to picnic outside the city. That is what the missals under the arms suggest to me, or the picnic baskets fastened to the bicycles, or some knapsacks. That reminds me of other picnics at home, before the war that already seem so distant! There are, of course, few *"Bourguignons"* who fail to make inviting hand-signs , even in our "sleeping cars" , unequivocal gestures that even a Czech who does not know a word of French can understand perfectly. Some of these young folk respond with friendly gestures, but with no trace of invitation. The others, more numerous, pursue their course, nose on the handlebars or gaze fixed straight ahead. Perhaps this is hostility, perhaps indifference. For all that, it does not disturb me, and that vision of such a beautiful Sunday still fills me with joy.

The train, which is still rolling slowly, loses speed, but now we are nearly in the city. Iridescent in the sun, the bell towers and multi-colored roof tiles give the whole city a festive air. Many bell towers and cupolas, many buildings with extremely beautiful architecture make me think of Vienna or Prague. I treasure the memory of a pretty postcard where the copper domes of the bell towers shine and all of the window panes reflect the sun to us as if the city is on fire! The train passes between the platforms of the station at a walking pace. It is Brno! On the platforms and around the station is a variegated crowd in all the colors of the women's dresses. But the train does not stop and the vision disappears as the train picks up speed. Again yet one more snapshot, very tidy, for my memories.

At about 11:30, no doubt, a little before noon, the train stops in open country and the field kitchen on its flatcar serves us soup. A good *"Eintopf"* [one-dish meal] of peas and bacon. The line stretches before the field kitchen with the sound of clattering mess kits, laughter and conversation. Those who already return with full mess kits do not wait, eating their repast while walking. But a *gourmet*, a bit affected, who also satisfies his eyes while he eats, makes a curious discovery! Wait a minute, he says! Raisins in my pea soup? The cook must have fooled himself at the bottom of the sack! But no! The raisins have wings? That is not possible! Good God, they are flies! Well then, what an outcry! And it spreads, even among those who have already swallowed practically all their ration. They do not go back for seconds. But that day there, the quartermaster sergeant listens, and also *Lieutenant* Jean V., *Rittmeister* von Rabenau and the others! That day I learn more abuses and terms that I do not know, and mostly in Walloon, than I have ever heard in all of my existence. Some of the excited men push the things far away. A little later we will be happy with another soup and a little supplementary edibles. All is not lost, neither the morale nor even the war, at least not yet!

By way of varying a bit the occupations with which we pass our time, two or three times I spend a bit of the journey in the company of comrades in the service on a flatcar armed with anti-aircraft machine guns on mounts. They go on duty at every change of guard throughout the 24 hours of the day to defend against any aerial attack. If I remember correctly, there were two heavy machine guns (*SMG*) on these wagons. Throughout the entire journey they have to be ready to go into action at any moment. The time passes slowly enough, and with monotony. Happily, the countrysides, as varied for us as they are new, provide much diversion, as do the conversations, which never lack subjects and, at times, a visit like mine. They are less comfortably set up than we are on our wagon full of straw, but that lasts no longer than 24 hours, 16 of which are in full sunlight, without protection, and it beats down hard. Those youngsters, for most of the time this duty falls to or is claimed by the 6th Company, still find the courage or the desire to sing their enthusiasm. That makes up for the lack of radio in the wagons or replaces the chatter of these young songsters who do not yet have the Iron Cross, but some of whom would end this first campaign under the wooden cross, of birch wood! One thinks of it at times, but without pathos, and today I have not forgotten, I have not forgotten them. Who among us fails to remember them?

We are now at the 29th or 30th of May, and soon we will delay no longer in catching up with our comrades who left before us, those of 8 August, 1941. For several days we have been in the USSR. We no longer meet the herds of half-wild horses galloping in the *puszta*[2] as in Hungary, nor the great stud farms frequented by horsemen without peer, whom we watched maneuver with astonishment and rapture. All that is past. The country is now nearly uniformly flat. A few *isbas*[3] with roofs of tin or straw, rare villages. A few female peasants, heavily loaded, for the men carry nothing. They are dressed poorly, dowdy. This is, indeed, the Soviet paradise? Perhaps we will see something better farther on? The railroad leads us right toward the forest, which we are approaching. Now we are there and the train, which slowed a bit too late and too far, comes to a sudden stop.

What is happening? I see men dashing to the right in the woods. Among them, the *Prévôt* John Hagemans.[4] He is in shorts, bare to the waist, carrying his helmet buckling his belt while running, submachine gun on his shoulder. It is the platoon which was on alert at that moment. There is always one, ready for action in any circumstances, in rotating duty. John Hagemans' men are all more or less equipped in the same manner, not very orthodox, but reacting quickly. Some shots come from the forest in our direction. Myself, I hear nothing up there on my wagon of straw, nor do my friends. The men penetrate the forest, fanning out as in an exercise and disappear. Everything is quiet, but, as a security measure, another platoon is put on the alert the length of the train and the anti-aircraft machine guns are aimed toward the forest. Sporadically we hear a few shots or the sound of a few bursts of submachine gun-fire. Then, nothing again! After a good quarter-hour, maybe half an hour, we hear voices; then I see the men of the platoon that had reconnoitered reappearing, one after another. They saw nothing, heard no more. Partisans? Hunters? Illusions? Who knows! All of the men return to their places on the train and it moves on. Woods, then the steppe for a change, then more woods, that is the Ukraine!

Today is 1 June, 1942. I do not remember seeing a single cloud since we left the *Regenwurmlager*. The weather is always very beautiful, very hot. Is this really the war? Am I not dreaming? Everything that I see, everything that I am experiencing, is it truly real? At times I ask myself! The train keeps rolling and the morning passes, then the hour of noon and the hour of the meal. When, at about 1400 or 1500 hours I sit up and emerge from our hole in the straw, I instinctively look toward the front. Immediately I see some grand metal structure. As we approach I ascertain that it is the superstructure of a bridge, a very large bridge. We are not on the immediate approaches of the

---

2   The *puszta* is the grassland biome on the Great Hungarian Plain, now widely cultivated, similar to the American great plains or the Eurasian steppe.

3   Russian log huts.

4   John Hagemans was the *Prévôt*, or Provost, of the *Jeunesses Rexistes* – the Rexist youth organization. After the first contingent of volunteers forming the *Légion Wallonie* had lost so heavily in the fighting in Russia that the *Légion* was in danger of disbandment, Léon Degrelle called on the Rexist Party for a new contingent. John Hagemans personally led a group of 150 or so teenage boys from the *Jeunesses Rexistes* that assembled on the Grand Place in Brussels on 10 March, 1942 and volunteered, *en masse*. John Hagemans, as former leader of the Rexist Youth, held a special place in the affections of the '*Bourguignons*'.

bridge and we discover the river. Large and majestic, it is the Dnieper! When the snow melts, or when there is heavy rain, it must be even larger, for the bridge extends far beyond both banks of the existing river. However, it is impressive enough as it is now.

This time we are certainly in the heart of this Ukraine. Then, immediately after, it is the city of Dniepropetrowsk, the first great Russian city that we have come to, for we did not enter Odessa, we bypassed it through its suburbs. We have already crossed the Pruth, the Dniester, the Bug and the Ingul, and this is the most imposing of all. The onion-shaped bell towers, the *isbas* in the suburbs and the mournful old structures, dilapidated and somber, at the heart of the city. The sun and the broad *allées* of hard-packed earth somewhat redeem the sadness and poverty of the whole. I speak of *allées*, for how can one call this sort of road a street or an avenue? Doors, casements, windows, of wood or of iron, where not the smallest atom of paint adheres, or, if a trace remains, it must date from before the October revolution! And that was in 1917. Everything is rusty, yes, that is the dominant impression, what lingers. Rust everywhere. Even the old bricks seem covered with rust, impregnated, saturated with rust. Not a single building that is new, or even more or less recent. Everything is old, old, old. All of it seems to date from the time of the Tsars and, doubtless, all of it really does date from that epoch. There may be a possible exception in one or another industrial structure, but that is not certain. I think of the "*Les Misérables*" of Victor Hugo. I believe it is worse here, and we are in 1942!

We enter the Dniepropetrowsk train station, a very big station with many tracks, like a marshaling yard. Lots of bustle, everyone is busy. The German personnel are active, the Slavs make haste slowly. Distributed on these tracks are lines and lines of goods-wagons, like ours, or older. Doors and windows latticed with barbed wire or, in part, nailed shut with planks. All of these wagons are packed with Russian prisoners. There are thousands and thousands of them. Perhaps 10 or a dozen trains, each made up of dozens of wagons and probably more than 40 men per wagon. How many? Hard to say. I see cigarettes and morsels of bread fly from our train toward that of the prisoners near us. Our halt in the Dniepropetrowsk station lasts a good two hours. It is with relief that we leave this spectacle, this sad city. When we are back in the country it seems to me that we breathe better. The depression of this city was suffocating. I have the sensation that now everything will become more serious, that the "easy" life will come to an end! Onward we roll, all day, and the same the next day, and the night returns. In the course of that, but much later, the train stops. We finish the night after a fashion, trying to get back to sleep, but we already know by the distant noise that our voyage on this new sort of "Orient-Express" stops here.

Embarkation for the front – 23 May, 1942.

A little emergency snack during a train stop.

Our train in Bessarabia, May 1942.

A small Rumanian train station and our cook, B.

4

Slaviansk: The Front is Not Much Farther

It is 3 June, 1942 and I already seem to have heard the sound of cannon in the distance, very far away, and to have seen the flicker in the sky that they produce. Right at this present moment this becomes infernally clear, and the front cannot be very distant. It is no longer really night, but not yet really day. The noises and sounds of life come to us, the sound of footsteps on the ballast. The sergeants of the day rouse the men. Henceforth commotion, all the noises rapidly increase. It is here that we disembark, we are at Slavjansk!

The sun emerges and climbs rapidly. Everyone washes up quickly at the pumps that we find at the approaches to the railroad station. The city seems important enough, but not comparable to Dniepropetrowsk. Less populated but quite spread out, like all the Russian agglomerations. As always, no paved roads. Nothing but sand, nothing but dirt. Everywhere the old hovels, old houses or sordid, shabby *isbas*, but this seems less sad than the big city. No time for extensive reflection, it is the great removal! We gather our stuff, buckle the knapsacks and bread bags. A few swear out of habit in situations like this, and there are the shouts of those who don't immediately find their things that they scattered about during the long trip. Those who lack order or method! It is always the same ones who have this sort of misfortune. Then everyone has to help in unloading the *matériel*, the horses, the carts, the field kitchens, weapons and foodstuffs! Everything is lined up along the tracks in a great turmoil, with lots of shouting and swearing, for sure, but also with great skill. We are there, ready to get going. And now?

While we are busily at work, there is a hullabaloo and a rumor spreads: the *Chef*[1] is there! Everyone converges on a building in front of which we can already see a compact group. *Eh oui*! The *Chef* is there. Lots of noise, hands extending and conversations. He has not changed much, but from the very start, one thing is most striking, of traits more pronounced, more noticeable. There is no more of the "student". It seems to me there is nothing else different. Always the same smile, and he talks to us with the same animation as he communicates his habitual enthusiasm. Already most of us are ready to go all the way to the feet of the Urals! We must acknowledge it, we must endorse it. And it is a fact, we will march far in the coming months. We do not linger in accomplishing the first day's march, and the first few hundred meters are done in column of threes, singing. Platoons and companies well formed. But as we leave the city the road no longer allows that, and soon two parallel files march down the road on opposite sides, sleeves rolled up, collars open and rifle carried in whatever position is comfortable for the moment.

Le Chef has taken his place at the head of the column and marches along with the men. Thus he accompanied the new recruits that we were for the first few kilometers before getting back in his saddle and riding on ahead to Brachovka, escorted by his *aides de camp*, all on horseback. As for

---

1 *Le Chef de Rex*, Léon Degrelle – 'Chief' of Rex – who joined the *Légion* he created as a common soldier, but is still the *Chef* of Rexism and the Rexist Party.

us, we proceed as in our exercise marches at the *Regenwurmlager*, but this time it is not an exercise. We march, we march, and I well know that, no doubt, that there is a little more solemnity at the bottom of my heart, but I feel good. My feet are comfortable in my hob-nailed boots. Watch out for blisters! We look at the countryside, flat, and resume our usual conversations. Regularly we halt for the accustomed 10 minutes. Everything is as we expected, everything is calm in this sector. The horizon is vast, and we can see far into the distance. Toward evening we see woods, a forest, ahead and to our right. Our column turns toward the woods, and finally we reach it and enter. Beech and oak, big trees, but also stands of mature forest that have grown from seedlings, and, of course, birch. We stack our arms and remove our knapsacks. By fours, we put up our tents. It must be said that we do this with our tent canvases, which are also our "macs", our rain-gear. In short, a very practical article of equipment.

While we are busy getting set up and while the field kitchen is preparing the meal, sounds of distant muffled explosions disturb the peace. Soon the whistles and two explosions shred the air in the woods where we are working. Two heavy artillery shells fall, but far from us. We are well-nigh astonished! An observation plane must have reported our progress toward the woods and radioed our presence there. Undoubtedly they want to impress us. We are not dreaming. We really are in Russia and it really is war! The forest soon regains its calm, but this time we smell powder for the first time, and it is not face powder! That is truly the first smell of the war that I remember perfectly and that I shall not forget. Leaning against trees, we chat while smoking a few cigarettes before going to sleep in our tents. The night passes uneventfully, protected by the sentries. At *Reveille* we get coffee from the field kitchen and a snack before the tents. No water, so no wash-up. We don our gear and set out. It seems that the artillery of the day before is 16 kilometers from the woods. Thus we regularly get the news, the details, and ask ourselves where they come from, for generally, they are exact and prove to be accurate. Our march resumes and again, now and then, we hear the sound of artillery coming from the southeast.

In the afternoon we approach a village, the very one occupied by our comrades, Brachovka! Bearing witness to our morale, a song breaks out, and those who are strolling about in Brachovka stop short. It is French that they hear. It is, indeed, the reinforcements that *le Chef* announced the previous day. We reach the first "old-timers" who stop to look at us. Each of us looks for familiar faces. I quickly find some, since I know well many of the first contingent. Old comrades, militants like myself, childhood friends or from secondary school. We are totally surprised, and disagreeably so, to see scowling faces and few smiles. Among my old comrades I have only one or two disappointments. Everything goes very well with the others, and I feel great joy, as do they, at our reunion. But it seems that there are, on the other hand, some among the friends of my company who receive some jibes or disagreeable remarks from some of the other "old-timers". It must be noted that the reception was pretty chilly on the part of some of the companions of 8 August, but not from all. One cannot generalize. Some of the "old-timers" observed that if we had not arrived, they would have been repatriated. This remark, which I heard several times, is true. But they experienced Gromovaya – Balka[2] and the harsh winter of 1941–42. This attitude surprises me, for we had hoped for a warmer reception, and that is not always the case, but I find no difficulty in

---

2 On 18 February, 1942 the *Légion Wallonie* approached and occupied Gromovaya – Balka under heavy Soviet artillery fire. On 28 February, after 10 days of incessant shelling, the Soviets attacked with two infantry regiments, supported by tanks. For 10 hours the *Légion Wallonie* blocked the passage of Gromovaya – Balka, achieving its first battle honor and mention in dispatches. In the fighting at Gromovaya – Balka, 71 were killed, 155 wounded, or 55 percent of the 411 men who were in that action – 150 having remained with the train at Grischino.

excusing them. Perhaps I will have the opportunity to find many old comrades with whom I had strong ties and most of whom will be pleased to see me.

Our two companies which have just arrived assembles, form up, and *Capitaine* Tchekoff approaches us. What demeanor! Strong, quite stocky, firmly seated on his horse. His language is virile – very, very virile. A welcome in his own style that does not displease me. We are provided lodgings, one *isba* for every squad (10 men). Our squad is assigned to an *isba* on the slope southeast of the village, near the mill. We are *Sergent* Fauville, our squad leader, the brothers Anthonis, A. Devaux, A. De Smedt, Raymond P., Emile E., Parmentier, a comrade whose name escapes me and myself, the nine fusiliers. We settle into this *isba* where there are also its normal inhabitants, the Russian family consisting of a couple, some years of age, a daughter with a young baby, whose husband undoubtedly is in the Red Army, and another daughter who, I think, is single. Also living in this *isba* are one horse, two cows, several nanny goats and a billy goat, and, in addition, the farmyard poultry. These animals live in the stable which is an integral part of the *isba*, with a door between it and the habitation. In winter, or whenever it is cold, this door stays open during the night to allow the warmth of the animals to circulate freely and to spread into the habitation, thereby helping to warm the house, but also contributing to the ambient fragrance! On the other hand, at all seasons of the year, an opening at the bottom of the door to the stable allows the poultry to circulate freely throughout the entire habitation! Since we sleep on the ground, chickens, ducks and geese pass over our bodies several times each night. At first we wake up in a wild attempt to wring the necks of these brazen fowls, but, after a while, we get used to it. After our first night, the day of 5 June serves for arms inspection, organization of equipment, receiving directives and formation of the new units. The day goes quickly.

In the midst of the following night we are awakened by a racket. What is going on? I see shadows come and go. They are our Russian hosts. They come and go from the stable to the dwelling and vice versa. I am now fully awake and, by the light of a sort of oil lamp, whose wick is made of a stalk of maize (*karasinka*), I see that the man lays a newborn calf on the wooden table. The woman and the daughters have old burlap bags with which they rub down the young calf. This *toilette* accomplished, they put the calf back by its mother. During this time the baby wakes up and bawls incessantly. Then the grandmother takes it on her knees while the mother prepares bread-soup for him. I watch her prepare a sort of milk and flour mixture in a pot heating on the stove, which they lit to warm up the calf. This is quickly done and, without even wiping it off with a cloth, the mother pours the contents of the pot on the table where, a few moments earlier, they had laid the calf! Then the grandmother picks up the bread-soup from the table with her index finger, rubs the two index fingers on each other two or three times, passing the bread-soup back and forth from the one to the other to cool it, and then she thrusts her finger, covered with this mixture, into the mouth of the infant, who seems to appreciate it despite all the above. *Bon appétit* little one! The operation continues thus until there is no more of the bread-soup on the table. I do believe that the infant fell back asleep, for I certainly did the same.

The next day the women go out to the fields and the man remains at home, as on many subsequent days. He then awaits the return of the women to prepare the meal, for of course, it is they who do the cooking and wash the dishes before returning to the field. All this time the man waits, rolling his cigarettes of *magorka* and meditates. His only occupation, his entire preoccupation, is the horse. I have rarely seen the men work. On the other hand, the women work hard! During this time the baby, who remains at home, is in a sort of square, low box, with a big cord at each corner whose ends come together above, fastened to an eye-headed nail in a ceiling beam. Thus the baby passes his first months suspended between heaven and earth. To put him to sleep one slowly turns the box until the cords are sufficiently twisted and then lets it go. This improvised cradle then turns back and forth nearly indefinitely! That gives time to do other things without being disturbed by the cries of the baby.

Our relations with our hosts are perfect. For them, the war seems to be over. They simply await the return of the son-in-law. They resume their accustomed ways. We share our comestibles and they share their ordinary meal with us: *kapusta* (cabbage), *kartochka* (potatoes), *maslo* (butter) and *moloko* (milk). Sometimes a chicken or a goose.

The following day, two or three Russian airplanes, "*Ratas*", fly over the village and, when we see the planes, we lie on our backs as instructed and all fire our rifles at the airplanes. They fly low, and, the fire of numerous rifles is dangerous for them. Then a German airplane arrives, all alone, and the Russians attempt to flee. The pursuit immediately begins and after a few tens of minutes, one of the Russian airplanes reappears, trailing a long stream of smoke, and crashes a little northwest of the village. We hurry there. Nothing stirs at our approach. We lean toward the panes of plexiglass. The pilot is dead in his cockpit. With some difficulty we remove his body and lay it on the grass of the prairie. Our doctor soon arrives and can only confirm the death. We collect the personal effects and papers on board (a bare minimum) which are sent to the division's headquarters.

With great curiosity, since this is the first time, we inspect the machine, very rudimentary, in truth, in its totality, and pay particular concern to the instruments. I immediately start to cut one of the red stars from one of the wings with my knife and others do the same with the different insignia on the wings, on the cockpit and the rear aileron. It must be stated that this is not difficult, for all of its surfaces are made of coarse cloth. Others dismount the dials, clock, altimeter, bank-indicator etc., or portions of the cockpit plexiglass. There are at least 10 of us thus gathering our first trophies of war. A few of us dig a grave and bury the aviator. We gather a few flowers from the field to cover his tomb and fire a salute in his honor. We are, in truth, a bit emotional. In order to avoid letting this show, each of us attempts to exhibit an air of detachment, or appears to be interested in something. It is the first tomb on our itinerary!

The following morning the residents of the village call to us and invite us to follow them. What is happening now? A few hundred meters from the village they point out to us a cow on the ground. She writhes about and is swollen like a gourd. Good Lord, do they think we are veterinarians? There is nothing we can do for this poor beast, no more than they can. Finally they ask us to put her down with a rifle shot. Indeed, that is all that can be done, and it is quickly done. The peasants tell us that this is already the third or fourth cow that has died like this in a few weeks. Later our doctor will give us several explanations confirming that the disease is incurable. For these poor people, most of whom have only a single cow, to see two die that had been saved for a better day is a catastrophe. *Chesko yedno, woïna*!

The following afternoon I write a letter or two home. At that moment, cries, distant noise, interrupt me and call me outside. There is also the sound of airplane engines. Decidedly there will not be a dull day in this out-of-the-way steppe. I dash toward the "*barza*". I know no more precise name for this sort of terrace that partially surrounds the *isba*. Just as on the day before, I see an airplane flying toward us, flying low and trailing a stream of black smoke. It burns, and the flames that surround it come from an engine. It is a much bigger airplane than the other time, and, like that one, it also crashes near the village. Now it is very close and we see the distinctive markings. It is a German airplane! A *Heinkel* 111. Good God! They are not getting out! The machine crashes immediately in a shower of sparks and we run, breathlessly, toward it to try to do something. But when we get near the airplane we quickly see that there is nothing more to do. The flames keep us a good dozen meters from the airplane and we have no way to extinguish them. We cannot come one step closer. We have to shield our faces from the heat with our arms and I can feel the flames scorch my arms through the cloth of my sleeves. It is necessary to fall back a bit. What tragic impotence!

The flames quickly die down, and three or four of us attempt to approach. All the same, it puts out a lot of heat, provided that nothing explodes, the fuel tanks or the ammunition! At present it is the metal that still radiates heat. Nevertheless, one of my bolder comrades tries to reach the cockpit and, after several attempts, to slide open the canopy, protecting his hands with his fatigue jacket. We can see well that he sweats big drops, but then he is able, with great difficulty, to get a hold on the body of one of the two occupants and to pull him against the edge of the cockpit. Three of us manage to pull the man outside and lay him on the ground. Then it is the pilot's turn. The two aviators are stretched out, side by side. They are nearly naked, their uniforms and flying suits burned off, and what remains is charred! It is only a little later that we realize the injuries to our hands, superficially burned, despite our precautions. But that is nothing serious. We were burned while grasping the bodies. Seeing them stretched out we better understand, they are truly roasted. The one is still big, entirely bloated. He has three bullet wounds in his chest, from which emerge bubbles, like boiling fat. The other is small, all shriveled up, charred, truly black!

It was their last mission … Ours begins now after the doctor is through. We dig two graves more near that of yesterday's Russian and bury two comrades in arms. Two wooden crosses are quickly made and planted, topped with the helmets found in the airplane. A few flowers, like the other day, and last respects. We fire a salute in honor. There are three young men who were still adversaries two days ago and who now rest, side by side, in their final repose. One is in his native earth, the other two in foreign soil, far from their own. Their families will receive the traditional telegram, *"Am Feinde für das Vaterland gefallen"* ["Fallen in the face of the enemy for the Fatherland"], and then their personal effects. Pathetic memories! For the Russian flier, I do not know how things are done, whether and how the families are informed. In any case, the drama, however accomplished, remains the same for the wife, Russian or German, for the parents, for the orphans. I am glad that I am not married, though I do have a little promise at home. If I was married I would feel less at ease, for all that I am able to say is that I feel serene at the moment. Today one has time for emotions, but tomorrow?

In the morning of the next day we move out on assignment for the infantry gun platoon, the artillery of the infantry. We are eight men and we are going to Slaviansk, or, more precisely, we are returning there to find horses. We take the same road as when we came, but this time cover it in a single day, a good stretch! We spend the night in Slaviansk and, after taking charge of the horses, we again set out on the road to Brachovka. Two of my comrades, who are already experienced horsemen, ride on horseback for the first kilometers. The others and myself each lead two horses by their halters. There are neither saddles nor bits. As the kilometers go by the muddy road tires us greatly and I too consider riding, but without stirrups and without a bit, that is not easy for a neophyte like myself. I give it a good try, without giving it a thought, like an idiot, attempting to use the earth and the mud like a stepping stone, but, of course, my legs immediately sink into the muck up to the calves. It is after the attempt that I reflect, and I think that I must find a tree.

After seven or eight kilometers a small tree emerges on the horizon and I quicken my pace. Once there, I first cut a branch in order to make a bit and I then lead one of the two horses to the chosen tree. I climb up two meters and slide onto the horse. I untie the other *en route*. Indeed, it goes better thus and the bit serves its purpose. It is, indeed, less tiring! After two good hours on the road I find that the horse has a distinctly prominent spine and I ask myself why horses do not come into this world with a built-in saddle. Nature has not foreseen everything! I do not dare to get off the horse, for there is not a single tree in sight that would allow me to remount. I decide to await a better occasion to eat, but a bit of walking would really be good for me, and even better for what I sit on.

A little later, no longer, I change my mind and decide that everyone should take a break to eat. In truth, that is good, for my legs are stiff and my lower back is hurting. We eat and stretch our legs a bit, but it isn't necessary to linger. Then, the devil take my pride, I ask a comrade to give me a hand up to put me on my horse. I was going to say, to put me in the saddle! And then, "gee-up" – in French, "*Hue*"! *En route* to Brachovka.

The ordeal resumes and I quickly confirm that it is not only my *derriére* that is suffering, but that my kidneys are also in trouble. I am unable to get used to it; it goes from bad to worse. I have the feeling that I am sitting on a rocky crest and, before we get to our destination, the back of the horse turns into a knife blade upon which my posterior reposes. I have, indeed, changed my position, one time more to the left, then more to the right. For a kilometer or two more toward the neck, then more to the rear, toward the rump. But there is no remedy. My Achilles' heel is there, where you think! It is with frantic relief that I see Brachovka appear on the horizon. As soon as we arrive, I prepare to dismount from my scaffold, but, after these four or five hours on horseback, I realize that I am going to have problems. To cap it all, there is *Capitaine* Tchekoff, who comes to meet us, on horseback, like us, but a thousand times more at ease, must I say? And him, he loves it and that is obvious! We straighten up to salute, at least I think so, at least I try. I have the impression that, at the moment, I am sitting on a saw blade. The *Capitaine* invites us to dismount. I am unable to accomplish the movement of lifting my leg, and already my forehead, my cheeks burn with shame. Stiff as a dead tree I pivot on my horse as on an axle and fall heavily to the earth. I have just enough time to behold the disgusted expression of the *Capitaine*, who turns away, distressed by my fashion of riding, but yet more by my fanciful way of getting off the horse. He must find it sickening, and I understand that. I already know that I shall not be in the cavalry, and that I shall never be honored with the rank of "*Rittmeister*"!

From 12-16 June we are kept busy with exercises and also reorganization and I take advantage of these few days to transfer from the infantry gun platoon, where I was assigned, to the *PAK* (anti-tank guns) and then to return to the infantry. I do not know which pleased me the most, but I believe that I developed somewhat of a lack of affinity with certain superiors of the artillery. Oh! Not anything big, but it was thus that I returned to be a *fantassin* [Tr. Note: GI, doughboy, Tommy, grunt …]. The Queen of all the arms, is it? At least that is what it says in one of our songs. A squad of infantry is formed which is to set out tomorrow to reinforce the Donetz Front, and I find myself there along with several "old-timers" and some of the newcomers of 10 March. Among others there is the adjutant and *Sergent* Y. Chenot and Generet. The last was killed after the war in Indochina in the ranks of the Foreign Legion, in other fighting.

On the 17th we march to the Donetz. The road that leads to the front is not a bed of roses. Along the way I see signs of recent fighting. An acrid smell irritates my throat; it comes from the destroyed, burned *isbas*. But another odor mingles with it, the stench of the corpses of men and horses which now mark our route. The atmosphere reeks! It is a smell that I shall never forget. Shell craters become more and more numerous, as does damaged equipment, guns and demolished carts, lorries and other vehicles that are burned or machine gunned. It is all Russian Army equipment. There only the chimney of an *isba* remains, pointing to the sky. Here a twisted section of wall, here and there ruins still smoking. This first sight makes me believe that the fighting has been heavy and that this was a hot spot. I am told that we are at Spachovka.

Today I will have my first baptism of fire! I am curious about it but my stomach knots and my heart beats fast every time that I think of it, for the hour of truth is now very close. I believe that I am afraid! Each time that my heartbeats quicken I try to stop thinking of it, but the moments of respite grow shorter and shorter as the crucial moment approaches. I observe the others to discover their thoughts, but everyone hides his fears, or else they do not have fear! My pride prevents me from asking the question; and then, in every way, they are all taciturn today! It is that which makes me think that we all react in the same way that I do and that no one would admit it for all the gold in the world! Words fall into the void, and when I make a joke to give the impression that none of this disturbs me, I am lucky if I get one or two brittle smiles in return, belated and, no doubt, out of courtesy. I believe that nobody is fooled!

Now we march in the woods and the Donetz flows quite near. The Russians are on the other bank and absolute silence is imperative. My heart beats wildly and I try hard to control it. It beats so hard at times that I fear that the Russians will hear it, or, at the very least, that my comrades will hear it. Am I really yellow? But, all the same, this is the first time that I have faced enemy fire! The leader of the squad and the leader of the platoon give orders softly, and with gestures. Ahead of us there is a touch of light in the woods. It is a clearing. We must advance with care and in extended order until we are a few meters from it. We must then cross this clearing by successive bounds, at the run, of course, and alternately, on the signal of our squad leader. My throat is dry and my pulse beats in my temples as I stop near a tree, right by the clearing. I kneel on the ground to regain my calm and to present a smaller target, and I see that the others are doing the same. Nothing stirs, and I see the Donetz, which flows silently a little lower. The Russians are there on the other bank! The river there is no more than 20 meters wide, it is right there. But I cannot lose sight of the squad leader, those are the orders. It is dangerous to give in to my curiosity for a moment and examine the surroundings.

The squad leader lifts his arm. Two men immediately stand up and leap as if spring-propelled. They dart into the clearing like hares. *Ah oui*! It is true, now it is my turn, and another comrade's. I emerge in the open space at the moment that the two first ones throw themselves to the ground and, when it is my turn, I lie down, or, in truth, I let myself fall. I already hear the sound of the next ones running. The two first are up again resuming the run. Almost immediately I do the same. The Russians opened fire as soon as we entered the clearing, but it is only now that I hear it, that I realize. In four or five bounds we are again, more or less, under cover, in the woods on the other side, but the Russians keep firing, at least for a few more instants. I did, of course, hear the whistle of the bullets as I ran, but I only realize it now! I catch my breath and confirm that the rhythm of my heart returned very quickly to normal, or nearly so. My fear is gone and I do not even know when it vanished. *Tiens*, that is curious! I believe that it happened at the moment when I went into action. *Oui*, I do believe that is true. Fifteen minutes ago I would not have believed it. I feel reassured, at least for the moment. It was taken from me without shame.

We resume our march in the woods and we head for the jump-off positions where we join up with the "old-timers" who have been there for several hours. We are directed to the fallback positions, behind a knoll, in the woods, for one does not have access to the frontline positions except under cover of night. It is necessary to cross an open space in sight of the enemy to reach the foxholes of the riflemen on the bank of the river. This dangerous passage is marked with a sign, "*Feindeinsicht*" [under enemy observation]. Access by daylight is too dangerous for the coming and going of the relief. At least half of them would likely lose their lives in the attempt. So we wait for night in the rest positions to go under fire, or, in any case, to go up into position.

I have somewhat regained my calm, or at least a sensation of stay of execution. In any case, it is no longer the same tension, but I do not analyze it rigorously. Perhaps it is deliberate, and on purpose, but I do not really attempt to figure it out. For whatever reason, I feel better than I did an hour or two earlier. The novelty of the present moment helps me to relax. We rejoin the "old-timers", haloed for us with the glory and the experience acquired during the last long hard winter, and that is already enough to ease our uncertainties. And then, there is the desire to prove that we are not lacking in courage.

We eat a bit, we chat, we speak of home, all while smoking a few cigarettes or a pipe. All of that helps us regain a bit of serenity, sufficient so that, when night comes and we gather to go forward in line, there is no more than the slightest tension. As ordered, there is complete silence when we ascend the crest of the knoll, then branch off with care to the right to cover the open ground that leads us, in line, a few meters from the Donetz. Those who are there rapidly leave their holes to make a place for us and follow the road back to the rear.

Now, I have been in this hole for 24 hours. By the way, I don't know what time it is, 2100 hours? 2200 hours, perhaps? Truly, I have no idea, and I no longer have a watch. However, it is not that the Russians took it from me. Its nervous system did not survive the rigors of instruction. Little by little it has fallen into insanity, gaining one day, losing the next. In brief, since it was no longer to be trusted, I granted it leave as we were passing a river whose name I no longer remember. I settle down for the night, but there is certainly no question of sleep. It is necessary to keep watch, but we keep watch in turn. I am in an individual foxhole, like the others, but certain of them are grouped together in a single position. There are positions that are linked by communications trenches, but not all. I gradually get used to the darkness, but it is very black and I can't distinguish much. The river, on the other hand, is omnipresent. Unlike everything else, I see it well, and I hear it even better. It is a soothing sound, untroubled by any other noise. Even the nocturnal birds seem on the lookout and live on guard. I do not hear them, or only very briefly. A few times the noise of the Donetz becomes louder, and I listen carefully, scrutinizing the surface of the river. It would not do for the Russians to cross it without my being aware. That would be bad for my health, and a catastrophe for my comrades.

The time of my watch drags on, and my anxiety increases with fatigue, then fades and reappears. Yet there are a lot of noises that I can neither identify nor locate. That is always why they are so disturbing. I try to distinguish something on the other bank, but with no success. It is too dark. To my right I believe that I see the pallor of a face, emerging from a hole, but I am not at all sure. To my left I think I have a confused impression of some sounds coming from a position where there are four or five men. It is possible, for there is a light machine gun (LMG) positioned there and also the squad leader. In front of me, not a sound, not a movement. There are moments when the silence is so oppressive that I would prefer a tempestuous explanation. But the time passes and, at the very moment when I hear a noise that I quickly locate, I distinguish a silhouette that approaches, crouching. It is a man who comes to let me know that I can sleep, but, preferably, keeping one eye open. He passes on to the next hole and then returns whence he came. It is my neighbor who is now on watch and this time I believe I can guess his position, there, where the courier who woke him up is right now. Is he the only one sleeping? As for myself, in any case, I don't know if I will be able to sleep. It seems to me that I should keep better watch than I did just now, for the arrival of the courier did take me a bit by surprise. Despite everything, I doze a bit, but the slightest sound causes me to sit up and open my eyes. Thus the night passes and is gone, and it is the sun that suddenly wakes me. I did end up falling asleep! I stretch my limbs to get rid of the numbness and regain my spirits. It is now 18 June.

Now to check out the topography of the sector by daylight. What is it really like? Above me, in the skylight that forms the opening of my foxhole, the branches of a few trees stand out against the depths of the blue sky. However, to discover the terrain extending around me I ought to sit up with care so as not to provide too easy a target to those across from me. Therefore I stand up with great care, just far enough to bring my eyes to the level of the parapet, and my first look is at the river, and on the opposite bank, in an attempt to discover the positions facing me. But nothing stirs, and nothing reveals the positions opposite me. Then, very slowly I scan the entire horizon all around me, and I scrutinize so closely that it hurts my eyes. It is only after four or five attempts that I finally think that I have discovered one or two hillocks that may hide the Russians, but there is not a movement to give them away.

The weather is fair and already hot, for the sun climbs very quickly above the horizon, despite the early hour of the morning. The individual foxhole that shelters me is no more than a few meters from the Donetz, which it is slightly above, two or three meters above water level. Grass, bushes and a few trees clothe the banks of the river where our positions are located, and the other bank is similar. I have just spotted at least two nests of Russians, for I saw movement at two different locations on the opposite bank. The closest of the two positions is, in my opinion, no more than 40 or 50 meters from mine. I also think that I heard the sound of voices, and my name is not Joan of Arc. The lapping of the river is always there, very soft, but one can guess the strength of the current. A few moments ago I was intrigued by the curious shapes of two forms caught in the dead branches fallen from the trees and dragging in the river. I just realized what they are: they are two bodies in the water, caught by the branches. They are not *Feldgrau*,[3] they are two Russian soldiers! Macabre company, but not noisy, and not in the way. In spite of myself I look at them frequently.

Suddenly I hear a shot and a whistle… but, *Bon Dieu*, it is me they are shooting at! I did not immediately realize what it was, but I caught on soon enough. I was imprudent in my attempt to better discover these Maccabees, and there would be one less in our ranks if the one who fired the shot had not been so maladroit. With an elite marksman, I would have been shot. A good lesson! One cannot relax his prudence for even an instant; it would be fatal. They are indeed lurking there, doing their best to do to me what I would do to them and to put a stop to my heartbeats! But, no more. They must stop watching me and relax their surveillance, for now they know exactly where I am. I must shift my foxhole a few meters to the left or to the right to mislead them. I locate some reference points for the night and place my rifle on the parapet. All the time I continue to observe the sector across from me, but more discreetly this time, and, every now and then, I make a little sign to my neighbors on the left or the right. The one to the right is a good 20 meters from me, the one on the left a little farther. There is a machine gun there.

I eat a morsel to pass the time and the day passes slowly with no more problems. I appreciate the relief that allows me to smoke a cigarette in the rear, for it is forbidden and too dangerous to smoke here, since there is no breeze to dissipate the smoke, and the hot air makes the smoke stagnate. There is no need to make their task any easier. I would have liked to send a few well-aimed bullets their way, but I find no occasion, and it would be idiotic to fire at random. I was just thinking that I should avoid firing at night, since the flash of the discharge would allow them to locate my position exactly, and it is risky for the relief. I feel more at ease this evening than yesterday in my position, for now I know the surroundings and the nature of the shadows that surround me. Yesterday it was unknown. This evening, on the other hand, I know that the Russians are really close, and the relief seems more dangerous than it seemed yesterday. So I tell myself "wait and see", but in German, of course! Once the night is really dark, I hear noises, and the sounds approach very quickly. It is the relief, no doubt, but I stay on guard. It really is one of our own. In a few minutes the comrade replaces me in the hole and, after a tap on the shoulder, I descend the slope, turning off to the right to rejoin the squad leader and the machine gun crew. A few minutes later we are back in the rest positions where we are served a hot meal. Everything was set for our return. It is good, and I have a good appetite. Sitting before the tent I smoke a cigarette. Half an hour later I stretch out to sleep.

19 June. At *Reveille* the sun is already up, but the hot coffee is good with the breakfast that I eat a few paces from the tent. We share our first impressions, talk of the positions facing us and compare what each of us was able to locate. My comrades also saw the corpses caught by the tree branches in the water and no longer quench their thirst with water drawn from the river with that upstream. Some of them also saw corpses carried by the current. Myself, I have not seen them. In the evening we go back to the forward positions again for 24 hours. This night the Russians send over a few bursts of fire. Doubtless they are nervous, and I feel good when, based on my observations of the

---

3   *Feldgrau* – field-gray – is the color of the German uniform.

night before, I can satisfy my desire to reply. I empty one or two clips and am content. This night, in the bottom of my hole, carefully concealing the flame, I light a pipe and savor it prudently. The time passes better that way. As was the case the day before yesterday, I am on guard for part of the night, half-asleep for the remainder.

20 June – and when day breaks the corpses are still there, and nothing seems to have changed since the other day. All the same, the distance seems to be a little closer today. Today I hear artillery and gunfire in the distance, on our left. I do not remember hearing it yesterday. The sun goes down and night falls quickly. We remain on guard. The scenario is the same as the night before. Already it is practically routine. Relief and return to the rear. This night there is a curious occurrence, dramatic for one of our comrades. Two "*Bourguignons*" who were bringing up rations from the rear through a little ravine ("*balka*") were surprised by Russians who had infiltrated or strayed into our rear. Loaded with rations, they followed the little ravine as usual. We believe that two Russians were hiding on the rim and jumped down as they passed. Comrade Lamote had his hair cut a little earlier and that saved his life. The Russians that jumped down on them attempted to grab them by their hair, and Lamote's forage cap was left in his attacker's hands while the latter passed above his head and landed on the ground in front of Lamote. Surprised, lost and ignorant of the number of the attackers, little Lamote had just one reflex, to flee without looking back, to flee desperately. After wandering haphazardly he got back to the lines with nothing worse than the loss of his hat, the rations and a great fright. Perhaps the attackers were famished? A patrol dispatched immediately found no trace of the missing comrade. He never returned. A warning for us all, and one more reason to maintain vigilance.

On 21 June, traveling in the afternoon with two comrades, I spend a moment at the grave of two "*Bourguignons*" killed a little earlier at the Donetz: Mathias Brossel and G. Sauveur. Two wooden crosses topped with a helmet. It is simple, it is poignant. For them, it is all over, for us, it all begins! There I felt that the sort of rancor that some of the "old-timers" seemed to nourish toward us vanished. We are accepted. That evening, at about 2300 hours, we evacuate the positions and cross the Donetz south of Isjum on pontoons. There is no resistance and we proceed toward Kupiansk, 22 kilometers distant, passing swamps and areas of sand. At 0250 hours that night, Isjum was to be attacked by outflanking it. Passing through Kupiansk on the Oskol we continue toward Kapitalovka, which we reach after an exhausting 19-and-a-half-hour march! Finally, we pitch our tents in some woods in the suburbs of Isjum, but since the city has already fallen, we have no need to intervene. Dead tired, exhausted, we sleep as much as we can. Some do not even have the strength to eat, and go to sleep immediately.

On the 26th we move out of the cantonment toward Brachovka, which we attain after a new 35-kilometer march. We left that village nine days earlier and I recognize it, but I am quartered in a different *isba*. This cantonment does not last long, for on the 28th we are already heading out toward Schurki, 15 kilometers northwest of Slaviansk. During this time the battle continues between the Donetz and the Don, and we are in reserve with the *97th Jäger Division*. The village of Schurki stretches along the hillside, and is smaller than Brachovka. Once more the units are reorganized and we do hard training exercises. Today, 30 June, an exercise in advancing under live fire from heavy machine guns. The machine guns are well-fixed in their adjustment, at least I hope so, ranged to a hair, verified, inspected, tested by the instructors. When everything is finally well in hand, we advance under their fire, crouching down, but without raising ourselves too much, at risk of being cut down by a burst of fire. The fire is set at 1.70 meters, precisely, but, one never knows. It is better not to exceed 1.50 meters. This little margin is not much. It is necessary to become accustomed, to season the men, but I am one of those who has already had my baptism of fire. More exercise in the ensuing days. Individual advance *en slalom* [zig-zagging], for targets wooden soldiers that topple when touched with the bayonet. The military administration even thought to transport this material here, a dozen kilometers from the front! The terrain chosen for the exercise is furrowed with little "*balkas*", or trenches, and covered with bushes. At each turn there is a target. It is necessary to complete the course as fast as possible, firing on certain targets, bayoneting the others. There is also firing on fixed targets from prone, kneeling and standing positions.

Our German instructor gives us a demonstration of *sang-froid*. He positions himself on a little knoll and has us take cover in the little "*balkas*" or trenches around it. Then he takes a grenade in his hand and removes the screw cap[4] before pulling on the cord. He places the live grenade, in his hand, on the top of his helmet and then remains motionless while he counts to six. He warns us to take cover before he gets to five, because at six, is the explosion. And, in fact, at six we hear the explosion. We immediately raise our heads to see what happened. The instructor is there, above us, uninjured, his helmet blackened on its upper part by the powder. Conclusive demonstration of self-control! Obviously, there must be no wind, not the slightest movement; the grenade must be perfectly balanced on the helmet. The experience should not be attempted with a rounded grenade!

The instructor then asks us, with a little smile, if there are any volunteers to try the experience? Despite the jitters, I want to try it, but I hesitate at the thought that the least movement, the most imperceptible trembling could make the live grenade fall at my feet. Then a comrade with less reflection volunteers, and, I no longer know how, but I join him. Now I cannot turn back or I will lose face. My comrade, Cobut or Cobeau, I believe, is in the same state of mind that I am, but I think that nothing in the world could make us admit our fear. At least, I believe that fear concerns me, and I do not believe that my companion is exempt from it. The instructor looks us over carefully and scrutinizes our eyes, and, at that moment, I ask myself if he wasn't hoping that no one would volunteer? But, after his challenge, perhaps offered rashly, he, too, cannot back down! So his only recourse is to ask us the question, "Are you sure you really want to do this?" He watches my companion and me and our simultaneous nods confirm our intention to the instructor. Quite possibly no sound would have come from our throats if it had been necessary to speak.

Our *Feldwebel's* slightly hesitant manner disappears and we forget our own concerns a bit as he now gives us his instructions: breathe calmly and deeply until your nerves are calm, but don't hesitate too much; legs a bit apart for a good stance, prime the grenade and place it on the helmet, holding it by the base, the stick upward; don't stir, don't breathe, tense the muscles of your neck. Don't forget to count, to count slowly to six, without hurrying! When he finishes speaking the men take shelter. The instructor prepares to do the same, but waits until the last moment, and remains quite close to us, undoubtedly to intervene if necessary, for he has taken on a great responsibility with rookies like us. I go first. I no longer know if I am afraid, but it seems to me that I am trembling a bit. I unscrew the cap, spread my legs and pull the cord, all, I have the impression, very quickly. I make sure that the grenade is stable on my helmet and loosen my fingers slowly, very slowly, hoping that it does not topple off or remain stuck between my fingers as I lower my arm. It seems to stay, and I hear nothing fall, and there is, obviously, no question of lowering my head to make sure. That would be truly too stupid. I count and arrive at six, but, undoubtedly, too quickly, for nothing happens. I hear a noise, but it is our *Feldwebel* taking cover. I resume my count, after a brief interruption, and, at eight: brrroum! A blow on my head like a sledgehammer, but not as strong as I imagined, or, maybe, it is because it is over so quickly! The noise? Like a cannon shot, but far away, and one that is prolonged as it seems to approach, and it is done!

---

4   The author uses '*dégoupiller*', which is usually translated as 'to remove a pin', but to activate the German *Stielhandgranate 24* or *39*, the standard German stick-grenade, which was used in this demonstration, one unscrews the metal cap at the end of the wooden handle and pulls on the porcelain bead – thereby pulling the igniter cord, which extends through the hollow wooden handle – giving a 4.5-second delay before bursting. The only difference between the '*24*' and '*39*' is that the latter had a longer wooden handle.

The instructor is beside me before I even realize it and gives me a good slap on the back. I believe that he is as relieved as I am! My comrades' heads emerge and turn to look at mine. I, in turn, take cover for Cobeau's experience. Again I am able to breathe normally without thinking about avoiding making a mistake, but it seems that I am still trembling a little. At least, at the critical moment, I think I did not tremble! But, already I hear the explosion of Cobeau's grenade, and, happily I am under cover, for my thoughts are still wandering and take me away from the present moment. My comrades get up and I do the same. Cobeau has also had his experience. We take a break and discuss it before we get back to the village.

3 July. In the evening a ceremony is announced for tomorrow. In German or in French, it tells us: brush our uniforms, polish the leather, clean arms. On 4 July the entire unit musters in the square for review. *General* Rupp, commander of the *97th Jäger Division*, of which we are a part, awards a great number of decorations and Eastern Front Ribbons[5] to the "old-timers" of 8 August. Our standards rest on our stacked rifles and impart an air of festivity and solemnity to the steppe which surrounds the village of Schurki. A German chaplain celebrates mass and all, I believe, take part, even the non-believers like me. During this time the German armored formations that have come down from the north move east of the Donetz toward the lower Don, encircling Rostov, which continues to resist before its final investment.

---

5   *Medaille 'Winterschlacht im Osten, 1941–42'* (Medal for the 'Winter Battle in the East, 1941–42') – awarded to all members of the military and non-military formations who had served on the Eastern Front for at least 14 days for combatants and 60 days for non-combatants between 15 November, 1941 and 15 April, 1942 (both dates inclusive).

Our arrival at Slaviansk in June 1942.

Capitaine Tchekoff welcomes us at Brachovka.

The Russian airplane shot down at Brachovka.

My squad at Brachovka in June 1942.

A bit of accordion music (June 1942).

En route to the review at Schurki.

My anti-tank gun, June 1942.

A wrecked Russian tank *en route* to the front.

A baptism of fire, as we move forward to our positions on the Donetz.

Our first Russian prisoners.

The graves of our comrades,
Brossel and Sauveur.

Le Chef and, on the other bank of the
Donetz, the Russians.

Crossing the Donetz.

The sands of the Donetz.

The Donetz behind us: now we will sweat.

The furnace and the sands.

5

The Advance

7 June, at 1600 hours, we move out of Schurki and, after a night-march, are billeted in Slaviansk, in the park. There are several white stucco buildings there, dilapidated, like everything we see. Everything here is stucco. In this park there is a series of trunks of statues of men, the heads of which are on the ground, pell-mell. It would be easy to put them back on matching trunks, like children's puzzles, all the statues are stereotypes. All these Stalins, Lenins and other notables of the regime have found their muscular opponents. The *Vaguemestre*[1] Tinant calls the roll and distributes the mail. And, for the first time in Russia, I receive news from home and many small packages of cigarettes. Maximum weight 100 grams. But I have a good dozen and I share them with my comrade, de Bruyn. And here I must make a little parenthetical remark. During our instruction, this buddy showed me a photo of his daughter, blond as wheat, and I told him that she was very much to my taste. Just between us, I must tell you that I married a brunette. De Bruyn shot right back at me, laughing, that she was not made for me, but, all the same, he gave me her address. Caught off-guard, and in a humorous style, I wrote to her that, poor and orphaned, I reproached her father for not sharing the contents of his packages, especially his cigarettes, with as much altruism as I suspected he had. I had not, at that time, received any packages myself. I had entirely forgotten this letter, as you can well imagine. That was four months ago and I thought nothing of it. It was with delighted astonishment that I received these packets, and a letter where she explained very sweetly that, to punish her father for his lack of camaraderie, she was sending his share to me. And, by way of hard luck, for I believe or I suppose that she also sent him something all the same, he did not get a single package for him. That is why, totally shamefaced and embarrassed, I shared them with him. Our other buddies had a good laugh out of it!

It is here, also, that I see the "*Prévot*" reappear, who had to return to a field hospital for an illness. He seems emaciated and the illness has left its mark strongly on his face. There is also a sort of salt lake where the water is so dense that one floats on it without making the least movement, and I am very astonished to see there for the first time Russian women bathing, and bathing without brassieres! The next day, 9 July, in the afternoon, we leave the cantonment for the banks of the Donetz, where we camp for the night. 10 July we break camp to cross the river. One part of the train crosses by ferry on a movable bridge built by German pioneers. The other, including me, crosses at a ford.

The banks at this location are extremely sandy, but, since the first part is sloping, we cross it with no great difficulty. The second part is different. The carts are really heavy and massive, so that the horses, which are, nevertheless, "Pomeranians", strong as elephants, cannot move forward more than a few centimeters at a time, until they are no longer able to move forward at all! Now the ordeal begins again for us! None of those who took part will ever forget it to his dying days, and whenever I am reminded, I sweat at the thought of it. Not only do we have to remove our knapsacks and gear from the carts, but we also have to unload all the rest: rations, ammunition, arms, which are not feathers. In brief, all that an army needs for a campaign it has to take with it.

---

1 *Vaguemestre* – a non-commissioned officer acting as regimental postmaster and baggagemaster.

And that means we have to carry it all, sinking in the sand over our boot-tops. The sand gets in them and makes movement all the more difficult. The sun beats down incredibly and the heat is torrid. The sweat pours forth and soaks us from head to foot. Everyone works, bare to the waist. We must push the carts in the sand toward the ford, and then across the large rocks that litter the bed of the river. The carts sway and capsize, throwing their driver into the water and we have to turn the vehicle right-side up with the help of trees that we must cut with an axe. The horses get frantic and rear, and we have to control these beasts that weigh more than 500 kilos, sometimes 700 kilos! The *matériel*, all that is on these vehicles, we have to transport at the ford, stumbling on the rocks, slipping or sinking into the mud, all the way to the far bank, tormented by myriads of mosquitoes! *Ma foi*, we could well collapse here. It is work for the Titans. We injure ourselves, our fingers get crushed, as do our feet, under the wheels of the carts. Cries, oaths, blows to make the horses move. We are all on the verge of exhaustion. Nevertheless, we must do whatever it takes to get everything across the river. We must continue! My throat is dry and the water in my canteen is as warm as the ambient air. Sand is everywhere and crunches between my teeth. It sticks to my body and mingles with the sweat. Breath comes hard and short, I suffocate! Here, too, the bodies of Russian soldiers float the length of the bank, but so what, we move toward where the current is flowing and rinse our mouths. I come to envy the men breaking rocks at Cayenne![2]

After hours and hours of work, loads and vehicles, all the trains are finally on the other bank. We attempt to move one or two loaded carts, but in vain! They do not move a meter forward, and the horses, which have worked as hard as we have, are foundered. Again we must unload, lug the loads that are heavier than lead one meter at a time and set them down on the other side of the dunes! The heat is such that the uniforms of the men who fall in the water, or the trousers that are moistened in crossing the ford, are dry in a quarter of an hour, but that is enough time to irritate the skin, as provoking as the chapping which does not disappear right away! Ten times, 20 times, 30 times it has been necessary to cross the ford to transport everything. What we have gone through is outrageous! The horses could not do it! It was necessary to slaughter some of them. I have to master myself, to control myself to maintain modesty and decency in describing what we have endured in these moments! In reality, it is indescribable. It is no longer on the scale of what is human. And still it is not done!

Once the reloaded carts are beyond the dunes, it is still necessary to push, to pull the carts, now burdened again with their loads for eight to 10 kilometers. I feel that I am no more than a skeleton with nerves, muscles and skin covering it, emptied of all liquid substance or even dampness, if it is not this sweat which does not dry up in an instant! One can well sponge oneself, but it pours immediately from all the pores. Of course, during all this we carry all of our kit: knapsack on our back, bread bag, gas mask, spade, rifle and bandolier of ammunition, 30 kilos at the very least, doubtless a bit more, and, as a bonus, always, to relieve the horses, we also push the heavy vehicles and guns ahead of us! But who will come to relieve us? "*Infanterie! Du bist die schönste aller Waffen*"? [in German, "Infantry, You are the most beautiful of all arms of the service"] At this moment I would give a lot to be in the *Luftwaffe*.

Those who still have the strength jeer and swear, but march all the same, and push like the others who can no longer jeer or swear. We have to push and pull like this for another eight to 10 kilometers, but now with occasional respites, for here and there we reach sections of the route where the ground is a little more solid. This provides a bit of relief, but not rest, by any means. And for us it seems that we go on forever. Most of us by now have blisters on our feet. And now, to distract us, another form of torture, and more fatigue! It is not astonishing, after all this, that our

---

2 The *Bagne de Cayenne* – the Cayenne Prison Colony (or Devil's Island).

feet are soaked by the hours of labor crossing the ford. Our torn blisters quickly expose bare flesh which immediately suppurates. My comrade, Mol, can no longer take it and receives authorization from the adjutant, Chenot, to ride on a cart for the rest of the stage. I am not fat, but he looks like he has lost 10 kilos since yesterday. Truly, his features are drawn, marked by fatigue and suffering. What do I look like? I have no idea, and little concern. I prefer not to know! I have too much to do with my blisters and try every means to find the best way, the least painful way to place my feet for each step. God knows, but these efforts must add to the fatigue and make the march yet more frightful! March or die, old friend, you have no choice. But I ask why I have two blisters on my right foot and only one on the left! Is the left already favored? I follow my road, step by step, kilometer after kilometer, and this time it is my comrade Beauraing who falls into step with me, if I dare to say so. As the evening arrives, exhausted, dead tired, we arrive in a village whose name I lack the courage to ask. Dehydrated, we drink anything that we can get our hands on, mostly water, also a bit of milk and we drop to the ground. I think I am asleep before I even touch the ground. We sleep like logs. The next day, 11 July, we resume our march, but very painfully, for my blisters are bleeding.

Thus, somehow or other, we reach Krasny – Liman. Crossing a little square of beaten earth, shaded by a few trees, a woman and a young man approach us. They talk to us immediately in perfect German! We give them a questioning look. The woman, who appears to be between 40 and 50 years old, explains that they are German by origin and hope to get back to Germany as soon as possible. Her husband, an engineer, worked in Russia for many years, but was already deported before the war. She has no idea where, for she has never received any news. Is he still alive? She and her son were sent here to live. Previously they lived in Rostov. Their clothes are well tailored, and that is what struck us when we saw them coming toward us, for they were conspicuous for their bearing and style. Seen up close, I see that their clothes have been through a lot of cleaning and darning since they were new! No doubt that was all that was left of their former condition.

The woman then asks us what she should do to be repatriated with her son. I advise her to wait for the establishment of a "*Kommandantur*" in the village in order to plead her case. That should not cause much delay, for I have seen the installation of the German military administration in villages before the fighting forces have even finished capturing them! German organization is unequaled, and never wavered right up to the end of the war. We chat a bit with these interlocutors, who ask us a wealth of questions about Germany and the war, and they are astonished to find foreign volunteers in the ranks of the German Army. We encourage them and before we part they embrace us and the woman kisses us. The Russians, on the threshold of their *isba*, offer us drinks and we quench our thirst endlessly. Then the German woman and her son give us a last wave of the hand from the far side of the square. I truly believe that I drank two or three liters of water, and I would drink yet more, but we have to continue our journey. We only have to follow the troops, all of whom proceed in the same direction. We go right through Krasny – Liman, but the march becomes impossible. Since the sweat dries a bit on our feet, our socks stick and immediately adhere to the sores produced by our blisters. We decide to rest for a bit and knock on a door. The people receive us very politely, as is the custom, and offer us food. Totally done in and sore, we decide to spend the night there. Truly it is impossible to go on. The infected sores are not pleasant to look at! We wash in a barrel behind the house and I then feel light, light, freed of all the dust of the road. I also start to wash my underwear, which certainly needs it, but the "*kasaika*" and her two daughters want to do that for us. We allow them to wash our sores and to bandage them – after which we collapse into sleep.

When we wake up the sun has already been up for a long time and it is extremely hot. We wash up and I shave for the first time in at least three days. I feel truly better now. Our hosts offer us *sautéed* potatoes and chicken, which neither of us two would dream of refusing, and then curds (*kisli-moloko*), a veritable feast! I realize that one often has a hot meal in the morning here. Our underwear is dry and clean. That is pleasing. But as for putting our feet in our shoes! That is a new torture. Nevertheless, with great care and much pain we finally put on our shoes. It is now 12 July and we must go on!

During the night scabs have formed on our sores and the first few kilometers are all the more painful. Inevitably, they peel off as we march, and it takes time, not to endure it but to get used to it. We march all day, always under a leaden sun, in the dust of our steps or that raised by a cart that passes us. Of course we are unable to march very fast and I do not know how many kilometers we cover this day in getting to Lissitchansk. We search for and find a pleasant enough *isba*, despite our modest tastes. Always a very good welcome, on the table, the fare of people who are used to having little. We have learned to be satisfied with this very frugal repast, and, at the same time, to appreciate certain dishes. A *purée* of *kapusta* (cabbage) and a few morsels of boiled meat. But, before eating I must, as usual, get rid of the dust of the road, for it is not possible to eat thus. Each evening of the journey it is the same, the dust and sand glued by sweat forms a crust on all exposed parts of the body. Otherwise, we are bronzed, tanned by the sun. But the nostrils and the throat are also coated with dust, to say nothing of the eyes, where it sticks as on fly paper. Many buckets of water are the remedy for this filth, and the Russians, who practically make a bucket brigade to provide us with water, don't come back to watch our consumption of this liquid element. For them, a mug takes care of their needs, I invent nothing; it is the strict truth. Their quart mugs, one in the mouth, and then they send one or two spurts of water in the hollow of the two hands held together in the shape of a conch shell and immediately pass their hands over the face. According to their more or less advanced conception of bodily hygiene, they may or may not repeat the operation a second time. And their *toilette* is done. Then they put their cap or their *chapka* back on – assuming they took if off before washing themselves – and remain covered thus for the rest of the day. As for the women, this sort of headgear is replaced by the eternal scarf, knotted under the chin or around the neck, with more or less felicity, not to say elegance, often with a different style according to region.

After the meal, it is time to sleep. The misery of my sores wakes me two or three times during the night. These are painful enough shooting pains, and on feeling them in the darkness, they seem quite swollen to me. With the help of fatigue, I manage to go back to sleep. Upon awakening the pain is even greater, and I discover that the region surrounding the sore, for it is now no more than one, is bordered by blue and mauve colors. I also believe that I am running a temperature. But there is nothing to be done; I must go on, always continue. "Ever forward"! We have already fallen far enough behind our company! A quick wash-up, eat a bit of bread with milk. It is all that there is. I think I shall burst in trying to put my boots on; I feel that I fainted twice! Haven't I endured enough already? All the same, I feel that I am tougher than that. But you would have to see the sores, for there are several new ones. I do not need to be disappointed in myself. That would be the worst thing. So, a grimace that attempts to be a smile for the sake of my comrade, Beauraing. I pull on my boot and the laces and I get up, saying, "Let's go!" Farewell and thanks to our hosts of a night and I push open the door. Immediately the sun blinds us and already the heat envelops us. We are on the road. Our steps immediately stir up the dust. The sun makes iridescent the grains of dust that settle very slowly behind us. We are on a new stage of our journey, but since the bread bag is empty we have to think about taking on fresh stores. I think we must find a train station, and people have no trouble showing us where one is. There, to nobody's surprise, we find a sort of canteen, or "*Truppenbetreungsstelle*" [troop welfare center], where the nurses and a *Feldwebel* have no difficulty giving us some bread, sausage, butter, cigarettes, candies and some "*Kaffee-Ersatz*" to refill our canteens. Seeing me limp, a nurse asks me what is wrong and wants to see my sores. When the bandages, which stick, are removed, the blood mixes with pus and drips on the ground. "*Mensch! So können Sie doch nicht weiter! Sie müssen gleich in's Lazarett!*" ["Man, you can't go on like this! You must go to the hospital immediately!"] She points out the field hospital to us and sends a male nurse along with us to make sure we go there. She is really nice, and, as a result, to say nothing of seeing that the others pity my condition, my scruples melt away like snow in the sun. And, without feeling any guilt, I allow myself to be led to the hospital.

It is a building that is in good condition, ground floor and one story above, doubtless once a school or a party office. Straw mattresses on the ground, but everything is very clean. A lightbulb hangs from the ceiling at the end of its cord. Is there already electricity there? Doctors, male and female nurses receive us very kindly. We are their first patients from a corps of foreign volunteers. Temperature, 38° and a bit [100°F]… They moisten our bandages with Ribanol, a yellow liquid disinfectant, for within a half-hour, they are already sticking to the sores. As soon as the sores are exposed, they give us injections and the nurses begin anew to wash the sores with brushes and soft soap. I bawl in pain, but my nurse, and I already say "my", is so pretty and cares for me with such a smile that I am ashamed of it, so then I clench my teeth. This takes a good half-hour, and afterwards I can wash myself in a small adjoining room. Then the doctor comes and gives instructions to the nurses: new disinfection of the sores, bandages, Atabrine for malaria. They then serve us *bouillon* and biscuits. An hour later, dinner: goulash and mashed potatoes. Then a fruit *compote*. It has been a long time since we have had such a meal. We must rest, lying down, for three or four days to promote skin formation over the sores and to rest our legs. After that, we can get up and circulate a bit. It is with pleasure that we give a hand to the hospital personnel. We empty bedpans and urinals, sweep and wipe things down. In brief, we make ourselves useful. I feel that I want to make amends for my stay in the hospital. We also chat with the wounded on the ground floor. We are on the upper floor, along with those suffering from dysentery and other maladies. In the five or six rooms on the ground floor there are 20 wounded, injured at the Donetz or in the fighting that ensued. Upstairs we are a dozen.

20 July, fully recovered, clean uniforms and new underwear, we leave the hospital, our bread bags well filled. We have no trouble following the traces of the *Légion*, since, most of the time, the route is well posted with the insignia of the units; ours is *Bataillon 373*. Thus we cover the kilometers! We march all day, sometimes by night, to avoid the worst of the heat. We pass through Kirovo on the 22nd and find lodging at Torskaja in the evening. By the evening of the 23rd we are at Tarvosovka, the 24th we pass Tchenovoka to arrive at Novo-Astrakan, the 25th Tchankikaja, the 26th Prognos and we spend the night of the 27th at Dubrowojé. We are at Kamenka on the 28th. The heat remains sweltering and adds to our fatigue, but the sores are forgotten. Nearly everywhere we find German food, and sometimes, in addition, we are fed by the householder. In such a case we share our pittance with our hosts, and they seem to really appreciate it, certainly for the change. The men are infatuated with our cigarettes and the youngsters with our candies. Often the mothers tell me that their children have never tasted or even seen such things.

Aside from our sores, what we have suffered most from in these recent days is thirst. The villages are farther apart, rarer, too, depending on the region, and our canteens are soon emptied. In any case, in this heat, the water that is fresh when we fill them is hot within a quarter of an hour and no longer quenches the thirst.

On the 29th we leave Kamenka and, a few kilometers from the city, a military car passes us and stops to pick us up. It is empty. We are three, including the driver. God, how restful to advance like this, without marching for once. We feel like tourists, and the jolts of the road do not disturb us. No more than the dust that lines the interior of the car. We have known worse, we have eaten more than that. It is inevitable, for this dust penetrates everywhere, all the more since the driver, to avoid suffocation, has lowered two windows in the front and two or four in the rear. We are seated in the back of the car, where we get a little more air, hot air, for sure, but air, all the same. At about 1700 hours we arrive in the suburbs of Krasnié – Sulin and decide to call it a day. There are four or five *isbas* there, a bit out of the way, and we head for them. We quickly meet up with a dozen German and Rumanian soldiers, with an officer, who are already there. Since we have nothing much in our bread bags, it is the householder who serves us chickens, ducks and *kartochkas*, or potatoes.

I do not like peeling potatoes, and leave this work to others more skilled in that. I see a fellow who is making a clumsy attempt to cut the head off a young cock, and I show him how I have seen the Russians do it, who, no doubt, do not have knives. I take the chicken's neck between my index finger and second finger, the head in the hollow of the palm. With a circular movement I rotate the chicken at arm's length, and very rapidly. In less than 30 seconds I feel the body separate from the head, and, with a sharp blow, I separate the last tendons; then immediately squeeze the neck hard so that I am not covered with blood spurting in the bird's dying convulsions. In all honesty, I do not enjoy this, but, urchin that I am, I wanted to show off my knowledge and dexterity to these old veterans. I then do the same with another chicken, then with a duck, and then leave the work to the others, who want to try out the method. The duck is tougher. It is the two Rumanians and a German who finish the job.

A full hour later we are all sitting around, on the ground, and each of us eats nearly a whole chicken or duck, after drinking the *bouillon* in which they were cooked. There are 15 of us and there are the remains of 12 hens, ducks or cocks. We ate well, but the *bouillon* was very greasy. That is why several of us have urgent calls of nature! It is important, every time that the occasion offers, to eat more than what is merely necessary to restore our equilibrium, for we never know when we will have to go one or two days without eating, or reduced to a bare minimum. A morsel of hard bread and a little water or milk for the days that are most sumptuous. That is the usual. At times, nothing at all! It is a good idea to take precautions. The car pursues its journey, but in a different direction than ours. We lodge here this evening. We talk a bit more around the fire, which dies out, and the Rumanian officer, who speaks good French, is quite happy to be able to speak this language which he has little occasion to use. A chap of the *97th*, originally from the Klagenfurt area, gets out his harmonica and offers us a cozy hour of nostalgia. On the distant road, a few very rare convoys hasten toward their destinations, and, behind them, the dust settles, very slowly in the setting sun, which still illuminates the steppe with its last oblique rays. The shadows lengthen and calm settles sweetly over this peaceful countryside. We do not believe at this moment that there is a war; that men are falling at the front this very instant. Here, in the apotheosis of the evening, the harmonica makes us dream. What are my family doing at home, what are my dearest ones thinking of at this very moment? Myself, I live a precious moment of time!

Night falls rapidly at these latitudes, and the shadows fade before they disappear, to give way to the silence of the night. Only the glow of the cigarettes, or the long, thin Rumanian cigars at times furtively illuminate a face, faces that are young and serene, or those of older comrades, grave but reassuring. To prepare us to sleep, the Austrian comrade plays us the *"Zapfenstreich"*, *Taps*, the last melody of the evening, the lights-out. Calmly, a bit moved, we all leave to go to sleep. The two Rumanians and a German stay with us in the same *isba*. At about 0700 or 0800 hours in the morning the sounds of traffic wake us up. I go outside and already find two or three Germans engaging in their morning ablutions. On a road, 200-300 meters away, interminable columns proceed, doubtless toward the front, fresh troops to relieve the ones that captured Rostov, as well as *matériel* and ammunition. I feel remorse at being here and do not delay after washing up and breakfast. *En route*, the *"Vormarsch"*, the advance, continues, and the comrades of an evening, of a single night, separate, each one to follow his destiny. *"Auf Wiedersehen, Hals und Beinbruch,"* or *"Servus"*[3] for those of the south.

---

3   German, 'Till we meet again, break a leg…' or '*Servus*' is the standard greeting or farewell of Austrians and Bavarians.

The terrain is hilly, and when I see a panorama from a height, I can guess the meanders of the road in the distance by following the columns of dust which rise high into the sky. As there is not one atom of wind, not the slightest breath of air, these columns of dust sketch in the sky in the same sections of the road with all the bends and forks. One sees well these columns of dust that cross in identical fashion at the intersection below, but one can only guess, enveloped in the thick air at the ground. All the same, it is curious to observe. A little before noon, from a height near the road, I distinguish a very important agglomeration through this heavy, dusty atmosphere. It is a city, an extremely great city. It can only be Rostov. There are tall structures, grain silos as well as industries. I finally determine that we really are not far from the city. The hot air, the sandy dust that is constantly hanging in the air, omnipresent, this haze of heat produces such a density in the atmosphere that it actually makes the air thick, so that at first sight the city seems to be far away.

By about 1400 to 1500 hours we are in the center of the city, after passing through the miserable suburbs. The city is no less so when seen up close. Leprous and decrepit. The old tramways are immobile, abandoned. Curious. We climb onto them., look at them more closely. The seats are worn and torn, the planks battered, paint peeling, wretched! "Eh! Beauraing, come see this!" At the conductor's place, on what I will call the "dashboard", is written in all the letters of the font: *ACEC*[4] Unbelievable, but there it is. We continue with our inspection and finding nothing else new, return to the road. There is much destruction resulting from the fighting: Russian tanks, cannon, all knocked out. A sign, "*Kommandantur*", already! That always helps to find food, and we do not neglect it. After which we head for the exit from the city, pursuing our road.

Shortly after leaving the city, however, I want to find the explanation for a goings-on that intrigues me. There is a procession of soldiers of all branches of the service that is heading for an old building and returning, painstakingly carrying mess tins and all sorts of other containers, ranging from helmets to jam jars of all sorts. These containers are full to the brim with a brown liquid that I cannot immediately identify. My first thought is of honey, but the liquid is too fluid for that. I ask a fellow, who tells me that it is beer! No time to waste, I must go there! It has been more than two months since I have seen any. It is not that I am a boozer, but thirst has tortured us all so much, and, in addition, since our departure from the *Regenwurmlager*, the beverages have had little variety: coffee, tea, milk, water, nothing else, and, most often, water. I must taste that when the occasion offers. My life as a soldier, short as it is, has already taught me one thing: never let an opportunity go by, or you may kick yourself about it later!

As we approach the beer garden the stale odor that tickles our nostrils leaves no doubt about the nature of the liquid. We follow the corridor taken by all of those in the procession that seem already familiar with the place, and go down the steps of a staircase that leads to the basement, but which is not lit by any more than the intermittent flame of a lighter or a match, struck by one of the disciples in this curious procession, transient flickers that illuminate little and do not allow one to distinguish anything significant. I count the steps, but why, since I have no idea how many there are. I, too, pull out my lighter and strike a flame now and then. After several flashes I have gone down several more steps and think that I have reached the ground of the cellar, for, by the flame of the lighter I make out a uniformly level surface. I continue my journey on the basis of that glimpse, and … Splash! I fall full-length into this mass of liquid! I have tumbled down two or three steps, hidden by the level of the beer that has spread out through all of the cellar. The explanation? It is simple: the taps are not closed, or can no longer be closed and most important, the holes in the vats that are missed by the 'customers' in the long lines before a few taps.

---

4   *Ateliers de Constructions Electriques de Charleroi* (abbrev. ACEC) was a manufacturer of electrical generation, transmission, transport, lighting and industrial equipment with origins dating to the late 19th century in Charleroi, Belgium.

I get up again, totally surprised at what just happened to me, to find out that only one part of my head has not been immersed. As for the rest, I am like a sponge. Here I am, beautiful, but momentarily refreshed. The moment of surprise passes, I start to laugh and Beauraing mingles his laughter with mine. All the same, I think that at the moment I fell I swore, or, at least, said something bad. I would be astonished if I had not. Since it all happened in the dark, at least I have not lost my dignity as a warrior. There is some consolation in that, or there should be, after all! We do not interrupt our progression toward the vats of beer for anything. We can hear the noise of those who are providing for themselves there. First I have to find my lighter, which slipped from my hands at the moment that I fell, and, curiously, I quickly put my hand on it, in this 30 or 40 centimeters of beer, despite the darkness. It does me no good right then, but I will take care of it later.

Past the corner of a corridor, I see lights and shadows. There are fellows there who have candles, and one or another of them has the consideration to leave a lighted one in place. It is thus that we see the silhouettes of four or five enormous vats of beer, whose contents slowly flow from the taps and some other openings into the corridors of the basement. Each of us fills our canteen and mess kit and gropes our way back to the exit. The return is easier, for after turning the corner it is easy to head for the light that comes from outside. Once up the stairs it is easy to find the exit. It is time to orient myself and to empty the mess tin of beer, too much of an encumbrance for walking. It is, quite frankly, vile! Insipid, tasteless, flat, for there is no head, less fresh than water, but, all the same, I drink it down. After going through all this, even though it was free for the taking, if at the risk of an atrocious death in a sea of beer, I am not going to then foolishly pour out this beverage that we have brought this far on the pretext that it is vile. So, we then drink it, useful for the thirsts to come, but with a grimace. And we laugh again about our, especially my, misadventure, for Beauraing, behind me, had time to avoid falling. Why must I always be in front, especially since André is bigger and much heftier than I am? No matter what, I never learn my lesson!

We drink, but my thirst is not quenched. It is the coolness of the cellar that did me good. Ill at ease, in a uniform soaked with beer, I feel sticky from head to foot, but we must go on. Always forward! We look for and find signs at the exit of the city, and move on toward an unknown future. A few hundred meters farther a tank which is about to pass us by stops, and the commander invites us to climb on board. Stroke of luck, these are the tank men that we met up with in leaving the beer garden, and that we have sweetly and politely greeted. They had a good laugh over my adventure and, no doubt, avoided having the same for themselves. La Fontaine was right: I speak of the writer of fables, and not of a buddy who had the same name. You will immediately understand my hope, "A good deed is never lost." He must be the one who said that!

Crowded on the tank along with several other infantrymen I am forgetting the incident in the cellar when, suddenly, a fly, then 10, then 100 land on me, drawn by my new style of perfume! Then a war without mercy begins, but also as vain as it is senseless. There are six of us on the tank, and there are hundreds of flies! My allies and I pitilessly crush all those that land on me, but there are even more that we miss in our frenzy, and they return in greater numbers every time. Exhausted after half an hour, our blows become feebler and less precise. The flies have won, we surrender the ground. I satisfy myself with doing the best I can to keep them from my face and the nape of my neck. We cannot wear ourselves out farther in futile combat that cannot succeed! We advance, the tank rolls and we conserve our strength and our legs. The suspension of the tank is evidently not that of the car of the other day. Already it is not that luxurious. What is more, here we are sitting on steel; these are not upholstered seats. The tanks are sheet steel, which is not so hard, but, assuredly, less effective for their primary function.

When, in passing through a village, we discover a well, we take a brief halt to refresh ourselves once more, for the heat remains stifling. My uniform is already dry, but it has not lost the smell of the beer, and there are always the flies. I take advantage of the opportunity to ask my companions to pour buckets of water over my head and all my body, without restraint, and also without taking off my clothes. I empty my pockets, but I realize that is stupid, because everything in them has already been well soaked. In comparison to the ambient air, the water seems cold as ice, but that is a relief. I than wring out my jacket and pants, and I repeat the rinsing. I then slip them all on, after drying them anew.

Ten minutes later we are rolling again to then arrive at Kamensk! I believe that we are not on the right road; we are going in the wrong direction. We therefore consult with our tanker friends who are going to get orders, and we consider what we should do. While we wait, we billet ourselves with a householder, after refreshment at the city commissariat. The following day we are back on the road again. In the afternoon I have a sudden violent nosebleed. No doubt due to the heat! Fortunately, a village is nearby, but it seems to be abandoned. The *isbas* are all shut up. From an instinct of politeness I knock on the door. Then more heavily. Not a sound, no response. *Alors*, greater measures, I kick it with my feet. And, to my astonishment, the door opens, not from my blows, but by the hand of a *moujik*! He looks at us timidly, but is reassured when he understands that I merely want some fresh water to assuage my nosebleed. *Voda? Da, da*! And immediately I am brought a bucket of water from the well. Finally, when the bleeding lets up, I tear off a corner of my handkerchief which I dampen and stuff in my nostril. All the family is presently gathered in the room. Their fear has vanished and they offer us a drink of curdled milk. That is, in fact, the best thing there is for thirst! We are sorry to leave. These people, no doubt, went to earth when the Russians left and we are the first "*Nimetztki*" (Germans) that they have seen, since they take us for Germans. That evening, 31 July, we are billeted in Danilovka.

And on 1 August we move on to arrive at Novo – Tcherkask, a little northeast of Rostov, at about 1800 hours, which we left with the tankers two days ago. We made a journey for nothing. We are warmly welcomed by a good lady and her two daughters in front of a one-story house, with an aspect that is both tidy and extremely clean. They live precisely on one floor. I am captivated, for the older daughter is beautiful, she is the prettiest "*Tanagra*" that I have ever met. Without any exaggeration! She is a goddess! I can only compare her with one of those precious statues. Her skin is bronzed, just to the right degree, while most of the others have darker skin. Her eyes are dark blue, sea-green, I have never seen their like. An expression I can never forget, hair nearly black. Furthermore, a figure to tempt a saint to damnation! And all the world knows that I am not forward. She gives me smiles by the hundred, and just one of them is enough to make me melt. *Bon Dieu*, what is happening to me? It is the first time that a woman or a young Russian girl aroused my desire, turned my head. I had never believed such a thing was possible, after all the others that left me cold, if not disgusted! I always have my camera, but, alas, no film, and that I shall always regret. So I make as if I did, I take phantom pictures of all the family, then of the goddess all alone. And then I ask André to take pictures of us, her and me. It is a chance to take her by the shoulder first, then by the waist.

The house is extremely tidy, everything freshly whitewashed, not a fly, real curtains. No luxury, but everything is stylish. And that is, certainly, great luxury compared to all that I have seen to date, since I crossed the frontier, the last frontier. The mother serves us perfumed tea in real teacups, if you will! She places maize pancakes on genuine porcelain plates, prettily decorated. There are cakes of sugar, and that, too, is the first time that I have seen them in Russia. But I am not interested in that, only the girl fascinates me. Every time that I look at her I meet her eyes and confirm that she has not taken her eyes off me. I do not want to seem presumptuous, but no girl has ever looked at me like that! With a thousand precautions, I take her hand, and she does not pull it back. On the contrary, it is she who tightens the grip and her gaze has the softness of velvet. The mother has seen what is going on and smiles very kindly throughout at the two of us, even though I, embarrassed, am about to let go of her hand and pretend innocence. This complicity of the mother accentuates my trouble, and now not even an axe could separate our hands.

The mother prepares a meal and insists that we partake. I am not hungry. I soar in the ether, but I do not dare to refuse. I eat, but I do not really know what I swallow, I am elsewhere. Hurrying to finish so that I can take that hand again, released with regrets in fear of not being able to recover it. The meal finished, side by side, pressed close to one another, we sit on a bench along the wall. One arm around her neck, my hand resting on her shoulder, with the other I have taken hers again, our hands resting on her knee. What euphoria! The curve of her hip pressed tight against mine, the war could continue like this for a hundred years, and then I would sign up again for another 30 years. Her mother offers us cigarettes. That, too, is the first time that I have seen this in Russia, and that it is a Russian woman who offers them to me! They are not German cigarettes. One more time I cannot refuse for fear of hurting her feelings, but I hasten to finish it to resume my dream. I hesitate in order to savor the grasp I must release in order to take the cigarette, but I keep her hand. I then resume my former position and pursued my dream.

I kiss the girl very chastely, and her mother says nothing! I kiss her again, and again, but each time at a decent interval, fearing to break the fragile equilibrium, to lose the mother's good will. I no longer fear that the daughter will pull back. I perceived her agreement, I have won her confidence. I fear far more to hurt the mother. We remain like this for minutes, or for hours, I truly have no idea.

"Now, time to go to bed?" Oh, not yet! I no longer know that Beauraing even exists, that he is there! What dolt would interrupt like this! Shatter a dream, and why? To go to sleep! I ask you… In truth, André is a very nice boy, and I admire him greatly. Simply, he is bored, and the time seems very long to him. Doubtless, it is late. We get up, desolated, but our hands stay together and the girl shows us to our room. For there are rooms and doors that one can open and close. The girls give us their room. They will go to sleep with the mother. André leaves for a moment, perhaps out of discretion, I gather up all my courage to ask my goddess to share my bed, her bed. Gestures do much to make up for my lack of Russian vocabulary. She is neither indignant, nor offended. She simply indicates that I must ask her mother. Swallowing my saliva, I decide to do so, and, very sweetly and very maternally, the mother makes me understand that I will be gone the next day and that her daughter will take the risks. With her hand she makes a gesture which I think I well understand which has nothing trivial about it at that moment. She holds her hand open and flat, horizontally at the level of her forehead and makes a gesture from left to right (you will fill in the rest!) I do not know if I could insist, but I believe that I quickly and completely understand everything: don't spoil it now, keep everything pure. All the same, my soul dies, but I am determined above all to leave a good memory with these people, with this mother who understands, who has given us such a marvelous welcome, who has done so much good for these two boys of 18 and 19 years!

I kissed the mother, who has gone toward her room, and the daughter stays a moment longer in mine. I kiss her again, with far greater passion and less propriety, but without going too far. I kiss her many times, enormously, and André returns. She rejoins her mother and her sister. Calm returns to the house, but not in my heart, and I lie there in my torment! Each of us has our own bed, André and me, with bedclothes and pillows, but for what good? I would stretch out anywhere. I do not sleep much, but I dream, dream enormously, dream wide awake.

The sounds of the house wake us in the morning. Mother and her daughters are already up and I see my Dulcinea who washes up in the living room. She is not naked, but wears only a light blouse, and her gestures as she washes herself conscientiously uncover the treasures that I shall never possess. I see her back and watch her with no shame. Am I a fool? How could I close my eyes this night, even for an instant? All the same, our door was never closed this night. But I suspect that it is not entirely by accident that things are the way they are. She slips on a skirt while turning and sees that I am watching her. No doubt I blush, but she smiles at me, with a knowing eye, and my embarrassment vanishes. When we enter the other room, two buckets of water are ready for us to wash, well rinsed and filled with clear water. Now we are clean and civilized! Then we go to the table and my heart already throbs, for I realize that soon there will be a moment of grace, a fleeting moment of bliss in all this great upheaval.

For a moment I again clasp this hand, trembling more than yesterday, for I know that soon it will all be over, that I shall only preserve a memory in my heart and a pocket full of nostalgia. Once the meal is done, all the motives are good to draw out the time, to postpone the separation, but nothing can do that, the moment comes! We all embrace and our gazes meet. I see tears, even in the mother's eyes. And my hand instinctively caresses her cheek. I hold my brunette with the sea-green eyes very tightly, and lose my breath as I embrace her. *Adieu* my little Circassian! We then leave very quickly; we quicken our pace and do not look back for a good distance so as not to see the tears. They are there, the three of them, at the top of the few steps, and, no doubt, they have not ceased to wave farewell to us. The road curves here and will efface it all. One last wave, one last look ... sad. I believe that I have just accomplished my only, or my most beautiful, act of heroism in my war!

It is done. I am off, anew, to the war, but I am not bellicose. We proceed anew but in the deepest silence. Are we afraid of torturing ourselves? Or is it to pursue a dream? There are no more dreams there about being a soldier. Then we march, and me, I become angry! We march fast, too fast, for more than once Beauraing asks me to slacken the pace. Toward 1700 hours I realize that we have gone astray a second time. We find no signs, not the least indication! Imbecile that I am, I have marched straight ahead without giving a thought to where we were going, lost in my thoughts. We are in the back of beyond, not a soul in sight, not even a shadow! Nothing on the horizon. There is not much to reflect on, and that is not my custom in such circumstances. Action is required. Where did we leave the good road? Impossible to determine. We decide to continue onward, for I do not like to double back.

We have done well, for within less than an hour a village appears on the horizon, to the right. We hit our target. In order to get there we have to leave the road and take something that looks like a footpath. The village is on the slope of a hill facing southwest, and I count no more than 20 *isbas*. I can now make out people who come and go in the village, and soon, two men approach us, shouting and gesticulating. They ask us what we want, and are very agitated! Initially I believe that their cries are hostile, but the intonation does not support that. They seem to want to stop our progress. Do they want to stop us from entering the village and warn us of the presence of Soviet troops? Nevertheless, we will have to lodge somewhere for the night!

The men now approach us with infinite precautions, zig-zagging wildly, but never ceasing their shouting. But what sort of game are they playing? What is this circus? They are now little more than a hundred meters from us and gesture toward the ground! Finally we stop and stand, quite intrigued, and it is at this moment that I understand one of the words that they cry out and incessantly repeat: "Mine!" Breathless, we look at the ground, but see nothing at first. As we study it more, we discover what look like blisters on the ground, topped with a sort of bunch of matches surrounded by little tufts of grass. Good God, mines!!! We would never have thought of that, and these peasants have saved our skins, most certainly. Nailed to the spot, we dare neither advance nor retreat. Minutely I inspect the surroundings and determine that there are many, and many more behind us. We have had a fortunate escape! We have crossed at least 30 meters of mine field. The two peasants are now quite close to us and point out the dangerous places. They know the safe passages! This field of mines extends for a hundred meters and primarily contains infantry mines. Anti-tank mines are not, in principle, dangerous to us, for they require more than 70 or

80 kilograms to trigger them! We follow the footsteps of the two men who throw furtive, curious glances at us and who talk together. I think that they took us for Russian soldiers but are just realizing that we are wearing German uniforms. Several times I hear the word "*Nimetzki*" or "*Nemetzki*" (German). What will they do; what should we say? Are they friends or enemies? How will they react at the village? We keep on guard, but it is impossible to draw our pistols, for that would be a hostile gesture toward these villagers, or indicate a lack of *sang-froid*. That is what we debate between us in a neutral voice as we approach the village, and with an air of detachment so as not to reveal our doubts. I am in my element, for this is the kind of risk that I love, and I run this risk in full knowledge of the cause. Will there be weapons there? Or Russian soldiers in civilian clothing? Soon we will see.

When we arrive at the village, our guides talk to the other residents and the same word comes up repeatedly in their conversation. They look at us with a little curiosity, but not too much. To the contrary, our "*Wallonie*" shoulder patch intrigues them, and soon, with a questioning forefinger, the question is put to us in all simplicity. For better or for worse, we try to explain that we are Belgian, but they do not seem to understand, or are not convinced. "*Belgiski? Nes naï, ni pou ni maï!*" ("Belgian? I do not know, I do not understand!") I get another idea, and I say to them, "*Franzoski*". Ah! *ja snaiou!* They understand! And smiles reappear, soon followed by a meal. But, as before, it is the women who offer us salt and bread. I understand that this is a gesture of welcome. I feel that we are safe. I also believe that we are the first strange uniforms that they have seen; the war has bypassed this village, perhaps thanks to the mine field that, doubtless, protected a unit of the Red Army that was billeted in the village before it withdrew. The meal done, we ask if we can wash ourselves and the women busy themselves heating a little water to temper the chill of the water from the well, poured in great basins carved from whole tree trunks.

Since nobody shows any signs of withdrawing to allow us to undress and wash, I make gestures of undressing myself, thinking that they will go, but not at all! They remain standing there, and arrange our things. They even help us wash our heads, backs and feet. We are the only ones who blush a bit, for our nudity does not embarrass them a bit! It is also a custom of theirs to bathe their guests! The next morning we obtain eggs, milk, flour and honey. All this goes into an enormous omelet, of which we can only eat a small part. We fill our mess tins full and the bread our hosts have given us goes into our bread bags. It is a good white bread, well leavened, very dense, with a good taste. Apparently it will be better for us in the Kouban than in any of the other regions we have traversed so far. The men help us to orient ourselves. We are in the Korosin region and we must head toward the southeast. That is the direction that the Russian troop took when they left, and it is in that same direction that we must pursue them, since that is our mission! We keep our eyes open, all the same, since Russian elements may still be in the sector in villages like this which have not been visited or occupied by our troops!

Behind us, the village has disappeared, hidden by the hills. Each time we reach the summit of one of these, the others appear, separated each time by gently sloping valleys, but with slopes that we must descend under the sun and in the temperature of a furnace. No more villages in sight during the hours that we march at a stretch, but fields of sunflowers as far as the eye can see! Kilometers and kilometers, Russian kilometers! To pass the time, since we have no other distractions, we pick the flowers and eat the seeds, the Russian "*chemiskis*", and we march. All things considered, a Russian division could hide itself in these fields and we would not see them. The extent of these plantings is that great! At times the fields of maize alternate with those of sunflowers, but always on the grand scale. But, if we change the motor fuel with such ease, passing from "*chemiski*" to "*koukourouze*" (maize), our pace is always the same; the one is no more exciting than the other.

We march with short halts, for there is not the least patch of shade, not the shade of a tree and we do not stop to eat at noon because we are not hungry. Thirst, on the other hand, is always present and we hoard the contents of our canteens, for we never know in this wilderness, far from the routes traveled by troops, when we will come upon another water point or a village! No matter how fresh and fit we were when we set out in the morning, within half an hour our cloths are already sticking to our skin. On the roads that we are now taking there is less dust, since we are the only travelers. The calm is as impressive as the infinite space! In the afternoon I think I am having a hallucination, or that I am a victim of sunstroke. I hear voices, women's voices! There are many little cries, amused laughs, yet I see nothing and André sees no more than I do.

We turn and head toward the place where these clamors seem to come from, and suddenly discover a huge hole! In the bottom there is a little lake, and four girls who are bathing there in the simplest of apparel! How was this depression in the terrain formed? It is as if an enormous meteorite formed it when it fell! I see no other explanation. The diameter at the top is certainly more than 200 meters. We are there, at the top, on the rim, when the girls see us. The cries redouble, and one of them hastens to the bank, grabs the clothes left there and takes them back into the water where they all dress in haste, without, however, being able to hide everything from us. We ask them the way to the village, and only have to follow them. They walk 20 to 30 paces ahead of us and show no signs of embarrassment. Two of them are not bad at all. I have just seen them in detail, even if only briefly. Their wet dresses cling to their bodies and we allow ourselves a few remarks, in French, of course. For their part, there is no shortage of squeals, and occasionally they turn toward us. I ask myself what they are saying. I would be curious to know! I have not forgotten Novo – Tcherkask and my little Circassienne, and I remain good, but I don't really know why.

We billet ourselves toward the center of the village, where the inhabitants receive us as amiably as usual, and before eating we decide that we will also bathe in the little lake we just discovered. It is only the second chance we have had to bathe since our arrival in Russia. The last time was at Slaviansk, in the salt lake, very salty. The other dips were in the fords, but no baths.

It is marvelous to feel the freshness of the water on my skin, after the heat of the day and the fatigue of the road. I feel like continuing our march, but that would not be prudent, and we decide not to, since we are far from the regular axes of movement and in an unknown land. After eating with our hosts, they offer us a place to sleep, after exchanging a few words about war and peace. Once more I confirm that all of the people we have met by chance in our peregrinations seem to be satisfied with the departure of the Russian soldiers and with our arrival and tell us so repeatedly. Most tell us that they are not Russian; they are Ukrainian, Circassian, Caucasian, or whatever, but not Russian! I get the feeling everywhere that totally confirms this impression and what these people tell us. Except, perhaps, in the big cities, where we generally have had only the briefest contacts with the people, if any. In the morning, after the meal, *au revoir*! *Da suidania* (or *da sudania*) *panianka, adieu pan, adieu barijna* (madame, monsieur, mademoiselle, or the equivalent). We resume our journey.

3 or 4 August we continue by Japlowskajé and Jablonskaya and there regain the frequented roads and their clouds of dust! We have seen from afar these familiar clouds and heard the sounds of the marching columns. On the 5th we are at Nelikowska where a very cultured woman invites us into her home. She offers us orange-blossom tea and corn pancakes and raspberry jam! Everything is fragrant, savory, even if there was a slight taste of soap in the pancakes. That (the soap) is made from poorly-refined oil, for everything is made from oil. We learn unknown flavors, we rediscover forgotten tastes. Here there are also several pieces of furniture and tableware, and the great samovar enthroned on the table. How different from the poverty of the Ukrainian villages, despite the agricultural richness of the Ukrainian plain!

On the 7th we cross the Don and lodge at Kalinine. Here the Don is about a kilometer in breadth, and it is always very impressive to cross such a river. Each time I have the impression that I am changing continents, entering another world! On the 8th we arrive at Nischi – Saloni and stop there. In strolling about the village we find an inhabited *isba* and, moreover, two horses whinnying in the stable! We question our hosts, but they are evasive. Do these horses belong to the foreigners? To the partisans? I form an idea, but I do not yet mention it to anyone. We spend the night and I talk of it with André, if we should transfer to the cavalry? He looks at me and is taken by the idea. I see it in his smile! As we finish our breakfast and bring it up with our hosts, they do not seem perturbed by the idea. They talk together and I also obtain a *"panjewagon"* (a sort of Russian cart) with no great discussion. They even prepare the harness!

Half an hour later, two *"Bourguignons"*, sitting on a *"panjewagon"*, leave Nischi – Saloni in a very good mood. In addition, there is bread, corn and bacon in the cart, and we don't even have to carry them! A new experience indeed! I think it is pointless to go into detail about how the kilometers seem to be shorter and our day's marches considerably longer! We have more leisure to better enjoy the countryside and we no longer fear the hills. Of late these are more numerous and steeper. It is quite reasonable that we reach Belaja – Glina in the evening without excessive fatigue, but quite thirsty. The next morning we leave the village with three horses, two in harness and one tied to the cart in reserve. That is why we decide to call it a day in the afternoon at Raskaja, where I find a forge in full activity. Our German comrades of the *97th* cheerfully transform the carts. They fix them up and equip them with metal wheels, far more practical because they are much lighter. We quickly fraternize and that is how it is that, the next morning, we leave Raskaja with four horses and two carts, one of which has steel wheels. I seriously envision providing each *"Bourguignon"* with his own individual means of transportation. I have suffered too much, myself, as a foot soldier.

This evening, at Jelinka, a new windfall, and what a windfall! I discover a camel near an *isba*. So now I become a horse-trader. After two hours of bargaining, I have one less horse, the best-looking one, but I now have a camel and another cart! The next day I drive a cart harnessed to a camel with a horse in tow. André drives a cart harnessed to two horses and tows the third cart. I see the road between the camel's feet, truly, he is big and the cart low. It is in this outfit that we reach Tischkaja in the evening, where we billet ourselves. *En route*, I know not why, but we have lots of time for reflection. I think that I was an adolescent until 10 May, 1940, of the start of the war, of my departure for Germany in March of 1941, of my joining the *Légion* in April 1942! What a journey I have taken, both literally and figuratively. What things have happened! And I am only 19 years old! Or is it 18? Do I really know still? I think of my years as a student, of my school comrades. What are they doing? What kind of life are they living? I envision the employees, the functionaries who go to their work, day after day, an entire day cooped up in their offices. I think of all the people who live a skimpy, insignificant little life. May they forgive me, but that makes me think of wood lice. Oftentimes it is not their fault, and I do not mean this in a pejorative sense. They have not found the ideal that gives a sense of living, perhaps they are timid? The life that I have chosen is truly more exalting, endowed with meaning. I am truly more certain to be useful for something! I would not exchange my life for theirs.

The next day we cross the Laba river, one more river, and we can make out very well the first foothills of the Caucasus in the distance! I laugh to myself when I see the heads of the soldiers who stop to see us pass in such a turnout! Some are astonished, others dumbfounded, but in the end they laugh just as much as we do. My camel advances imperturbably and, at times, the horses get out of breath trying to follow, for the pace of the camel is too fast for their walk and not fast enough for their trot. So, every now and then I wait, to allow André to catch up. Sometimes it is André who makes his horses trot to catch up with me. For five hours the two of us have formed a mounted unit, we make good progress, and evening finds us in a very small hamlet lost in this immensity! In actual fact, we are most imprudent, just the two of us, with no established contacts, with such an outfit, to lodge thus, isolated, at the mercy of the first partisan to come along. As a soldier, one should always sleep with one eye open. But there is a God who looks after fools like us, or in any case there are no more Bolsheviks.

The bridge has been blown up,
but we are still able to cross.

Jean F. – 17 years old, but shaped
by a harsh school.

One of our wagons during the "*Vormarsch*" [advance].

One kilometer after another.

The courier Jacques D. (bronzed) and his motorcycle take a break.

Into the Caucasus in September 1942.

After the shower comes the mud.

The road is long, but our morale is made of steel.

A little pause in a village of the Kouban.

Sharing the mess tin with a shy child.

Thirst is constant.

Passing through Rostov on the Don.

The German cemetery after the recapture of Rostov.

The horses are also tired.

A 10-minute rest.

After a day's march of
40 kilometers and two
hours of rest, we are
off again.

Our "*ordinaire*" (usual meal) – a feast for these Russian children.

The Ukraine 1942 "*Vormarsch*" [advance]. (Roger De Goy, comp. *Legión Belge Wallonie: Historique* – an unpublished manuscript in calligraphy, 1948. Written by interned Belgian veterans in 1946–47; one of five originals in the author's possession – privately printed in typescript c. 1990)

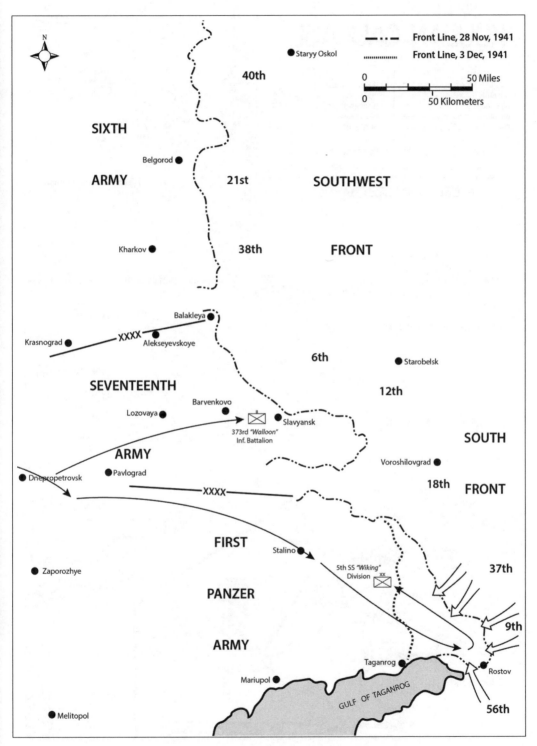

The Southern Front of the war in Russia, 1941–42.

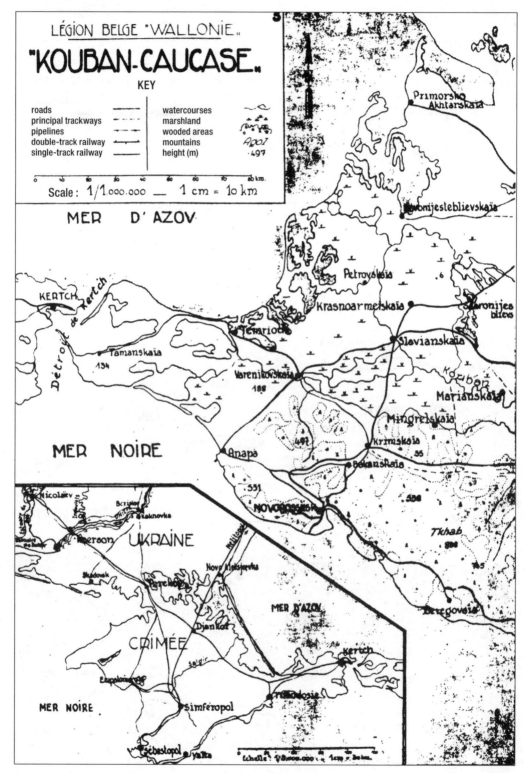

Kouban – Caucasus.

6

The Return of the Prodigal Son

On the 14th we resume the road toward Maïkop, which we reach in the afternoon. There is a little bridge to cross and, what a surprise! Who is on the other side? Our commander! Beside him is *Lieutenant* Jean V. and, a little behind him, an old buddy, Guy W. We both put on a very dignified air when we approach our commander.

To me he says, "*Eh bien,* Kaisergruber! What is all this about?" waving his hand at my outfit.

"That, *mon Commandeur,* is a camel!"

"Yes, I see that" – neither positively nor negatively – "but where does this animal come from?"

"I received it."

"*Eh bien*! Go take it back to the one who gave it to you!"

"*Mon Commandeur,* that is two or three days' journey from here."

"So what, do what I tell you."

"Good, *mon Commandeur,* but in that case I will need '*Marschverpflegung*' (food for the journey)."

"In that case, go to the *fourrier* [quartermaster sergeant]."

"*Merci, mon Commandeur.*"

During this brief dialogue I am unable to see the head of *Lieutenant* Jean V., who is a little to my right after I descended from the cart to present myself to *Commandeur* Lippert, but, on the other hand, I was able to see the hilarious face of my comrade W.! He showed us where to find the *fourrier* and a great many of our comrades come to greet us on the way, bursting with laughter. We receive rations and leave the city toward the suburbs. Obviously, we have already decided not to go too far. The men of the "*Tross*" (baggage train) have been forewarned and immediately take charge of the two carts and two horses. We then proceed a few hundred meters toward the outskirts and I accost some people in hopes of exchanging the far too conspicuous camel for a more discreet horse! The exchange is quickly concluded.

We had thought to seize the occasion to take another 48 hours' vacation from discipline, but decided to rejoin our company, which we immediately find with pleasure: the *3rd Compagnie*. In order to avoid attracting attention and running the risk of meeting our commander, we wait for nightfall to slip into the cantonment. Thus it is that, shortly after, we find a billet where *Adjudant* Dassy and other comrades, including Chavannes, already were. Our recent wanderings have worn us out, and we waste no time going to sleep. There are two comrades who have found the comfort of a bed, and well that they did. As for us, we are content with hard ground.

In the depths of my slumber, blasts of a whistle and I think I hear the bugle, at least if I am not dreaming. I am awakened. The courier Paquet, *Capitaine* Tchekov's orderly, bursts in and tells us that there is a state of alert; that we must prepare to move out! I have only enjoyed a part of my night's sleep, but what can I do? I have nearly forgotten my military state. You can well imagine that the month of individual tourism and total freedom that we experienced has removed us far from the constraints of discipline! It is hard, but that's the way it is. We chose it, so we must comply! Everyone looks for his things, his equipment in the dark, and those who are already up bump their feet into the ribs of those who are still lying down. We assemble in front of the *isbas* on the road and the column moves out within half an hour. Decidedly, I am not rested!

It seems that we are heading toward Tuapse and that is no secret! We proceed in the night and ascend the first foothills of the so greatly yearned for Caucasus Mountains. We talk little, for we are tired and the mountain has us panting. Dawn breaks, chases away the night and the sun makes shadows of the marching columns. Little by little it dissipates the mists of morning and outlines the crests that loom in the distance. We march and we climb, our throats are dry. Thorny bushes covered with round yellow berries border the road and tempt us to quench our thirst. I taste them, since nobody else will take the risk. They are bitter, very bitter, but they quench my thirst. I munch three or four. They are hard, but no more, one never knows. We climb and we climb, and the panorama enlarges. We can see farther and farther, and as before, the clouds of dust rise high into the sky above the columns that move down in the valley. And, lower down, to the left of the road, I see a shepherd and his flock on a high plateau, but it is 200-300 meters below us. Of course I saw the flock first; then the shepherd, and the dogs that harass the animals that want to scatter.

In the afternoon a city emerges in the distance, through the haze. First I make out minarets and cupolas, then the rest of the city. We are already in Islam! These are the first minarets that I have seen, and I think of Aladdin's land. But our experience has none of the Thousand and One Nights! We continue to climb, and in the evening we pitch our tents on a crest. The night is cooler. We feel that we are at an altitude, even though it is not yet very high.

The following morning we climb a little more, then descend, and then resume climbing. The city in the valley below is Abadischowskaja. At noon we reach a crest that should be wooded, but there is little left now. In effect, it now consists only of stripped tree trunks and trees lying on the ground, as if the woods had been mowed down by some giant. The blast of the shells or bombs has torn nearly all the leaves off the trees and the rare bushes that remain! It is as if a cataclysm struck the hill, an almost lunar landscape! The foxholes of the infantry and the shell craters overlap, and both hold cadavers by the dozen – Russian and German, pell-mell. The positions have changed hands, back and forth, several times, and we must occupy them in our turn. There are several corpses in every hole. In the one where I crouch there are two Russian corpses and one German, one upon another. On the parapet is an open can of meat and an orange Bakelite butter dish that still contains butter, melted and rancid. In the bread bags there is bread. So, to pass the time, we eat. We rest there for maybe two hours before receiving orders to move on. It is the 1st Platoon of the *3rd Compagnie* that is going to take positions to screen the left flank. We depart, leaving behind us the countryside of the apocalypse. The 1st Platoon found a live Russian concealed among the corpses – a Russian who will enlarge the ranks of our auxiliaries.

We descend for a good half-hour; then climb again for at least two hours, and more of the same. The march is exhausting. The heavy "*Tross*" [unit/baggage train] has taken another route along the line of the Maïkop – Tuapse railroad, and only the light "*Tross*" is following more or less the same itinerary as us. That is why we have to carry all of our equipment and why the march is more arduous. Nevertheless, at Maïkop we have been promoted to "*Leichtgebirgsjäger*" (light mountain troops), carrying no more than the bare minimum so as to be extremely mobile!

At present we pass interminable files of Russian prisoners, carrying on their backs tins of water tied to a sort of backpack made of planks. There are thousands of them! The columns form like serpents that wind in the mountains and we can make them out from afar. Then, we meet them as we descend toward Maïkop and double the traffic on these mountain footpaths.

It is impressive to see, and makes me think of termites on a human scale. Now the footpath descends no more, it climbs interminably, in stages at times, but we never cease to climb. At the end of the day we reach a point named "Hill 233". It is a sort of grand basin, right in the mountains, and heavily wooded. It is also the terminus of the column of "water bearer" prisoners, for there, to the left, we find a mountain of "canisters". These cans of water are guarded by armed men, and taking some is out of the question. It is our halting place, and we pitch our tents one more time. A field kitchen serves us coffee and we are issued rations. It is here that, for the first time, I see and eat bread baked before the war, in 1939! The markings on the cellophane bear witness to it! We eat in front of the tents, sitting on a tree trunk. In the center of the basin, in a hollow tree trunk, runs a little spring. But it runs drop by drop, and we wait in line. It takes a 15-minute wait to fill a quart cup. The line will continue all night, for sure! Nevertheless, at *Reveille*, ill at ease with a five or six-day beard, I use part of the coffee I receive this morning to shave and remove the whiskers from my face. It takes courage to choose between thirst and hygiene. The 1st Platoon of our company, the 3rd, rejoins us during the day. Shortly thereafter the 1st and 3rd Platoons (mine) are designated for a reinforced reconnaissance patrol (*Spähtrupp*). It is a group with a good 30 men, with *Lieutenant* Jean V. and *Adjudant* Robert D., which vanishes into the extremely dense forest. We enter it by a footpath that descends and climbs again, but which, does, indeed, descend, and in total silence.

The mission seems to be important. It is also perilous, no doubt, otherwise they would never have formed such an important group. Here the front is everywhere, and it is necessary to be on guard everywhere at all times. A village or a strongpoint that we leave can be back in enemy hands again soon afterward. Henceforth, that is how it will constantly be. In the mountains there is no "*HKL*" (*Hauptkampflinie* – main line of resistance, MLR) and we are only "at home" in the locale we occupy at the moment. Afterward … The forest is somber and deserted, the silence of the dead reigns! Only in spots does the sun pierce the foliage and project a few patches of light in the undergrowth or in the rare clearings. All of a sudden, after a full hour's march, the column stops dead and we are on full alert, one knee on the ground, hidden behind a tree, or prone among the shrubs. The four machine guns immediately take up firing positions. We hold our breath and scrutinize the woods. We do not chamber rounds in the rifles that already have rounds in the magazine, so as to avoid making the slightest sound. The submachine guns are different; they can be armed without making a sound. Below, ahead, to the right, a wisp of smoke, very thin, but nothing stirs. We remain like that, three, five, 10 minutes? Then, directed by gestures, we fan out and advance very slowly, with all care, all our senses on the alert. The dying fire is there, in arm's reach, beside it a pot in which the water is hot. They attempted to extinguish the fire in haste, without completely succeeding. Three meters distant is a "Maxim" machine gun on wheels, with its loaded drum, ready for action. Farther away are other arms. The state of things makes it clear that the camp was recently abandoned in haste. They saw our approach and decamped, without thinking of defending themselves. All the same, we advance with prudence, for they may well have calmed down a bit farther on and be waiting for us! There, to the left, a corpse; then we see five, 20; in front, and also to the right, there are dozens. Finally we count nearly an entire company. In any case, there are well over a hundred! Most of them have been shot in the back. Doubtless they took position here and were surprised in the night from the rear. The spectacle is dismal. The engagement must have taken place two days ago or more, and the corpses are already covered with flies and bloated. They teem under the uniforms. Evidently, with this heat and the humidity of the undergrowth … A ray of sun touches a corpse, illuminates a petrified face. Blood everywhere. It is black, dried on the wounds and around the holes in the uniforms. We rummage around to come up with some "*Soldbücher*" (paybooks) and identity discs, but we can do no more. No doubt we have neither the time nor the possibility of burying these comrades; others will take care of that later! There are also Russian bodies, but there are less of them. We would never have seen these dead right off, for the color of the uniforms, Russian or German, blend in too well with the grass, the soil and the underbrush. What a hecatomb! We move on a bit, just in case, before returning the way we had come, mission accomplished, probably. No doubt it was necessary to find what happened to a company of the *97th* that had vanished in the wild!

After three hours' absence we returned to "Hill 233" and the leaders report to headquarters and deliver their report. Shortly thereafter the battalion moves out. We climb the escarpments; we climb yet another good hour before we descend again into the valley on the other side, to arrive in the evening at the Maïkop – Tuapse railroad, near the village of Apscheronskaja. There are long-range guns there in firing position, no doubt aimed at Tuapse. One of them has burst, and its muzzle looks like a peeled banana! We pitch our tents on the railroad ballast and it rains. The temperature cools off rapidly and we take shelter in the tents for the night.

On the morning of 17 August we resume climbing and heavy rain alternates with occasional clearing. The march is extremely arduous. We slip on the muddy path; we stumble on the rocks and slide off damp roots whose bark has been stripped off by hundreds of boots. They are slick, slimy with mud left by other feet. These roots intertwine and emerge from the ground to spread snares for our steps. When we slip, we often slide back several meters and knock over sacks from which oaths emerge, and which are, themselves, precariously balanced. It is their posture, hunched over under the rain that gives these comrades, wrapped in their waterproof canvas, the appearance of sacks. It is a dog's life, but we must go forward. In the evening we get to Pruskaja. The *1st Compagnie* was engaged there, reinforced by the machine gunners of the *4th*, which cleared the road of Russian resistance. This night we occupy the village.

On 18 August we resume our road one more time, and in what has nearly become habitual for us, we climb before we descend again, immediately to climb again. The descent is hardly less fatiguing, since we have to hold back and brace ourselves with our hamstrings. The legs get tired, but we are a bit less breathless. The 3rd Platoon is rear-guard, and we descend along a mountain stream. In the afternoon we catch up with a squad of our heavy mortars, who advance with great effort. We hear them long before we see them, for the horse-drawn infantry cart makes a lot of noise on the rocky ground.

I joyfully meet three old comrades who, what's more, lived in the same quarter of the suburbs of Brussels as myself. One of the three, Max M., is still in good health; the other two, Arthur V. and Jean J., are not doing so well, especially the last. Malaria and intense fever for Jean J., dysentery for Arthur. Our Russian auxiliary, Ivan, an ex-prisoner, also seems to be holding out. Our column quickly catches up and passes them. As for myself, I join them, and, seeing my platoon follow the road, I hail my platoon leader, *Chef de Groupe* S., talk with my *adjudant* and am told that the mortar squad is not part of our company and that I must go with the company.

Since I have confirmed the precarious state of the health of the men of that group, I resolve that I cannot abandon them, and I let my platoon leader know my decision. They warn me of sanctions and even of a court martial, but I stay!

Little by little my platoon moves off and vanishes ahead of us in the forest. The four of us remain, plus Ivan. It is, indeed, difficult to move the infantry cart forward in such terrain. Forest, boulders, torrents. The horses toil, but we also do so more than them. We must push constantly, help the wheels make it through the rocks, hold back during the descents. It is not a sinecure, we are short of breath, we sweat, we wear ourselves out! What is more, we are no more than three able-bodied men, including Ivan. Jean is absolutely incapable of doing anything and Arthur is not much better.

In places the forest is extremely dense, broken up by rocks so big that it becomes impracticable for the infantry cart. Accordingly we follow the bed of the torrent, which is not much better, but, at least, wide enough to let the cart get through. There, also, we have to push or pull to get over the boulders, the rocks and all the rough terrain and that has its problems. There are places where it takes more than an hour to move 200-300 meters! At times we have to leave the bed of the torrent and proceed on the crest, on the edge of a precipice that is on our right, the only practicable place, if I may say so, for there are always rocks, holes and tree trunks to get over to make our way. At one moment the horses have to strain to overcome some obstacle and then, continuing with their dash, with no possibility of stopping or restraining them, they stumble and topple over, taking the cart with them, for sure. We close our eyes, hearing nothing but the noise of the fall and of the horse-shoes on the rock. That can certainly be heard for hundreds of meters, and if there are any Russians nearby, they will have no trouble finding us. And, with a noise like that, they might well think that there is an entire company and keep their distance! All the same, we have to go see what happened, for the noise has stopped and we realize that something unexpected has happened. In fact, the team has not gone far down the slope of the ravine. One or two trees stopped it. The terrified horses are on one side, the inert infantry cart on the other side of the tree trunks. Another miracle! With infinite precautions we secure the infantry cart so that it cannot topple farther and pass the horses' reins before Max releases the harness holding the horses to the cart. Then, slowly, with lots of shouting and straining we manage to lead the horses onto the crest, and then the infantry cart. Written like this, it seems simple, but God knows how we sweated! Broken fingernails, cut fingers, scraped by branches, we are exhausted, but we keep on. First, of course, we have to repair the traces and the reins, cobble up all that was demolished in the fall and stroke the horses to calm them.

Now we follow the sound of the guns, for that is the only form of orientation we have to rejoin the front. Jean has a good 40° of fever [104°F] and Arthur's dysentery forces him to make one stop after another. He no longer takes the trouble to re-button his clothes, but we advance! Night comes, suddenly, as always in these latitudes, and our advance becomes even more arduous. We can no longer see the rocks and roots on which we stumble! Happily, at times the moonlight penetrates between the trees and helps us a bit. Finally, beyond the forest in front of us, we make out clearings and we arrive at a little plain. Shortly after getting out of the forest we are surprised to discover unexpected activity! By the light of the moon we make out moving vehicles and others that are stopped. I think I can hear the sound of engines and recognize the silhouettes of armored vehicles among the other horse-drawn vehicles. I am not sure, because they are far away, but I firmly believe they are there. I also see shadows that come and go and move about near the column. We can also hear voices, but are unable to make out what language they are speaking there. We are on the alert! Are they Russian or German? No matter how we strain our ears, we cannot say. Suddenly white flares are discharged by this convoy, climbing into the sky, hissing, then slowly falling, hanging from their parachutes, illuminating the landscape. Instantly we freeze in place, in whatever position we were in, for our shadows must not move, and thus we can be confused with a bush, a tree, or whatever! Once the last flare has fallen to earth, we lie down and await a suitable moment to move. It is then that Max decides to send Ivan to reconnoiter. He is, in effect, the only one who risks nothing. He then moves off, at first slowly, with caution, then resolutely, toward the convoy. We watch as best we can, but we cannot make out anything. We wait! A quarter-hour later, Ivan returns. They are Russians! He spoke to them. It is a unit of the Red Army. It would have been impossible to assure ourselves of it in the darkness and without getting too near. All the less so since Russian soldiers are often dressed in truly fanciful fashion or so disparate that, even in daylight, it is sometimes difficult to distinguish them from civilians. I could not see why a column of civilians would be there, in the night, or why they would use flares, but we had to make sure, it was vital for us. What could we do? Wait and not stir? Faithful Ivan! Still dressed as on the day when he was captured, he was able to mix freely with the others without being noticed and then return to warn us of the danger. We owe him a debt of gratitude! He could have stayed with his own people, or even have denounced us!

Our patience is soon rewarded. Soon the column moves on and disappears in the night, to our left. Shortly thereafter we get up to follow our own route, but to the right. It starts to rain again, but within a short time, happily, we reach a house that we did not even see until we were within 30 meters because of the darkness and the rain. Without inhibition we knock on the door, and, right away, the door opens. Naively we ask the people if there are soldiers here or in the neighborhood, but they do not understand. They speak no more Russian than we do. They employ another idiom. They are Armenian. We do not complicate things. We are taking a big risk, but what else can we do? The people do, indeed, speak of *Nimetzki*, but it may be that they merely are repeating the word that we have just spoken. We decide to stay there, with no other precautions or reconnaissance in the village. At least this way we are not attracting any attention, in case the Russians do occupy the village. The two sick people sleep on the "*pitzki*" (Russian stove).[1] Max and I sleep against the entrance door, so that we will be warned if anyone tries to enter or leave. Who knows? It is always possible that someone here might try to warn the others of our presence. In any case, we have to allow for the possibility if we want to live to grow old! We sleep naked, wrapped in our covers, giving our clothes time to dry. We sleep with one eye open, but we do sleep. In the morning we eat a hasty morsel before setting out to reconnoiter the village, Max and me. What precautions do you want to take in this situation? They are necessary, for if there are Russians in the houses that we approach, they could easily put paid to our account once and for all! We are not Sioux Indians, and we approach as if there was nothing to fear! Happily, we do not go very far before we meet Germans, and, shortly, the men of my own platoon, who arrived here yesterday, before us. The Germans, very surprised to find us here, hasten to lead us to their headquarters, where we are received like saviors! They fix "*Kartoffelpuffer*" (sort of potato pancakes) for us and, during this time, the commander of the place gives us the following details: we are at the command post of Regiment "Nobis", and there are no proper combatants there to speak of. There are only administrators, train elements and stretcher bearers, with only rifles, a few submachine guns and pistols. They have been surrounded for two or three days, and *Commandeur* Nobis can't get over seeing us! We explain to him how we got here thanks to the darkness of the night; that we passed through the lines without realizing it; that the Russians are retreating, harassed or pursued from all sides. In any case, he testifies to his pleasure at seeing us, while we eat what has been prepared in our honor. Imagine, a quartet of combatants who fall from the heavens with machine gunners and (what luxury!) a mortar. He is delighted that we will fill out his defenses, reinforcing his corpsmen and other "*Verwaltungslandsers*" (administrative soldiers). Of course, that is what we are going to do very quickly. The village is practically in a wooded basin, only the southeast corner offers a little clear land. The *isbas* on the north and east of the village are right against the forest, and we take our position in an *isba* at the extreme northeast of the village. The trees surround the *isba* on two sides and come right up to it. The side facing the village comprises a sort of veranda and we spend part of our days there when we are not on guard. Several meters from the house on the left there is a bread oven where we bake the pears that constantly drop on our heads. There are a great many pear trees, whose pears fall ceaselessly, and we put them in the oven as we have seen the Russians do, *pardon*, the Armenians. They are inedible when raw, but when baked in the oven or dried they are passable. We also eat the plums, which the people have set out to dry on the slope of the roof exposed to the sun. Thus we pass the time when we are not on guard.

I am busy near the oven in question when, I don't know why, my alert senses, no doubt, I raise my eyes in the direction of the forest and I see a man in a leather jacket watching me! He is pressed against a tree, and partly hidden. It seems that there is a second, a little farther away, but it is the first that catches my eye. He is 30 meters from me, no more, and we look at each other like two

---

1   The Russian '*pitzki*' was a large mass of brick with a fire chamber and air passages so that the entire mass warmed up. It was large enough so that the entire family could bed down on it and keep warm at night.

china dogs! *Ma foi*! It is a Russian soldier! But what is he doing there? My weapon is in the house, and I play it cool, arms dangling at my sides. I call out to him, "*idi souda*" (come here). It is all that I can do to keep up appearances and show my self-assurance. The fellow turns and scampers off. I run to the house, take my rifle and, at the same time, alert my buddies. One of them also saw the one or more fellows who ran away, but, disarmed like me, he leaped into the house and also got his arm. Three or four of us take up the pursuit, but see no more of them. We pursue in the direction that they took, but we are soon out of breath, because the ground rises steeply in leaving the village in the bowl. We run, we march, for at least 20 minutes, but find no trace, they have evaporated. Ten or 15 seconds were enough for them to gain their distance or take cover! Perhaps, after all, they were attempting to surrender, and became afraid at the last moment? I cannot have had too frightening an air, disarmed and cooking the pears like a proper housekeeper!

On the road back we meet a group of mounted Cossacks. These cavaliers are employed around here in chasing partisans. They understand quickly what just took place and immediately take off in pursuit of the fugitives. We return to the village, greatly disappointed. We cannot leave our weapons for a single moment!

The next day we receive an Astrakhan billy goat and our friend Arthur, who did the butchering, carves it properly for us. It is nothing great, but it is a change in our daily meal! The comrades who pull guard duty this night, in the orchard, have a cold sweat. Regularly, objects fall around them. They think of grenades, but nothing explodes! It is a while before they determine with laughter that it is the pears falling, as I had found out for myself during the day. That is easy to say, but at that moment, in the dark, they did not realize it right away!

On the 20th I must rejoin my squad in the platoon. I change my billet. The weather is execrable. It rains and we bathe in the mud. In the evening the squad leader, S., accompanies me to show me the position where I am to stand guard. It is still clear, but not for long with such rain! *Eh bien*! The location was chosen well. After marching at least 300 meters and crossing the river (Pcheka, I believe) on a tree trunk that is polished smooth and very slippery I am on high ground in the midst of an old cemetery! The squad leader does not tarry, and I understand. It rains incessantly, not in torrents, but steady and regular, a heavy rain that permits 20 meters' visibility, but more than that, a rain that makes so much noise that it is impossible to hear anything less than, perhaps, a cannon in the distance. Since I have time, and before night suddenly falls, I examine the surroundings a bit, at least what I can see since the rain reduces my horizon greatly. It is very important to learn a bit about the topography of my position so that, in an emergency, I can find the best defensive position, the best firing position. I determine that there is no position that is particularly good, a few big gravestones, yes, but as for the rest, nothing but old crosses of worm-eaten wood or rusty iron. It seems that there is nothing here but very old graves. It is a long time since anyone was buried here, or there have been no deaths in the village for more than 50 years! I quickly made the rounds of this field of repose where none of the inscriptions are still legible. I should be relieved at midnight, which means I have to stay here in this unending rain for four hours. I wear my waterproof sheet. The water runs off of it to the ground, but often into my boots. My helmet keeps the water from running down my neck; that is always protected. The darkness is now total, and I sit down on a rock, facing west, but attentive in all directions, for the enemy can come from anywhere. Upon reflection, which takes place since I have nothing else to do, I tell myself that, in fact, I am here to warn my comrades in the village in the event of a visit from undesirable guests. My shots will alert them in time to take up defensive positions at the entrance to the village. As for myself …? That is not very cheerful, but there is no injustice, since each has his turn to take the risk.

Time flows, slowly, very slowly, and the rain never stops. Have I been here for 10 minutes or an hour? I have no idea and I no longer have a watch. There are also some trees here that I just saw, as old as the crosses in the cemetery, and every time that a fruit falls to the ground, I jump, as did my comrades who stood guard yesterday during the night in the village. When will it be midnight? If only the rain would cease! The time seems shorter the less I think. Now and then an animal creeps through the grass or the bushes. I hear a rustling, but can distinguish no more. A squirrel, a hedgehog or a fox? I have seen more than one by daylight. At times also the beating wings of a nocturnal bird. All of this is only supposition, but this is how I learn to interpret the sounds.

It is certainly past midnight now, but, no matter how acutely I listen, no matter how I peer into the darkness, there is no sign of my relief. What are they doing down there? Nice to be warm and sheltered. The minutes pass and, no doubt, the hours, too, but I have no way to measure the time. How can I know? All that I can do is wait, but I prefer to wait for nothing and think that I shall be there forever, that is less aggravating! Soon day will dawn, but it remains just as dark, just as dark and rainy! I do believe that my waterproof sheet leaks, but my jacket moistens so slowly that the water has time to reach my body temperature. Later, much later, I feel the cold and I think that it is the sign of approaching dawn. It is always slightly before daylight comes that the temperature chills, or that is the moment that the organism chooses to react! The rhythm reverses. When, at last, the night grows less dark, when the day dawns, faint and uncertain, the rain keeps falling in the same fashion. I wait patiently for a long time, certainly more than an hour after daybreak, before I hear the sound of someone approaching. That should be my relief, at least I hope so, for the Russians would take more care to make less noise. But nothing is certain, and I remain on my guard, in the shelter of a rock. I gaze, wide-eyed, and scrutinize the limited horizon through the rain in the direction that the noise seems to come from. A sound of footsteps. Now I hear them better, a sound of footsteps, of slipping, of muffled oaths. No doubt now, it is the relief, but it is five more minutes before I see the familiar silhouette of a comrade's helmet emerge from the curtain of rain. Before I even have time to ask a question, he explains: Gérard D. was supposed to relieve me at midnight, and the squad leader explained to him how to get here. Gérard set out bravely in the face of the darkness of the night and the rain. He was crossing the river on a tree trunk, got to the middle, when he slipped and fell into the river. He made it to the bank and wandered a bit before getting back to his starting point, where he recounted his misadventure. Soaked to the bone, he refused to try again. The squad leader, S., rather than leading the relief to me himself, since he was the only one who knew my position exactly, considered that it would be better to wait until morning to relieve me! I thought that I had been forgotten in my position or, for some reason, he did not care! Thus it was that I stood 12 hours on guard in the cemetery in rain that would disgust a duck.

I came back down, slipping in the mud, crashing into bushes, shivering and soaked. I crossed the river on the tree trunk, with a thousand precautions, but if I had fallen there, I could not have been more soaked than I was. Simply, the water that was on me was not as cold as that in the river. I will spare you the report I made on arriving at the command post, and, especially, the language in which I made it! I made no friends that day. Half an hour later – that was how long it took me to say what was in my heart – I enter an *isba*, have the "*pitzki*" lit to dry my clothes and I am in my briefs. In truth, not even that, for they needed to be dried too. My clothes are on the "*pitzki*", including my briefs, and I am wrapped in my blanket. I demand complete silence from my hosts, and I forbid them to open the door for anyone, not for the entire Red Army, not even for a general. I do not know if they understand me, but I snooze in peace, my lower back to the heat. When I wake up the fragrance of roast chicken tickles my nostrils. I open my eyes and discover that there is sun. It is already on the decline. It is already late afternoon! The good woman makes me understand that she has prepared the chicken for me. I go to the veranda to get some fresh air and to shave. When I return I put on my dry clothes and sit at the table. Then I go to inform my squad leader where he can find me if he needs to and I return to the *isba* where, an hour later, I go back to bed. When I am awakened for a new spell of guard duty it is 0400 hours in the morning and I am on duty until 0800 hours. There is still plenty of mud, but at least it has stopped raining, and I am no longer on guard at the cemetery. I am a bit on the other side of the river.

Life here continues in this fashion until 25 August, That morning we are informed that the sector has been cleaned up and cleared of Russians and that we are going to rejoin the battalion. I and my comrades of the heavy mortar go to take our leave at the command post. Nobis, the commander, gives us for the insignia of the regiment the *"Spielhahnfeder"* [Blackcock feather], an escutcheon in white metal, decorated with the plume of the fighting cock. A gesture of friendship, a token of gratitude, it is not a decoration.

We return to the road, with less rain, more sun, and, to complete our cheer, the setting is marvelous. Very beautiful, but it is the Caucasus, and that includes hard climbing at times. In the afternoon we get to a hamlet, a little village whose name I do not know, a dirt road lined with 15 *isbas* on both sides. There is a plethora of fruit, fruit trees that are good for our health, for we all suffer from scurvy. The locals receive us very cordially, offering us bread, butter and honey, and allow us to gather all the fruit that we want. There is no shortage of food in this village, and, if it was not for the sound of guns in the distance, we could believe we were on a mission like the explorers or ethnologists, since the village is so peaceful, and the environment so wild! This night we sleep peacefully with the insouciance of youth, even though the enemy could be anywhere around. All the same, we place two men on guard.

When the sun rises on this forgotten corner of the Caucasus, we shake ourselves, wash, eat a bit and get back on the road. The view is majestic. All of the landscapes are of epic proportions, yesterday infinite plains stretching to the horizon without end, today forests that swallow us up. These mountains hide yet more without end. On every side we discover even more of them that we also cross, one after another, covered with sweat, chafed sore by our straps.

I do not know why, but I imagine a moment when, seen from on high, this little group of *"Bourguignons"*, immersed in the green desert that engulfs us, this sort of Amazon, represents something insignificant, absurdly low on the scale of the universe. Yet we are there, each of us with his own personal and very tangible problems. Perhaps it is the awareness of being so small and of representing so much that gives us the strength to be what we are and to do what we do with such determination, day after day. Tomorrow is another day. Our enlistment causes us to surpass ourselves whenever we can, on the human scale, for we are not Gods. It is the distress that forges our determination. When the day's march is long or heavy, we avoid conversation so as not to get out of breath, and it is the time for reflection, for philosophy. That restores the spirit and assuages the pains, or, at least, reduces our awareness of them. In effect, the "Russian" sores have put in their appearance. We also call them *"Fleckfieber"* [spotted fever], but I do not know if that term is appropriate. They are small whitish blisters, lighter than the skin, which end up with a little black point. We cannot help but scratch them, exposing bare flesh, and it is inflamed. Thus the torture starts. The sores extend and eat into the flesh, deeper every day. Sometimes there is fever, or is it malaria? At times, Atabrine reduces the fever, but Ribanol does not heal the sores. The areas that suffer most are those where clothing rubs, socks, belt and boots. Lice, inseparable companions, lay their eggs in these sores, and the problem escalates. As for me, I have a tendon at the back of my ankle that is practically denuded. It is not that it is really painful, except in marching, when my feet heat up, but how to avoid scratching it? At the end of the day our weakened organisms do not have all the resources needed to combat these maladies, which come, in turn, or simultaneously, to undermine our health. In addition to the Russian sores, dysentery, malaria, scurvy or other afflictions manage to weaken our constitutions, sap the strength out of these bodies that have been so hardened, so well trained. Even though most of us are still holding out, at least till now, there have already been evacuations. It is in these conditions that we reach Koubano – Armianski.

7

Koubano – Armianski: Caucasus

On 26 August our little group makes its entrance at Koubano – Armianski, where the main body of our unit is. Arthur V.E. confirms the disappearance of his rifle. Suffering from shingles, he lightened his load as much as he could, consigning his possessions to the ammunition wagon.

The bumps and jolts of the road have shaken it off and, *voilà*, Arthur is without his weapon! Ordinarily that would be a court martial offense or, in any case, an extreme penalty, but nobody noticed it before it was found, two days later – the rifle emerging from a pothole full of water at the entrance of the village. Arthur has, truly, had a lucky escape, and it is now time to restore the condition of his most precious possession, at least the most precious in the eyes of his superiors.

I move in with my comrades of the mortar platoon as if nothing had happened in an *isba* on the heights to the left of the village on the edge of the forest. The village is in a large clearing, shaped like a basin, like so many others, crossed by a stream that comes from the east. The population, Tscherkesse and Armenian, is a friendly population, we feel that well. Orders confirm that! The instructions are very strict, no "*Zabralages*" (thefts) of food, no propositioning girls, and if they proposition us…? Offenses on our part will receive exemplary punishment!

The situation of the village is not ideal, indeed, it is frankly dangerous. Koubano – Armianski is dominated to the north, east and south by wooded ridges. Only the southeast presents a little embrasure, somewhat removed, but with a little "*balka*" (ravine) and the stream, which exits thence. Here there is no longer a front line. Each village is the front. A village may be occupied, at times by us, at times by the Russians, but one never knows until one approaches if it is occupied or not, and by whom? There are villages in front of us that are held by us, and others to our rear that are held by the Russians. The space between the villages belongs to whomever who ventures there, and only for the moment that they are there. It is the new kind of war that we must get used to! The guard duties and patrols are numerous and fatiguing, the patrols murderous. Our strategic situation is extremely precarious, but the village is agreeable and the population courteous.

This night Max and I stand guard between the forest and the last houses, the two of us calm and relaxed, despite everything, but not inattentive! The next morning I descend to the bottom of the village and shave, wash at the bank of the stream where I meet one or two comrades who have come to do the same. As we are talking after washing up, we see unaccustomed activity in the east part of the village, in the direction of the command post, which leads us to check it out. There we find groups that are in animated conversation. A patrol has just arrived there from Tcherjakov and has announced the death of "*Prévôt*" John Hagemans [see earlier footnote on John Hagemans] and other comrades who were killed at Tcherjakov during an encounter with the Russians.

This loss is a heavy blow for us, for we all appreciate John Hagemans, a modern-day cavalier, but it is an especially heavy blow for the youngsters for whom he was truly their leader and friend. Although I did not see them, I am sure that tears must have been shed in private, and that fists were clenched in pockets. We are all soldiers, already hardened, it is true, but some are so young! And, after all, there is nothing humiliating in shedding tears, in weeping for a friend!

Thus we learn of the death of 15 of our comrades, and that 50 to 60 of ours were wounded in the fighting. It does not appear that there were any killed or wounded outside the boundaries of the village, at least on our side. In actual fact, there may well have been some wounded outside the village limits, but those who were killed died defending the village that had been surrounded against the assaults of the Russians who were attempting to recapture it. I also learn in the same fashion that the village had been captured at the very moment when the Russians were distributing soup, and that right after the assault, the same Russian cooks found themselves facing a line of "*Bourguignons*" with their mess tins, there, where a few moments earlier their compatriots had stood in line. An amusing caprice of the war, less gay, I presume, for the Russians who missed their soup that day.

In the afternoon we receive another patrol from Tcherjakov whose mission was mopping up the woods between the two villages and maintaining contact with us. We learn that Pierre Taverne was killed during an encounter between this patrol and the Russians who infest the woods. He was just 15-and-a-half years old when he was struck down in these forests of the Caucasus. His father is with us and his grief bowled me over. We are not used to seeing a man cry, and all the efforts that he makes to control himself, to contain his tears, are in vain, which make this sight even more insupportable for me. Embarrassed at indiscreetly witnessing this scene, I turn away to hide my shame, my shame at being powerless to do anything! The father appears to be well past 40 at the very least, maybe over 50, but today he looks much older. Even before the death of his son he seemed aged to us, with no pejorative intention, but we were so young! That is why we sometimes had a tendency to chaff him, saying that he was talking drivel. It must have taken an enormous amount of courage to enlist at his age and thus stay beside his son. But that was beyond the ability of our infant brains to comprehend, to appreciate his true valor!

The next day we receive a new surprise: our comrade Jourdain, whom we believed dead, had been put in an *isba* with the other dead, awaiting the right moment for burial. It was not possible to dig graves right away, since the village was under incessant enemy fire. Early in the morning one of our comrades sees a sudden movement among those whom everyone believes dead. Jourdain himself asks him why he was put there with the dead. The doctor is called immediately, who listens to his heart and decides to have him evacuated to a hospital in the rear. We place him on a "*panjewagon*" but it is a corpse that arrives at the field hospital. Our comrade Jourdain had no more than a brief stay of execution. The bumps in the road did him in. He had a minuscule grenade fragment in his heart, and no one understood this ephemeral resurrection! The "*Bourguignon*" who saw him sit up among the dead never saw him again, nor did the doctor. The doctor stated that Jourdain had no chance at all of surviving.

These last weeks, especially these last few days, have seen the effective strength of our battalion melt away like snow in the sun. The battalion, with an authorized strength of more than 800 men, was down to no more than about 500 by mid-August. Today, after deducting the dead, the wounded and other evacuees, there are maybe no more than 300. Nevertheless, we are holding positions usually assigned to a normal, complete battalion.

On the afternoon of the 28th, the combat group that was at Tcherjakov arrives at Koubano. It was relieved by two companies of the "*Wiking*" [*5th SS Division Wiking*, designated a *Panzergrenadier Division* in November 1942]. It is our first contact with this *SS* unit, in which we find another Flemish comrade, Victor V.D.B. For me, it will also be the occasion when I discover their tracked motorcycles!

I rejoin my platoon in the *3rd Compagnie* and join my squad in its billet east of the village. Behind the *isba* are a few acres of vineyard, and, right behind that, the forest. Always this forest is immense, majestic, nearly impenetrable. A hole has been cut in the roof of the *isba* for a lookout post with a machine gun. The location is unhealthy, the house dangerously situated.

There have been too many lost and killed, and it is necessary to strengthen our security. That is why it is decided to double this post with a guard below the house, between it and the vineyard. This vineyard provides marvelous cover for all attackers. The ramification of the trunks of the vines are almost like a tunnel, for at about one meter above the soil they are pruned and trained to extend laterally in both directions. That is how the Russians, taking advantage of this cover, have already succeeded in approaching the guard post and throwing a grenade into it, which, fortunately, the man on guard was able to throw back out. This situation is really bad for us, for we are truly so few at present that we stand guard four nights out of five for the entire night so long as it is dark. That is to say, from 2130 or 2200 hours until 0330 or 0400 hours in the morning. During the day, one man on guard is enough at the *isba* and one at the *kolkhoze* [collective farm] southwest of the village. At that location there is a little "*balka*" through which the Russians can reach the village without being seen and fall upon us without warning! This situation allows two men to sleep while all the others are on watch. This solution is preferable to relieving one man, one single man, on guard. Toward 0330 or 0400 hours, as day breaks, these four men lie down to sleep, and the ones that were sleeping relieve them, but with only one at each post. Thus we alternate the guards, standing guard two nights, then one night of rest, and daytime guard duty. One day things become even more complicated. The men on guard at the *kolkhoze* dozed off, no doubt, and were awakened by two Russian soldiers who wanted to surrender! You see the situation? If the only punishment of the two men is deprivation of *petits-vivres* [1] for a certain time and a severe warning, it is because higher-ups duly considered their state of exhaustion and lack of sleep of these young solders. At other times, this would have resulted in a court martial and assignment to a disciplinary company. Thus it is that we must find men to patrol this "*balka*" – at least during the night. Due to fatigue and nerves during this period, fusillades, justified or not, often break out suddenly in the middle of the night. Frequently one burst of machine gun fire triggers another, and yet more join the fusillade from all corners of the village. Perhaps it was a stray dog, or a wandering cow that provoked the fire, and, more than once, at dawn, the trophy of one or another gives rise to jibes and grins aimed at the nervous machine gunners. But how can one distinguish, in a moonless night, between a cow or a dog or some sort of assailant? It is more the noise that gives the alert than a silhouette. Rather than risk surprise, they open fire.

On the 29th a patrol leaves Kouban with the mission of finding and bringing back the remains of Pierre Taverne. The father is the first to claim his place among the volunteers. It is certain that they will bring back our comrade, unless they are killed to the last man. The patrol departs in silence and disappears in the forest by the gullied footpath that climbs toward the edge of the forest, south of the village. When it reappears in the afternoon, emerging from the woods, we immediately notice the improvised litter that the men carry. We know then that our comrade has been brought back. I descend to the road that the patrol takes, heading for the command post. When they silently pass, I gaze at the waterproof sheets, wrapped around two rifles. Two feet stick out at one end, a tuft of hair at the other. It is our friend – a 15-and-a-half-year-old kid, a man. And there, right behind, is the papa, his eye riveted on this form that sways with the footsteps, wrapped in this shroud. Later, much later, I shall go and simply shake his hand. Right now, I cannot interrupt his thoughts, I am afraid to provoke tears. Each of us slowly returns to what he was doing, waiting for the ceremony of farewell. Later, all the rest of the battalion, except for the guard, will

---

1   In the German Army, the *Spieß*, or *Kompanifeldwebel* ('top sergeant'), had a chest of what were called *Marketenderware*, or, in French, *petits-vivres* [salt, sugar, coffee, dried vegetables, schnapps, wine or vodka etc.]. He distributed these at regular intervals, or on special occasions.

assemble in a horseshoe around the hastily-dug grave, the prayer for the dead, a salvo of honor. "*Ich hatt' einen Kameraden!*"[2] Yet another leaves us, the youngest!

That night I stand guard as usual after having all of two hours' sleep. At a little after 0400 hours in the morning I am relieved and collapse to sleep. When the noise, the light, the sun wake me up it is 0800 hours. Because rations only get to us with difficulty and late, I conceive a project. Before we got to Koubano we passed through a little village or hamlet where we spent the night, and of which I have good memories, no doubt because we received a good welcome there and all that we needed so that we did not waste away! Not that I am a great eater, but everything that we ate there was very passable and we have found no better since setting foot on Russian soil. On the other hand, it seemed that there was enough there to feed a lot of people. I came up with a project to turn this to my comrades' advantage and give them a surprise.

That is why I shared this idea with my excellent friend, Raymond P. He is a part of the little group of musketeers that we have known since 1941. As is well known, there were four musketeers, and closely united. They have names: Emile M. from Spa, Alfred D. from Charleroi, Raymond P. and myself. Then we adopted a fifth, Armand D. of Liège, with no difficulty.

Raymond and I decide between the two of us to set out on a private mission, but for public (and alimentary) utility. Thus it is that, at about 1000 or 1100 hours in the morning, we depart on horseback toward the southwest in a most discreet fashion. The horses are borrowed from the villagers, for we thought it futile to ask the "*Tross*" for them, you can understand why! It was far better and more prudent this way. Russian horses are not shoed, and, fortunately, make less noise! For our entire itinerary everything is calm and we do not meet a living soul. A good hour later we arrive at the village, where everything seems equally calm, and we head toward the *isba* where I spent the night a few days earlier. We dismount and tie our horses to the pillars of the porch railing, then knock and enter to greet my former hosts. Immediately I see from their faces that something is wrong! Raymond and I exchange puzzled looks, even a bit uneasy. All the inhabitants of the *isba* are suddenly talking all at once, nervously, but without raising their voices. We do not understand much except for "*krasni*" and "*sovietski*". The "*pan*" takes us by the sleeve and leads us toward a side window of the house, but keeping us back some distance from the window pane. He points out six or seven horses tied near another *isba* no more than 50 or 60 meters distant! In an instant a thousand thoughts cross our minds. Did they not see us arrive? How could that be possible? Maybe they did see us and are going to attempt to surprise us? We do not need to alarm our hosts with our weapons; they might think we were drawing them because of them. We will remain on guard and not draw our weapons. We observe the road and our surroundings through the other windows, but nothing stirs. Perhaps they were too occupied and were making too much noise, themselves? Why didn't they think to set a guard outside? Were they as thoughtless as we were? That is impossible? How are we going to break contact and leave, the two of us with two rifles which are not automatic and with two pistols? Surely they are better horsemen than we, even if they are not Cossacks. We are mere foot soldiers who ride like sacks! We are in a fine jam! I feel guilty for having involved my friend Raymond in this adventure. Obviously, there can be no thought of carrying out our project. We don't need to gather moss here, but how to get away? Should we depart on foot, leading the horses and mount in the saddles later? Or should we get in the saddles right here? We take our route of departure in a dead angle where they cannot see us for the first 150 to 200 meters, and we decide to get in the saddle right away, so as not to lose time later if they spot us. If they have already seen us and set up an ambush somewhere, everything is already over. If they discover us at the moment of our flight, everything will change. In case of need, we

---

2 '*Ich hatt' einen Kameraden*' ('I had a comrade') is a traditional lament of the German Armed Forces.

can fall from the saddle and attempt to defend ourselves, if the horses have not already thrown us off, wretched horsemen that we are. In any case, if they discover us we will not have much chance of shooting our way out of here.

All the same, the people fill our pockets with plums and slip a big loaf of white bread inside our jackets. While the rest of the family keeps watch at the windows, the "*pan*" and an urchin help us get in the saddle and untie the horses. Happily the road turns a bit and the Russians cannot see us from the *isba* where they are. Very cautiously, slowly, and with much care to make the least possible noise, we start out, keeping in the shelter of the screen provided by the houses, with constant furtive looks to our rear. Two-hundred meters are behind us, 300, 500. They can no longer see us; we are hidden from their view. We urge on the horses. My heart now beats more reasonably, but I do not know just when it stopped beating wildly. I am no longer sweating, I do not sweat, maybe I never did sweat? At least the sweat has already evaporated under the sun? We cannot help but turn around every moment, ever fearing the appearance of a horde of Cossacks on our trail! We cannot imagine that we were not seen, since we did not try to hide when we entered the village. Thanks to the villagers for not denouncing us, or you would never have heard my story.

An hour later we enter Koubano even more discreetly than we left it. We only tell a few intimate friends what we have done, those with whom we share our bread and the plums. Now we go to rest and to forget our emotions, for, of course, this evening we stand guard.

For 30 August and 1-2 September, guard duty as usual, and, as usual, toward 1000 hours in the morning, contact patrols with Tcherjakov or Poporotny, another village with fruits, including a variety of double plums, like Siamese twins, that intrigue me. Since they are good, I soon give up asking questions on this subject and am content to eat them. It is a fact that we eat far more fruits than other things and, with the intestinal upset that we have known for several months, we are never free of dysentery. Within a few days we have lost all of the weight that is possible, to a point where we can no longer get any thinner. Up to 15 or 20 times a day we run toward the vineyard, which is an ideal latrine. Furthermore, while squatting, one can harvest the grapes without moving. As soon as it is swallowed, it returns to the foot of the vine that bore it. In effect, the grape merely passes through the body without delaying there, nothing holds it back. One is truly stricken by dysentery and since there is no medication that has any effect, nobody is concerned anymore about what they eat. On the other hand, the soldier eats what he finds when his rations do not arrive or are late! I do really believe that even if one were to eat concrete or granite, our body would transform them into water. There is that dysentery, there is that fatigue from the daily guard duties and patrols, there is that intestinal imbalance, but there are also the lice and the Russian sores. Despite all that, it is also necessary to take time from what is available for rest to go once a day to the infirmary to have the sores cleaned. We stand in line, and when our turn comes to be cleaned, they don't take the time to remove the bandages, they merely pour Ribanol from the bottle onto the bandages. In any case, we quickly realize that this does nothing. On the other hand, when our rations arrive, along with the foodstuff, we often receive two or three little bottles of vodka, and what we do with it is our own business. Along with several of our comrades we get the idea of using this beverage to treat our sores. *Alors*, for the information of doctors, I must attest that it is formidable. After pouring half a liter a day on the sores, and not by the oral route, I most emphatically state that everything is taken care of in eight to 10 days; there is nothing visible where the sores had been except a few spots on the skin. Anyway, I do not like vodka … at least, I did not at that time! And, in regard to drink, something very curious happened to one of my comrades. I was marching behind him on one of our innumerable routine patrols when I thought I discovered a new model of canteen. My own canteen is concave on one face and convex on the other, like all the others that I have seen up to this point, but the canteen of my comrade, who is in front of me, is shaped like a balloon, completely round and spherical. That intrigues me to the point where I cannot help but call his attention to it. It should hold at least double what mine does! Astonished, he feels it and seizes it quickly to take it off his belt. He wants to open it but is unable to. His repeated efforts are in vain. He tells me that, before leaving, he filled it from his hosts' barrel and that it is full of wine. I noticed that all of the villagers make their own wine. But this wine is in full fermentation, and that is what has inflated his canteen. I advise him to get rid of it, for I am afraid of what will happen. I need not say it twice, and he throws it far away. When it hits the tree that he aimed at, it explodes violently, hurling fragments of aluminum in all directions. I think that we all hit the ground out of reflex as we would do for a grenade. Its remains are at the foot of the tree, the neck with the stopper still screwed on tight and a quantity of torn fragments of aluminum, torn to shreds. He will never put wine in his canteen again, if he is able to get another.

On 4 September, at the end of the morning, we assemble a strong patrol, all of Platoon "Denie" for a reconnaissance mission. We are to check out the terrain toward Ismaïlovka to find out whether the village is held by the enemy. This village is a few kilometers northwest of Koubano. In the group there are, among others, two veterans of the *Légion étrangère*, the French Foreign Legion: *adjudant* Dusevoir and the brothers Loupart. These comrades wear decorations won in another uniform. They display patches that make one dream: Tonkin, Sahara, Morocco, Rif. The presence of these "old-timers", men with experience, moreover, always reassures us. A man of the village serves as our guide. I believe it is the *starostat* (the mayor) of the village. As soon as the orders are issued, the column moves out and silence rules. We are not to return without completing the mission. The order is perfectly followed, and once we enter the forest, not a word is exchanged. If a dead branch breaks underfoot, the outraged glares of the nearby marchers instantly focus on the offender. These reproving looks make the perpetrator feel guilty and make him more prudent. The weather is beautiful and it is hot, but the foliage gives us shade and a delightful coolness. If we could only walk as tourists and fully enjoy this practically virgin nature. What a marvelous, intact region! What nostalgic memories we would have later! Whenever someone believes they hear a noise or think they can make out something abnormal, the column immediately stops. We freeze, one knee on the ground, or screened by a tree while the flank guards or the men at the head carefully scrutinize the surroundings or check out with binoculars what caught their attention. It may be the unaccustomed silhouette of a stump, the flight of an animal at the sound of our footsteps or the call of a bird that has been disturbed. As soon as we are reassured, the column moves on again. We continue thus for about an hour, maybe a bit more. At that moment we see through the trees a touch of brightness, the hint of a clearing that becomes more definite and enlarges bit by bit. We slow our march and two men move out ahead to reconnoiter. We are now at the edge of the forest and the clearing extends before us. The village is on a sort of mound in the middle of the cleared area, a few patches of maize as everywhere in Russia and a sort of thicket, a big copse between us and the village. We move out into the clearing, in full sunlight. A woman's voice suddenly cries out, *Nimetski*! I did not see this woman before she cried out and she now runs toward an *isba*. Three Russian soldiers immediately appear and head for the thicket, where they disappear. Our comrade Paquet, *Capitaine* Tchekov's orderly, turns and moves toward the thicket, calling to the Russians to surrender. I get the impression that they want to comply. They allow Paquet to approach them. All of a sudden, contrary to all expectations and logic, they open fire with their submachine guns and Paquet falls to the ground. Another comrade, farther back, is also hit. It is Jacques P. We rush to form a semi-circle around the thicket and fire our weapons a bit at random, since the Russians have gone to ground there. They don't hold out and come out of the copse, crying out, their hands up and surrender. One of them is wounded in the foot or the leg. He limps and grimaces. Some of our men rush to Paquet, along with our medical orderly. He is lying, face-down on the ground, lifeless. His blood flows slowly, staining the ground around his head. He has been hit in his forehead, he is dead! Jacques P. has been lucky, very lucky. A bullet slightly wounded his chest after having shredded his identity disk, hanging around his neck. He has no more than a scratch on his right pectoral. Other men surround the prisoners. What were they thinking of? Did they think they would make us flee? It was senseless to fire on us. Killing one of our men and wounding another and then to surrender! They should have either surrendered right off, or have fought to the death. They should have known that they had no chance at all of escaping! Did they misjudge the situation? I do not understand.

The medical orderly cares for Jacques P., then the wounded prisoner, and our men assemble a makeshift litter to carry our friend Paquet. One man watches the prisoners, and I go with the others to comb the village, but there is nothing, not a Russian soldier to be found. There is no need to wait. If there had been any they would certainly have come to the aid of their comrades, at least if they had not already fled. We rejoin the little group near the thicket of trees and, after a short pause and deliberation, we take the road back to Koubano, which we get back to in an hour-and-a-half, maybe two hours later.

On emerging from the forest we meet our first outposts and answer the usual questions in such a situation where we bring back dead or wounded. Who is it? Is he dead? Thus, gradually, everyone in the battalion learns what has happened. The body is left at the infirmary, not far from the command post near the other graves already lined up there. *Adjudant* Denie, leader of the patrol, goes immediately to report to the commander. We go to rest in light of the usual night guard duty.

This night my comrade on guard tells me a little story that took place a few days earlier at Tcherjakov. When the Russians are not firing on our positions they attempt to infiltrate to surprise our men. Thus, when the firing stops, our *"Bourguignons'"* suspicions are greatly aroused. One of our comrades in position not far from the *kolkhoze* heard some disturbing noises and warned his neighbors. One of them, Gilbert Delrue, well known by all for his loud mouth, his big shoe size, but also for his courage and his mettle, got up immediately and headed confidently toward the *kolkhoze*, his light machine gun slung around his neck. Arriving soundlessly before one of the doors, he kicked it open, immediately spraying the interior with a generous burst of fire, right down to his last round! Sure of his good work, he immediately inspected the premises, assisted by the comrades who had been drawn by the sound of his fusillade, to count the bodies. Alas! They only found seven or eight horses, dead or in agony, among them that of their *chef de file*, their file leader, "Caucase" as he was called, the horse of the *Chef*. When Gilbert saw the *Chef* he announced, with entire seriousness, standing at attention, "*Chef*, Caucase is dead for the peace and well-being of Europe! Along with several of his fellows!" The *Chef* did not punish him severely for it, but it was talked of in the *Légion* long afterward!

On 7 September there is a new special mission to the village of Nikolsk, west of Koubano. When I say "special", I mean that it is a patrol different from those that maintain contact with other units or other villages that we occupy, or for escorting rations. A good 20 men-strong, the patrol moves out along the "*balka*", which winds in a large valley, before entering the forest, which extends here as nearly everywhere, and shelters numerous villages and hamlets. The patrol advances without a sound beneath the tall foliage and it seems that even the birds are holding their breath. The silence, or, I should say, the total lack of noise, is such that at times it becomes oppressive. As is usual during our incursions into an unknown or dangerous zone, the group stops to determine its position or study the terrain before committing itself. This sort of halt is repeated as often as seems prudent. As a footnote to such halts, I, and other comrades suffering from dysentery, use the halts to isolate myself, after which it is necessary to quicken one's pace, without running, so as not to make noise and to rejoin the group. At times like this one must be very attentive, for one is all alone and left behind. More than once a little group of Russian soldiers, aware of their inferior numbers or on account of their situation have allowed the main body of a patrol to pass them by and then attacked those who were separated, the laggards.

It is during one of these necessary halts that I suddenly hear shots rend the air and disturb the quietude. One is always surprised in this sort of situation, for one does not know right off where the shots are coming from, nor whom they are aimed at. Nor is it easy to tell how far away they are because of the resonance or the echo in the woods. I quickly turn and run in the direction in which I have just seen my comrades disappear. I was not that sure of finding them, one never is in such a situation, but I finally see them, dispersed at the edge of the woods. I learn that they were fired on when they emerged from the forest and that one of ours fell, but my interlocutor does not know who. A few minutes pass and I see a little group on the left, two or three men who run toward us. Lulls now follow sporadic bursts of fire. There is discussion among the little group over there. Finally we are motioned to fall back into the woods. We regroup a few minutes later 200-300 meters from the clearing. It is then that I learn that the name of the comrade who was killed is Ernst! This boy enlisted on 8 August, 1941 and was discharged for health reasons, epileptic seizures. I don't know how, but he succeeded in enlisting for a second time, with us on 10 March, 1942. *En route* to the front he fell from the train, but, fortunately, was uninjured. All of a sudden I think that he went to a lot of trouble to come and be killed here. The instruction that began in March, the life at the front, the beautiful summer. I am not yet 20 years old, and already the verb 'to live' is now conjugated for him in the past participle. When the sun sets this evening over Koubano, there will be one more grave alongside the other mounds! The Nikolsk mission is over, it was necessary to know if the village was occupied, if there was any resistance there. It seems that it was expected that we would find at least an enemy platoon, while, in the event, there was a battalion or at least two companies.

8, 9 and 10 September, the days follow one another with no real change: guard duty, the usual patrols, endemic fatigue! This afternoon I am on guard in the granary of the *kolkhoze* with my comrade Raymond T. when the sound of a "*panjewagon*" catches our attention. It is our cook Van Oost, accompanied by his assistant and three Russian women. They are 50 meters from us and are heading toward the exit of the village. Two or 300 meters away, on the left, there is an indentation in the woods that shelters a field of potatoes and another of maize. No doubt they are going there to gather materials for feeding us. They go on their way and we cease watching them. A quarter of an hour, maybe half an hour goes by since they passed. Heart-rending cries surprise and chill us. A glance toward the woods, the women appear, running back and screaming. I see one, two, then three men leave the village on the run and head for the field where Van Oost is. I hasten down the ladder and am on the road, soon followed by one or two comrades. All out of breath, we reach the field. The comrades who preceded us are leaning over a form on the ground, and two of them scour the entrance to the forest. Our comrade Van Oost is stretched out, his back on the ground, eyes closed, his features contorted in a grimace. The spectacle is horrible; he has seven or eight bayonet wounds in his abdomen. His jacket is open, his shirt shredded, spotted with fresh blood, his pants low on his hips. Pink foam emerges from his mouth in spurts, and the flies are already landing on his face. Is he dead? Does he still live? I have no idea, but the body moves a little, contracts at times. We put him on the cart and take the road back to the village in all haste! In the alerted village there is already confusion. Every available man is assembled to scour the woods and find the perpetrators of this blow. Two-hundred men, perhaps, who comb the woods for hours. Van Oost is taken to the infirmary, but he is already dead, for sure. Toward evening a group brings in two men who were hiding in the woods. One wears part of a naval uniform. Are they the ones or not? Interrogation at the command post provides nothing, and the prisoners are taken to the division headquarters. When the sun sinks one more time over Koubano there are five graves lined up by the command post. Sunset at Koubano is always an apotheosis of gold and purple, but Van Oost will see it no more. For the others, life continues as before, even though it is someone else who gives them their soup.

Each dawn is a new birth, for no one is ever sure of seeing another day break, of living another whole day. Perhaps it is this precarious equilibrium between life and death that makes us so appreciate the rare moments of release from tension in this hostile, but so marvelous landscape! The lack of sleep, the fatigue overwhelms us, true, the loss of a comrade and these graves that multiply do yet more. The uncertainty … And yet! All of this has not yet broken us, we still hold on, even if, at times, some waver, but regain their courage.

One of these five graves is that of a young Russian, killed accidentally in a mortar firing exercise a few days before. At that moment I was with my friends of the mortar platoon, west of the village. The platoon was to determine a firing position that would provide the best angle relating to a critical point located to the northeast. They were to wait to see the Russians appear at that precise location with the intention of attacking Koubano. A range was given, estimated and a bit under, no doubt. The commander was skeptical and added 50 meters since the estimated range really seemed under to him. Despite all that, the first round hit a house on the edge of the woods, killing the young Russian. The villagers believed that it was a bomb, dropped by a Russian airplane, for an airplane had just flown over us, high in the sky, by pure good luck. Nobody thought it useful to disillusion them, it was better thus. *Russki smajot nié karosh*, we told them! (No guarantee as to the spelling. We have learned a bit of Russian, but phonetically). We buried this innocent victim with military honors, and the villagers appreciated it.

At this moment yet another curious event took place. A comrade named Tilman, but whom we nicknamed 'Little Sister", disappeared from his patrol during an engagement with the Russians. Two or three days later he reappeared, smiling with that angelic, slightly naive, laugh that was especially his. He had wandered through the woods during that time, not daring to approach villages that he did not know for fear of finding them occupied by the Russians, until he found our *3rd Compagnie*.

On 14 September a patrol moved out that morning toward Poporoty (also called Poporotny) to bring back the rations detail. In the afternoon, comrade Bouvay, the machine gunner of the patrol, emerged from the woods, totally out of breath, wild-eyed, clothes in disorder. Not without difficulty, for he was badly shaken, bit by bit we got the details from him. The patrol was attacked after it had left Poporotny for Koubano and was totally taken by surprise. Definitely, experience had not taught them the lesson! Several of the men of the patrol had put their weapons on a "*panjewagon*" so they wouldn't have to carry them. Thus the patrol was entirely at the mercy of its attackers and was massacred as if it were in a slaughter house! Bouvay believed he was the sole survivor and had little idea how he made it here. A rescue patrol was immediately organized and took the field to attempt the impossible. Then the anxious waiting began, and discussion. What stupidity! What carelessness! Who was the leader of the patrol who is responsible for all this? In any case, warnings of severe disciplinary action come to us from the command post and Bouvay was the first to be so informed!

When the rescue patrol returned, late in the afternoon, the news was disappointing. It brought back three dead, which it laid on the carts with our rations, resting on the food that we receive in the evening. There was no sign of life except for the horses, one of which was wounded and had to be dispatched. What happened to the others? The dead, whom they laid down in front of the command post, were named Lequeux, Tellier and Denain. Two of the three, veterans of 8 August, had just returned the day before from a brief leave home, and that was why they were included in that patrol, having missed the amount of fatigue duties that we had accumulated, let alone engagements. None of us knew how many took part in this patrol, but the result was catastrophic: three dead, one survivor, and how many missing? Certainly they must know how many at the command post. This evening, eight graves are lined up at the edge of the road that passes through Koubano, and flowers on the first ones have not yet faded! Many of us have no bread, and my comrade and squad leader is famished, to the point where I see him take a loaf of bread that has traces of blood on it, cut out the bloody portion and throw it far away and sink his teeth into the intact remainder!

The days pass and life continues in the familiar rhythm of guard duty and patrols. It is always necessary to escort the wire-patrols that go out to repair the communications lines cut during the night by the enemy. We must tirelessly maintain regular contact with the neighboring villages to prevent the enemy from moving into them and from getting too bold. We must regularly escort the supply parties or other missions. There is no chance to sleep more than four hours, perhaps five, and that is the exception. Every time it is interrupted. Happily, the weather continues to be good!

I do not know what thoughts depressed the spirits of comrade De Sloover at this point, but the scene seemed almost like a joke! However it turned out otherwise. I must say that this comrade was, let us say, an original. One afternoon he comes toward us, buckling his belt with canteen and bread bag. "Good, I am leaving," says he.

"*Ah*! *Oui*? And where are you going?"

"I am getting out of here, I have had enough!"

That is all that we can learn. We watch and look at him with a little smile of amusement, sort of like a wink of the eye. De Sloover turns his back on us and goes toward the road, which he takes heading north and disappears from our view. At the time, we give no more thought to it, since, basically, that is just the sort of thing he would do. But, when he cannot be found when it is time to stand guard, we must inform the commander of the company, who listens incredulously! Nevertheless, there is the evidence! De Sloover is not there and we do not see him again, not the next day, never. Nobody ever hears any word of him!

October arrives, and, though there are still many beautiful fall days, the nights are cooler and rain puts in its appearance and falls now and then. To shield us from the rain we have our tent canvasses, but we do not have our hoods, to protect us from the cold. They are with the "*Tross lourd*" [heavy baggage], which has taken a different road than ours, that in the valley.

9 or 10 October: at the time of the fighting at Tcherjakov, the bodies of all of our fallen comrades were gathered and buried, all but two, those of our companions Chavanne and Lempereur. Since our command refuses to abandon anyone, even the dead, numerous patrols have already combed through all of the sector, but always in vain! Since it is now clear that we will be leaving Koubano in a matter of days or even hours, our commander has decided to make one last attempt. The men are chosen, and my squad is included. The leader of the patrol, or the mission, is my squad leader, Georges P. The force, 10 or 12 men. Thus it is that this morning we leave Koubano for this last mission, a final duty!

Each time that I enter this forest I have the impression that I am crossing the threshold of one of those old cathedrals, elaborated over the centuries, that generation after generation have erected, stone upon stone during the decades. Everything makes me think of it, the silence everywhere, and the penumbra too. Truly, the transition is grand. The sun shining outside, and hot, too, and here, near darkness and coolness. These tree trunks so tall and straight, impressively thick, and the vault far above that hides the sky from us. A ray of sunshine pierces the foliage and illuminates a detail. I see there the stained glass windows, iridescent with the light. The contemplation that this forest inspires in us, our situation, for we are aware that some of us may not return. The column stretches out in single file so as not to offer too compact, and, thereby, too easy a target, but also not too extended and fragile. There have been too many cases of fatal negligence, and our squad leader takes all precautions. He calls for two volunteers to take point, and I volunteer, along with my comrade Raymond T. Georges P. seems astonished and I get the impression that he is perhaps a little vexed, despite my lack of sensitivity. I do not know why, but I get the idea that he distrusts me, that he doubts my courage. It is true that, until Maïkop, I made my own war in a rather independent and personal manner, and on the rare occasions that I was able to avoid marching, I preferred to go on wheels, but that was because I could do it and that it would cause no one harm. It was not a tragedy. It was not of my own desire that I became a "straggler" during part of the "*Vormarsch*", and I rejoined my unit before its first engagements. But it is true that I enjoyed my independence and discovering Russia in my own fashion. In brief, Raymond T. and I went ahead, followed by all the patrol. I am well aware of the fact that the *avant-garde*, the point, generally serves as a target for the enemy and thereby alerts its comrades who then, in principle, have time to take position and reply effectively. I figure that it is my turn, and that, quite simply and without boasting, but also without evident humility, is why I volunteered, for that is my character. I feel that I am in a state of grace, but do not ask myself why. I do not know! We advance with caution, but without delay, being careful not to break dead branches, all our senses alert, attentive to everything. The eye sweeps everything, like a searchlight, stopping for an instant on every detail that seems hostile. A glance, at times, to the vault above, for danger can come from on high, too. It has happened that the enemy has hidden there to drop grenades at the moment that we pass below. It is to say that danger lurks everywhere, it bathes us. It might be buried, to surge suddenly behind us in the direction that we came from! Everything seems strangely calm, but this calm is at times all the more agonizing because it seems unreal! If some animal does not make itself evident, one can believe that there are no more, that they have been chased away by some other presence. We advance at a steady pace and I feel that I am calm, more sure of myself. I observe in detail and I see everything. The situation does not prevent me from constantly admiring this marvelous forest, and from discovering, on each patrol, yet new amazing objects of wonder. There is a trunk lying on the ground, at my knees, that collapses into dust when my foot touches it, and I think of how it has been there for a hundred years, or maybe far longer, to disappear thus at the touch of a foot, and without a sound! A little farther another trunk that I already know well, and that I must skirt. Here I know of two occasions, at least, where our men have allowed themselves to be surprised and taken! But today, nothing… perhaps farther on? We keep on guard! We approach the clearing that I also know. We must go along its left side and get past it. There are three or four trees in its first third, still young, and not yet as big as the others. Scattered here and there are several big stones and rocks covered with moss. I shall never forget this clearing, which I compare with Eden. Even though I find it beautiful, it is, at once, peaceful and wild. I have passed it many times, but never have I lingered there. That would be dangerous to expose myself thus, as on a podium, under the spots of sunlight, with the enemy crouching in the shade of the undergrowth, the enemy who is on the watch for us and only waits for that. We pause as we leave the edge of the woods to study the shade of the trees on the other side of the clearing, but nothing abnormal catches our attention and we resume our march. When we reach Tcherjakov it seems entirely natural to me that we got there without mishap.

The village is unrecognizable. The "*Wiking*", which relieved us, has fortified the entire village and tied the houses together with trenches. We make a halt and have a bit of a chat with our German comrades. We spend a moment at the graves of our "*Bourguignon*" comrades buried there, including "*le Prévôt*". Then we leave the left side of the village and go back into the foliage of the forest, there where our comrade Georges P. is sure that we will find the bodies of our two that were killed. We must search conscientiously, for the vegetation may have covered them, and go forward, meter by meter. Finally a cry, I think it is Georges: "Here!" He has just found one of the bodies, stretched out between two fallen trees. We discover the second, a moment later, not far from the first. Mission accomplished, but not yet completed! One thing strikes me regarding the first body. All of the parts that are exposed to the air seem intact, the skin diaphanous. But, on closer examination, as I have already seen in other cases, the maggots pullulate beneath the tissues and give a sort of life to this sorry skin, to this that was a young being like us, a friend full of life, once so strong in his ideals that he could have moved mountains. This is all that remains of him! We spread out the tent canvasses on which we will place them, and we work our way, with some difficulty, between the two fallen trees. One comrade lifts the head to pass his arm under the body, and the head comes off in his hands, the helmet on the skull and a part of the backbone that remains solidly attached to the head! The scene is macabre, but we are hardened, and the unhappy Chavanne is capable of anything. This first part of the body is placed on the tent canvas and we lift what is left of the corpse by gripping the uniform. What remains of it is a magma, trickling out of the sleeves, the bottom of the coat and the legs of the pants. It is a liquefied corpse that we place on the tent canvas. The others have done the same with the remains of Lempereur. I have prepared myself, since the stench makes me nauseous, but it doesn't do so. We then return to Tcherjakov, carefully carrying these burdens, for fear that they will come apart before we get there, or that we will lose a part. We dig the graves alongside those of our comrades who have fallen here. Our last respects, a farewell to our German comrades and we take the road back to Koubano. The return, like our trip out, proceeds without incident, and the squad leader goes to deliver his report on the mission.

8

Toward New Horizons

On 12 October, as evening falls and in the rain, we leave Koubano – Armianski, not without regrets. Despite everything! Despite the extremely hard and constant service that is ours, despite our dead, we regret leaving Koubano because we have had time to get used to it. We feel a little bit at home here.

For the first few kilometers we are animated, for we have now been sedentary for a month-and-a-half, if I may express it this way without laughing, and this evening we are on the move again. Just now? Tomorrow? That is the unknown! That is what excites and fascinates us always. We are not *blasé* about our fantastic adventure. The animation diminishes, the conversations run dry as the kilometers pass. Each of us takes what shelter he can under his canvas, for the rain is heavy and cold! The soil gives way more and more often under our feet, we have the impression that we are marching on butter. The efforts to avoid falling are more fatiguing than the march itself, and the path climbs and descends to enliven our pleasure. Water trickles off the canvas and seeps into my boots, the mud sticks to the soles and then to the uppers of my boots, then to my pants, as if it is undertaking to submerge us! With the help of capillarity we will be soaked to the neck in a couple of hours, if not sooner. To the extent that the soggy uniform keeps in body heat it is endurable, but when the wind penetrates beneath the canvas, everything chills and the body freezes. Nevertheless, we must keep on marching. Early in the morning we arrive, chilled to the marrow, at the bank of a river, of a little torrent, and we camp there. The soil, covered with dead leaves, is sodden, and it is there that we pitch our tents. A little fine rain is falling that penetrates and drenches us.

It is in these conditions that we must uncover ourselves and use our canvas to make the tents. We have only our jackets and a light shirt, our pants and shorts on our bodies. On our feet we have our boots or mountain shoes and socks with holes. We are averse to getting under our tents, soaked as we are, to catch our deaths of cold! We must not stand still, we must keep moving so that the wind can dry out our wet clothes. We try to build a fire! But with what? Everything is soaked! We can make the attempt, and live in a moment of illusion. Everyone tries to find some bits of grass that are more or less dry, or, at least, not as soggy as the others. In a cranny, or between the roots of a tree, among the rocks, or under the denser thickets. Some twigs and bits of dead wood. One finds a last letter in his pocket that he has jealously saved, awaiting the next. Another discovers a few sheets of cigarette paper that he saved in his wallet, hoping to find some tobacco some day! Don't risk everything. Don't use it all in a single attempt. We clear the dead leaves from a little place in the sun and minutely prepare the saving fire, as the first men on earth did centuries ago. But, perhaps they did not then do it in the rain. The fire is lit on this little hearth, and I see, with fear, the paper that burns up, but does not pass the flame to the twigs. Only a few blades of grass catch fire, and immediately collapse in ashes. The fire dies out! Another attempt fails, and a third also. Comrades have collected blades of grass and roll them in their hands, or slip them into their pockets to dry them a bit, and do the same with the little bits of dead wood collected here and there. Finally we manage to keep going a few hesitant flames, tiny and weak. But the fire does not grow, does not attain any size. It cannot do anything like that!

Inspired by grace, at least so I believe, I take the detonator out of a grenade, then, resolutely, I remove another. I insert the two into the heart of this slender hope for fire with a thousand precautions. We move back a meter-and-a-half or two, but nothing happens. I approach it before the last flame disappears and start to blow on the fire. One time, five times, 20 times, then, all of a sudden: bang! I get up, dazed! Ten hilarious faces look at me, convulsed with laughter. *Ma foi*, that makes them laugh! So much the better, after all, that they still have morale, that they are not inert. When a buddy hands me his little metal mirror I understand better and I join in the laughter. It is not beautiful to look at, but it is a riot! The bang scattered that embryonic fire. Whatever else it did not do, my initiative has inspired the spirit of creativity. Some of my comrades open a few cartridges, gather the remnants of the fire and pour the powder on it, which immediately catches fire. Everyone gathers anything that will burn and feeds the fire very progressively. Thus, with a lot of trouble, we finally attain a small fire, but there is always more smoke than flames, and it does not warm us up very much. The chaps cough and rub their eyes, but do not give up their place at the fire for any pretext.

It is time to wash myself, for my face irritates me. My face is black, as with soot, and dozens of little fragments of aluminum are sticking in my skin. Georges P., a good soul, attempts to pull them out with his fingernails. Truly, these fragments are small, and it is not easy, for his fingers are fat and tremble with the cold. When he has finished I only need to wash my face vigorously at the edge of the river. Now I need to warm up a bit. Like the others, I take off my jacket and wring it out with the help of a comrade, but only come up with a few drops. God only knows that it is soaked.

I put it back on and, just like my comrades, I alternate presenting one side and then the other to the relative warmth of the flames. The side presented warms a bit, while the other shivers, and, vice versa, when I turn and present the other side to the fire. Too bad that the smoke does not warm me, or I would already be dry! Finally, I cough, and a good fit of coughing also helps to warm me!

We share the few crumbs of bread that one or another finds in the bottom of his bread bag and we more or less, mostly less, warm up the dregs of whatever dubious beverage is left in one canteen or another. We then refill them at the river, and there, at least, we will be certain that it is water, the same that has not ceased to fall on us from the sky.

We then finish up by seeking the shelter of our tents and catching a bit of sleep, but not without organizing the guard. That we know!

Toward evening, we are back on the road, without having had much rest. It rains always, it is cold, our legs are heavy, but we march. My friend Roger G. and I talk about pralines, the pralines that we relished before the war at Godl's house ... Shhhh! No advertising. We speak of what we have nearly forgotten, but, all the same, we can dream a bit! Is this to give us courage, or to make us slaver? If only we already had a bit of dry bread, stale, even moldy!

The conversations die away, we are exhausted, we march in silence, our thoughts turned inward, trying to find a little rest there. I really think that we sleep while marching that night! We wake up when the column ahead of us stops and we bump our heads on the helmet of the man ahead of us and stop moving forward. Perhaps it is not true sleep, but we doze without thinking of anything, our heads empty and our feet follow, one after the other, out of habit! Eyes shut, we cover, I won't say kilometers, but at least hundreds of meters that one has no memory of afterward, and when one bumps into a man or a rock, it really is like waking from sleep!

Toward the middle of the night we are crossing a plateau when we receive the order to rest. We are warned that it will not last long and that there is no place to pitch the tents. There is no choice, and, when you are exhausted, you stretch out on the ground in the field on our right, in the hollow of a furrow, helmet under your head. By chance, but I ask myself why, my neighbor has a horse blanket, which he shares with me. We cover ourselves and sleep, despite the rain, which does not stop. Always this light rain, like mist. I awake with a start, surprised by the call and, three minutes later, the march resumes. It seems that I slept for two hours! The ground was sodden, but, fortunately, the water did not collect in the bottom of the furrows. The rain stops and dawn starts to break, a dirty, gray dawn, when we receive a new order to rest. I sit, or allow myself to fall, on a damp rock at the edge of the road and I suddenly think that the *"Les Misérables"* of Victor Hugo had a pretty good life compared to ours! No doubt I think of that because we have a *sergent* in our battalion who bears that illustrious name and who has, himself, drawn attention to the identity of names! Am I not wrong, even in these circumstances, in wracking my brain in always trying to find a relationship between things and events? But I think that this happens in spite of myself.

Later, when we move on, the sky starts to clear and, here and there, a ray of sunlight shines which starts to dry out the ridges and gilds the wet leaves, which scintillate as they are stirred by the wind. I really think that today is the 14th, and Kouban already seems far away. The time ought to be measured not by the kilometers traversed, but by the fatigue, by the effort required, but that is only an idea. Fortunately, the clearings are more numerous and allow the combination of sun and wind to dry our uniforms, for we are ill at ease in these clinging wet clothes.

The mud, which is also drying out, comes loose in places and falls back as dust. We have been marching for a good two or three hours, and the road climbs constantly and we are out of breath again. Just now we notice a pipeline. We march alongside it at times. It runs the length of the mountain, crosses declivities, passing from one slope to the other, suspended in the air. To gain time, but, especially, as a shortcut, many of the men decide to walk on the pipeline. The mud that sticks to our boots makes this perilous. The pipes are hardly more than 30 or 40 centimeters in diameter and are already greasy and slippery on their own, for they exude the viscous liquid that flows within them. And then we, sitting astride these pipelines, bruise the coccyx rather than try it on our feet. For what? To save a few meters, a few dozen meters of hairpin bends in the road? And this, 30 or 40 meters above the ravine! Bah! At least the aches will be different and will distract us from our other pains! We meet innumerable Russian prisoners who file past in columns, as has been the case since our first marches in the Caucasus, but this time they carry ammunition and all sorts of supplies. They appear to be better fed than we are, even if they are no less tired.

The march goes on interminably, if not indefatigably, interrupted by rests, more or less long, more or less brief, but always too short, for we never have time to recuperate. Day dawns on the 15th, and then comes the night, with more rain. While marching this night I feel that I have a fever, but I tell myself that it is the fatigue, the lack of sleep. The ridge that we have just crossed was named "The Mountain of Storms", no doubt inspired by the good weather it produces.

The 16th dawns pale, one of those early mornings when one would like to see night come right away, to go to bed, to sleep, to think of nothing and wait for a more auspicious day where one could be less melancholy. But all day we march in the rain, except for a few rare respites. When day fades one more time we reach a railroad line which soon vanishes into a tunnel. It is the line from Tuapse and it makes me daydream, for I think that it must be better there. Here, we are at Schadichenskaja. We pitch our tents on the railroad ballast, drained by the pebbles, for it is the only place in any way practicable. On the down-slope, there is a dead horse, like those scattered along our itinerary, but this one will not be a total loss. The *"Bourguignons"* have already started to cut off steaks, which they cook as best they can on fires sheltered by the big rocks. Others prefer the shelter of the tents, bringing rocks heated on the fire into them, cooking their slices of horse-meat in where it is dry, for it rains constantly, if perhaps I have not already said so?

Since my fever does not go down, I go to see Doctor A., whom I just spotted. I have only 38° [100°F]. It is mild, and remains so. Medication is reserved for serious illnesses. We pass the night in our tents and we finally sleep for an entire night, even if we sleep poorly on the ground, our clothes always soggy.

On the morning of 17 October we are lined up along the way and, as we start to move out, I see a group of "*Bourguignons*" a little apart. I am told that they are going to be evacuated, most of them sick with jaundice. As for us, the march resumes and rain alternates with clearing, or maybe the clear spells alternate with the showers, for I cannot remember which we started with. In the course of the afternoon we enter a valley which extends into the distance and narrows as it rises and loses itself in the forest. Here, too, there are a lot of dead horses scattered on the ground that mark our path. At present, only the mules and the little Russian horses, and also some 300 "*Bourguignons*" hold out! There is not a one of the hefty Pomeranian, Brabançon or Mecklenburg horses! The half-starved "*Bourguignons*" that are there have, nevertheless, helped them and lightened their loads as best they could! We head toward the ridge by way of the narrowing valley, leaving behind the field kitchen, the *PAK* and other heavy weapons. The road climbs the length of the slopes and the muddy soil does not make the climb any easier. We have to find a foothold on a stone or a rock, or use a tree or a branch to help us along. The mules manage well enough, but the few horses require our assistance, as if things were not already difficult enough for us! We brace ourselves against a tree and pull on the reins with all our remaining strength. For hours we climb and labor, short of breath. We reach the ridge crest that we are to guard one hour before night falls and pitch our tents there. Once the tents are set, the work done, I am shivering, my back is cold. I try to warm myself up in every way, swinging my arms and beating my thighs. Our tent, by pure luck, is only a few meters from those of the commander, of the *Chef*, and of *Lieutenant* Jean V. The commander questions me and listens to what is happening with me. How does he know that I am sick? Five minutes later *Lieutenant* V. brings me a well-filled canteen sent to me by my neighbors, my compassionate superiors. It is vodka and I, who have not yet drunk any vodka, or in any case, very little, put the canteen to my lips and drink three quarters of it right off. The first gulp goes down, and I savor the beverage, but the rest has no more effect on me than water, or hardly more. Ten minutes later I feel entirely well, able to hike all the way to the summit of Mount Elbrus. Very satisfied, I empty the canteen before going to bed, all the happier because I have evaded guard duty. (May my comrades forgive me!)

During the night I wake up, retching. I have to get up before it is too late to avoid soiling my comrades or the tent. We are all completely naked, each rolled up in his blanket to avoid itching from the lice. As I well know, I am taking a risk, for even though it is damp, it is not comparable with the cold and humidity of the valley. I crouch and go outside the tent, dressed as I am, very simply, and throw up everything that is in me entirely at ease. I ask myself what I can have in my stomach, since we have not really eaten in eight days! I am not cold, the temperature seems quite mild to me. A voice surprises me! It is the commander. "What is this?" I vaguely make out his silhouette, for the night is very dark.

"It is me, *mon Commandeur*, Kaisergruber."

"Have you lost your mind? Get back in your tent at once!"

"It is not my mind that I am losing, *mon Commandeur*, I am not cold and I am afraid of soiling my comrades!"

"Get back in there!" It is clear, it is firmly put. I have no choice but to obey! I go back in the tent, but I remain at the entrance, prepared for any eventuality, and I quickly go back to sleep in spite of the thirst that grips me. When I wake up in the morning I am thirsty and hungry, but thirsty above all! My bread bag is empty and the canteen is dry. However, I spot some drums of petrol, some of which are upright and retain two or three centimeters of water, thanks to their rims. The water is clear, except for traces of petrol on the surface. My thirst is so great that I do not hesitate for long, and, more or less avoiding the traces of fuel, I suck up the water with pursed lips. My comrades do the same. The Russian orderly of one of our officers has discovered, I have no idea where, one or two handfuls of some sort of flour, and in the adjoining tent, where there is still a little water in the canteens, we set to making *crêpes*. Primitive as they are, it is a Godsend when they bring us some. What wisdom to have been parsimonious with the contents of their canteens, but they are adults, and we are impulsive kids. The day is rainy, like all of its predecessors, and the night goes as did the day, immutably. I do not have to stand guard this night either. In the morning our stomachs awaken at the same time that we do. Perhaps it is they that awakened us. Hunger and thirst twist our guts, but nothing appears; no rations in sight! The rain has refilled our watering troughs of the day before, and we quench our thirst as best we can. We find, to our dismay, that the horses have eaten a third of the pole of a cart! The poor beasts are no better provided for than we are. They have also eaten the lower branches of the trees around them. The drivers cut down a tree and make a new pole. My comrades collect acorns, and I do the same. There are few. We talk of pralines, and, *voilà*, we are eating acorns, entirely happy to have found them.

At about 1100 hours a little group comes toward us, coming up from the valley. Hurrah! They carry thermoses on their backs. We are saved! The thermoses are not even off their backs and we have already surrounded them. But what a deception! It is not soup, it is only coffee. We say bad things about the cook, without knowing if he has anything to cook! At least it is hot, and that is good, in any case. One small gulp for each man. At the start of the afternoon we set up a reconnaissance patrol, and, since I have gone two nights without having to stand guard, I am included. I do not feel bad, but my head is as empty as my stomach. I follow the others like a sheep, without knowing where we are going, nor seeing where I go, which earns me a couple of spectacular tumbles, and I stumble at least 20 times. I do not know how long we have marched when we finally halt, beyond a ridge, on a little shelf from which we can make out a very large valley in the distance. But we must be careful, for there is *"Feindeinsicht"* (the enemy can see us). It seems that there on the horizon is Tuapse, seven or 17 kilometers as the crow flies, but I have not measured it. I am astonished, for it does not seem any better than here. We don't see anything special, for there is mist, and the sky is entirely gray. We hear airplanes, then muffled explosions. Now we can make out clouds of smoke, denser than the mist and the clouds, plumes that grow and become impressive. We even believe that we see flames. These are the *Stukas* that have bombed the petrol tanks at Tuapse. When we have had a good look we turn and go back the way we came. When we get back to our jump-off positions someone pours a brown and yellow liquid into our mess tins, hardly thicker than *"Kaffee-Ersatz"*. When the person serving me sees my questioning look he says, "It seems that it is soup?"

"Ah! Oui?" I can think of nothing else to say and I swallow this eleven-hour-old *bouillon* that is no more than tepid! That will provide a little ballast in the event of a high wind, for I can't weigh very much, no more than my comrades. All the same, we manage to force a laugh, even if only a weak one. After a new night, day breaks again, and despite everything, I have more difficulty getting up, for the fever has returned. No doubt I have perspired here on the patrol and gotten a chill watching the fireworks over Tuapse from this shelf exposed to the winds. *Bon Dieu*, but my back is cold and I have trouble breathing! How long this day is and how I would love to sleep! Finally night comes, but I do not sleep well, and only in short stretches, for I have a backache.

Shortly after *Reveille* I learn that we are going back down toward the valley, that we are leaving the heights of the Pschich. What joy! I must see the medical officer without delay. When we get down there we rejoin our comrades that we left five or six days ago. They have established the positions and are living in the "bunkers" dug out of the side of the mountain, but the water that runs down from above forces them to bail their bunkers out at regular intervals, even during the night, for the water finally submerges the branches with which they covered the floors of their shelters. The friends that I rejoin, when I visit them, no doubt find that I do not look well, that I seem undernourished. Emile M. and Raymond P. offer me the only specialty of the house, a good loin of horse. I am not in a condition to be difficult, and I gladly accept the invitation to their table!

All the same, I turn away when I see them cut the strips of meat from the same carcass that was already there the previous week and that I saw when climbing to the positions. It is not raining for an instant. There is even a ray of sunlight, and all the men coming down from above settle down where they can to catch a bit of sleep. Since there is water, everyone quenches their thirst, but the commander decides to send a party to find food at any cost, for it is not possible to continue like this, our stomachs sunken for many days. The men are in danger of falling like flies, and the ranks are already so thinned! *Voici*! Raymond offers me the "steak" that Emile has just grilled. It has no less allure than most of the morsels of meat that I have eaten in recent months. It fills the lid of my mess tin. At the moment that I eat it I force myself to think of other things and to avoid looking at the horse that provided it, but it attracts my gaze in spite of myself. I prefer to change my place and turn my back on it. No matter what, the image of the horse returns to me, or at least what is left of it, what remains of this poor carcass, devoured by all, one cut at a time, undoubtedly each according to the taste of the diner. I try, in vain, to think of other things while working with might and main to cut up this flesh! Tell me the truth, Emile! You did not make a mistake and cut this morsel from the saddle or the harness? I get the impression that you forgot to undress the animal before operating on it! All the same, I do my best to make a start on this morsel of leather! Well grilled, as it is, I see that my friend is experienced. The odor of carrion is not too perceptible. My stomach has something to work on, and that is the essential!

The ration party returns at about 1300 hours with potatoes on a "*panjewagon*" with a couple of sacks on top. Depending on their size, the potatoes are cut in halves or quarters and thrown pell-mell into the field kitchen with big red beans, peas, broad beans and a sort of semolina. Some bits of "thoroughbred" are also put in for good measure. One hour later we relish an "*Eintopf*" such as I have never eaten, and for which I shall never find the equal, the flavor! Soon afterward we are on the road again, descending into the valley where we return to Schirvanksaja. The fever, which seemed to have let up, and the pain in my back return, as if the preoccupation with more vital things had absorbed my attention in the meantime. My aches have been modest, and the nourishment that we just had, has perhaps also nourished the fever and the malady. When we finally arrive, for the second time, at the Maïkop – Tuapse railroad that we left eight days earlier, I find that I am, once more, in the same pitiable state. I go to revisit Doctor A. He is there on the railway ballast right where I saw him eight days ago. Even before my turn arrives, he calls to me and tells me, "Wait there, I will have you evacuated," and gives me a thermometer: 38.7° [101.7°F]. I am happy, I admit, but I do not dare to show it. For shame before my comrades? Or out of fear that it would put it all in question? No doubt a little of both. Yes, that is it, a little of both! I see my comrades, Emile, Raymond, Paul, the others. I am a little ashamed, in spite of myself. I am going to leave them, I am going to leave my squad where we understand each other well. Despite everything, it is a wrench, a separation. We have been together so long, we have shared so many joys and miseries. I try not to think too much! I am afraid to let my emotions show, a tear? *Oui*, I said it, too bad. But it is the truth. One cannot always be master of one's emotions, 24 hours a day, seven days a week for month after month. Two lorries are there and we are motioned to climb on board. I say my farewells, but I don't dare hesitate. A few handshakes, a few slaps on the back, a wink of an eye. If you return to Belgium, go see my parents, says Emile, and he gives me their address in Spa. I never wrote it down, but, regardless, I never forgot it. I promise him, I swear to it … and I keep my word.

9

21 October, 1942: Evacuated

The lorries rumble off and jolt over the bumpy road, and my comrades vanish into the countryside at twilight. We are about 20 men in this lorry and, undoubtedly, as many in the other, Germans and a few "*Bourguignons*". There is a little conversation, but nobody really wants to prolong the conversation. I believe that each one hopes for a bit of calm, to turn inward, to strike a balance, to consider plans, perhaps in any case, to dream. This morning, the heights of the Psisch, this evening, the ballast and the tunnel at Schirvanskaja. All of that seems truly distant, as if wrapped in fog, and it has only been an hour since we left our comrades! Human nature is curious.

The bumps prevent us from sleeping, but words or conversations are infrequent. During the night, at about 0200 hours, we arrive at the Maïkop "*Hauptverbandplats*" [clearing station], aching all over, but happy to know that we shall soon enjoy the warmth of a bed. This will be the first time since 23 May, with maybe one or two exceptions.

The "*Sanitäter*" and the "*Schwester*" [medical orderlies and female nurses] help us down from the lorries and, already, we feel surrounded with care and attention, it is marvelous! Wounded, some on stretchers, are removed from the other lorry. I believe that one died *en route*. Ten minutes later we are in bed, our clothes being disinfected in the autoclave. Temperature, pulse, a cup of tea, a pill, and then I fall asleep. It is good to let go of everything, to finally relax after so many exhausting months, under tension day and night. Here, it does not rain, it is dry and the lightbulb in the ceiling gives the effect of the sun!

22 October: *Reveille* at 1000 hours. I did not even dream! Temperature, medicine, wash-up. There are no orders to carry out, nothing but smiles and kindness. At about 1400 hours we depart in a medical column. A dozen lorries. At about 2000 hours we arrive at the *Revier* (infirmary) at Usti – Labinskaja.

I have slept so much since my evacuation, wakened only for care and meals, that my notes for the next 10 or 15 days are vague, imprecise. I have some clear memories, others less so. The dates may be off by a day or two, but it is true that the weather and the dates are unimportant. All that mattered at that time was the rest and the care! I had to catch up on all those nights without sleep and to benefit from the warmth of a bed or of a simple straw mattress to dry out my body from all the humidity it absorbed in the last month! The lorries took us to a medical train, the train to a hospital. It was at Maïkop, or maybe Stavropol, for I heard both of these names in a state of semi-sleep. Maybe even a day or two in the hospitals of each of these cities. In any case, I made sure to point out on my "*Krankenzettel*" (certification of illness, evacuee) the mention of "*Heimat-Lazarett*" (homeland hospital).

It must have been 29 October that a *JU 52* airplane carried us to the Crimea, landed at Simféropol – South and took off again, after replenishment for it and for us. After a rather short flight we landed again, this time in the Ukraine, but I do not know the name of the place. A medical train was waiting for us. So long as they don't take us back where we came from. It seems, in effect, that we have gone in a circle. But, since we hear talk of encirclement of the Caucasus, that is not surprising.

But no, the journey continues toward the west. We can let go of our cares, others have taken charge of us, concern themselves with us. Although I am not cured, I feel cured. Today all my maladies and my fever seem supportable! All that remains for me to do is to vanquish these two enemies. Yesterday, in addition, I had to face hunger, thirst, cold, mud … all united against me alone.

The remainder of my itinerary consists of no more than a succession of little and great joys that I did not realize could still exist. The devotion, the efficiency, the marvelous kindness of these "*DRK Schwestern*" [German Red Cross nurses], the medical orderlies also, and the doctors, for sure! But I must give first place to those hidden guardian angels that immediately take charge of all the needs of each of the wounded, of every sick man, individually, as if we are the only wounded or sick man that they have to care for. The men and women truly put themselves out. That is the impression they give me! I cannot ever say it enough. Did we thank them sufficiently? I have only met one camel[1] among the "*Schwestern*" and, yet… It is easy to confuse a camel with a dromedary, the one has two humps, the other has but one! I do not yet know where I am going to land, or where this voyage will end, and I am curious about it. I learn from a doctor that I have had a relapse of my pleurisy. That is what I was afraid of, but I am not surprised. We lived two long weeks outdoors, in the rain, with no changes of clothes, no way of getting warm!

I do not blame anyone for the course of this voyage, tedious for another, but I enjoy every moment. Dniépropétrowsk, Tarnopol. Lublin, Katowitz, Breslau, Mannheim, Karlsruhe and, on 4 November, we arrive at Bad – Triberg in the Black Forest.

Some of the wounded, some of the sick left the train *en route* and stayed in other hospitals. My hospital, here – already I say "mine" – is the *Hôtel Sonne*, and all of the hotels have been transformed into "*Reserve -Lazarett*" [general hospitals], and care for the ill and wounded. Intensive care, alternating hot and cold compresses for three or four days in succession, pills of all colors, injections of all sizes. "*Weintraubenzucker*" [dextrose] in particular, they are the biggest!

It turns out that I also have jaundice! But pleurisy and jaundice, combined, seem downright benign to me after all that I have gone through!

On about 20 November I am able to take my place, along with the others, at the dining tables on the ground floor. True family life, with civilized repasts! But I especially marvel and would rather tell you about all that makes me happy today, but that is of no interest to anyone except me, instead of talking of the front, from which I come and for which I enlisted! Know, however, that the little treatments continue, that I have an excellent regime because of the jaundice, that the hotel was nicely decorated with wreathes of fir ornamented with pine cones. Already they are preparing for Christmas, and that, from the room that the three of us share, I have a splendid view of the Black Forest, which already wears a sumptuous cover of white. Oh yes, and I was going to forget to say that our "*Oberschwester*" was divine! And not old! She lived in Srt. Georg, near Villingen, but I cannot tell you more, because I never knew her exact address!

On 30 November I receive my Christmas package, which the army gives all its soldiers, early – and, on 1 December, I embark for Brussels, with the help of a medical orderly who carries my package, the only one, and who reserves a good place on the train for me. It is a gesture of pure courtesy, for nothing prevents me from carrying it myself. Perhaps it may also be due to my status as a foreign volunteer, for I doubt if all soldiers in my condition are blessed with the same favor.

This little package, beside me on the bench, is my only wealth, all that I have, but it seems like more when I am surrounded with such solicitude.

---

1   Equivalent, in English, to saying something like 'She's a real cow'.

Stuttgart, Frankfurt, Maaseik, always detours, and finally Brussels, where I arrive on 2 December. I see my father, moved and glad to see me. One night in my bed, and then, on the 3rd, I report to the military hospital at the *avenue de la Couronne.* There I meet a dozen of my comrades, P. Mezzeta, *Adjudant* Mathieu, Hans, R. Baudouin, E. Poot, R. Marchal, Pourbaix and others too, including a certain Raskin, whom I have never met and who will later be executed. But, at this moment, I feel the same bonds of comradeship with him as with all the others, including those whom I have never met until here. Raskin was infiltrated into our ranks for reasons that I do not know, but which had nothing to do with our motivation.

At the moment I do not know it, but I have just completed the campaign that was the most exalting – hard assuredly, but not the most dramatic, nor the most murderous, and woe to those who survived and are going to take part in the campaigns that lie ahead!

The comrades who lost their lives in this first campaign died with their illusions intact. Happily they did not know that they had offered their lives, sacrificed their "20 years" in vain. But certainly they did not haggle, they did not calculate! And then, is it not necessary to say that nothing, absolutely nothing, is in vain?

10

Conclusion of the Campaign in the Caucasus: Prelude to Another

December 1942: I am still at the military hospital until the 19th. The nurses and medical orderlies ought to bear well with our jokes and exuberance! They do not have to laugh every day, unlike us, but they have the advantage of being in good health, while, for us, it is sometimes painful to laugh, some because of their stitches, others, like me, with a tube that reaches into the stomach for a very necessary washing.

In brief, this 19 December I go on convalescence, to take a fresh-air cure! For real! A fresh-air cure! After I have lived in the fresh air for the last eight months! For the last months at the front I have lived nowhere but in the fresh air, lots of air, and with water on top of that. Much water and very little food.

A few days earlier the doctor, by chance the same one who checked me out before my departure for the front, told me that he would send me for a fresh-air cure and gave me the choice: Bavaria, the Tirol or … Spa! Obviously, my decision was instant, since chance offered me this possibility. Indeed, I would have loved to see Bavaria or the Tirol, with which I was unfamiliar, but it offered me a unique occasion to keep my word, to please my friend Emile.

On the afternoon of the 19th I arrive at the *Hôtel Normandy*, in Spa, with the following treatment: two hours of walking in the morning, the same in the afternoon, with a siesta in between. Here, the oldest and, at the same time, the man with the highest rank, convalescing like us, is a 60-year-old artillery major who treats us a little like his children. Very polite, paternal, he is the one who presides at the dinner table at the *Hôtel Rosette*, for it is there that we eat. His formula, when all are present, standing behind their seats, is "*Guten hunger!*" (Good appetite) Then we sit and are allowed to serve ourselves. The dinners are perfect, without being *gourmet*, and a good share of us, like myself, follow a diet prescribed by their doctor. I follow the prudent diet voluntarily, the one prescribed! All of the staff at the restaurant, except the administration, are civilian and Belgian, and extremely friendly!

The next afternoon I look for the *rue Brixhe*, where Emile's parents live. When I ask a passerby for directions to the street, he asks who I am looking for and as soon as I tell him the name, his face lights up, Ah, they will be happy! Emile is getting married today! I am totally taken aback. Emile had told me nothing of this, and, furthermore, I am amazed that he returned home so soon after me, if not at the same time! I hesitate a bit, but I tell myself that it is absolutely necessary to go there, hoping to give him a good surprise! Furthermore, he would never forgive me if I didn't. The passerby shows me where it is. I go up the few steps of the stairs and ring the bell. Only then do I fully realize my feelings, and I swallow my emotions before the door opens.

A young woman whom I have never seen opens the door and cries, "It is Fernand!" I am astounded! How does she know me? I do not have time to ask myself questions, for already a dozen persons surround and embrace me. Right away I am facing the father and mother of my friend, I guess, I am certain of it! They embrace me with so much affection, as if I was their own son, that I am deeply moved. But a soldier should be strong and hard, and not show this kind of feelings! The mother, the father, everyone puts me at ease. They give me the place of honor, they set another place. Truly, I am confused. I already know that it is not Emile who is getting married. My informant confused the first names. It is his brother, A. I am embarrassed to have imposed myself on their celebration, but my shame fades rapidly in the face of this simple, spontaneous, warm hospitality! I ask them how in the devil do they know that it is me? Were they expecting my visit? No, absolutely not, but Emile told them so much about me in his letters that it could have been no one else but me. Already they *tutoie* me[1] and I am entirely at ease. The tarts appear, all sorts of tarts, with rice, with sugar, with fruits. It is wartime, and it is difficult to do better, it is perfect! Emile's parents are charming, more so than I could imagine! I have to promise to come see them every day, or, at least, every other day.

In the ensuing days we take many walks, Emile's Papa and me. Sometimes A. joins us, and, on occasion, his wife, Josée. Sometimes Carl, a German friend, also accompanies us. Emile's father explains the forest to me, which he obviously loves, like all of nature. He tells me the legends of la Fagne.[2] He shows me all the local walks, Balmoral, the lake of Warefaaz, Nivezé, Sart, Creppe, Géronstère... We amuse ourselves firing the *P 38*[3] at stumps.

I spend three marvelous weeks and quickly regain pounds of weight and my color. I have no regrets about Bavaria or the Tirol. I share my Christmas and New Year's celebrations with Emile's parents and my German comrades. I must be everywhere. Everyone wants me to be theirs. *Mon Dieu*, may I not be engulfed by pride! Emile's Papa does not consider the streets safe. Once night falls, he absolutely insists on accompanying me to the hotel after every visit with them! I try in every way to dissuade him, but with no success! The only course left for me is, each time, after I have gone into the hotel, I come back out shortly and discreetly follow him to make sure that he gets home safely. Thus I watch him, marching ahead of me with a confident step that belies his age, his *Fagnard* [see footnote on la Fagne] walking stick firm in his hand. He proudly showed me an old percussion pistol, and it is that with which he intends to assure my safety. Thus, every evening, you can be sure, I walk this distance three times, which gives good evidence of the success of my cure. I could never forgive myself if something happened to him.

During my sojourn he introduces me to everyone, people of modest means and the local authorities. Among others, I spend an afternoon with the parents of a comrade, Léonard I., of Italian origin. His two little sisters play duets for me on the piano in a very well-practiced manner, and then curtsey to me as if I was someone important. Truly charming, if a bit embarrassing to my modesty. I knew Léonard well. He was evacuated after the Tcherjakov fighting following a bout of hysterics. He remained, paralyzed, for three long months in a Munich hospital, where he later married his nurse. I maintained contact with Emile's parents by letter as long as possible. His Papa died in captivity at Merksplas.[4] I saw his Mama whenever possible after 1950, and until her death. She still worked at a hotel in Spa at 70 years old, constrained thereto by her financial situation! Wonderful people, I have only the best memories of you!

---

1   *Tutoyer* – use the familiar '*tu*' rather than the formal '*vous*'. In French, one only uses the familiar form with intimate family and friends.
2   La Fagne (French for the Fen) is a swampy natural region in southern Belgium and northern France – mostly in the provinces of Namur and Hainaut in Wallonia.
3   *P 38* – a 9 mm semi-automatic German service pistol model (*9 mm Pistole 38*).
4   The municipality of Merksplas, 40 kilometers from Antwerp, is mostly known for its prison – one of the biggest in Belgium – where the author will later be imprisoned.

On 9 January, 1943 I say *"au revoir"*, not *"adieu"*,[5] to my friends in Spa and I take the train to Brussels and return to the military hospital. On the 10th they make me enter the *"Chirurgie Abteilung"* [surgery section], since, suddenly, in the last two days at Spa, one of my "Russian sores" became infected and resembled a phlegmon.[6] I have minor surgery and a course of treatment for the afflictions, which seem to me to be cured. In March I am entitled to several days of leave, and, on the 16th, I enter the *Chef's* guard. It is at that moment that we guarantee the security during the burial of Paul Colin, director of the *"Nouveau Journal"*, who was assassinated three days earlier. While serving in the *Chef's* guard, I run into companions such as P. Minet, J. Gilson, Beysselo, Fauville, Antson and others. The family N. take care of supplies for the *Chef.* The father, the mother, and the young daughter. Do I really have to tell you that it is the young daughter that I know best? It is all good, all honorable. If I remember the parents well, I can tell you that I remember the daughter even better, who, even though she is an old lady today, is still able to keep the attention of young grandparents like me.[7] I request to rejoin my comrades before they return to the front and, on 13 April, I embark for Meseritz.

On the 15th I am already on the train for Brussels, for it seems that I am entitled to my leave from the Caucasus. The few days in March, when I left the hospital, were, in fact, a convalescent leave, and did not replace my normal leave that my comrades enjoyed.

Fifteen days passed quickly, and on 30 April I am, once more, on the train to Meseritz. Arriving in the afternoon at the Meseritz barracks I am extremely astonished to meet there seven or eight fellows from my quarter of the outskirts, and even friends that I knew at Cologne in 1941, during my time at *l'École Humboldt* or at the factory. Several of them came from very different political horizons than mine, some, at times, from the very antipodes of my beliefs. Less than a year earlier I found it necessary to come to blows with two of them! Nevertheless, they come right toward me, happy to see a "veteran". Yes, I am already a veteran for some of them, at least for those that came after me. For me, they are comrades, like the others, and I am the same for them.

On 5 May we leave Meseritz for the camp at Pieske. A space in the pine forest, 200-300 meters on a side, was used for the construction of the camp and its facilities. It is a countryside of moors and heath, ornamented with an extremely beautiful lake and sprinkled, here and there, with forests of pine and birch. The barracks are comfortable enough and neat, despite everything. There are flower beds and well laid out paths. There I meet other comrades of the *Formations de Combat*[8] *de Bruxelles*: M. Willem and Georges V.E. in particular. The exercises are resumed, and there are marches, by day and by night, sometimes on the same occasion.

This month of May is marvelous, and reminds me of that of 1940. The exercises do not exhaust us, thanks to our enthusiasm, which allows us to still find time and energy to swim in the lake, near the camp. Since the army neglected to provide us with swim trunks, we never have to wait for them to dry. Perhaps that is why we are observed, from the other side of the lake where there is a camp of *BDM* (*Bund Deutsche Mädel*, Association of Young German Women). We can see the camp from our bank, but I have never caught the *BDM* watching us. Perhaps it is that, in my innocence, I do not believe that they do so! What, on the other hand, does fascinate me is the magnificence of the sunsets and the thrilling bugle calls when our friends, Milcamps and Willy K., sound *Taps*, played with imagination as a duet! The delicate orchestration of the setting sun and the bugle calls are in perfect harmony, it is the apotheosis of a happy and well filled day! At this

---

5   *'Au revoir'* means 'until we meet again'; *'adieu'* is equivalent to 'goodbye'.
6   phlegmon is a suppurating inflammation that infiltrates the tissues and may develop into an abscess.
7   Remember, the author was writing this in 1991 – at which point he was 68.
8   The *Formations de Combat* were created on 9 July, 1940 by the Rexist Party. With this new paramilitary group, they hoped it would become the militia of any future official Belgian Walloon collaborationist party.

moment, everything stops in the camp! Every *"Bourguignon"* stops what he is doing, conversations simply cease! Everyone meditates for a moment, the fellows leave the barracks or open wide the windows, but all in complete silence. Sometimes I have even seen eyes filled with tears. All of you who were there, you remember. In any case, I have never forgotten, the memory remains engraved in me. A treat for the ears, a vision of paradise! The sun slowly sinks, and its last rays cast an oblique touch on the tips of the pines, on the heather and, at last, the day ends, illuminating the sand like a carpet of golden sequins, passing to red, then violet, finally giving way, as if with regrets, to the realm of the night.

The nights are mild, but the dawns chilly, in this land at the limits of the frontier. No need to rock us to fall asleep. At daybreak, the bugle sounds *Reveille*, brutally rousing us from slumber and this bugle call does not charm me like the other that I spoke of! A new day arises that will bring us its little joys, succeeded by little trials and thus again, until 1 June. One of the little trials is a night in prison, or, to be more precise, 24 hours, in fact. A team of volunteers was formed that were to go to East Prussia to prepare new cantonments for the *Légion*. We were a dozen, all of whom spoke German. That was one of the conditions to be a part of this mission. The leader was *Adjudant* Hecq and my comrades were, Emile M., from Spa, Eugène M., a Luxembourger, F. Deponthière, Chapus, some others and myself.

I was waiting for the moment of departure in my room and was alone. It was the hour to salute the flag and my roommates were all there. The officer of the day, who inspects the paths before reporting to the assembly located at the entrance of the camp, where the flagpoles are, sees me and tells me to pick up the horse dung that had been left there in front of my barrack by one of our four-legged friends. I inform the officer that I must depart immediately on a mission. He becomes aggressive and I determine that he is not entirely sober. It is true. We have been provided here with an abundant canteen: candies, chocolate, alcohol, and who knows what else? But I know, on the other hand, that the officer of the day has not been abusing the bonbons or the chocolate. That is why I rebel and simply refuse to follow the formal order that is given to me. I refuse to submit to an order under these conditions. What do you want? At that age one lacks tolerance! A few minutes later my comrade, Guy W., who is a non-commissioned officer of the guard for 24 hours, comes to get me, accompanied by one of the guards, and asks me to follow them. Thus it is that I find myself in prison, in an incredible promiscuity! There is a trio there, the Cornéli brothers and Marius, the latter Italian, who have drunk to excess and have soiled the prison with their vomit. It is everywhere, and its stench makes me nauseous to the point where I feel that I, myself, shall "catch" intoxication from them! I find a corner of the bench to sit on, after toppling one of the drunkards, who are unaware of anything, but am unable to close an eye all night, for the fellows snore so loudly! At 1100 hours the following morning I report to *Commandeur* Lippert, who listens to me, and I can see that he thinks as I do but cannot let it show, nor give me satisfaction. It is hard to swallow, but I cannot expect it of him. The *Commandeur*, whom we all respect, has never committed the slightest injustice! You can rejoin our company, he tells me, but all nominations for appointment and promotions will be postponed for you for a year. We will leave it at that. Nothing will be entered in your *"Soldbuch"* [paybook]. I am content and I think that I got off well. In fact, I never have thought of putting a stripe on my sleeve, of getting promoted someday, and it hardly concerns me. I spent a bad night, but that is over, forgotten, no regrets! I see that I was wrong in my expectation that my company commander would have been able to defend me and get me out of prison before night, but he did not do it. That is why I request him to let me change companies, explaining my reasons to him.

Thus it is that I go from the *PAK* to the *"Pionniers"*, having, hitherto, exercised my talents in the *3rd Compagnie*. I think that I have said that I love change, and I have found a good reason! No doubt I am to become familiar with all the arms of the service.

This first June produces a great development that we all take note of, a change that will hence-forth give a new direction to our enlistment, to our entire future! This first day of June we are honored with the visit of *Reichsführer* H. Himmler! He arrives on board a *"Tatra"* automobile,[9] entirely silver, with the futuristic lines of a fast racing car. He is not alone, you can be sure, his suite is numerous and high ranking, *General* Berger, in particular. What is striking from the very begin-ning is the absence of all protocol, nothing stiff, none of the habitual rigidity of ceremonies and presenting arms. It impresses us, obviously, but does not put us ill at ease. Everyone can see him close up, he shakes many hand. I remember his blue eyes, very clear, piercing. I have the impres-sion of x-ray eyes, that Himmler sizes you up at a glance. He announces to us that we have become a part of the *Waffen-SS* and I feel a very understandable pride, as is the case, I believe, with all of my comrades. As I see it, this passage into the *Waffen-SS* is like a promotion, nothing less! In the ensuing hours all of the *Légion* passes a physical examination, and you can be sure that our hearts beat rapidly for fear of being refused entry to this new family that fascinates us.

During this visit I suddenly hear, *"Sie da! Kommen Sie mal her!"* ("You there, come a little closer!") I turn and see that it is our comrade, J. Marber, that is being called. When Marber is three paces from the officer, the latter picks up an instrument to measure Marber's facial angle and approaches him. I understand! Our comrade Marber is Jewish, I know it, we all know it. He has never hidden it, but that never caused a problem with us. It seems that, today, that is no longer the case. At least that is what I think. Having measured the facial angle, I think that I hear the officer ask our comrade the question, "Jewish?" And Marber replies, *"Ja!"* Marber has been questioned in the same manner as any of us would have been, neither more nor less courteously, and he is demobilized with just as much courtesy. He is returned to Belgium two days later and is never subsequently inconvenienced. I, myself, can confirm that I later met J. Marber in the 1960's in a sports store in Brussels, Midi-Sports, to be more precise.

I return to Pieske, where the passage to the *Waffen-SS* is the subject of all conversation, and those that do not concern it have little of interest! Now we do not go to East Prussia. I simply missed a trip. Life goes on as before 1 June, possibly with a little more zeal for, no doubt, we feel a moral obligation to justify our promotion.

When, on 28 June, we entrain for Wildflecken, we all feel that we have taken a new step. As for me, I think that it is a logical evolution of our enlistment. Stalingrad was in February, we do not forget that, but we see that development as an episode, no more, even if the situation must place constraints on the future. In fact, we think little or nothing of it, and our morale remains unshakeable. We have confidence in our leaders, in those who have taken on the defense of our Western World. It is in this spirit that, the next day, 29 June, we detrain and take up our quarters in the Wildflecken camp.

We have been entirely satisfied, even astonished, with the barracks or camps that we have frequented to date. They have been rational, clean, cheerful, in a word, hospitable. But what to say about Wildflecken? A barracks? It does not resemble one. A camp? Not at all! Splendid pavilions scattered in a superb forest setting, at 800 meters' altitude. Ground floor and one story above, painted in eggshell colors. Lined up harmoniously along the roads, without any austerity. No geometric alignment, well fitted to the site. The basements of the pavilions are in country stone, the sloping roofs covered with gray slate. The roads are paved with asphalt and there are no rectan-gular sectors more than 1-200 meters in size, except for the length of the *Adolf Hitler Platz*, where the officers' mess is located and the assembly hall. Woods of fir trees separate the buildings from

---

9   The *Tatra 87* was built by the Czechoslovakian *Tatra* motor company and was one of the fastest production
    cars of its time – noted for its aerodynamic streamlining.

each other. In brief, a four-star establishment! And we really see a great deal of the stars. Mainly while on exercises, which are very hard. On the "*Spiegel*" [collar patches] and the epaulets of the officers, who are very numerous here. We do a lot of saluting, but "*Dienst ist Dienst, und Schnaps ist Schnaps*" ["Duty is Duty, and Schnaps is Schnaps"]. There are 10 or 12 canteens for our pleasure, athletic fields, as if the training exercises were not enough? Movie theater and [stage] theater, in short, everything that is needed for relaxation in addition to the appropriate military installations. When speaking of the cinema and the theater, that makes me think that we have among our comrades chaps who call them "*Théatre*", "*Kino*" (cinema in German), "*Cabaret*", "*Taverne*" and I am doubtless, omitting some!

It is here at Wildflecken that, on 2 July, 1942 for the first time I don my *Waffen-SS* uniform, which gives us additional obligations, less rights, all of which confuses me. One day the entire platoon is punished, I do not know why, and assembles before the pavilion in full gear, with full knapsack, empty bread bag, weapons, gas mask, shovel, nothing lacking! The only things we are not carrying are the armoires and furniture from the rooms. The "*Monsieur Loyal*"[10] who directs this circus is *Adjudant* Thir, one of the specialists in this form of diversion, along with the *adjudants* Jehay and Dohay, whose names have a certain air of kinship! When one of them presides over the festivities, every one of us knows exactly what to expect! A new uniform can be worn threadbare in a good hour, or can be reduced to shreds in 15 minutes! The temperature is 25 to 27° [76–80°F]. To put us in condition and warm us up a bit before the grand performances we start with those that are more banal and more simple. A bit of marching and drill, quarter-turn, half-turn, sling arms, shoulder arms, present arms. Attention, at ease. I abridge, for, just thinking of it, I am already out of breath.

Then, running-pace, down on your face, anything for a bit of variety and to avoid somnolence. When you throw yourself on the ground, you may well believe that one does not choose the place where one falls. *Alors*, in addition to the exhaustion, abrasions and ecchymoses [hematomas], stones bruise our ribs, dead branches malignantly poke holes in our skin, impertinent grasses penetrate our nostrils clear to the sinuses, and the dust that engulfs us everywhere dries our throats and mucous membranes, but not our sweat! In less than 10 minutes the best athlete would normally give up the ghost. We, we keep on for an hour, an hour-and-a-half, two hours! Which, undoubtedly, annoys this *adjudant* of misery. When he asks us, shouting, to reassemble again, we think that it is all over. We will be able, at last, to breathe, to calm the gasping breath that burns the sore throat. "Put on your gas masks!" What?! Futile to protest, absolutely not that! Otherwise, not a word, not a sound escapes our lips, nobody has the strength. We do as ordered. Once the masks are adjusted, we march, we run, we do the "down on your faces". We are back to ground zero! As if everything that we have done so far counts for nothing!

Twenty minutes later, "Attention!" New hope! This time, is it done? No, not even time to breathe, to reflect! Climb the trees! When we are all up there, perched like monkeys, but far less at ease, the order comes from below: "Sing!" And louder, *Nom de Dieu*! *Alors*! Am I a nightingale, or am I mad? Perhaps both, after all! Like the others, certainly, I have slightly loosened my mask to get a bit more oxygen with less effort, to avoid suffocation and to clear the lenses of the mask, which were totally fogged. But watch out! Anybody who is caught trying this trick resumes this exercise this evening or tomorrow, at the risk of replacing this instructor with another one. *Alors*, to avoid drinking more this evening or tomorrow, drain the chalice to the dregs today and be prudent! This sort of punitive exercise is not a daily occurrence, but it is not that rare. Alas for those, it is often

---

10 In the world of the circus in France, '*Monsieur Loyal*' has become the generic name for the ringmaster – deriving from an actual circus family of the first half of the 19th century in France.

the same ones that are punished. As for me, I usually manage to avoid it well enough, but I do not have the enthusiasm of the addicts. Don't think that I am complaining! Everyday life is enough for me, with its usual exercises, its marches, its great moments and its servitude, which leave very little time for reveries or blissful ease.

Alors, Sunday, the only day of rest, without exercises and with minimal service. Do you know what I do? *Eh, bien*! Along with five or six of my comrades, I descend toward Wildflecken, which we pass through to then mount the other slope of the valley and climb all the way to the "*Kreuzberg*", a Calvary [wayside cross] at the high point of 928 meters! A round trip of 16 to 18 kilometers, and by no means easy, for we don't follow the road, which is yet longer. Happily, before returning, there is a way to quench our thirsts with a good beer at the establishment next door to the convent, built a short distance from the summit. When I explain this to my German friends, they say we are crazy! Perhaps you think the same, and you are not wrong.

Others prefer to go to Bischofsheim, Gersfeld or Brückenau to stuff themselves with pastries in the "*Konditorei*", or "tea-room", in French! Or, again, to meet the girls of the village there, sometimes both distractions simultaneously for the more exacting. As for myself, I prefer nature, and if one meets the girls there, that is even better.

On about 15 July all those who are able to drive an automobile, a lorry or to pilot a motorcycle are ordered to report. I seize the stroke of good luck and join the ranks. And that is why, on 18 or 19 July, I find myself in the train, *en route* to Kraków, or Cracovie, along with 40 of my comrades of all branches of the service. My comrade J. Talbot, a good buddy, who is, at the same time, an excellent horseman, is in charge of the detachment, but that, doubtless, is not the reason he has been designated responsible for our group. At Kraków, the barracks that house us also house elements from other units, but we are the only foreigners among the Germans. All, however, belong to the *Waffen-SS*. I am immediately appointed as "*Dolmetscher*", or "interpreter", which entitles me to be housed with the non-commissioned officers, with *Sergent* Talbot, even though I am still *caporal*. There is a slight problem at the start: evidently I do not know the translation of technical terms, of mechanical pieces. But, happily, among the "*Bourguignon*" students there is a very good mechanic who gives me the French translations of all of the mechanical elements that the instructor speaks of and whose pictures are on the boards I have to deal with.

I rapidly find a few comrades among the German *sergents* and *adjudants* that are our instructors, and, at the same time, become the driver of the German commander, a *Sturmbannführer*. That allows me to have tea with him nearly every afternoon on the Krakau square, under the arcades. Other officers often join us and all have the good taste to refuse to let me take part in paying the check. I can, instead, spend my pay in the company of my comrades. I have a good job and the days pass agreeably, except for the two first Sundays!

On those days I am, in effect, between the hammer and the anvil! Don't forget that we are dealing with the "*Bourguignons*"! The first Sunday there is an assembly in the lateral court, near the garages, at 1000 hours in the morning, instead of the 0800 hours during the week. *Sergent* Talbot has assembled the men to present them to the *premier lieutenant*. I am on the left, and a little behind Talbot. Attention, Present Arms, At Ease. The *Obersturmführer* gives orders after saluting the troop, and I translate: From 1000 to 1200 hours, maintain and wash the lorries and motorcycles! An event then transpires that no one expects, the Germans even less than myself, and which, without doubt, has never been seen in the German Army: one, then two, then five or 10 men demand to speak and tell us that it is Sunday and that they want to attend mass!

All, with maybe one or two exceptions, then express the same desire. Among them there are at least a dozen who have never set foot in a church, I would swear, or, at least, not since their communion. I am extremely embarrassed by the situation and I look toward Talbot, who is just as embarrassed as I am, who gestures that I should translate, regardless. I turn toward the

Obersturmführer who looks straight at me with an enquiring eye, intrigued by what has just taken place. I tell him that the men have just told us, Talbot and me. I see that the *Obersturmführer* is incredulous at first, perplexed, and a bit disconcerted. Apparently he has never met such a situation! He calls me close to him and asks me if this is a joke. I explain to him, as best as I can, that we have a chaplain, which astonishes him, and that he conducts masses for us at the brigade whenever he is able. He reflects for an instant, then has me announce to the troop that there will be an assembly in 20 minutes for the mass. He has, thus, decided to accede to the demand of the "*Bourguignons*". Curious! I have never seen an officer yield in such a situation!

At 1040 hours we are *en route* to the church, in well-ordered ranks, singing from a heart filled with joy! Talbot commands the detachment and the *Obersturmführer* accompanies us, as well as the two instructors, one of whom is my comrade Joep. Joep is hilarious, and tells me he has never seen anything like this, never! Joep is a wonderful chap of the *LAH*, the *Führer's* guard.[11] His black hair brushed back, skin bronzed, he must be 1 m 95 or 2 meters tall [6' 6" – 6' 8"]. He can bellow like a madman or laugh like a kid. This is a first-rate experience for him, living with the "*Bourguignons*". He will certainly talk about this someday to his grandchildren, in the evening at reunions. When we arrive at the cathedral… why couldn't we have gone to some little anonymous parish? … All the Poles, and there are many, line up flabbergasted! They have certainly never seen anything like this! Halt, break ranks, and the "*Bourguignons*" enter the church with great discipline, standing aside, being polite to the Poles and granting them priority, but all enter the church. It is true that the instructors are there, outside the church, and are going to wait there until the end of the service. I remain with them and Talbot, chatting until the end of the service. Then, assembly and return to the barracks, singing. The Poles who were present that day at the mass will also talk about this day! Such doings will never be forgotten whether one is German or Polish!

What happens the next Sunday is not to be forgotten and shows that our German comrades are not devoid of a sense of humor. The previous Sunday's digression certainly surprised them, but it failed to provoke any outburst of temper, as we might have feared, nor was there any sign that they held it against us. This Sunday, then, assembly at 1000 hours, like the previous Sunday. Presentation of the troops, at ease. All of the instructors are there, and I ask myself what is going to happen. The *Obersturmführer* advances and asks me to tell the men who want to attend mass to move to the left. With a very few exceptions, everyone moves to the left. He then asks me to tell the men who want to attend the movies to move to the right. Two or three of the isolated ones who had kept their places do that. I have to laugh in spite of myself, especially when I see the astounded look on the faces of the "*Bourguignons*". At this moment, without the least shame, I see a dozen who move from left to right. I think that the instructors are going to react, but no, nothing! Just as if they had seen nothing, they tell us to form ranks, and one detachment goes to mass, the other heads for the movie theater at the barracks. With Joep, the instructor, and at his request, I accompany the detachment to the church. The "*Bourguignon*" who remained alone, and did not choose to go to the movies or to attend mass, was freed from duty and was able to go into the city!

The third Sunday, there is almost the same scenario: to the left for mass, and about a dozen choose that. Then a little variation: those who remain in the ranks do a quarter-turn to the right and off to the garages. Wash and maintain vehicles! All go in good order and in a good humor. The humor of the ones was accepted by the others, and vice versa. The "*Bourguignons*", good players, accept the lesson. The following Sunday, there is no service. Maintenance takes place Saturday afternoon, movies for those who so desire Saturday evening, and Sunday is completely free.

---

11 *LSSAH – 1.SS-Panzer-Division Leibstandarte SS Adolf Hitler.*

As for the rest, every day of the week we have theory in the morning and leave in the afternoon for the training tracks, which is to say, the land on the route to Katowitz. I lead the moving column in the commander's *Mercedes "Kübel"* [command car] and he gives directions to the rest of the column with little signs. For the first days I learn like everyone else. Then I am released from the instruction, having passed my tests. Thus I can accompany the commander in the city.

Also, in the meantime, I form a friendship with comrade Potiaux, a former prisoner of war, a hefty man of 85 kilograms [187 lbs], who arrived at the *Légion* after our return from the Caucasus. Since we now have liberty on Sunday, he likes to idle around the market in the morning. However, since we are forbidden to go out alone, since soldiers have been assassinated in the city, he asks me to accompany him. I like that and this becomes our Sunday morning distraction. Curious market! They sell a little of everything there, live chickens and ducks, birds, cheese, vegetables, but it seems to me that there are many more booths where they sell and serve vodka and other forms of alcohol, and also gambling tables where one plays for money. There are all sorts of games where the *zlotys* pass from one pocket to another as soon as the dice fall or the cards are laid down. More people gather around these last booths than at those that sell victuals. There is much drinking, as is clear from the number of drunks that we meet, who walk alongside us or who are slumped nearly everywhere or who are lying under the trestle-tables. Several times we are knocked down accidentally, in which case we make nothing of it so as not to provoke a futile squabble, but when it happens once or twice more, we determine that we are being knocked down for the fun of it and we repulse the fellows without hesitation, but without useless brutality. Nothing serious happens, for the people undoubtedly find us quite resolute not to let them step on our toes too openly. We keep our cool, but also keep on our guard. When I meet Joep there he asks if we are out of our minds! The two of us are walking in this crowd where we could be stabbed without anyone knowing it but the victim, himself. But this amuses us, and we return every Sunday morning right up to our last Sunday in Kraków.

On 30 August we leave Kraków, *"Führerschein"* [driving license] in our pockets, good for driving automobiles, lorries up to 30 tons and motorcycles, solo or with side-car. The commander and the instructors have come to know us, with our qualities and our faults. We are sorry to part, we have made friends. A good memory, an agreeable sojourn!

At the beginning of September we resume the routine of instruction at Wildflecken and we go to pick up new *matériel* at the railroad station, the *BMW* 750 side-car, the *Zündapp* 250 cc solo, and a few *Victoria* 600 cc motorcycles, which spit fire!

Since I have a brother who works at IG. Farben at Aken/Elbe, near Magdeburg, I obtain four days' leave and, on 6 September, I take the train at Bischofsheim. I have to get up at 0430 hours in the morning, for it is eight or nine kilometers to the railway station and I have to get there on foot. Since I can expect no *Reveille*, I sleep with one eye open and wake up every half-hour so that I get up in time. At 0515 hours I set out with my comrade, Raymond V., whom I invited. At 0700 hours we are on the platform, and at 0730 hours the train pulls out: Fulda, Eisenach, Gotha, Erefurt, Leipzig, Halle/Saale, Köthen, Aken/Elbe, with two changes of train. Finally, with joy, I see my older brother and my sister-in-law whom I have not seen for two years! I meet their son, who is only a few months old, who was born here.

I am introduced to the engineers at the factory, to friends and acquaintances, and I take the opportunity to go see a childhood friend, a girl, who works at Dessau and whose brother is also in the *Légion*.

In celebration of my stay at my brother's house I cook for them *"Kartoffel-Knödel"* (potato-balls), but my recipe left something to be desired, for these *boulettes* are so heavy that, when swallowed, they fall right down to your heels! These few days' respite are pleasant, but they pass quickly and on the evening of the 8th we embark on the train at 2000 hours to return. Warnings and bombing forces a detour, and we return via Halberstadt, then Halle/Saale, where we have to change trains. At about 0300 hours we eat a *"Griess-Suppe"* (semolina soup) at the station canteen. The atmosphere of these German stations in full wartime is quite unique. Who remembers it? But, without a doubt, it is the same in all countries at war. Everything is blacked out, of course. The lamp globes are painted blue, shedding scant light on the always-crowded platforms. The window panes and glass domes are also daubed with blue. Faces are ghastly in this dark shadow. The only way to tell civilians from military is by the cut of their clothes, by their silhouettes, or by their leather. There are lots of military, on the platforms, in the canteen. At this hour, those that can, catch a bit of sleep wherever they are able to. There are sailors, aviators, infantry, all branches of the service gathered in this military canteen, humanized by the *"Schwestern"* [nurses] of the *DRK* [the German Red Cross]. In the breach, day and night, always a friendly word, one kindness or another, the fairies of the abode. A couple of fellows are asleep in a corner, head on knees, knapsack on the ground, within reach. Others sleep, stretched out on the benches, some leaning forward, arms on the table and head resting on them. The loud-speakers softly play the popular airs, airs that we all know, the songs of Zara Leander, of Ilse Werner… songs interrupted by *communiquées*, the spoken news, or announcement of an alert. Many are asleep, while new arrivals go to the counter, to the turnstiles, look for a one-dish meal, or coffee. There is never total quiet, but everything is muffled. Even the sailor who is snoring there. He snores discreetly one might say, head on his seabag, accordion in its case resting on the ground under his bent knees.

The rare conversations, the narrative of a leave? Of a previous enlistment? The search for a friend? One makes friends of an hour or two, sure of never meeting again! Fellow-feeling, all the same. What has happened to you all, shadows met, shadows who told me of your families, of your homes? Other memories are the slogans in all the train stations: "The enemy is listening", "Wheels must roll for Victory", "Someone is always hatching plots", or the advertisements: "Why is Juno Round", "Good shave, good humor!" So many images graven in my memory!

At 0630 hours a train for Leipzig and Frankfurt/Main is announced by the loud-speakers. We need to catch it and leave the warmth of this canteen, its odors of stale tobacco, of coffee and of one-dish dinner. Outside it is cold on the platforms where there is a whisper of morning breeze. Dozens of pairs of boots or hob-nailed shoes hasten, clattering on the asphalt of the platforms and the steps of the carriages. Everyone finds a place. Raymond and I find two that face each other. In the meantime day has dawned, but the warmth of the compartment encourages sleep. We do not really sleep, and when I open an eye it is to glance out the window. We would not believe we were at war if it was not for the *"Flak"* around the cities that we pass through and the ruins here and there in the cities. After another change of train and we finally get to Bischofsheim, from which we walk to Wildflecken, as we left it four days ago. Here there is no trace of the war, not a ruin to bear it witness.

I resume life at Wildflecken. I must say that it is far easier to traverse these thousand hills of Thüringen on a motorcycle than on foot, and that is why this sort of exercise is far more pleasing to me than forced singing in the top of a pine tree. The valley of the Fulda soon has no more secrets for us, when, in a few days, we can cover more kilometers than the infantry can in weeks. It takes no more than half an hour to catch my breath at the summit of the *"Kreuzberg"* or of the *"Wasserkuppe"* to admire the countryside stretched at our feet. This is far more agreeable! But do not, for a minute, think that I disavow the infantry. I have had good moments there, especially during the *"Zigaretten-Pause"*, filled with charm and far from the roads and well-trodden paths! No, that was something else!

One Sunday afternoon, the *Schirrmeister* [maintenance sergeant] Fuchs and I set out together for the *"Wasserkuppe"*. He has taken me for a friend and, in a conversation, I told him that I would love to take a glider flight. We often see these great white or tan gliders, slender as dragonflies, soar over the region. A day or two earlier he told me that he has made arrangements and that we can go this Sunday. We depart at the wheel of a big "*Horch*" automobile, destined for the *TTR* (*troupes de transmissions*, signal troops). With the top down, we have all the air we want, and I am impressed with its engine. I am able to take the wheel, and to drive with pleasure. In a quarter of an hour we are at the summit of the "*Wasserkuppe*" where I park our "torpedo" right beside a hangar full of gliders. We enter the office, in a wooden barracks, where Fuchs introduces himself. There are four or five men of the *Luftwaffe* there, and others of the *H.J.* (Hitler Youth) Introductions, talk. Fuchs and the *Luftwaffe sous-Lieutenant* find that they have mutual friends. Everything goes very well.

Half an hour later we are on the field near the gliders. Classy machines to the tips of their wings! Biplanes, monoplanes, totally marvelous! I know that today I am going to glide. A biplane which has just let loose a glider approaches us after a nosedive. He comes to a stop 30 meters from us and it is a kid in knee breeches who gets out. He wears a Hitler Youth uniform, a great pull-over sweater over it, like all the youngsters on the field, except for the *Luftwaffe* fellows. Fuchs asks him how old he is. Seventeen years! Fuchs and I take our places, each of us in the front of a glider with twin controls, but it is two of the kids who take their places in the rear and who will do the piloting. The planes that will tow take position to be hooked up and, five minutes later, we are off the ground after about 100 meters of bumps. We are very quickly at an altitude of 200, 300 meters where we are released and bank. Softly, and with no effort, the glider rapidly climbs to 500, 600 meters. It is marvelous, what calm, what a sensation of relaxation. The only sensation is the sound of the wind on the wings. I realize a childhood dream that was interrupted by the war. I was actually a member of the air-scouts at the "*Maison des Ailes*" [House of Wings], *avenue Marnix*, for several weeks just before the war, and the outbreak of war ruined all my hopes. Today I take a little revenge, of a sort, but I am not the pilot. The "*Wasserkuppe*" is, it seems, one of the best places in Germany for this sort of sport. Nearly always it has ascending air currents! We fly for nearly an hour and reach 900 meters above sea level. There is practically no turbulence, the sky is serene. I see the camp, the "*Kreuzberg*", the entire valley of the Fulda from up in the air. This is worth the effort! When we land I feel light, truly relaxed. The *Luftwaffe* offers us a drink and we stay with them until 1800 hours, whereupon we return to Wildflecken. I learned that Hanna Reitsch spent time at the "*Wasserkuppe*" and paid school fees there.

On 2 October I go on a mission to Frankfurt/Main and the vicinity, accompanied by comrade Lagrasse. We go to find and obtain parts for our motorcycles. *Schirrmeister* Fuchs' automobile drops us off at the railroad station in Brückenau very early in the morning. We are in Frankfurt before 1000 hours. At 1100 hours we arrive in the outskirts, near the Niederrad, in a residential quarter where we obtain a first lot of parts that we then leave at the baggage room of the main railroad station. In the afternoon we head toward Mainz. Thus, in the course of three hours, we go to Höchst at Hanau and Offenbach at Wiesbadden, each time leaving the parts that we get at the baggage room. The industry has, in effect, dispersed its inventory all around the outskirts in a multitude of big houses, little workshops and unused garages to avoid heavy losses resulting from the bombing. That gives us a chance for a little tourism. We spend two nights in hotels with our *Übernachtungs-Scheins* (lodging certificates), and the last, of four or five, in a sort of dormitory for soldiers in the immediate neighborhood of the station. On 5 October we take a walk, this time for pleasure, and, a little past noon, we get on the train for Brückenau where we arrive at about 1500 hours. The station master telephones Wildflecken at my request and, at about 1700 hours, the lorry arrives that will take us back to Wildflecken with our packages.

One day in October it is announced that, the next day, at daybreak, one of our comrades, named De Wilde, will be executed by the firing squad. I do not know him, but we learn that he had deserted twice, and that on the second occasion he disposed of his weapons for motives that we do not know but that the German court martial must have known. In addition, he was found guilty of numerous acts of indiscipline, more or less grave. The accumulation of these acts, and, most certainly, the second desertion and the disposal of his weapons is what earned him the supreme penalty. Nobody, I believe, is happy with the sentence, but I think that everyone understands it. The conduct of comrade De Wilde was not worthy of a volunteer, especially in time of war. This sentence would be applied in any army in the world, even to a conscript, without waiting for a second desertion. However, he showed himself more worthy at the time of his execution, and it is due him to say that.

At dawn of this day, when the *U.V.D.* [*Unteroffizier von Dienst* – non-com of the day] turns us out, a great feverishness is evident everywhere. On the other hand, there are few words spoken. Everything takes place in unusual silence. No smiles, none of the customary jokes. The emotion is real. If we were not required to be present at the execution, for the example, no one would attend.

Day has just broken when the companies assemble, each before its pavilion as usual. The units converge toward the place of execution in silence, but the sound of the footsteps of the marching troops echo louder than usual on these morning paths. We march along the buildings that house the stables and the trains-vehicles toward the firing range, and the lingering fog of this autumn morning dissipates under the first rays of the sun when we come out on the parade ground between the firing ranges. At the far end of this parade ground stands the stake that draws all our attention. All eyes are riveted on this stake that stands out against the fir trees that cover the hill at the far end of the plain. We see nothing else! Had it not been for its tragic destination, nobody would notice it! A little shiver runs up the spine of all these brave warriors, more accustomed to combat than executions! Silence is total, religious, the dry commands alone break the silence. They crack like slaps in the face! As they arrive, the companies form three sides of a great square where nearly 2,000 men assemble to watch one of their own die who was not able to hold his place! The sun is now there, but still so pale that it cannot warm the air of this chilly early morning. Is the chill that causes all these hardened men to shiver that of the morning or of the emotion? All is in place for the sacrifice of propitiation! We hear the sound of an engine in the distance, approaching rapidly. A canvas-covered lorry appears and stops a little aside, to our right. Some men get out and escort the condemned, dressed in linen, his head bare. They remove his jacket and he advances toward the stake, chest bare. The chaplain approaches and talks to him. De Wilde is in perfect control of himself, pale but showing no signs of fright! The men in the ranks are as pale as he is. He is tied to the stake and offered a blindfold, which he emphatically refuses. During this time the execution party is placed in position. The men chosen for this duty have refractory reputations, hard heads, the least disciplined of the *2nd Compagnie*. Among them are two men that I met in the prison at the *Regenwurmlager*, Italians. *Capitaine* D., commander of this company, commands the party. De Wilde asks permission to address his comrades, but it is refused. We see him spit out the cigarette that was offered to him and, while the firing squad gets ready, he cries out in a strong and confident voice, "Comrades, aim for the heart, *vive la Légion, vivent les légionnaires!*" At this very moment the salvo sounds and I see the body stiffen and jump under the impacts, before sagging, held by the bonds. An *adjudant de service* approaches the stake and cuts the bonds. The corpse immediately collapses, face forward, and the officer who commanded the firing squad gives him the *coup de grâce*. At the shot, the body moves in a final convulsion and the military doctor leans over it to confirm the death.

It is finished, all over and, *voilà*, my neighbor on the right sinks down to the rear, without anyone having time to catch him. He is stretched out on the ground, his face pale. D. was unable to stand the trial, he has passed out, quite foolishly! Someone loosens his necktie and exposes his neck. A comrade slaps him and D. revives. Shortly afterward the company medic accompanies him back to the barracks while the companies, in formation, make a quarter-turn right to pass by the corpse before they too return to their barracks. Today's activities are similar to those of any other day, but the atmosphere is entirely different. Some visibly avoid talking about the morning's events, others, on the other hand, discuss it. Thus we learn many things that we did not know in the morning about the last moments of the condemned.

It was the evening of the day before that De Wilde was told of his execution. He did not have a negative reaction. On the contrary, he gave every sign of euphoria! On the other hand, those who kept company with him during the last night were, it seems, more depressed than he was. What is certain, and that I confirmed, is his behavior on entering the lorry that was to take him to the place of execution and which also carried his coffin, under a canvas that had been thrown over it. He pulled off the canvas, lay down in the coffin to check its fit and said that he found it correct. He then did a headstand on the open coffin, supporting his hands on the side walls of the casket. He did not stop joking. We were told something else that remains unverifiable: "They" are supposed to have left the door of his prison open all night to allow him to escape, and he is supposed to have refused that possibility! Nobody has ever been able to either confirm or deny this hypothesis, but I have trouble believing it. The event fades into the background, in any case, as the days pass and activities redouble that lead up to 10 November!

For a day or two we have known that our departure for the front is imminent. We do not yet know, but we can guess from the preparations, from the enthusiastic activity of the entire brigade. Trunks are packed, everywhere there is the sound of boxes being nailed shut. Everything piles up in the corridors. Our lorries carry archives, armory, small articles of all sorts to the railroad station. I drive an officer, bring back another, carry an order or look for someone in the camp. Rolling stock is already waiting there, under guard of a duty detachment. I make six or seven round trips between the camp and the railroad station. It is another great moment for us and, were it not for the fatigue of such a day, we would stay awake all night, excited by the vision of the imminent new departure. The night is short. And, with *Reveille*, the commotion resumes. The buildings are nearly empty now and echo more than usual. These are the things that are striking, since one gets used to a place, as to a routine.

I guide two lorries to the railroad station, then two motorcycles that are loaded on the flat wagons, where everything is secured conscientiously under the vigilant eye of our *Schirrmeister*. In the afternoon our train departs, between loading platforms still heaped with the *matériel* of the companies that will follow or are crowded with the villagers who have come to bid us farewell. There are many girls, for sure, but also those who are not so young and also men whose age still spares them from armed service, at least for the time being.

I have no ties here, at least, not of the sentimental sort. It is easier to depart in that condition. Perhaps I wanted this, subconsciously, if not deliberately? Some trains left before us, others will follow, six in all I believe, today and tomorrow.

They left us at Tcherjakov.

Léon Degrelle called this Rexist rally in the *Palais des Sports* in Brussels during the first furlough of the *Légion*, which began in December 1942.

The end of leave from the Caucasus.

The encampment at Pieske in May 1943.

1 June, 1943 – passage into the *Waffen-SS*.

The passage into the *Waffen-SS*.

11

New Winter Campaign: Tcherkassy

On 11 November, 1943 the *SS-Sturmbrigade Wallonien* heads toward the east. *En route* to who knows where? The weather is gray and cold, with intermittent rain. Decidedly, it is not like our first voyage to the front in 1942! This time, be it noted, the anti-aircraft defense of the train is assured by two 2 cm quadruple *"Flak"* mounted on flat rail wagons. The wagons are equipped with heaters; it is no longer spring. It is indispensable but it takes up space in the center of the wagon, which forces us to crowd into the reduced space. At night it is comfortable enough, for, crowded together, there is less heat lost. During the day it is more annoying, for it is not possible for all of the men to remain squatting in their place for the entire day. During stops we take advantage of the moment to stretch our legs, we flounder through the water and the mud when we leave the ballast.

We pass through Fulda, Eisenach, Erfurt and Dresden. The stops are numerous, and often long. The trains are also numerous, in both directions, which is the reason for our slow progress. There is traffic on the rails by night and day. There are civilian trains, but mostly military trains *en route* to the front or returning, also trains for men on leave. They are, generally, the fastest. We pass Görlitz and pass through Breslau, then southeast toward Kraków and, due east, through Premysl. We ask where we are going, for we know nothing. It takes five or six days to reach Lemberg! Here, Father Christmas, ahead of the calendar, has left winter outfits for us. Felt boots, Balaclava helmets,[1] fur-lined gloves, *"Übermantels"* [winter overcoats]. So the wagon has a bit more in it, for these are all bulky, especially the overcoats and boots. There is white outer clothing, camouflage for the snow, and the rest takes less space. It is a good thing to have all this, for this time it is certain that we will spend the winter in Russia!

We have left Lemberg and are headed south. Will we, perchance, go to the Crimea? Some say so! That would be grand, but who knows? And, in that case, why would we have been issued all this winter gear, which the Crimean climate does not require? In any case, on the 18th or 19th we reach Iasi and Kichinev, then Tiraspol. Could the optimists be right? In that case, so much the better. In any case, we are not far from Odessa. On the scale of Russia, one could say that we are in its suburbs! Alas! Three times alas! Our train makes a hairpin turn and heads back to the north, toward Kiev!

On the 20th or 21st we arrive at Uman, where our itinerary bears a bit to the east. One thing intrigues us now. The sound of artillery fire reaches us as strongly from our right as from our left! The sound increases precisely at the rate that we advance toward the east or northeast. During the night of 22 November our train halts in the Korsun railroad station in the rain, falling snow and a cold wind. In the distance, in the city itself, at various points on the horizon can be seen the red glow of fires. At the very least, thus, we are at the diapasons[2] and there has been no prelude! With

---

1 A Balaclava helmet is a knitted cloth headgear covering the entire head, with only part of the face exposed. Today, it would probably be called a ski-mask.
2 The diapasons are the medium-scaled organ pipes – often prominently featured in the *façades* of pipe organs.

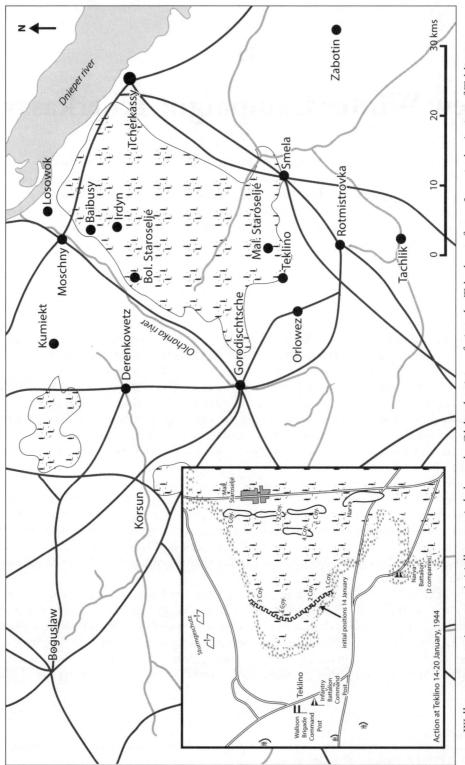

Walloon strongpoints were initially occupied along the Olchanka river – facing the Tcherkassy forest. Inset is the Action of Teklino – 14-20 January, 1944. (Redrawn by George Anderson based upon maps sourced from Doc. F. Hellebaut/Arch. E. de Bruyne)

no preliminaries we are plunged right into the heart of the subject, the center of the action. The train has brought us to this terminal, right near the front.

Detraining commences immediately, in the rain, in the wind, and it is no sinecure. At least, in such a night, the Russian Air Force does not come to welcome us. That is all that would be needed to fill our glass to overflowing. The work of unloading warms us up, except for our fingers, and the rain soaks us, without quenching our thirst. We then move out in infernal mud on a track which, at this point, is no longer even that and which we are taking, for the first time, in the heart of darkness. There is no public street lighting, of course. Do not forget that we are in Russia. I have never seen public street lighting in Russia, but, perhaps, they have it in the big cities. In any case, even if there had been, we are at war and it would be blacked out or out of service. In any case, there is nothing but the slender beam of light from my motorcycle headlamp, itself blacked out, that helps me to see more clearly. There is no more sidewalk to guide us. It is only when one of us falls into the ditch that one can say with certainty that we have left the good road. Fortunately, the stage of the march is not long, even if it does take hours, and we halt to get some rest in a village named Arbousino.

On the morning of 23 November we resume our journey, our second, or better put, our second mud bath! It astonishes me that mud baths are supposed to be good for the health! One would think that, at present, our motorization would make the task less difficult. In principle, it should do so, but you shall soon see that it does nothing of the kind, and I can assure you that the lorries and all this motorized equipment is much harder to push than our primitive "*panjewagon*"! We did not think of this when we were issued all of this fine *matériel*. It is not for nothing that one speaks of heavy equipment. Ah! If we had only had this *matériel* in the summer of 1942!

Some vehicles pass without problems, but those that follow find themselves facing a rutted road, and one must remember that all these vehicles are heavily loaded, and that some are towing artillery. The tracked vehicles tow it well, with a few exceptions, and then return to pull those out of the mud that did not. In brief, we are soon covered with a layer of mud from head to toe. We even slip inside our boots, where this treacle has infiltrated, for in the places where the lorries get bogged, the mud is often knee-deep, if not more, when one puts his foot in a hole. The "*Zugmaschinen*" [prime movers], which are big tracked vehicles that can transport an entire platoon, work like mad! These tracked mastodons also pull the 8.8 cm "*Flak*", our great anti-aircraft guns, and are the guardian angels of these helpless columns, marching in this universe of mud. The soil is a clay-loam, heavy and impermeable, which does not allow the rain to infiltrate and prevents drainage, a clay similar to what is used by sculptors to rough out their works, and soon we look like their rough statues, for we are covered with mud. We flounder, we slip, we swim in this filth! And, furthermore, if only it was just ourselves! But no, we must push the vehicles that are in trouble, and brace ourselves in this mud, find a firm footing to support our effort! Few of us have not fallen flat, two or three times at least, in this cold and glutinous mass that insinuates everywhere, right to the skin, under our clothes. Happily, I have my motorcyclist's oilskin greatcoat.

My *BMW* side-car, driven by two wheels, makes pretty good progress, like the *Volkswagen* "*Kübel*" or the "*Schwimmwagon*" [amphibious *Volkswagen*], except when the mud is deeper than 50 to 60 cm, but is totally incapable of carrying heavy weights. Thus everyone leaves his vehicle to help the big ones and takes upon himself the hardest work. The "*Zugmaschinen*" return in their tracks, having towed the guns that they pull farther on, and pull the other vehicles from their bad situations.

When I regain my motorcycle, my feet, my entire body covered with mud, the handgrips, the saddle, the entire machine has the air of a clay sculpture. Not all of the sections of our march are this bad, but none are good. Later, we enter the Beloserjé woods. The track takes a new form, less mud bat large surfaces that are under water. Here the German pioneers have built a corduroy road for hundreds of meters of round logs taken from the woods. In places these round logs float and sink 30 or 40, even 50 cm into the water when one treads on them or under the wheels of the vehicles. But they are secured to each other and remain solidly together. I note that this track in the woods has blockhouses and bunkers, also of round logs, scattered along it every 100 or 200 meters, sometimes more, sometimes less, to function as the tie-points of the road. Certainly, this is not without good reason. In the distance, the artillery has resumed its fire. In this regard, I have repeatedly noticed something curious: quite often it is only at the moment when the fire resumes after a period of calm that one notices that it stopped for a while. One gets used to anything, even in such matters! One notices when the fire opens up, then one gets used to it, but one is not conscious of the moment when it ceases.

The moment that we leave the forest there is a big market town in front of us, it is Beloserjé, which we pass through. Troops are billeted everywhere. We leave the village and we are out on the steppe again. The sector is a bit rolling, but the hills are modest. Some sections of our route are still very difficult, others less so when the relief is sloping or a bit more elevated. On the afternoon of the 23rd we reach the village of Baibusy, a little elevated in comparison with its surroundings. My company, the headquarters company, will settle down here. The other elements of the brigade, which arrived before us, are already settled. The cantonments that we are assigned are northeast of the village, and I waste no time reporting there.

12

Our Second Campaign:
My First Winter

The *isba* that is assigned to me at Baibusy is at the edge of the steppe, isolated from the others. Like all of the *isbas*, its door faces west. Thirty meters to the northeast is the closest habitation, 100 meters in the same direction is the one that houses the commander of my *compagnie*, *Capitaine* Anthonissen. The nearest neighbors to the north are a bit more than 50 meters distant, partially enclosed by a bit of hedge and a few little posts and rails, a good meter high. To the west is the road, a mud track, grooved by hundreds of ruts, that passes through the village.

I recover my kit from one of the lorries, throw it in my side-car and go to put it in my *isba*. Like all the others it is a makeshift cob-wall structure, covered with a sort of straw that is not thatch. The *isba* is infested with lice, shabby, like all its neighbors. Ten meters to the left is a little building, even more makeshift, which seems to shelter a not-so-numerous flock of poultry and a few cords of firewood. Below, 10 or 15 meters from the house, is the well with the typical well-sweep, one end on the ground, the other pointing toward the sky, seeming to indicate a point in the heavens.

I knock and I enter, meeting all the miasmas, all the malodorous effluvia that suffocate you and surprise you, even though they are habitual. It is a mixture of odors of cabbage, unrefined and unrefrigerated sunflower oil, of humid soot when the "*pitzki*" (stove) is not fired up and of the fire when it is lit. The smell of sweat mixes with all this, not the result of any sort of work, and the smell of the livestock in the adjoining room. I enter and close the door. *Eh*! *bien*, believe me, you get used to it after a while. I don't say that you do not smell it, just that it only strikes you on occasion, or after you have been outdoors for some time.

In front of me there is a bundle of rags, about 1 meter 60 centimeters tall, surmounted by a white scarf. When I look closer I discover a woman's face, an ageless face. Later I will learn that she is about 30 years old. At the window is the face of a woman of 45 years, at least. Beside her is a kid of seven or eight. She calls him Cola. I infer that his name is Nicolas. He wears a sort of *chapka* [Russian hat], even indoors. I think that most of them sleep in their *chapka*. When the youngster takes off his hat I see that his head has been recently shaved, but that his brown hair is already emerging. Both of them have their feet and legs wrapped in old rags or jute cut from old sacks. This spectacle is the same everywhere.

They give me a friendly greeting, with a little timid smile. Out of courtesy I ask where her husband is, the "*pan*". She replies, evasively, "*Woina*", the war. I deduce from that that he must be a soldier, but you never know. I set down my things and arrange them in a corner. I indicate to the *mamka* that I would like to shave, and, as usual, I am offered a glass of water. I quickly set out to explain to her that I need at least 100 times that much, and hot, to boot. Twenty minutes later the water is boiling on the "*pitzki*" and she puts the long, low washbasin, carved from a tree trunk, in the middle of the room. She pours the hot water in it. I add cold water, exhausting at one time at least a week's worth of her reserve of water.

I start to undress, but she does not budge. I warn her that I am going to strip completely. She smiles and remains where she is. In actual fact, it was the same during my first campaign, why should it be any different today? I put my feet in the washbasin and sit down. She then approaches, takes my soap and starts to carefully wash me, without the slightest embarrassment, totally at ease. She is delighted with the scent of my soap, its sweetness. It is, however, the wartime soap of the supply service, green, and it floats in the water. I, myself, never noticed that this sort of soap had any particular scent, and I offer it to her. When she has finished soaping me she rinses me off with a glass and then dries my back, then handing me the towel for me to take care of the other side. She is very happy that I gave her the soap and indicates it to me by bowing her head. I get dressed, but the legs of my muddy pants are not yet dry. I scraped off what I could. It will dry overnight. When my body is clean, I feel that my soul is, too!

I go back out and leave on foot, leaving my motorcycle in front of the *isba*, since I am not going far, two houses farther up, where the *capitaine* is staying. I report and place myself at his command. He tells me to return for orders in an hour. I take advantage of this time to visit the adjoining *isbas* and see who is staying there. I find other men of the motorcycle platoon and also of the *TTR* [*troupes de transmissions*, signal troops], *Adjudant* Lentiez, *Sergent* Winandy and their men. An hour later I report again to the *capitaine's* house, where I meet *Sergent* De Meersman, of the armory. I am told to go back to Korsun to find a part of the convoy which arrived late, in particular the two lorries of the armory.

Night, or, at least, darkness, is approaching when I set out. I head toward Beloserjé, and, *en route*, I slip, I slide, I skid. I change ruts, rather by chance, thinking I will sink in less here on the right, but then, farther on, it is the left that seems more practicable, for no particular reason, simply "by guess". I come across several vehicles, both ours and the Germans, even mechanized chaps who prefer to transform themselves to infantry, but not the lorries I am looking for. I discover one of the two in Beloserjé and encourage it to set out toward Baibusy. I then continue toward Korsun and, three or four kilometers from the village, despite the noise of my motorcycle, I here shouts at the same time as I make out the slender beams of blacked-out headlamps. The light is faint, but enough to give me the impression of a lake, indeed, an ocean of mud that seems even worse than it was this morning. The water has not ceased to flow into this low point over the hours. I hesitate to proceed, but, all the same, I advance another 1-200 meters before stopping. I leave my motorcycle there and, using my service electric torch, I set out on foot toward the vehicles. The mud has re-entered my boots before I get there. At the start I took precautions, rendered futile at present. Nevertheless, I make no bones about getting there.

There are at least 20 vehicles there, German and "*Bourguignons*", and among them is the second vehicle that I am looking for. I try to help, I let the fellows know that I am going to send them semi-tracked vehicles, "*Zugmaschinen*", and I take the road back to Baibusy. When I arrive it is past 0100 hours in the morning. I go to wake up the *capitaine's* orderly and the *capitaine* at the same time. I can thereby confirm that he wears pyjamas, that these actually do still exist and that he has been able to keep them with him to this point. I ask him for authorization to send the "*Zugmaschinen*" to help the fellows in the steppe, to which he agrees with no difficulty. I then report to the northeast exit of the village where, this afternoon, I saw the vehicles concentrated. A guard points out where *Schirrmeister* Fuchs, the *chef du matériel*, lodges and I wake him in his turn. He gets up, gets dressed and goes to wake some drivers, himself. As for myself, I return to my own lodgings. I have awakened enough of the world for one night.

I do not knock before entering, for I tell myself that my hostess is asleep. I enter without making a sound and light my electric torch. There is no one in the room, but something stirs on the "*pitzki*", behind the chimney. There is soft talking. There seem to be more people than before. A shadow emerges, and I shine my light on it. It is the *mamka*, but there are other shadows behind her. I make out two old people: a man and a woman. The *mamka* gets down off the stove, lifts her petticoats and pulls out a heap of old rags. I ask myself what she wants when she holds the rags out at arm's length to me. Good people, sensitive souls, you can skip the next few lines! She draws my attention to the rags that she shows me and I shine my lamp on them. They are full of blood! I tell myself that she is wounded, that I must do something, find Caufrier, one of our medics! I try to find out what has happened, but my Russian vocabulary is extremely limited. It has been a year since I have had any practice. I do not know if I have understood what she wants to tell me, or if I have guessed, but it all quickly becomes clear to me. She is simply menstruating!

But why did she show me all this? I ask myself if she is afraid of being raped and wishes to dissuade me from so doing? Anything is possible. At the very least, maybe she did not immediately recognize me and thought she had to deal with someone else, perhaps a Russian. Perhaps at some time or another during the night the partisans who live a celibate life in the adjoining forests come here to find the pleasure that they are denied in the woods. I certainly hope that she did not for a minute believe that I could not resist her charms. Tomorrow I must make her understand that she does not run the slightest risk!

When I finally stretch out on the ground, rolled up in my blankets, it is close to 0300 hours in the morning. I will wash tomorrow, or, to put it better, a little later. When I wake up it must be 0800 hours. The old people have disappeared. My hostess explains later that, in these times, she does not dare to remain alone in the house at night. I go to the well, myself, to get water to wash and shave, and at the same time, refill the *mamka's* stock of water, and she washes my back once more – after which I report to *Capitaine* Anthonissen. He thanks me for my mission of yesterday and of that night. What courtesy, what politeness, and he congratulates me. All of the vehicles arrived safe and sound. He entrusts me with the office of "*Divisions-Kradmelder*" [division motor-cycle messenger] – and my duties: communications with the division headquarters and, of course, all of the other duties of the staff motorcyclist. Henceforth I will make the Baibusy – Beloserjé (or some other) shuttle practically every day, at times, twice a day or at night. Tomorrow morning I shall drive the *capitaine* to Beloserjé.

The next morning, at about 0900 hours, he takes his place in my side-car and looks at me, saying, "Attention, no mud on me!" I look at him in my turn, incredulous, and swallow my saliva! Before we have even left the village I tell him that I cannot promise to reach Beloserjé today, since I have to moderate my speed to avoid splashing him. At that very moment I see the first spots of mud on his face. He throws me a severe look, but says, right away, "Good, get going!" I did not count the spots of mud upon our arrival at the headquarters, but he had quite a few. He never again made that sort of remark when I drove him places, for he realized, no doubt, that when he comes with me it is because his own vehicle cannot take him, or he needs to get someplace, whether it is because there is too much mud or that it is a place that is inaccessible in a vehicle. It is true that I only had to drive him four or five times, as well as, several times, later, to tour the defensive positions at Baibusy, and the bunkers built by our pioneers west of the Olchanka. That day, however, there was snow. Today we still live in the realm of mud!

In the sector that we occupy there is practically no defensive construction, aside from a few little sections of muddy trenches filled with water. Our pioneers, about 70 in number, have enough to do building bunkers reinforced with tree trunks cut in the forest. By day, they saw up the round logs and prepare the work. At night they build their fortifications. This is the only rational way to organize their work, for the Russians can see everything and shell it with their artillery. They have the strategic advantage and are safe from observation in the forest of Tcherkassy on the other side of the Olchanka, a little river about 15 meters wide, sometimes a bit more, sometimes a bit less. All of our positions, on the other hand, are exposed, echeloned in the steppe, facing the river, which enters the Dniepr northeast of Baibusy.

This forest of Tcherkassy is filled to the brim with enemy troops. Previously there was an important drop of Russian paratroops in the region, which the German troops in the sector vigorously pursued, causing them enormous losses. Several thousand of them joined the partisans that were already there. At the moment of which I speak, the regular forces had linked up with them, which meant there were a lot of troops facing us, but the regular army was mostly toward the south, around the actual city of Tcherkassy. That is to say that the Russians have all the advantages, both strategic and in numbers, of which they have always had the latter.

What is most curious here is that the villagers tell us much about the troops facing us, which on the other hand, are themselves aided by the villagers, perhaps the same ones that give us information! That is something that is hard to understand. For it is certain that these men of the woods spend every night in Baibusy, restock their provisions and get information, no doubt both at the same time. Things have reached a point where it is decided to evacuate all the genuine residents of the village to the rear. Thus it is that one night the men of the brigade are chosen to search all the village for them and assemble them. In the morning I am astonished to find how many men are in Baibusy! I have seen very few until now, and, from that, I deduce that they have avoided notice. They are directed to the rear with their bundles and food for the journey.

The first snow falls before mid-December, and, for the first time, I see the country completely covered in white. Frost hardens the ground; movements are less painful and more rapid. Every day now it is necessary to break the ice on the wells with the help of a pickaxe to get water, and I take care of this to spare the poor *mamka* this work, for which she thanks me. When the layer of ice is too thick, I throw in a grenade, which I have had to do two or three times. Often I also take advantage of a few free moments to restock the woodpile, for the *mamka* has a hard time doing this. It is true that the edge of the axe cuts little better than the back! To do this I borrowed an axe from the armory, and I work miracles in this domain, and, furthermore, the exercise warms me up.

My life is thus divided between the tasks of a warrior and domestic tasks, whenever I find the time. In my *isba* the foodstuffs are held in common, we share the food. The *panianka* [mother of the house], one also sometimes says the *kasaika*, the kid and me, eat German bread and *le bordj à la russe*. For the most part, my jam goes to the kid, as with my candy, the "drops" or the chocolate, when we get it. I save a little for myself. Sometimes Nicolas manages to make me angry because he eats it all at one time. One time I catch him in the act with candy in his hand. He dares to say that it isn't true, but I see that he has the look of a dog that has been beaten and, in spite of myself, I feel sorry for him and almost feel that I am in the wrong! He has never received sweets before, at least from other soldiers before me. He had to go through a war to eat them, or even to know of their existence!

The rations we receive are very suitable, and my Russian hosts accommodate themselves very well to them. They like the change from the ordinary, as I like the Russian specialties that I taste. Certain preparations, if I may put it this way, are at times quite acceptable. As I watch the *panianka* attend to her duties I feel as if I am reliving the age of the cavemen or am in the heart of a primitive tribe at the source of the Amazon, setting aside the climate, of course! To boil her cabbages (*kapustas*) she has a sort of wooden handle, like a rake handle, that ends in a sort of S-shaped piece of metal. Then, for at least an hour, she crushes two or three cabbages thrown in a wooden trough with this rudimentary instrument. The cabbage is then cooked in water with salt and will be served, mixed in the soup, or enriched with a few morsels of lard or meat. She also prepares ahead of time a sort of millet, which she husks, for hours, in the bottom of the trough with the help of a wooden pestle. When cooked in water, she will strain it carefully and poor it into the earthenware pots. Finally, as needed, it is taken out with a wooden spoon. It is put in the *bordj*, one adds the meat, one can also reheat it with milk and make of it a sort of *crème* or *soupe au lait*.

A roughly-squared wooden table, a bench, a rustic stool, Oh, such abundance! A set of shelves. There you have it, all the furniture, then they sleep on the "*pitzki*". A cauldron or two, two or three earthenware pots, a pan, one or two wooden spoons, a knife, a tub to wash the laundry and one or two others, also wooden, to pound or crush the foodstuffs, when they are not the same ones that serve for all purposes. That is the entire household! Ah! I almost forgot the wooden bucket to bring water from the well. But sometimes a single bucket serves several dwellings. All the same, you will never convince me that all these necessary or indispensable things for a household, utensils or furniture, have been worn out or deteriorated in two years of war! Nor the clothes. No, there have never been more, and what remains often dates from the time of the Tsars. The revolution has brought them nothing!

I have seen even poorer households, and some, though quite rare, that are a little better equipped. A cow, a dozen chickens and three or four ducks, that is their entire fortune, though their most precious treasure is the one or another icon that has survived the ages, the purges and the revolution. There are millions of such households; it is the entire Ukraine, nearly all of Russia, and it is all alike. Farther south or to the southeast I have sometimes met people that were better off, but barely. As for the land itself, it is always the great Russia, and many of us still cherish the nostalgia. The steppe is immense and marvelous under its mantel of white when the sun makes it infinitely iridescent! It is mysterious and oppressive when the fog or the rain hides the horizon. But always it fascinates. That is why I so love my duty, which is to furrow the country in all weather, in all conditions, alone on my motorcycle.

On 13 December, in the last hours of the night, a patrol of the *1st Compagnie* under the young but brilliant *Lieutenant* van Eyser, embarks on the inflatable rubber rafts of the pioneers and crosses the Olchanka river. They are 30 men whose mission is to reconnoiter behind the Russian lines, where our aviation has reported a partisan camp and a significant concentration of tanks. On the other bank the men of the patrol disappear, vanishing in silence. Protected by their white camouflage they blend perfectly into the snow-covered countryside. In the evening my *TTR* [signals] friends give me disturbing news, which has quickly made the rounds of the cantonments and positions. The van Eyser operation has turned into a catastrophe! Of the 30 men, only eight made it back to our lines, and four of those were seriously wounded! There was a mistake in orientation and they were surrounded by a multitude of partisans and others, including many women. They defended themselves with great courage, but that was not enough. *Lieutenant* van Eyser was among the first to fall, *Caporal-Chef* Bataille threw himself on a grenade to avoid being captured alive by the Russians. When *sous-Officier* Decamp fell in his turn, there was only one non-commissioned officer left! The eight survivors, and, especially, the four seriously wounded, required the courage of desperation and the will to survive no matter what in order to break contact and make it back to our lines. After wandering for two days behind enemy lines, two other survivors reached our positions at Mochny. They had not eaten or slept since the patrol departed and had to crawl for two days to slip through the net without being discovered! Ten out of the 30 made it back!

After hearing the accounts of the survivors, it appears that the drama originated from the excessive boldness of two or three of the group, over and above the error in their itinerary. Their mission was reconnaissance and, if possible, to bring back prisoners. They were not to fire except in extreme emergency and only in self-defense and to disengage. However, it seems that some of them attacked a bunker from the rear, thus alerting the entire partisan colony. They showed great courage, but orders are sacred. We lost 20 comrades to an excess of combativeness, to too much bravery!

It is a very curious winter that we are experiencing here. The periods of freeze and thaw alternate in succession. The temperature ranges from −20°, −25°, even one night of −27° [−4, −13, −16°F] in a few days, if not in a matter of hours, to thaw and rain, and then immediately dropping to −15° [5°F]. It snows again and adds to the accumulation that has not had time to melt. At times it reaches 50-60 cm. Two days of thaw and the circulation of vehicles reduces the snowpack to 20 cm of frozen snow and an ice rink that allows me beautiful skids without having to worry about traffic. Thus there are days where the only vehicles that can get about are tracked vehicles and a few motorcycles.

On 22 December I learn that this night a strong contingent of the brigade is going to attempt another audacious *coup de main* against the village of Irdyn, south of Baibusy. The next day, in the afternoon, I learn that the operation was entirely successful and some comrades of the *3rd Compagnie*, who arrive at Baibusy, coming from Bolchoï Staroseljé, tell me of the exploit. The *2nd* and *3rd Compagnies*, with an attached squad of pioneers armed with flame throwers, penetrated the zone occupied by the Russians, crossing a partially frozen swamp, wading calf-deep. The Russians, doubtless thinking themselves well protected by this natural obstacle, did not watch it, and the *"Bourguignons"* were thus able to bypass the village and attack it from the rear. The surprised Russians fought, nevertheless, but the survivors finally had to fall back before the furious assaults of the *"Bourguignons"*, who then set the village ablaze with the flame throwers. As evening fell they returned by the same route through the swamps. German assault-guns (*Sturmgeschütze*) that had accompanied them at the start of their mission, but which had been unable to accompany them farther due to the nature of the terrain, were waiting for them on the other side of the swamp. These tracked assault guns were able to cover their return with their fire. Irdyn, which was always a bastion, is destroyed, an enemy strongpoint that can no longer menace us from the south. We lost three killed and seven wounded.

You can be sure that, every day, patrols and *coups de main* by the brigade succeeded each other, and that the brigade thus rapidly acquired an excellent reputation with the *Waffen-SS*. The cold is brisk on this Christmas Eve and the clear, brilliant moon drives the shadows from the silent steppe. In the *isba* we keep the fire burning and, on the primitive table I spread out my paper and I do my best to write home. The *karasinka* barely illuminates my sheet of paper, which I slide up against the base of the lamp if I am to see at all. The slightest draft makes the flame flicker, and I must wait for it to stabilize before I resume my writing. It is, in fact, a corn stalk bathed in oil, and it gives scant light. I put on paper the things that one does not say, that discretion prevents me from sharing with my friends, with my comrades. When I take a break and then return, I see my shadow, distorted and flickering on the wall, extending on the ceiling, this ceiling where the flies wander that are attracted by the chickens that walk around in the adjoining room.

Suddenly I see myself again in the same situation, but more than a thousand kilometers from here, in Koubano – Armianski, in the heart of the Caucasus, in September 1942! Just like today, I was writing by the light of a similar oil lamp that cast my shadow in identical fashion, but it was still summer there. So long as I remained motionless, the ceiling and the upper part of the walls seemed painted black, the room plunged in silence. But when I made a gesture that was a little bit abrupt, or when I straightened up, the entire room started to move, the whitewash on the ceiling and the walls appeared anew and the buzzing of the flies filled the air... It was, in fact, the thousands of flies that lit on and covered the upper portions of the room. The slightest gesture disturbed them and they took off, filling the *isba* with the sound of their swarm. It was insane, incredible at first, but, as I said, one gets used to anything. In the morning one opens the door and the woman, shaking a corn stalk with its leaves, chases 95 percent of them out. They calmly return when the doors are opened and, in the evening, they are all back at home, not a one missing.

They are there today, but far less of them, comparatively, for it is winter. I have no desire to celebrate Christmas and volunteer to stand guard this night. That will allow a comrade to rest or to celebrate, if he wishes. I think that I have a good life, at least I like what I am doing, so I should be pretty good. At about 2200 hours someone knocks on my door and Auguste D. is framed in the door opening. I find Auguste to be a bit original. A good man, big and stalwart, but a bit round-shouldered, lanky. He must be between 35 and 40 years old. I think that he told me he has several kids, two daughters, I think. I remember that at Wildflecken I was always astonished at the length of the letters that he received and I asked him if he conceived his children by mail. He smiled blissfully, but don't be fooled. He came from the Charleroi region where he was an engineer.

One day, smiling as usual, he showed me one of these letters, no less than three pages. It was the household accounts! He explained to me in all seriousness that he did not allow the women the freedom to spend the money carelessly. I also remember another story where Auguste made me laugh. Perched on his motorcycle, ready to leave for one errand or another, he saw me and, with a vibrant "*Au Chef*" [to the chief], waving his left hand, he gave it the gas with his right, but more than he should have. His motorcycle reared up, tossing the great Auguste to the ground, tangled in his *accoutrements*, and his motorcycle finished by leaping a good 20 meters further! Otherwise, even when he was rolling, with his long legs, one always had the impression that his feet were still dragging on the ground.

We go to stand guard together. Since the temperature is –25° [–7°F] I put on my overcoat over my motorcyclist's waterproof and put on my felt boots. The cold assaults us on the doorstep. We set out on the road that passes through the village, 10 meters from my *isba* as we march with care, there where the snow is not well packed, for there are no nails on the soles of the felt boots, and the road is terribly slippery. Hands in pockets, in spite of the fur-lined gloves, submachine gun on my shoulder. Auguste, himself, happily armed with a rifle. We amble on, side by side, talking in a low voice through the chin-piece of our Balaclava helmets, for the cold is bitter and dries the throat, and the last nasal hairs. When we stop a moment in silence, we hear the freezing! The snow crunches even when we do not step on it. Dry crunching comes from everywhere, the joists of the houses, the trees, the bushes, the wood of the fences, everything cracks and groans, everything seems to suffer from the cold. The sky is clear and filled with stars, the moonlight makes shadows, as clear as those made by the sun; it is so bright! The snow sparkles marvelously under such bright rays. When, at the end of the footpath between the *isbas*, we reach the steppe, it looks to us like a sea of black, stretching to infinity! Before us, on the left, a black void, it is the edge of the forest, a few hundred meters distant. We contemplate this fairytale spectacle in admiration, despite the cold. We resume marching, for in such weather one gets cold quickly and needs to warm up quickly. We march, always elbow to elbow, when, suddenly, Auguste loses his balance and slips. A bullet whistles past my left ear! It does not miss me by much! – But Auguste! Are you crazy or what? You haven't engaged the safety! I just told you not to hold your rifle like that, with your finger on the trigger, and, on top of all this, through the cloth of your pocket! Auguste lies there looking at me and smiling in an angelic or idiotic manner, make your choice. I look at him in the moonlight, as in full daylight. I give him a good bawling out and my anger subsides. I have neither the desire or take pleasure in getting angry.

We resume our round, but it is a good half-hour before either of us speaks a word. That is how one can be stupidly killed by a careless buddy, at more than 1,000-2,000 meters from the actual front line! A little later, we take turns in entering my *isba*, which is right on our route, to warm up a bit, our gloved hands right on the earthen wall of the stove, our backside sitting on top of it, avoiding, of course, the cast-iron plate in the center. For this brief instant the other keeps watch outside, observing the surroundings.

When, at about midnight, having resumed our march in the meantime, we find ourselves east of the village, a growling, then, more perceptibly, the sound of artillery fire comes distinctly from behind us. We turn around immediately and see light, to the east or northeast, like lightning. They are not very distinct, for the sky is clear, but the sound of the explosions is definite, and they get louder. What is happening? Are the Russians attacking? It is entirely possible, for it is well within their accustomed behavior. We hold our breath, we pause for a moment. As the firing continues we go back to the northeast of the village to better see from there what is happening, but also to get closer to a source of information, that is, the *isba* of the company commander and the *TTR*, the communications people who are in a position to listen to the messages of all our outpost units. The firing diminishes in intensity and, when we arrive at the captain's *isba*, our relief is there. It is waiting for us. They know no more than we do about what is going on, and Auguste and I each return to our respective lodgings. The uncertainty, the lack of news, tends to put me ill at ease. I do not want to be surprised asleep, for, in fact, Russian tanks crossing the Olchanka could easily be here in less than 10 minutes. All the same, I end up falling asleep quickly.

In the morning someone knocks at my door. It is a pioneer sent to me by the *capitaine*. I must drive him to Gorodischtsche where he needs to have two mine detectors repaired. I am to pick him up in half an hour in front of the company office. At 0830 I meet Rémy in front of the command post and we place the detectors in the side-car. He takes his place on the rattle-trap. At that moment *Capitaine* Anthonissen comes out of the office. Don't go off like that, he tells me. Mount an *LMG* (light machine gun) on the side-car mounting. I am not going to dispute an order. I well know that this is not done, but I can't help saying, "You know, *mon commandant*, that I have already passed through these woods at least 30 times, and nearly every time alone, even at night, and I have never had a machine gun!"

"Go to the armorers and mount a machine gun there!"

"*Oui, commandant!*"

Half an hour later we leave Baibusy, Rémy very ill at ease in the side-car encumbered with the mine detectors, the machine gun loaded with a belt, two ammunition boxes tied onto the back of the side-car. We cross the steppe that leads to Beloserjé and take the road that passes through the woods toward Drabovka and Derenkowez. We soon arrive at the corduroy section of the road. Despite the intense cold of the preceding night, which dropped again to at least −10°, −12° [14°F, 10°F] and despite the sun, there are always some difficult sections where the thin layer of ice has given way under the wheels of the vehicles that went before us. These are the places where the soil is peaty.

Except for one or another, where signs of life are apparent, most of the bunkers that are scattered along the road appear to be empty. From others, we receive friendly greetings. Look there, Rémy, ahead, to the left a lorry is stopped. But it is damaged! It is one of ours! It has our emblems. *Bon Dieu*, what has happened? Tires shredded or torn off, axles bent, wood broken, metal parts twisted! I dismount to look closer. The lorry is unoccupied, empty, nobody around. We move on.

"In my opinion, Rémy, it has run on a mine. I can see no other explanation! Hurry up and get those things fixed that you have there. They might be useful for our return!"

In the distance it gets lighter among the trees, the end of the forest. Soon we will be out on the steppe again, then Derenkowez. But what is happening? All of a sudden the motorcycle slows down, it is in trouble. I give it gas, but in vain! It is not the condition of the road that is the cause, nor the mud, nor the snow. I disengage the clutch and shift to neutral; I dismount. I do not really know a great deal about mechanical things. I look at it, I tinker with it a bit, I pull on the wires, I take out a sparkplug and thereby discover that the engine is abnormally hot, and smell burnt oil. Ah! S**t! I am out of oil! What should I do? There is no one in sight. Should I wait? A vehicle could pass by in 10 minutes, but I might also wait two days! The edge of the woods is not far, for sure, but the vicinity is not reassuring. The empty bunkers, the truck that ran on a mine. I must take all these into account. A great many partisans or others infest these woods, regularly set mines here, sometimes attack units or convoys that pass through it. That is why there are the bunkers. So far, I have always had luck, passing through these woods with no problems. Doubtless a single man does not interest them and is not worth triggering an alert. That must be why, until now, I have always passed through this forest with no trouble! Rémy releases the catch that prevents the machine gun from swinging on its pivot, he pulls the operating handle back a few times to open the breech block and makes sure that the grease is not frozen, but everything seems in good order. It is better to be prepared than to be surprised in an emergency that it does not function, if one even has the time to be astonished at that moment.

I remount the motorcycle and kick the starter: the engine turns over! Not without difficulty, but it turns. Now it is a matter of going slowly and stopping the engine every time before it gets too hot. Fortunately, it is cold. We stop every 300-400 meters and, each time, I give the engine time to cool down. The low temperature today helps us. Finally we get to Derenkowez. I ask the Germans whom we meet. No! No *Werkstatt*, no workshop. But there is one at Gorodischtsche, they tell me. Good, there is no other solution, we have to get there. But, as we slowly make our way forward, I sense that the motor is having more and more trouble, we have to stop more and more frequently and for ever-increasing amounts of time. Finally the pistons refuse to move at all, they are stuck, like us, it has had it! Even Nabokow, two to three kilometers before Gorodischtsche, is not yet in sight. There are still at least 10 to 12 kilometers before we reach our destination.

Thank God, or I don't know who, a lorry approaches and stops. The comrade of the *Wiking* division will tow me. Less than half an hour later, he stops in front of a *Wiking* workshop, motorcycle broken down and the same for the mine detectors. An *Unterscharführer* [sergeant] in mechanic's clothes approaches us and I explain my problem to him. Good, they will see what they can do. Leave the motorcycle and return tomorrow evening. He tells us where we have to take the mine detectors and we go there right away. After that we look for lodging, but not without difficulty, for the town is full to the gills. We finally find bed and board. The following morning we report to a "*Schreibstube*" (company office) where we ask them to let our unit know so that they do not worry about us. In the evening the work is not finished and we spend another night here. The following day we are able to head back at about 1000 hours in the morning. All the same, the mechanics worked quickly. If I fully understand, they had to replace the cylinders and piston-rings and rebore the engine.

As we head back the sun is shining and it isn't so cold. We pass through Nabokow and take the same route that we came by rather than changing our route via Bolchoï – Staroseljé. I do not know that route as well and I do not know what condition it is in. But I do know that from Bolchoï – Staroseljé to Staroseljé it is hardly more than a footpath. I have gone that way once or twice. So I choose Derenkowez, then the forest and the corduroy road. The lorry is no longer there. We get to Beloserjé, or nearly, for the motor suddenly breaks down again, just as before! Now what! This is downright unbelievable! I don't wait. I stop immediately and determine that there is not a drop of oil in the crankcase, once more! What sort of a f**k-up is this? Did someone forget? This is inexcusable! Was there an oil leak at a joint? Anything is possible, but I get angry. I should have checked the oil level before leaving, but who would imagine such a thing? It just came out of the shop. I shall long remember this mission! We slowly move on toward Beloserjé. We have just passed the last bunker before exiting the forest when we hear a fusillade behind us, but far off! I stop a moment and we scan the forest in the direction of the bunker, but we see nothing from here. In any case, the firing comes from much farther away! We see nothing and move on. You don't try to do anything with a motorcycle in this condition.

As we go through Beloserjé I make a slight detour to the division headquarters, where I report the firing. When we leave I see one of our lorries. It belongs to our company *fourrier* [quartermaster sergeant]. I ask Lux, a fellow from the Tournai area, to give me a tow, and that is how we get back to Baibusy, where Lux tows us to the vehicle park. I explain, totally crestfallen, our difficulties to *Schirrmeister* Fuchs. He tells me to leave my motorcycle and to come back here tomorrow morning at 0800 hours. I then go to report to *Capitaine* Anthonissen, but I dread this a bit. He listens to me with a severe air, which is habitual for him, but he does not blame me at all. On the other hand, his orderly, Derzelles, does that for the captain, and that idiot proves to be most disagreeable. But what right does he have? Also, I let him know at least as severely what he can do about it. I have often observed this phenomenon, that an orderly tends to assimilate the rank of the one he serves! That may impress some, but not me!

When I get up the next morning, at about 0700 hours, it freezes anew enough to crack stone, −17°? -20°? [0°, −4°F] At 0800 hours I report to the *Schirrmeister* and am directed to my motor-cycle, which is under the shelter of the roof constructed specially so that they can work on vehicles even if it rains or snows. It is a simple roof, set on posts, open to all the winds! When the blizzard blows the snow blows in under this roof just as freely as the wind. What's more, it is built on the high ground northeast of the village, to the right of the road from Mochny, just before the *kolk-hose*. There is a great barrel where the waste oil burns so that the mechanics can warm their hands every now and then. It burns well and intensely, but one cannot feel the heat even a meter away, you must really hold your hands 50 centimeters from the flame to feel any warmth. I notice that to start diesel vehicles they burn straw, and even the soil, under the engines.[1]

The *Schirrmeister* gives me a mechanic, and it is the same one who translated the technical terms for me that I could not translate, myself, into French at Kraków. He is a very polite boy and, in addition, an excellent mechanic, and, what courage! It is necessary to work in gloves, there is no choice, but do not, for a moment, think that this prevents cold hands. Furthermore, it is very difficult [to work in gloves] but indispensable. The slightest contact of skin with a metal part or a tool that is not protected with a wooden handle or some other insulating material, and your skin adheres to the metal and remains frozen to it. When the frozen sore warms up in a more temperate location, you jump through the ceiling, you curse the entire earth, for the pain is insufferable! All it takes is one moment of inattention, but, despite everything, something will surprise one at some point, despite all the warnings and reminders! We work like this all morning in the wind, in the cold. I am frozen, even my feet in my felt boots. That does not happen when we march. I lean over, I straighten up, but only my hands work. Just before noon, everything is disassembled and left to soak. I hasten to go and get something to eat, and my friend Drion brings me a formidable, and quite hot, one-dish meal. My two hands hold my mess tin tightly, warming up quickly, and my fingers tingle like a new form of torture. But the pain subsides, as does my hunger. This soup does good things for me!

When I return to the shop at about 1330 hours, Fuchs tells me that I can go back to my quarters. The mechanics will carry on from here. I cannot be of any help to them. Out of sympathy I stay near my comrades and determine that this brave *Schirrmeister* has no fear of working in any sort of weather. For me, this is the image of true heroism, of everyday heroism, one of the innumerable facets of humble heroism! Let us never forget it!

When I return to my quarters I meet Drion and *Adjudant* Deravet, who accompanies me at my invitation. I did well, for when I enter "*chez moi*", I find there a brood of young girls, visiting neighbors. They are singing when we arrive, accompanied by a balalaïka, and we immediately ask them to continue. They sing these nostalgic airs very well, extremely beautiful melodies that well reflect the Slavic soul, that harmonize well with the country, the climate, with our situation. It all is an atmosphere that we remember perfectly. When they pause for an instant, it is to munch the *chemiskis* (roasted sunflower seeds), hundreds of whose husks already litter the ground. We drink tea and offer candies to this improvised choir. A beautiful afternoon follows a less agreeable morning. Whatever we are doing, that is not what we are here for, and I cannot help but think of those who are toiling to maintain the vehicles of the brigade.

---

1   Straw or petrol-soaked ground was burned under the diesel engines to warm them for starting.

This night the wind whistles violently and I see the snow stick to the window panes. When I get up in the morning, the windows on the northern and eastern side are entirely covered with a thick layer of snow. We cannot see outside. I go to the well to fetch water and there is a new layer of 20 to 25 cm of snow on top of what is already packed.

On 29 December I go to Beloserjé, deliver documents, but, since my motorcycle is not yet repaired, I drive *Adjudant* Deravet's *Mercedes "Kübel"*. The weather is not ideal to go there with the Victoria solo [motorcycle] that I could just as well use. When I return in the afternoon, I have the pleasure of meeting the comrades who are returning from the positions and will lodge here for a few days with me. They are J. Coppée, Debaisieux, Willy Cox, G. Bourgeois and two or three others. I shall have company for the New Year! I ask the *panianka* to invite for tomorrow evening the neighbor's daughters and the mothers, if they so wish, since the fathers are gone. She does not need to invite the grandfathers, but if they, too, wish to come, they will be welcome.

The next evening they are there, six or seven of them, with two balalaïkas, a grandfather with his violin and three *mamkas*. With all of us, that is quite a crowd, but that is no problem. Comrade Cox has a chromatic harmonica that he plays very well, and he joins the orchestra. It is quite a hit with our Russian guests when he plays a solo. The musical ensemble is perfect, the *ambiance* sympathetic. We enjoy an excellent evening! For the first time, I dance with the young Russian girls. One is slender, without being bony, the others plumper, but not disagreeably. Not too free, not too shy, just right for good company. They are polite, and do not refuse a single dance. We give them candies, cigarettes and chocolate. We have just received abundant packages for the holidays. I enjoy watching them smoke. One of them has moistened her cigarette for half its length.

Precisely at midnight, at the moment of the New Year, the thunder breaks forth all at the same moment and the entire eastern horizon is lit up. The *barichnias* (young girls) are all afraid and press close against us, or is it a pretext? Here is yet another confirmation, true here as in Germany under the bombing. In these circumstances many civilians approach soldiers, as if the uniform reassures them, gives them shelter, as if each soldier is invincible, as if nothing can harm them! Outdoors are the fireworks. We interrupt the embraces and hurry outside. We quickly realize that it is not the front that is ablaze! It is the *"Bourguignons"* who celebrate the New Year in their manner – despite the ban on pointless expenditure of ammunition. The sky above the positions held by the brigade is streaked with the light of tracer bullets, of projectiles of every sort for 20 kilometers! The intensity dies down, the ardor subsides, after a few last isolated, delayed shots, order returns. The embraces can resume, the party too. The girls have forgotten their fears, smiles efface dread. The party over, we walk home our guests, who are afraid to return alone. Fear of our patrols? Or fear of the partisans? We are now in 1944!

Days of calm alternate with more lively ones, small and big events come in turn. As the New Year begins, there is a *coup de main* by the brigade against the village of Sakrevka. This operation follows others that are not dissimilar to it. An assault troop, consisting of infantry from the *2nd* and *3rd Compagnies*, accompanied by a squad of pioneers and a few *Sturmgeschütze* (tracked assault guns), launches a surprise attack on this strongly defended village, filing through a mine field. All in all, a hundred men I think. Surprise favors the *"Bourguignons"*, but the Russian defenders react ferociously and the *"Bourguignons"* have to attack the redoubts, one after another, in hand-to-hand fighting and destroy them. The operation succeeds perfectly, and the *"Bourguignons"* bring in 30 prisoners, there is even talk of more than 80, of booty: three anti-tank guns and small arms. The other defenders are in flight, or wiped out. Our losses are three killed, five severely wounded, and a group of five communications men missing. Among them is Hanusse. I think I remember that this is the evening that our friend Willy Cox, who lives in the same *isba* with me, is missing at roll-call! All of those who live here return except for Willy, dead or missing! This evening there will be less spirit, much less spirit in the sad cottage. There must be a reason. Willy will no longer be one of us, even if he remains present in our thoughts! I see him again, still dancing with such spirit the day of the New Year, and playing the harmonica with such talent. He has left us, like so many others!

In the middle of the night a noise wakes us up. Someone is knocking at the door, but, waking from deep sleep, it takes a moment to identify the sound. It is dark in the room. I make out the snowflakes driven by the wind that trace white lines framed by the little windows and limit the horizon to a meter, at best. One of my buddies unbars the door, which he opens, and a pocket torch illuminates the visitor. It is Cox! Returning! He has more the aspect of one returning from the dead in the flickering light of the pocket torch, with his service spectacles, those that one wears under a gas mask, encircled by white metal and held to the ears by two rubber bands. Moreover, he is covered with snow that sticks to his eyebrows, to the lenses of his spectacles and all over. He seems pale, like a cadaver, but a cadaver that grins at us and we all smile at this friend regained, expressing our joy by slapping his back or patting his shoulders. Now, tell us all about it! It is simple. In the fire of the action and of the confusion, he suddenly found himself all alone northeast of the village with a sprained ankle, separated from the others. He did not realize right off that the mission was completed, that the silhouettes he could make out in the distance were already returning to our lines. He strayed a bit, but, all the same, made it to the footbridge at Baibusy, with a thousand precautions, and regained our lines. That's all, simply told! Today he got out of it! Alas! Six weeks later I will hear of his death at Novo – Buda when I arrive at Schanderovka!

I have learned that one of my old comrades is in an isolated position with another pioneer for his only companion along the Olchanka [river], far from all of the other strongpoints. Their mission is to watch and maintain the network of mines that protects a sector between Mochny and Baibusy. Returning from a mission at Mochny, I decide to drop in on them on my way. I have been vaguely told where they are positioned. Since all of the bunkers are dug into the ground and covered with a thick blanket of snow, they are not visibly different from, or only barely different from, the other little natural hillocks. In mid-journey, about half-way between the two villages, I turn off to the left, right out onto the steppe, toward the Olchanka.

I must be careful, for out in the open in this entirely white landscape my motorcycle and I make a good target for the Russians. In fact, I don't think much about it and the Russians don't fire, perhaps so as not to give away their position. I find my pioneer friends without much trouble. They have heard the sound of my motorcycle, even in the distance. Two men wave to me from the trench that leads to their bunker, hidden under the snow. I park my motorcycle behind a little hillock, in the hollow behind a break in the terrain and go to the bunker.

Their joy is great, and mine, too, but they rarely see anyone. Sometimes at night the *fourrier* brings them provisions for several days, and then they go for days and nights without seeing anyone. I come at a good time, they say, for they have prepared a fat hare, that dropped on them from heaven during the night, like a little pig. The poor beast, thanks to his substantial weight, jumped on a mine during the night. They were alarmed, thinking that an enemy patrol was attempting to get through the minefield to pay them a little surprise courtesy call! They crawled out into the field to see what was going on and thus came across the midday repast that I am about to share with them, thereby accounting for the explosion of a mine. I spent at least two hours with them, giving them news of our buddies and of the village. I then take leave of my friend, Max, and of the other comrade, Evrard, if I remember well, and get back on the road to Baibusy.

A day or two later the comrades who have been living with me depart. They go back to occupy the positions. For several days we have heard noises, alarming rumors. Russian pressure is becoming more menacing to the northeast than to the south. The brigade occupies a dangerous sector here, extremely exposed, a salient thrusting into the Russian dispositions on the Dniepr. That is one of the reasons for all the *coups de main*, of these operations by patrols of the brigade to probe the enemy and attempt to learn what he is preparing, to locate and identify his forces and his troop concentrations, and to take prisoners who can provide us with information.

F. Desmul, *KTF* [*Kompanie Trupp Führer* – leader of the headquarters company] for *Capitaine* Anthonissen's *compagnie*, who has gone on a mission to Belgium, has just been replaced by G. Bourgeois. The latter left Baibusy with his group, and that is why the *capitaine* has entrusted me with the post of *KTF*. On this occasion he asked me to cease living alone in my *isba*. Thereupon I asked my friend, Joseph Drion, to join me and he accepted my invitation with undisguised pleasure. Among others, my present duties include organizing and keeping track of the guards and patrols in the Baibusy area. I get up once or twice during the night to inspect these patrols and guards at the vehicle park, at the armory, at the ammunition dump and at the company headquarters. The *mamka*, who seems to sense just as much as we do the latent, but indefinite, pressure, does not dare to go out alone at night to take care of physiological necessities. *Alors*, she wakes me up, she too, and I have to accompany her. Decidedly, I shall have done everything in this war! She does not want me to turn my back on her, to take my eyes off her. Better to protect her, I shall tell you how this matter is accomplished. Allow me to paint the picture for you! She stops 10 meters from the house, with me about three meters behind her. The two of us scrutinize the shadows for a moment, listening with care. Once reassured, she slightly spreads her legs and slightly bends her knees. She then pulls up her long skirt with her two hands, one in front, the other in back, to free it from her body. And then what follows takes place very naturally, without shame or embarrassment. After which, with dignity, each returns to their respective bed, though, myself, I take advantage of the opportunity to make my rounds and inspect the guards.

I ask myself how the *kasaika* can know so much about the worsening situation when none of the villagers are able to leave Baibusy and since I, myself, never discuss it with her. I have never felt even the least trace of hostility from her, the slightest animosity. On the contrary, she has said to me more than once, while looking me straight in the eye, "Ah, *maladoï*," or something like that ("you are so young…") and she says it in a maternal way.

A few days later, in the evening, a heavy explosion makes us jump, not truly big, but not far from the village. Joseph and I go out and see a glimmer from the far side and to the right of the *kolkhose*, toward the Olchanka. We follow the road toward the exit from the village, from which we can see a fire but cannot distinguish anything precise about it. The next day we learn that the pioneers have blown up two German lorries which, by mistake, were off for a drive among the Russians and, having succeeded, with great dexterity, in regaining the Olchanka after drawing enemy fire, they mistook the foot bridge that the pioneers had built for the bridge at Bolchoï – Staroselje. In crossing the deck, of course, they ended up with their noses in the river. The pioneers were able to pull the fellows out of their bad situation, but not the lorries. To avoid leaving them and their contents for the Russians to remove and carry off, they blew them all up! That is the explanation of the diverse events of the night before.

Nearly every day is marked by similar events. Sometimes we are astonished at the moment, but then, later, there are perfectly natural explanations. That is why anxiety never lasts for long. We develop the simple habit of remaining on guard, of never losing our *sang-froid*, and most of these young warriors are less than 20 years old. It is the lesson of experience, the elementary education of the dangerous life that we have chosen. I have developed the habit of living in the present moment, one day at a time, of dealing with problems one by one in the order of their importance. This is the only way not to lose one's head, and, quite possibly, one's life at the same time.

I must also briefly narrate the story of little Noël, recall him to those that knew him, but who may have forgotten. On Christmas Day, part of the motorcycle platoon was at the front, at Losowok, I believe, under Soviet artillery fire. The Russian shells blew down some of the *isbas* like houses of cards, and my comrades were able to pull a kid out of the ruins of one of them, a poor, howling youngster, horrified, in nothing but rags, but uninjured! He must have been nine years old, and shed hot tears while clinging to the arms and legs of those who had just saved him. They then uncovered the shattered bodies of the father and mother of the little wretch. They buried the father and mother. They adopted the kid. All the men managed to put together a miniature outfit in field-gray and a forage cap. They clothed and shod him as best they could, very properly, as if he was their own kid, the child of the entire platoon. To feed him each gave a part of his ration, saving for him all their candies, all of their sweets. All of these old or young warriors filled in for his mama! Eager for the tenderness of which they had been deprived, they cared for the child, jealously protecting him at the heart of the platoon. The child lived with them in the front line in their shelters and, of necessity, was denied the education we would have desired for our own children. Not knowing his real name, or desiring to know it, he was baptized "Noël", for the day when he was found and befriended.

The child lived perhaps in the *ambiance* of duty care, learning all the foul words of our language, it is true. I have heard him say them, but did he understand them? I greatly doubt it! Yes, certainly someone taught him to smoke, I saw that too. It seems, but this I never saw, it is the chaplain[2] that told me this, that sometimes someone gave him beverages that an infant of his age should not have known. Granted, his education was, perhaps, less than brilliant, but the kid seemed happy to have a family where he could grow up, and all these adoring fathers, who would die for him! I have seen it, I assure you, and nobody else among the villages offered to care for him.

One day the chaplain came to take him away from his adoptive papas, to save him from this relative promiscuity! And the child's smiles disappeared. I later saw this kid wandering around in Baibusy like a soul in torment, less joy in his face than I ever saw when he was in the heart of his adoptive family. No doubt the kid no longer heard the bad words, perhaps no longer smoked, except for what he could do in hiding. He now lived with the chaplain and his orderly, and I suppose that the child went to mass every day. A few times he came home with me when he saw me in the positions at Losowok where the motorcycle platoon was at that time, and he knew that I was his friend, since I was the friend of his friends. I even took him along with me on my motorcycle two or three times on missions that were free of danger. He was a good kid, a poor kid. I remember him, I have never forgotten him.

When, later, I tried to learn what had become of this poor youngster, I regretted that I had tried to find out! I was distressed, like all those who had surrounded little Noël with their affection and, to whom the child, without even knowing it, had returned a hundredfold what they had given him. For a fleeting moment he had provided these warriors, so deprived of affection, the opportunity to express their love for him, their deepest sentiments. Instinctively they had poured forth on this child this overflowing love and affection that had accumulated in them for lack of an object to absorb it, a being to whom they could offer it.

I later learned that the chaplain had embarked, no doubt at Korsun, on one of the last airplanes to leave the Tcherkassy pocket, carrying out the wounded, and that the child Noël was abandoned. Nobody saw him again, not one of those that I asked. What happened to him? Is he still alive, or was he killed in the final moments? In any case, he never arrived at Schanderovka!

In all honesty, I must say that much later, after I wrote the story of little Noël, I learned the version told by this chaplain. I take pains to insert it here, even though this version leaves me totally unconvinced. I will tell you why. This chaplain said to *Lieutenant* R., who was at the time the leader of the motorcycle platoon, but is today, in orders as Brother P., that he did not abandon

---

2   The chaplain, *Abbé* Louis Fierens, kept a journal during his entire service with the *Légion Wallonie* and, after its conversion to the *Waffen-SS, SS-Brigade Wallonie*, which was published as *39 – 45, Carnets de Guerre, Prêtre chez les SS* (Paris – Brussels: Jourdan Éditions, 2011).

the child, whom he entrusted to the tankers at the start of the breakout because he did not believe that he would be able to get the child out of the encirclement. I say here that I do not believe this version, but am entirely ready to hear anyone who can confirm it. Two "*Bourguignons*" have told me that the chaplain got on the airplane at Korsun. I never saw the chaplain again after Belosejé nor, more significantly, at Schanderovka, which was an obligatory way-station – and not a one of the wounded who were housed in the *kolkhose* at Schanderovka that I was able to meet again ever saw the chaplain there. It is there, in particular, that he would have been by predilection. Furthermore, nobody, of all whom I have asked, ever saw the chaplain during the breakout, and God knows how many I have asked about it. And, in conclusion, I ask myself why he would have entrusted the child to the German tankers, since any one of the "*Bourguignons*" would have cared for the child as if he was his own. Did this chaplain really distrust us? Why, in that case, did he try to rejoin us?

Where are you, Noël? Am I really stupid? If you are alive today, you are called Dimitri, Boris, or possibly Sergievitch.[3]

This is the astonishing story, moving, in any case, for me, but absolutely authentic, of a child among the soldiers, among the other children who took him for their little brother! Counting at least a hundred lines, it is short, but the child was only nine years old! That is also short!

I also remember that other child, one of ours, who was 17 years old. I was, according to myself, going to cheerfully attain my own 21 years in a few days, and my 17 years already seemed in the truly distant past! This young comrade, whose name escapes me, tall, slender, with pure chestnut hair, one stripe on his shoulder, was surprised by the *compagnie adjudant*, sleeping while on guard. He was at great risk, court martial, a disciplinary company! I then saw *Capitaine* Anthonissen, always with the severe mien, who was said to be uncompromising, who passed for being a hard man, a hard character... I saw the *capitaine* take this kid under his protection, keep him close to him, to punish him, he said! I saw this "hard" man, understanding, paternal for this young comrade who was at the front for the first time. I was not fooled, my intuition did not delude me. The man that I admired, the superior who was respected by all, this *capitaine*, had feelings that the war had not extinguished. Veteran *capitaine* of the Belgian Army, come from a POW camp, this man was one of us and we were his. Passing homage to this officer of the elite who would be killed himself a few weeks later, him too!

My memory is stuffed with heaps of little events, of scattered memories, but very precise, that I have never read of and that I must recall to those who, perhaps no longer remember them. I think it is good to pass these memories on to posterity. They are a part of our history, of the glory one scoffs at. See! I can always pull myself together and keep a correct tone of good company.

A day does not go by without talk of intrusions by partisans at night, in Baibusy. It is certain that they come for information, as well as for provisions. The steppe extends northeast of Baibusy in all its immensity. The rolling terrain provides cover here and there, a few hamlets, a few scattered *isbas* by twos or threes in the shelter of the hillocks. We are going out on a mission to

---

3 Author's Note – The initial distribution of my book in French has resulted in two statements that allow me to add a correction to the account that I have given on these pages of the affair of our little Noël. I do this without restriction, indeed with pleasure, for the truth has its rights for us more than for any other. It is a duty. My comrades Alex S. and Raymond V.L. have assured me that they did see little Noël in the company of the chaplain on the afternoon of 17 February, at the end of the breakout, and that, accordingly, the chaplain must have entrusted the child to the German tankmen after that. [Tr. Note: This is in complete agreement with the account given by Louis Fierens, the chaplain, in his *39 – 45 Carnets de Guerre, Prêtre chez les SS* describing his time with the *Brigade d'Assaut Wallonie* during the Tcherkassy fighting and breakout. His account states that he and Noël remained in the pocket and took part in the final breakout. He then turned the child over to a German tank crew after they had made it back within German lines.]

reconnoiter the above sector where we do not have a single soldier, not a position. I have never gone to look in that direction. It is necessary to make sure that the partisans do not hide there. Our group consists of a dozen men. To avoid attracting attention, to avoid warning of our arrival by the sound of engines, we are provided with three sleighs drawn by horses. Two are harnessed as *troikas*, the other with two horses, and we have two reserve horses tied to the sleighs. Such precautions are not always futile. A dazzling sun lights our route, but it is very cold, at least –20° [–4°F]. The hairs in my nose are like stalactites, they are so stiff that it is painful when I rub my nose to keep it from freezing. For the first few moments we amuse ourselves by making noise, "*Nou! Nou! Davai!*"[4] We race. Then, more wisely, we proceed in line ahead and in silence. The sun on the snow blinds us, virgin snow without a trace of a footprint or other sign. No one has passed here since the last snowfall. Nothing on the horizon, only the blanket of snow, undulating into infinity, clinging to the irregularities in the terrain, the little hills what are scattered throughout the winter landscape. It is majestic, and strikingly calm! What a winter vacation! We do not believe there is a war on. I often have this impression, despite the risks of being surprised at any moment, like today or when I am on a mission, crossing the steppe or the woods all alone, where there are certainly partisans, where others have been surprised. Ahead of us on the left, a knoll that is a little higher than the others hides the horizon. We turn off to climb it and reach the crest. From there we discover a *cirque*, a basin where five *isbas* nestle, two on the left in front of us and three farther off, on the right. I head for the two first ones with my comrade Herbecq, nicknamed "*Gnole*" ["Hooch"] – I don't know why, for he does not drink – and two other companions. The two other sleighs, one of which is driven by Derzelles, the *capitaine's* orderly, head for the three others, a few hundred meters to the right.

The basin, quite round, is maybe 2,000 to 2,500 meters in diameter. As we examine this countryside, scrutinizing every aspect of this haven of peace, for we are here to observe, several of us suddenly report two little dark silhouettes standing out against the snow climbing the opposite slope in the distance. They are about two kilometers from us, a little less from our comrades who are headed for the *isbas* below on the right. We all shout, almost at the same moment, "*Stoi!, Idi souda!*" ("Halt, come here!") The sound of our cries carries and reverberates in the basin, and the echo returns our words, but the little black points in the snow start to run, act as if they didn't hear us. The only weapons we have, rifles, submachine guns, pistols and grenades, cannot do much at that distance. So, for what it's worth, we fire a few rifle shots in their direction, without much visible effect. One time only, the silhouettes lie down, fall to the ground, doubtless one round was a bit better aimed, for the sights on our rifles are only graduated to 800 meters, if I remember correctly. The two men continue their flight, reach the crest, and disappear behind it as if swallowed by a great white wave of the ocean. There is no thought of pursuit, pointless. What could we possibly accomplish?

We visit, we search the *isbas* without finding anything suspicious. We interrogate the inhabitants, but in vain. We get nothing from them. They say they do not know the two black points that have just disappeared and who chose to depart just as we arrived. Partisans? Soldiers? Two men of the village who took fear at our approach? Why? We did not see which *isba* the two men came out of. We do not know what the residents of the *isbas* said to our comrades on the other slope of the basin. For myself, I think that someone was keeping watch at the top of the crest and warned of our approach, just soon enough to permit them to get away ahead of us. If we had come on motorcycles or on other motor vehicles they would have had time to disappear before our arrival, but, doubtless, they never thought that we would also be able to come on sleighs, with less noise.

---

4 This is how a Frenchman encourages his horse – '*Nou! Nou!*' – and the Russian ('*Davai!*', or 'Faster!').

The other comrades rejoin us about an hour later, after searching the three most distant *isbas*. Turn and turn-about, one or two men guard our horses and sleighs, scanning the environs to avoid any disagreeable surprises. The enemy could have men hidden here or there in holes that we do not see and could surprise us at the most unexpected moment. If someone wanted our sleighs, we could not do much about it. We are to post a guard at the summit of one of the crests, for we would be unable, from inside this basin, to see anything going on outside of it. We warm ourselves up in an *isba*, talking and smoking. Three women and a kid who are there in the room watch us, fearful and curious. I would bet a lot that these people know something that we don't! For they must know that they have nothing to fear from us if they have no thought of harming us. We take the road back to Baibusy at the very moment when the sun sets behind one of the hills. We merely have to follow the tracks we left when we came, which lead us right back home. At Baibusy, as the days pass, talk mounts. There are increasing signs of Soviet pressure on our rear, of the danger of encirclement! At the level of the troops, there are certainly no more than rumors. We are not party to the secrets of the headquarters. All the same, I learn that, a hundred kilometers to our rear, Soviet armies have linked up to cut the main front line (*HKL, Hauptkampflinie* – MLR, main line of resistance). During this time, the vise also tightened from the north and south. It is in these conditions that the Battle of Teklino opened.

Wildflecken (on the *"Kreuzberg"*), June 1943.

Our train *en route* to Korsun and Tcherkassy, November 1943.

A Rumanian city – seen from the train.

En route to Korsun in November 1943.

A "*Bourguignon*" must be able to do anything.

Me at Baibusy in
December 1943.

"*Bourguignons*" and horse dealers.

One of our anti-tank guns.

The *TTR* – the communications men laying a line.

A position at Mochny.

13

The Fighting at Teklino

The Russians, certainly hoping to overwhelm us, try every means to cut up the units facing them, one might say in their midst, and which still show themselves to be aggressive. They are always ferociously combative despite their precarious position. Two Russian regiments have managed to capture a wooded sector northeast of Teklino and have firmly established themselves in this forest, one point of which juts to the southeast toward the village of Teklino. They are attempting to cut our supply routes. The danger is serious and extremely precise! That is why, on 8 January, the Germans launched a counter-offensive with unfortunate results. The Russians succeeded in establishing themselves solidly, fortifying with all the resources the forest offers.

On 11 and 12 January the *Germania Regiment* and the *Narwa Bataillon* of the *Wiking Division* launched a second counter-attack that failed, like the first one. The *Chef* [Léon Degrelle] then suggests to *Général* Gille [*SS-Brigadeführer* Herbert Otto Gille], commander of the *Wiking Division* to which we are justly proud to belong, that he hurl his men of the "*Wallonie*" into a new offensive! The general accepts with pleasure, a pleasure with, perhaps, a tinge of skepticism, despite the confidence with which he views our brigade and the acts of valor and bravery that have proven the mettle of the "*Bourguignons*". As witness to this skepticism, just before arriving at their jump-off positions between the village and the woods, the "*Bourguignons*" find this sign posted:

ZIRKUS WALLONÏEN
Vorstellung morgen von 6 bis 8
Eingang frei!

(WALLOON CIRCUS
Performance tomorrow from 6:00 to 8:00
Admission free!)

That is well calculated to excite the "*Bourguignons*"! And they intend to demonstrate to their German comrades that their passion can succeed there where they have failed! Four companies of infantry, accompanied by pioneers and the motorcycle platoon, which will intervene later, will attempt to recapture the terrain and to force the Russians back to their starting positions. The "*Bourguignons*" feel that their honor is at stake, and that is not an empty statement. They are aware that the battle will be very hard. They know it from all that they have seen or heard, here and there, in the course of events, in conversations and in bits and pieces, and, above all, from the failure of the two consecutive offensives. They have no illusions. Uncertainty grips some, fear assails others, but they paralyze none and the men would let you tear out their tongues before they would admit that they are afraid! That is true courage.

These are all things that I learned from watching and listening. The tone of the conversations is different, their faces are not the usual. All of this is evident to someone who observes them and knows them, even though I know well that everyone is trying in one way or another to hide his uncertainty. The men wait silently for the moment of the assault, chewing over their thoughts.

On 14 January, at a little after 0600 hours in the morning, the attack order is issued and the assault companies advance toward the margin of the forest where the enemy awaits them. It is not only the Russians that oppose them; they must also overcome the difficulties of the terrain. There is a thick blanket of snow, at least 40 cm, hardened by ice but not hardened enough to prevent them from sinking in, and the trees and branches that cover the ground, the result of the previous assaults, make the advance even more difficult. Men fall, left lying on the ground from the start, and the advance grinds to a halt after two hours of effort, more or less 500 to 600 meters from the jump-off positions. The Russian artillery fires point blank over open sights on our men. There is no more question of advancing even one pace. The *1st Compagnie* has to fall back, to give up part of the terrain conquered at such a price! A violent Russian counter-attack forces a large part of the attackers to fall back to a point 200 meters from their jump-off positions. One platoon, that of *Adjudant* Sapin, has, in the meantime, succeeded in breaking through on the right, overwhelming the Russians and firmly establishing itself in their positions. Cut off from all contact with our other elements, he has to stop and change direction in order to bring his platoon safe and sound back into our lines!

At 1300 hours there is a new assault by our men, who recapture the ground just lost and, in addition, in hand-to-hand fighting capture the light artillery positions that nailed them to the ground this morning. They have to stay there until 1600 hours. A platoon of the *1st Compagnie* is decimated by fire from Russian rocket launchers. Thirty men at a single blow! The battle is even rougher than the "*Bourguignons*" had expected. In the *mêlée* contact is lost again between the two wings, for the woods grow wider as the advance proceeds. Another platoon lost 15 men in an instant, half of its forces, in an attempt to re-establish contact with one of the wings.

The brigade receives orders to pitch camp on its positions and not to give up a single inch of ground at any price. The temperature is extremely cold, –25° [–7°F], it is even said that it falls to –30° [–22°F] that night! The ground is too hard to dig, and our men who are attacking have no shelter other than the inextricable tangle of trees and branches cut down by the firing, no mattress but the snow, hardened by freezing. Their *décor* is a vision of the apocalypse: their German comrades of the *Wiking Division* crucified on the trees, their sex organs cut off and stuffed in their mouths, secured at times by iron wire! These are the victims of the previous assaults, poor puppets frozen stiff. The "*Bourguignons*" know what to expect if they fall into enemy hands alive!

During the night of the 14th/15th contact is re-established between the different elements, and there, where it is lacking, reinforcements arrive to seal the breaches. The pioneers then lay mines to provide a bit better protection to the most exposed positions. The day of the 15th serves to reinforce as best we can the positions achieved, but some men have to be evacuated with frostbitten hands or feet. Russian-attempted counter-attacks are repulsed. The "*Bourguignons*" spend their second night in this forest, littered with corpses that are frozen stiff. The temperature has not moderated. On the 16th *Général* Gille comes in person to check on the situation and to congratulate the chilled combatants. He has them provided with chocolate and cognac to warm them up. But the "*Bourguignons*" also realize that a fresh assault is not far off.

During this time I am always at Baibusy, but, on the 16th, I am sent to Beloserjé and to Gorodischtsche, with orders to then continue toward Orlowez and place myself at the disposal of *Lieutenant* Renier, who commands the motorcycle platoon, from which I had been detached, without, however, becoming a total stranger. He seems to have work for a motorcyclist there! The order comes to me from *Adjudant* Deravet, and I must inform Scarcériaux or Staquet at the company office that I have arrived with the envelopes. Decidedly they seem to be preoccupied with my health or to be concerned about it!

It is late and night has long since fallen when I reach Orlowez and do not find *Lieutenant* Renier. However, I meet *Sergent* Hombert. The motorcycle platoon has been sent to reinforce Teklino, and I only find the Germans of the *Wiking Division* and a few "*Bourguignons*" of the trains elements, as well as the local cuisine. I stay in an *isba* with the *Wiking* medics and two "*Bourguignons*", one with a wounded ankle, the other with two frostbitten feet. I learn from them that there are also pioneers in the village. I am tired, but I do not sleep well, doubtless due to nervousness. They have told me so much, talked so much about Teklino! I keep waking up. It is true that the "*Bourguignon*" with the frostbitten feet groans in his sleep. He is able to sleep, he is exhausted, he comes from the front lines. I think that I shall go there tomorrow. Another fellow snores, one of the *Wiking*. I believe that he is a cook – at least he is the one who feeds the wounded. The one who snores has no more trouble sleeping than the one who suffers and moans, but me, I can't sleep anymore! Nevertheless, it is night. I smoke, I reflect. I can neither sleep nor stay where I am. I get up, I go outside. The cold immediately takes my breath away. It was so nice inside! I take a few steps without turning, for I am afraid of being unable to find my lodging again. I do not know Orlowez, I have only been through it twice, and 10 minutes later I am back at my *isba*. The snoring *Wiking* wakes up and sits up. We start a conversation and he, too, talks to me about the "*Wallons*" at Teklino, in a fashion more laudatory than otherwise. I tell him that I am also going there, and he looks at me with admiration. I can't shrug it off right now, but I am not at all proud.

For fear of being unable to start my motorcycle, I go to the outhouse where I parked it and take out the spark plugs. I have, of course, taken the precaution of wearing my gloves. I go back inside and put the spark plugs on the stove, which is still hot, and which the German comrade revives. He then goes out, saying that he is going to find something to eat. When he returns he is not alone. They are three, and they set down three large thermoses by the door. This is for your comrades, they tell me. They give me bread, a mess tin of one-dish-meal-*Eintopf* (at this hour of the morning!), coffee, sausage and butter. It is about 0530, maybe 0600 hours in the morning. Only one man is still sleeping, the others are awake. After eating I go to replace the sparkplugs in my motorcycle and I mount it. Two chaps come with me to push. The two comrades require no urging, and push enthusiastically. Ten, 20 meters and it starts. I make a half-turn, the thermoses are placed in the side-car. They say farewell, *Schuss*! *Hals und Beinbruch*![1] It is still night when I leave Orlowez.

I am not alone; two lorries follow a little behind me, with rations, no doubt. It is also cold. Fortunately there are hot air vents on the hand-grips of my motorcycle. The road is hard and slippery. Is it the cold that makes it so? My nervous tension has vanished. I am wide awake right now. When I reach Teklino the sky starts to clear up, little by little. Day will break soon, but the village is not asleep. Vehicles, the coming and going of soldiers liven up the village in spite of the early morning hour. I see vehicles with emblems proclaiming the presence of high-ranking officers, artillery pieces, *caissons* of ammunition nearly everywhere, lorries, some tanks. There is the area command post, marked by emblems, a group of a few men in a discussion. Finally I find a few "*Bourguignons*", an *Adjudant* among them. I ask directions to the [company] command post which they point out, a little farther on, on the right side of the road. I report there and ask where I should take the thermoses for my comrades. They point north, to the plain where I will find everyone at the edge of the forest. I engage the clutch and set off in the indicated direction, following the tracks on the frozen snow, in a slightly inward-curving steppe. In the distance, on the left, two lorries are stopped, surrounded by men who appear to be loading them. As I was just approaching Teklino,

---

1   This is a standard German phrase – equivalent to 'Luck! Break a leg' or, literally: '[Good] shot! Break [your] neck and leg'.

I heard a heavy fusillade and intermittent artillery fire. I think that these noises have not stopped, but it seems that I forgot about them in my preoccupation. Now I hear them again, and quite well indeed. I am not fooling myself. The lorries that I saw are in a sort of bowl, near the point of woods, about 200 meters away from me. Now I think I see what they are loading into these vehicles, and, when I am a bit closer, my apprehensions are confirmed. These are the dead that my companions pile up in the canvas-covered lorries. Bodies stiff in death, frozen stiff. Suddenly I have the sensation that it is much colder!

One of my comrades tells me they have already loaded 175 bodies, Germans, "*Bourguignons*", lots of "*Bourguignons*"! I avoid looking at the faces, as if I prefer not to know until later which of my friends are dead here. We take the body by the feet and under the shoulders to place it in the lorries, stiff as a tree stump. The last of each load have to be toppled over the rails. Sometimes a corpse which is on the top of the heap comes loose and topples, slides and strikes against the other bodies, lower down, with a dull noise. It is dismal! The sound, much more than the sight of the body that falls. It is hardly what one wants to see just before going up to the front line, but I have accepted it, no question of denying it, at the risk of deceiving myself. One can, when necessary, deceive a friend, an acquaintance, and not see him again. It may not be glorious, but, at least, there is the excuse that it is human. To be ashamed of your own self, that is quite different, for one always ends up by coming back to it sooner or later when you are alone and, in the long run, that becomes unbearable.

I catch the attention of a *sergent* who is directing the macabre fatigue-party and ask him what to do with the thermoses I have. I can leave them here, he is quite happy to be able to give a hot drink to his men, and will then have the thermoses carried forward by those who go to look for bodies. Another *sous-officier* [non-commissioned officer] is there who collects men to go up to the front line and help our comrades, and I join them. I am a staff-motorcyclist and my mission is not to go there, but, since yesterday, I do not know what is driving me. Perhaps it is the stories I have heard that constrain me. But the *sergent* that I was just talking to doesn't have to go either, yet, nevertheless, he, too, goes. The spectacle of all these dead comrades might have been able to dissuade me, but since 15 of our men are going up to the line at this very instant, I can find no excuse that will satisfy me.

We move along the margin of the forest to the right and then start to climb the slope that leads into the forest, toward the north. When I look back, I see my motorcycle near the lorries and two other lorries arriving from Teklino. I think that these are the ones that followed me from Orlowez. Progress is not easy. I sink in the snow. I have to make it over a heap of obstacles, bend down to pass under others. Branches, downed trees, on the ground or leaning, shell holes, where the powder has blackened the surrounding snow, the first bodies. There, two "*fledgrau*" corpses resting on a Russian, united in death, welded together by the ice! I remember all that I have been told, I have the impression of *déja vu*, of having already seen all that is presented to me today. These foxholes from which a head and an arm emerge, there a Russian, his trunk resting on the parapet, his legs in the hole, and neck and shoulder bloody. The effort of marching has warmed my body. But my hands remain cold and my ears tingle. This devastated woods does not block the north wind that turns the breath to frost as it leaves the lips! We advance quickly enough, nevertheless, and, in the distance, but less and less distant, the sound of gunfire stops and starts again incessantly. I have to hold my submachine gun, slung around my neck, clutch it to my body, for it sways with the rhythm of my steps, and the butt slaps my hip, the barrel hits my jaw.

There is a bunker, and there is another. Bodies in front, others behind. The body of a Russian lies across the entrance. A few meters farther on is that of a "*Bourguignon*", the "*Wallonie*" shoulder patch quite visible! One cannot go 100 meters without finding bodies, sometimes in clusters. In my opinion, in the hour that we have marched, we have crossed at least three crests. We can clearly smell the characteristic odor of gunpowder, the sounds of gunfire are now quite close. We hear talking, at times orders are shouted, in French, thank God! We climb one more crest, the slope seems longer, but not as steep as the previous ones. Everywhere there is the same desolation, dead in brown khaki, others in field-gray. Germans, Russians, *"Bourguignons"*, all mingled in death. I can distinguish the recently killed from the others, simply because they are not covered by snow or hoar-frost like the ones that have been lying there for several days.

Here is the crest of the ridge where we quickly locate our men who are advancing while scouring the coppices, the foxholes, seeking to drive out the Russians who might still be hiding there. We have not dawdled *en route*, but, nevertheless, we quicken our pace and rejoin our comrades in a few minutes. Bursts of fire, fusillades break out sporadically, first on the left, then to our right. We find ourselves among the men of the *4th Compagnie* at first, then of the *1st*. I think I recognize one or another pioneer. There are less corpses here, at least it seems so, less *feldgrau*, no more *"Bourguignon"*. At least I cannot identify any. Suddenly, in front of me on the left, dry cracks, bullets part the frigid air, I instinctively duck. Cries, the sound of running. Everyone hits the ground. Sounds of gunfire resonate everywhere at once. Behind me, in front of me. I no longer know who is firing, who is being fired on, where the firing comes from. I do not waste time thinking. Submachine gun in my hand, I dash with the others toward a thicker copse. No, it is a strongpoint that we are headed for, a sort of bunker from which come the bursts of fire.

We advance, running from tree to tree as fast as we can, which is to say not very fast, for the frozen snow grabs our boots. I slow down. Others, on the right, run, leaning forward to attack it from behind. I look forward anew, toward where the resistance is coming from and I suddenly see a Russian in a quilted jacket who is replacing the ammunition drum on his submachine gun, 20 meters from me. Between the two of us, but a little to the left, a *"Bourguigon"*, one knee on the ground, behind a tree that cannot hide him. I am looking only at him, for the Russian has his gaze fixed on him. I think that this *"Bourguignon"* has not seen the Russian. He is looking elsewhere, but the Russian is aiming at him! I do not have time to fire a burst before the Russian collapses, falling backward, dropping his submachine gun, at the same time that a dry popping grates upon my eardrums! I turn to the right, where the burst of gunfire came from and I see Damiani, at least I think it is him. It is his size and bearing, but the helmet changes faces. Our eyes meet for a moment and a see a slightly ironic smile. He seems to be saying to me, "You are not fast enough. I did it before you!" The *"Bourguigon"* on my left is relieved, for the firing from ahead of us is over. Taken from the rear by other comrades, the Russian nest of resistance is neutralized, and, doubtless, our comrade never knew that another saved his life that day. I was never able to identify him for, at that moment, I did not think of talking to him, having other more immediate and vital preoccupations. On the other hand, Damiani, the one I recognized, would not have liked me to tell him, for he would have been embarrassed about it! He will never learn of it, at least unless he reads my book and recognizes himself there. But I think that Damiani will never read what I write, for he too, is dead. I believe that he committed suicide near Breslau, at Lissa, on the bank of the Oder. He was seriously wounded in his private parts and would not have wished to survive under these conditions. He said that he was no longer a man. His shredded body was recovered on the riverbank. He had blown himself up, sitting on a grenade or on a charge of dynamite, which the pioneers regularly used in their work. He was a pioneer and this happened in the autumn of 1944! He was a very *chic* sort, an exemplary comrade. And I do not say this just because he is dead!

Life, death, friendship, all of these are so intimately intertwined! Everything happens so quickly in these circumstances that, frequently, you do not know where you are, who you are, everything, life especially, is no more than a question of reflexes. Every situation is truly fleeting! It seems to me that, at the moment of his fall, the submachine gun that the Russian dropped let loose a burst, for, as it fell, it jumped wildly. It is curious to realize that at such moments the mind can register such details and recall them so accurately years later.

The advance immediately resumes and the operation seems more and more to be combing the woods, just as we did during our training, but with danger added. Scattered bursts of fire, here and there, men shouting abruptly. A few minutes later, right opposite us, about 50 meters away forms suddenly stand up! I immediately recognize Russian uniforms, but already three or four bursts whistle past our ears and crash with a dry sound on the stumps, on the trees or get lost in the distance, whining through the frozen air. At almost the same instant all of our weapons crack in their turn, aiming to hit these uncertain silhouettes that flee as fast as they can run among the bare trees. They zig-zag, I lose sight of them, they reappear, because I make the mistake of trying to keep all of them at the same time in my field of view rather than to focus on one or another without losing them. This comes from the instinct of self-preservation, for, above all, one does not want to miss the one who is going to aim at us!

I fire from the hip while running, and, without stopping, I replace my empty magazine. Once or twice the Russians pause long enough to get off a burst to stop us in our course, then take off again. During one of these stops I see two that collapse and the others who scurry off. There are a dozen who, all of a sudden, vanish in a thicker part of the woods, which blocks our view and offers them safety. They have made a clean getaway! We slow down and my neighbor turns toward me. I see him stoop and pick up his helmet, adjust it on his head and return at the run. It is only now that I recognize him, it is Debaisieux. I have had neither the time nor the occasion to really look at him in the heat of the action until now. It is the appropriate phrase, for now we know the exact significance of this expression. We smile as we recognize each other. Like me, he is a member of the motorcycle platoon, but with another function.

We advance more slowly, with new prudence, for we do not want to be surprised and killed stupidly for lack of precautions! Even though the Russian resistance seems to have weakened, for all that the game is not necessarily won! We march, we stop, then, after carefully scrutinizing the woods, the copses, the slightest hole each time, we move on. We find nothing. They have disappeared into nature without leaving a trace. We study the footsteps in the snow, there are certainly enough of them and they scatter in all directions. We continue our pursuit to the crest, which we reach soon after. The other *"Bourguignons"* have also reached this crest at diverse points to the left and to the right. From afar an *adjudant* shouts to us to fall back a few paces to the shelter of the ridge line.

I do so and light a cigarette. When I look at Debaisieux a hole in his helmet draws my attention. He does not believe me when I point to it with my finger and ask him if the moths nibbled it. But, all the same, he takes it off, out of curiosity, and does not put it back on. There are, indeed, two holes, one in front on the left, the other on the back of the cap, at the level of the back seam. Apparently it is the same bullet that just knocked his helmet off when he simply thought it was a fortuitous fall from running into a branch. He smiles, but rather curiously. I think he has just realized that he had a close call! The order arrives to remain on the defensive and Debaisieux and I head toward a group that is forming to our left, six or seven men, including an *adjudant* and two *sergents*. I explain why I am here, for the same reason as the other *"Bourguignons"* who went into the line at the same time as me. Fifteen minutes later we are eight men going back down toward Teklino while our comrades above consolidate the positions. Well before arriving at the margin of the woods we meet again the *"Bourguignons"* who indefatigably continue to evacuate the dead. Now I understand better the origin of the curious traces left in the snow. They are the marks left by the bodies that are dragged down the hill, wrapped in tent canvases.

When I leave the woods I look for my motorcycle. I do not find it. It seems that *Adjudant* Demeersman took it to bring it to Teklino where it would be safer! Personally, I suspect that he took it so as not to have to wait for a lorry to leave for the village, or to avoid having to walk back on foot. Thinking that I will find my motorcycle at the bottom of the first slope, I start off briskly, but soon I feel fatigue in my calves, for I am afraid I shall have to make it back to Teklino on all fours. I now remember how tiring this laborious advance was in the frozen snow, even more difficult due to the obstacles that are scattered along our route. Finally I prefer to help in loading the bodies and head back on one of the lorries. There I am, an undertaker's assistant. These are comrades that I must load onto the lorries to bring them back to the trenches that the *intendance* [supply service] has dug for them in the rear. I do not recognize any of my friends among the dead. I am told several names, but I do not know any of them.

I get down from the lorry at Teklino village, for I see my motorcycle in front of the command post. The *Adjudant-Chef* Pede and Catrice, both from my company, are talking together in front of the command post. Pede tells me that I am expected at Baibusy, where I arrive as night falls, hoping that I will not get in trouble for my initiative at Teklino. *Adjudant* Deravet drops in on me and hands me an envelope that he wants me to translate into German. During the time that we have been here he has regularly come, once or twice a week, to ask this little service of me. Scarcériaux, the company secretary, sometimes asks the same of me. They each have a little girl-friend in Germany. My German is not perfect, but I manage well enough. The next day, 18 January, I arrive at Beloserjé and discern a certain effervescence at the division command post. That is to say that they are packing, they are loading the files. I am told that the headquarters is moving to Gorodischtsche. On the 19th, elements of other units that will replace us arrive at Baibusy. On the afternoon of the 20th we leave Baibusy for Beloserjé, where the company headquarters will be established. The *mamka* and little Nicolas embrace me! They are sad, truly sad, when I say farewell to them. I see quite clearly that this is not an act. In truth, we were quite close to each other and got along well, despite the entirely understandable little larcenies of the kid, that were of no importance. I loved him greatly! We will not return again, never! I turn a page, one more page of memories, but never without a little wrench. One more small wound, but there have been so many others already, one ends up on top of another, thus forming, as the days of events and trials go by, a carapace that allows one to survive many more without too much damage when the moment comes. If my age is still tender, it is necessary to protect myself. The heart, the skin, especially, must harden.

On 20 January, 1944 I move in at Beloserjé where I am billeted along with *Adjudant* Deravet and Drion in an *isba* north of the village at the edge of the road that forms an arc of a circle as it joins two others, the one that climbs toward the northeast toward Kumeiki and the one toward Mochny, to the northeast.

The situation now evolves day by day, one could say even hour by hour. This is what is called a "fluid situation"! In the days that follow I am assigned three or four missions to Gorodischtsche, since the division command post has been established there since the 20th. On other occasions, to Mochny and Derenkowez. During these days I am in Beloserjé only when I sleep, when, that is, I have a chance to catch a few hours of sleep now and then. At other times, I find lodging *en route* as my movements permit, at least when I can find time.

It is under these conditions that, on 27 January, shortly before leaving Gorodischtsche, I learn of our encirclement! In all honesty, I have been expecting this for some time, without, however, knowing too much about this possibility, but now it is certain, for I have just learned it at the division command post. For several days the noise of the fighting surrounded us, coming to us from the entire horizon! A little lump in the throat, nevertheless, but not the slightest sign of panic, not the least nervousness. The machine of war and all of its administration continues to turn as if nothing has happened. At the command post my travel order is signed, the stamps are always ready at hand, the "*Scheine*", or certificates, circulate as usual.

Nothing, absolutely nothing, has changed!

BLOODY SNOW

It is cold, the wind whistles and the snow is hard.
The steppe, after yesterday's battles,
Seems still to shudder and its soul is bruised
By the thunder of the canon that vomit fire.

On the endless plain where death is mistress,
Shadows stand out in this morning of fire,
Immobile, ghastly, in diverse poses
Where they congealed in the effort of their supreme farewell.

Yet the faces of these shadows
Where the ultimate suffering has contorted all the features
And these chaps who died in these hours of rage
Preserve in their hard eyes the vision of a heinous crime.

They are there by the thousands, on the frozen snow
Whose whiteness has been soiled by the falling bodies,
Creating on the virgin soil where an Army perished
A frightful scene of drama and woe.

And I suddenly dream, eyes filled with tears,
Of these men of twenty years, who died as heroes,
Deluded in their trust in the dubious arbitrament of war,
Strangers to this soil where their graves yawn.

But this one here has kept his smile,
And his eyes, open wide, seem fixed on me
So well that his gaze seems to want to tell me,
I am proud to die, my friend, embrace me.

And, bending my knee on the bloody snow,
Drawn by these suppliant eyes,
I press on these lips, in place of the absent one,
The kiss that the kid desired as he died.

My eyes then scan, anew, the plain,
I think of the dead of other days,
These tombs of soldiers fallen on foreign ground,
Where thousands find eternal rest.

And I curse the fate that begot the war,
creating for us this exile on foreign ground
Where so many children died, without their mother's farewell,
Seeking, in vain, a last kiss on their lips.

                    (Poem composed in prison by our comrade, J. S.)

The poem of an anonymous Russian soldier, found after the capture of a Ukrainian village:

WAIT FOR ME!

Wait for me, though it blows,
Wait for me, though it snows,
Though hard winters follow the falls!
Wait for me, when no other still awaits me.
Wait, when no one remembers the past.
Even when no letter comes from the distant front
... Wait for me!
Even when my mother, my son and my friends,
Fighting alongside me,
Have abandoned hope for my return.
And standing, offering a toast to my memory,
Stiff in that oppressive silence, do not drink! ...
Wait for me, for one day, even from the toils of death itself,
I shall return to you, who always waits for me...

14

The Encirclement

We are now encircled! The vice has closed on us. It was inevitable! We had to hold the Dnieper at all costs, retain the bridgehead, and the Russians, adopting German tactics, have committed considerable forces to cut our main line of resistance (MLR) which is, actually, about 80 to 100 kilometers behind us! Several army corps have attacked the pocket on all sides and are, at present, increasing the pressure of their thrusts, attempting to divide up the defenders to facilitate their subsequent annihilation.

Zhukov, Koniev, Malinowski, Bogdanof, the greatest generals of the Red Army, are engaged in our destruction. They are at our door and the 50,000 or so men that are in the pocket will have to brace up and stand fast against all the pressure, even though they are short of everything except courage!

When I report at Mochny, Derenkowez or Gorodischtsche, the front is presently at the gates of each village. If that is not yet the case for the last two settlements, it is only a few days away.

On 25 January the front of the *Brigade Wallonie* is extended, presently stretching 28 or 29 kilometers, even though the number of effective combatants shrinks daily. But it is the same for all the other formations. The *2nd Compagnie*, barely 80 men strong, evacuates its positions at Staroseljé to relieve the *Narwa Bataillon* at Losowok, which has been reduced to 130 men, though it should have at least 800 men! The motorcycle platoon takes up a position at Skity, reinforced with some heavy weapons. Everywhere it is necessary to hold the most important sectors, even though the number of combat-worthy men gets less and less! Every time that patrols are sent to probe Russian resistance the forces they find are more numerous and the evidence mounts each day ever more precisely confirming offensive intentions. Not one day, not one night passes without a battle developing at one or another of the cardinal points of the compass, most often at several points at the same time. Fires at all the points of the horizon are indicative. One group of *isbas* of a village has not even finished burning when a new blaze reddens the sky at another point. Losowok, which had to be evacuated in the face of superior forces, must be recaptured at any cost! The *2nd Compagnie* achieves partial success, but at what price – and with unparalleled courage, despite its shrunken numbers! The front is now provisionally stabilized with great difficulty at this place. Now it is the turn of our defenders at Mochny, Vernier's platoon of the *1st Compagnie*, to face the furious assault of the hordes that face them, starting at 2000 hours on 3 February. The 2 cm *"Flak"* engages in direct fire against the Russian infantry, while the more vulnerable infantry guns (*IG*) fall back to take position a little farther to the rear on the road. All of the combined fire begins to take the spirit out of the attack and the survivors retreat in the steppe to the east. Russian corpses litter the ground 50 meters from the infantry guns! At 2100 hours, just one hour after the start of the attack on Mochny, Vernier's platoon of the *1st Compagnie* is encircled on the extreme right of a suburb of Mochny. Nevertheless, our artillery is able to break the encirclement of this platoon by 2200 hours.

An order arrives by telephone from the command post of *Commandeur* Lippert to hold the positions at all costs until the *4th Compagnie* falls back. Displacement of the artillery begins at 2300 hours with enormous difficulty, and, at 0300 hours in the morning, it reaches Baibusy with all its *matériel*, but with serious damage to its vehicles. Nevertheless, this is how it will be nearly every day, for the *Brigade Wallonie* now has the delicate mission of rear guard. The salvation of the roughly 50,000 men who have been encircled will, to a large part, depend on its success. A heavy responsibility, a redoubtable privilege, but our German comrades, the high command, in particular, know that they can count on us. The "*Wallons*" themselves, know that they can count on their German comrades to open a passage to freedom and for yet other tasks.

In the afternoon the *1st Compagnie* was forced to fall back after being cut in two by violent Russian attacks. One part fell back on Baibusy, the other on Malenki – Mochny. In the course of falling back, the main defense was re-established for the time being on the Fossa river and the point of main concentration or "*Schwerpunkt*" shifted toward Staroseljé, now that Losowok and Mochny had been abandoned.

During the night of 3/4 February we evacuate Beloserjé. My motorcycle gave up the ghost this morning and I am now a foot-soldier! Drion and I have loaded the chests of the headquarters and various packs on a "*panjewagon*" and I am back in the situation I knew during the advance in 1942, but with less good weather. Today we have one more enemy, the climate, but it is a fantastic climate, truly awful. The temperature at times shifts back and forth across the freezing point several times a day, but doesn't fall low enough to rapidly freeze the ground and keep it hard long enough. Long enough, however, for us to suffer from the cold, but the road remains bad and adds to our difficulties.

We are not the only ones on the road that leads through the woods to Drabovka. A heterogeneous assemblage of vehicles precedes and follows us. Many heavy vehicles, lorries, artillery, carts like our own! We wallow again in the mud, the horses slip and fall on the corduroy road. Lorries and carts get mired, for at times they try to pass each other to try to better their position and must, thus, leave the corduroy road to take their chances in the muck whose depth one never knows. Then we must, once more, employ all our wiles to get out, work together and summon all our strength to get out of the bad situation. In places it takes us two or three hours to get through a single kilometer. At times a lorry or a tracked vehicle pulls a cart out of the mud, but sometimes, in the dead of night, we must detach the horses from several carts and harness them to a motorized vehicle to help get it to firmer ground. At least two or three times we thus see eight or 10 horses strain to pull a heavy vehicle out of a ditch, a vehicle that we must first unload, laying the load-heavy chests, artillery ammunition, on the other side of the road, sweating, sliding, in mud up to our calves or our knees.

Cries and oaths echo through the woods, in German, in French, even in Russian, for we say to ourselves that the poor beasts understand their "mother tongue" better – "*Nou! Hue! Davai! Verflucht Sakrament!*" – but I leave out a lot, especially when the reins break. The horses also slip and lose their footing like us, they get excited, lash out with their hooves in all directions and it is really difficult to avoid getting kicked. They get tangled in the traces, in the reins, and it is necessary, with great difficulty, to straighten out the ropes and straps. After a few swerves and uncontrolled slides the vehicle is put back on the good road. After which, in the profound darkness of the woods, we must unhitch the horses in order to hitch them up again to the carts. This sort of scene goes on all night, for even if the vehicles in front of and behind us would like to help, they are unable to because of all the other vehicles that prevent them from moving forward or backing up. It goes without saying that these incessant efforts exhaust even the strongest. And, in the meanwhile, even the weakest or the most exhausted must also endure this regime and a host of other torments, every day, every night, right up to the final outcome, fatal for some, salvation for the others!

Day after day, hour after hour, to do what must be done, even if you do not want to, if it is difficult, if the weather is bad. And to go on, even if no one is watching to congratulate you, without applause, without the promise of the least recompense, simply because it is necessary to do what you believe to be your duty! With the only satisfaction being to have taken part in a thankless task to the best of your ability and each one in his place. That is how every one of us has found the courage. And no one in the world, for all eternity will ever be able to take away from us this unique glory that we have acquired in the worst of our suffering, like a victory. According to this measure, all of the "*Bourguignons*", with few exceptions, have won these laurels that they never asked for and which they do not even claim! Nevertheless, I shall always remember that, if, in life, never is it always easy, on the other hand, never is it entirely impossible!

When, shortly after dawn, we leave the woods to arrive at Derenkowez, everywhere above us the sky is purple and gold, especially toward the east and northeast. These are the glow of the fires, the aftermath of the battles raging everywhere! Finally we enter the city where we find a jumble of men of all the units. It must be said that, at the start of the encirclement, a little earlier, the pocket that today contains the encircled troops was roughly equal in size to Belgium. It suddenly became evident to the high command that such extended positions were untenable for such a small number of men. It was necessary to accept the reduction in size of the pocket, but not just in any old way, and to avoid at any price the partition of the troops that the Russians were attempting. They have not succeeded in accomplishing that to this day. They are eager to do so!

On 28 and 29 January the Russian attacks come from the northeast, the west, and the southeast on Boguslav – Swenigorodka – Schpola. Then on Olschana, Korsun and Steblow, where vigorous counter-attacks repulse them, these localities being vital to us for our planned breakout. On 31 January the Russian attacks are general around the entire perimeter of the encirclement. On 1 February it is the same, except for the northeast sector. On 2 February the thrusts come from the south and north, and a little, also, from the east, and the same on the next day. But, on 3 and 4 February, the *III Panzerkorps* launches counter-attacks from the outside, coming from the south and southeast, which force the Russians to focus on them. At the same time the Russian Air Force drops leaflets on us inviting us to surrender! These leaflets are signed "Committee for Free Germany".[1]

Today, 4 February, the area of the pocket is less than one fourth of what it was on the first day of the encirclement! On 5, 6 and 7 February, Drion and I go into the front line east of Derenkowez with other men from all the units, mostly German, but also some "*Bourguignons*", six or seven. There is fear of a Russian breakthrough, which would be catastrophic for the future plans of the high command. We are here in these jump-off positions, for the Russians have already infiltrated the woods facing us. During this time, at Starosljé, other "*Bourguignons*" are fighting, one against five. Driven by the *Chef* [Degrelle] and the *Commandeur* [Lippert], they impetuously recapture the windmill hill that they had to relinquish in the morning.

My friend Drion has gone to the village to try to find something to eat. He returns at 0500 or 0600 hours, his pockets stuffed with brown sugar and a flask of pickled tomatoes and gherkins. He has seen Deravet who has told us to meet him in Derenkowez. First we eat our "emergency snack", well-steeped tomatoes and gherkins, and, for dessert, two or three handfuls of brown sugar! Here the sector is calm, but twice, yesterday and today, little groups of seven or eight men have left the woods across from us. They have come 100 meters in our direction, then thought better of it and moved off toward the left, parallel to the woods. A machine gun opened fire on the left, nailing the group to the ground. They got up, ran toward the woods, but the machine gun opened fire

---

1   The National Committee for a Free Germany (NKFD) was founded in Krasnogorsk – near Moscow – on 12 July, 1943 to give captured German soldiers and exiled German communists an opportunity to join an anti-Nazi organization. Two months later, a separate organization – the League of German Officers (*Bund Deutscher Offiziere*, or *BDO*) was founded – its primary task being to deliver propaganda aimed at the German armed forces.

again. Only two of them finally made it back to the shelter of the woods, but it was far away and I could not see it all. Farther to the north, but far to the left, the fusillades are more frequent, and much more sustained. Before night falls I inform our German comrades to the left and right that a superior officer has ordered us to Derenkowez. We get back on the road 200 meters behind our positions and proceed right toward the village.

Drion is unable to find the house specified by Deravet, though we searched for more than an hour. We find the house that is also occupied by some German comrades where we left the cart and horse in care of the "*pan*". We can always trust them, they care for the animals. After eating a bit of bread we head out again to look for *Adjudant* Deravet, whom we finally find in an *isba* to the left of an alley perpendicular to the main road. He informs us that a group of vehicles is stuck in the mud in the woods and on the road between Beloserjé and Derenkowez. He is happy to learn that we have his packs on our "*panjewagon*", that we are going to come and move in here. He congratulates us for our resourcefulness and efficiency.

The next morning, 8 February, Drion returns to the sugar refinery at Derenkowez and brings back a bread bag full of brown sugar. He also tells me that he found some gray packages there marked "*Raffinerie de Tierlemont*"![2] In the afternoon Drion and I head south from the village and return to the positions where we were yesterday. The situation is becoming increasingly critical. Everyone who is more or less fit for duty reports to the positions. In fact, we see wounded comrades, distinguishable by their bandages, who have come here to fire their shot! Yet others limp along the road toward other positions. The weather is execrable. It is cold, but not freezing. Driving bursts of rain are interspersed with snow squalls. We are plunged into a universe of mud, snow and water, above and below. Our cold, wet feet wallow through this magma in the bottom of the holes, the water and snow lash our faces. Our swollen hands, red and cracked, hold our weapons with great difficulty, with no real feeling in our hands. Every now and then a few Russian shells burst in the steppe before us and the echo of the explosions returns to us each time, returned by the woods and the hills facing us. Finally there are some better aimed bursts of fire that whistle past our ears and end up in the mud, in the snow behind us, toward the road.

Apparently the Russians want to probe our resistance. They are preparing for an attack, but for when? Right now? This evening? This night? Evening comes, then night, and, in turn, crouched in the hole, each of us tries to catch a bit of sleep. My hands pulled up in the sleeves of my motorcyclists' raincoat as best I can, pressed tight against my body, leaning forward with my legs folded, I manage to warm myself up a bit. But there is nothing I can do for my feet, submerged in the mud and the snow. The night is ominous and long with no end. Happily neither Drion nor I tend to pessimism, and we are able to laugh at our situation, at this distress, perhaps not as heartily as we might like, but with good hearts, nonetheless.

At dawn of this 9 February I eat a bit of hard bread, but with butter, with a jar of "*singe*" ["monkey", bully-beef] and washed down with iced coffee from the canteen. This morning we learn from the chaps that have come as reinforcements that the "*Bourguignons*" are still holding Staroseljé to the east and Mieliew to the southeast. At noon we know that the brigade has or is going to abandon these two locations, mission accomplished, and that those units will come to join us. While those units disengage at Staroseljé and Mieliew, they run into Russians who attempt to prevent them from linking up with us at Derenkowez. They have to clear their way and *Capitaine* Anthonissen is sent with an assault group (*Stosstrupp*) to attempt to relieve them by forcing the Russians to fight on another front. The captain never returns, nor any of the 30 men

2 Tierlemont (French), or Tienen (Dutch), is a city in Flemish Brabant, Flanders. It is the center of Belgian sugar production, with a huge sugar beet processing factory.

that went with him! I must honor the man of duty that he was, the company commander whom I truly appreciate for his profound qualities. It was not by chance that he volunteered to be among us. I must say it and hope that his family know it!

It is in these conditions that our units, practically encircled at Bolchoï – Staroseljé and Mieliew were, nevertheless, able to rejoin us, but not without losing some men and most of their *maté-riel*. During this time the Russians emerged from the woods facing us and assaulted our lines in compact masses. At first one or two bursts of fire come from our lines, but as the enemy approaches and shows his resolve to submerge us, everyone who can opens fire for all they are worth. All this crackles like a fire in very dry woods. At this moment everyone here at the front line certainly pulls his head down between his shoulders, for the air is cut by all sorts of projectiles. It takes luck not to be precisely in one of their trajectories! The assault mounts in intensity, but stagnates a little later. Our fire becomes more and more intense, as if fed by an inner fire, by every man's desire to go to the limit, not to die, but to regain our freedom, to escape the hammer that seeks to crush us on the spot, to pulverize us in this pocket. In less than half an hour many of the Russians are lying on the ground and get up no more, the others waver an instant, hesitate, and, little by little, start to retreat, dismayed by their welcome. As if encouraged by this retreat, we redouble our fire and aim for the silhouettes that are now running in the opposite direction, toward the woods that they had come out of. They may know that we are vulnerable, but they now also know from these last few days that we will go to the limit!

In the following afternoon we hear the sound of battle to our right, and at night there is a true corridor that forms, leading directly south, our only road of retreat! The village that is burning on our right is Arbousino. And the rain cannot conceal from us the effect of the glare on the low clouds, heavy with rain. If the road to Korsun is cut, that will be a catastrophe. Most of the men have had no sleep for three days, some for much longer, and all are exhausted, drained of their substance! I later learn that the *Westland Regiment* has retaken the position, clearing the threat from the Korsun road, our retreat route, that the Russians were no more than barely 200 meters from! But this road is still exposed, from both left and right, for the Russians are aware of its importance for us and we will be the last to take it. The brigade is always the rear guard, every moment at risk of the worst: breakthrough, annihilation. The weakness of one strongpoint, of one squad, even, at times, of a single man can topple everything in a moment, destroy us all definitively!

During the night we receive word, "We disengage before dawn!" What a relief! But when are we to sleep? I do not know what time it is when, finally, I am able to pull my feet out of this treacle in the bottom of the hole to immediately plunge them into that which covers the entire plain, including the road. We climb back up toward Derenkowez, and it is idiotic, I know, but I mean to retrieve "my" cart and "my" horses, my two little black horses. And, a miracle! I retrieve them. They have not been "*zabralés*" (borrowed). We lose time at the lodging, though it would be better not to gather moss here. Finally we are able to hit the road. All our possessions are on the "*panjew-agon*", and we don't have to march. *En route* toward Korsun we see, here and there, the artillery pieces that protect the road and our retreat, and also one or two reconnaissance armoured cars (*Panzerspähwagen*) that watch over us like guardian angels. Our joy does not last long. Already I regret having recovered the cart and team. We have made no more than two or three kilometers and already it is necessary to let go of my illusions. Once more it is we who must look after the horses instead of sleeping. And God knows that we are done in, exhausted for lack of sleep!

At first we push, we do our best, but fatigue sickens us! Then stupidly, we hit the horses to make them move forward, and they move forward before they stop a little farther on. Then we start again, to move forward a little more. Here I must tell you a joke which, no doubt, is not very funny, but I must still tell it, for it made me laugh to the point of tears for a moment. My friend, Joseph, has just avoided being kicked when he tried to stimulate one of our horses by twisting his tail. He then acts as if he is having a nervous fit, whinnies like a horse, and approaches one of them and bites its shoulder! I did not expect anything of it, and Joseph no more than myself, but the animal shied, feeling the bite. He actually bit the animal. I have to laugh in spite of myself, I have never seen a man bite his horse! I am sure that Joseph regrets it as much as I do. Certainly the horses do not have the same reasons we do to fall back, whence their small enthusiasm for this night-time march!

Harassed, exhausted, carrying all the weariness of the world on our shoulders, and those of our horses on top of that, we arrive at Korsun at the hour when the cocks should crow, but there are no more cocks at Korsun, no hens, no fowls of any sort. Nothing but exhausted men, their eyes red from lack of sleep. We leave our rig at one of the first houses we come to and go to flop down among other worn-out bodies that are crossing the threshold of a sort of school and are already asleep before they are 10 paces ahead of us! We have slept 12 hours straight without nightmares, without the slightest interruption, but I could easily sleep three times that and more! When I try to put my boots on I cannot do it, for my feet are swollen. It is true that it has been four days since I had a chance to take them off! After an insane time and a thousand attempts I finally get them on with the help of an old piece of cloth serving as a shoehorn. There is reason to howl, for I am hurting. I feel like I have put on boots that are at least two sizes too small. My feet were dry, but not so the boots nor the socks. Maybe they will dry out on my feet, at least I try to convince myself of that!

I have just learned that, on 8 February, a Russian parliamentary arrived at the lines facing the positions of the *112th Infanterie Division*, demanding the surrender of all the survivors of the *"Kessel"*, or encirclement. It was sent back with a *"Niet"*, *"nein"*, *"non"* – categorical no! In this case, he said, your total annihilation is only a question of hours! Another piece of news should certainly bring joy… to the Russians! The *III Panzerkorps*, which was attempting to link up with us, coming from the southeast, is running into major difficulties with the terrain, on top of strong enemy resistance.

It was still night, or, at least, not entirely day, when we arrived this morning. When I wake up this evening the day has already gone. We no longer really know how we live. We do not have the slightest notion of time, day and night are no more than natural phenomena. For a long time there have been no regular hours for eating to break the day before afternoon, there have been no more fixed points to lend order to the day. Now the quest for nourishment seems like a treasure hunt! We do not find it, unless by a miracle. We are four *"Bourguignons"* among German comrades. The others are elsewhere, scattered nearly everywhere. Drion and I go in search of food, and we each head in opposite directions to double our chances of finding something. I wander through a lunar landscape, among all sorts of ruins and wreckage. Remnants of charred walls, destroyed or burned vehicles, bodies of horses, craters of shells or bombs. I meet shadows that resemble phantoms. It is like the tragic opera, with scenery truer than nature, Wagnerian sound effects are provided by all the artillery that surrounds us, and, for illumination, the fires in the city and around us. A costly production!

I step over the ruins to change thoroughfares and hasten my tour of this Dantesque universe. I sink into the rubble, I slip and twist my ankles more often than usual, and when, weary and disgusted, I turn back, I discover a long, single-story building, extremely dilapidated, but pretty much spared by the war. From it come sounds of feverish activity. The building is but poorly lighted, and I have to go around it to find a door. I find it on the other side and there is a crowd pressing toward it. Is it the smell that has led me there? I do not know, but this shed is an army bakery. A dozen German soldiers are busy there and the vehicles before the door are loaded with bread by the drivers and those with them! Here we are, two inches from the end of the world, but all this functions and goes on as if nothing was happening. And it is only right that they do not demand ration stamps from us! In truth, the fellows are extremely kind and, regardless, give me three or four loaves of gray bread, a little larger than our "*pistolets*" [small French loaves]. Quite happy, I hurry to get back to the building where we slept, where I am supposed to meet Drion. I get lost and turned around before getting back on track. When I get there, Drion is not there, but I find three or four other "*Bourguignons*". Has he arrived? Where is he? I wait, I rack my brains and do not dare eat yet, do not dare to start alone on the fruits of my search. After a long wait I can stand it no longer, for I have forgotten the taste of bread for several days! I save a loaf for Joseph and give the other two to comrades who are there. Columns of infantry and also of vehicles pass by without a break on the road and, from the threshold I call in vain. There is no "Joseph" in the troop. Once more weariness overcomes me and I close my eyes. Oh! Only for a moment, while I wait for Joseph!

When I open my eyes it is light and it takes some time for me to remember that I am still waiting for Joseph, who has not returned. The "*Bourguignons*" have gone, but there are still two men there, and I swallow my remorse while sharing with them the loaf of bread that I was saving for Joseph. I find a pail to shave myself a bit, but no razor, no soap, not even a towel. A bit of my shirt takes care of that. It will dry soon, tucked into my pants. The three of us leave and join the troops that are leaving Korsun toward the southeast.

At the exit of the city we discover long columns that stretch out into the snow, all arms of the service mixed together, infantry and trains. We have not marched for an hour when, low on the horizon, Russian airplanes appear and strafe the column, raking it with their machine guns. We jump to the side and hit the dirt to get clear of the axis of their fire and then get back up to resume the march. The dead remain on the ground; the medics immediately tend to the wounded. A few minutes later the "*Samajots*" return and drop a few bombs. They are bolder now that there are none of our planes to chase them. For it was not that long ago that a single German fighter was enough to liven up three or four of theirs. I do not mean to say that they were all cowards, don't misunderstand me. But it is true for me to say that I have always seen that, even when they had superior numbers, the Russians were always the first to break off fighting. Today, certain of victory, they are bolder.

When we get up to get back on the road, ahead of us and behind us vehicles burn and columns of black smoke rise into the sky. Everywhere destroyed lorries and broken carts, bodies of horses block the road. Once more it is necessary to get to work, clear the road by toppling all the wreckage to the side. This is no easy matter for men exhausted, famished like us. Therefore we move forward, but slowly, and with great difficulty. The Russian planes return two more times and attack on all four of their passes, going and returning. Each time a few more men are left lying in the snow that will be their only sepulcher. When we pass, detouring around a burning vehicle, it warms us up as we go by, but the smoke and the acrid odor of burning rubber irritates our throats. These odors of fire, of rotting carcasses, of bodies and/or powder follow us everywhere; it is the odor of the war! It is night, at last, when we reach Stieblev, exhausted, but how could it be otherwise? Our hands are frozen, flayed by our labor. And always, nothing to chew on!

On 14 February, in the afternoon, I am back on the road from Stieblew to Schanderovka. The temperature has dropped again and the cold is penetrating. Today again, despite everything, we must get vehicles out of the mud and abandon others. Toward the end of the afternoon, at the edge of a pond, I come upon a stopped lorry. It is one of ours that has broken down. There I find the brothers Mi., J. Herbecq, André S., and one or two more. I am, indeed, hungry, but I am dying of thirst, and all the canteens are empty. Despite the cold the pond is not frozen, except for a few patches of ice. The stagnant water is covered by a thick layer of brown, green and bluish-green algae. I cannot resist it, and don't worry about typhus! I grab a rifle from the truck and tie my helmet to the end, which I move around on the surface of the water to push the algae aside as best I can. Then, with a brisk movement I let the water flow into the hollow of the helmet, which I pick up. The algae sticks to the bottom of the helmet and this viscous matter stretches out, trickles down and spreads out on the ground.

One of the brothers, Guy Mi., has discovered a little cardboard cone in the bottom of his bread bag which contains "lemon" powder, or citric acid, which we mix with the water in the helmet to hide the taste of the frogs! Some pinch their nose while drinking, or make the sign of the cross. The others prefer to taste what they are swallowing, without, however, draining the helmet to the dregs! In any case, there is something there to drink and to eat. Now all that remains is to be a bit patient to see which is stronger: the typhus or the constitution of a *Légionnaire*! I can assure you that none of us died, at least not from typhus.

Evening falls, and the temperature with it. It gets colder and colder. We all creep into the lorry and pull the canvas over us, and we pack in close to each other to avoid loss of our body heat, or should I say our human heat? Despite several awakenings due to the cold or to the noise of columns on the march, I was able to sleep a bit, to take some repose. When I wake up I have to do a lot of thrashing about and gesticulate with vigor in order to get rid of the stiffness and warm up a bit. A "*Bourguignon*" coming from Schanderovka and who came to Stieblew, tells us of the death of our *Commandeur, Lieutenant-Colonel* Lippert! This announcement appalls us, leaves us speechless. There is not a single *Légionnaire* who did not esteem his commander to the very highest. He was an exceptional man, a bit timid, but with quiet courage and steadfast, his integrity proof against any test. He lived in the same fashion as his men and did his best to do so. He ate like them, no more. I must stop here for he would already have had me stop, his modesty would not have permitted this for long.

Other news also upsets me. This "*Bourguignon*" tells me that Drion is wounded and is waiting for me at the *kolkhose* [collective]. How, then, did I lose track of Joseph, and how does he suddenly turn up there? This comrade also tells us of a series of deaths, including several excellent friends. My old friend Emile Müller of Spa, *Sergents* Lang and Pierre Duray, a childhood friend, and many more. He says that my friend Emile was killed at Novo – Buda, like the others. A tank alert had just been sounded. Emile, who was gun commander and was catching a moment of sleep in an *isba*, was up the moment the alert sounded to reconnoiter the nature of the danger and to inspect the sector with his binoculars through the window. At that very moment a tank round struck him in the chest. Thus one of my dearest and oldest friends in the *Légion* disappeared, hard and pure.

I have nothing more to do here, nothing to keep me here. I am pushed irresistibly forward. I say farewell to my comrades and head toward Schanderovka, which is only a few kilometers away. Now I am in a hurry to get there. Eager to depart, I march too fast, also, in part, because it is very cold and thus, at such a pace, I will warm up quickly. However, I have to ease up and settle into a less hurried pace, for I am getting out of breath and my throat is getting too dry as a result of breathing the extremely cold air too briskly.

I do not know what time it is when, at last, I see in the distance on the facing hill some houses among the other ruins. The road goes downhill. I cross a little "*balka*", or depression, and then go back uphill toward the village, which must be Schanderovka. There I first meet "*Bourguignons*". It really is Schanderovka, and the large, dark building on my right, built of planks and sheet metal, is the *kolkhose* and I go there immediately. I open one half of the double door and enter. Constantly looking to left and right in search of Drion, I quickly examine the entire place. It is dark here compared with outside where, despite the clouds, the snow reflects the slightest light. But my eyes adjust quickly. The roof, made of tin, or some sort of *Eternit*,[3] is about 10 meters above,

---

3 *Eternit* is a registered trademark for a fiber-cement, but the name is often used in a generic manner referring to fiber-cement. It is mainly used in roofing and siding, commonly appearing as a corrugated fiber-cement roofing similar in appearance to corrugated metal roofing.

maybe a bit more, supported by thick, exposed joists. The *kolkhose* is divided into two sections, and the wounded are collected here, lying on mountains of dried peas and lentils, all local. The ground, in the center part, is bare, or nearly so, for the weight of our men has dislodged quantities of peas and lentils from above, which form a moving carpet under my uncertain steps. These are whole dried peas, no broken ones. There are 50, maybe 80 wounded there? It is hard to say. Some quite genuine, others much less so. I do not see Joseph right away, and he does not recognize me immediately, for, while entering, I am only a silhouette in the opening of the door, standing out like a Chinese shadow on a background of snow. But there he is, hailing me from the top of his mountain of dried legumes in the back at the left. I approach him, walking in this mass that shifts away under my feet, and I must take 10 steps to get one step forward! When I get up to where he is I find that he does not look that bad, maybe a bit pale, but nothing alarming. I see his bandage on the wrist that he reaches out to help me up. A bullet passed through it but I do not know if the bone or the nerves, or a vein are damaged. To comfort him I tell him that, after all, he has a beautiful wound and will no longer have to fight. He smiles, but with a somewhat sad and sorry air that astonishes me. This is not like him! While I am thinking of something foolish to say, my gaze wanders over all the misery collected here on a background of still life. The *feldgrau* blends with that of the peas and lentils, but the bandages, contrasting with their whiteness, spotted with blood, are universally present, tragically red.

Arms in slings extend from uniforms with their sleeves cut off, feet and legs wrapped in strips of cloth like mummies. But there are also illogical extremities, that do not end with any foot, no hand, like broken porcelain dolls. They seem already resigned to this loss, but I am not yet so, and these are the victims, these are the ones who suffer! What a paradox. Joseph's voice comes to me in my *reverie*, an embarrassed voice, like that of a child who asks a favor. And I am astonished. For Joseph is 10 years older than me. Does he think that I am stronger than he is? I suppose that it is because I am healthy and he is handicapped. I try to extract us from this embarrassing situation with a joke, but Joseph tries to explain, awkwardly, shyly, he whom I have never seen suffer from this complex, that he is deeply convinced that he will never get out, that he will not survive the final test. I cannot believe my ears! He who is always so gay, so full of energy! He hands me his wallet, plump, very thick, where he has put all the mementos that he has left, all that he thinks is important for his mother. His mother, who was widowed in the previous war and who will lose her son, the only loved one she has left, in this modern crusade that he has undertaken as a duty! Laughing, kidding him about the importance of his wound, gently, but firmly, I push the wallet that he holds out to me back with my hand. He has a worried air, but, I refuse very firmly, and we resume the conversation. I spend a bit of time with him, I talk about one thing or another, and take advantage of the opportunity to talk with other companions. Finally I take my leave, promising him that I will return later.

I report to *Adjudant* Deravet, who is in the other part of the *kolkhose*. He seems quite happy to see me again and, since we are close enough, we idly talk a bit of all that has happened. Comrades from my company and from others join in the conversation. We discuss the commander and other comrades killed in the final fighting for Novo – Buda and talk of the fighting itself. Although the death of the commander has disturbed us all, his death has not in any way changed our desire to get out. To the contrary: indeed, it has galvanized us! I hear talk of "*le dernier carré*",[4] which gives rise to reminiscences, to ideas of glory, but which, all the same, sends a little shiver the entire

---

4   The 'Last Square'; the 'last stand' – referring back to Napoleonic times and earlier, when the surrounded infantry formed a hollow square and fought to the end against assailants from all sides.

length of the spine! This will also, they say, be the *"carré du Commandeur"*. The ensuing days will, perhaps, be a little less prosaic but, not to get ahead of ourselves, the essential will be to succeed!

I return for a moment to wish a good night to Drion and to other wounded comrades and I spend a little more time there. Comrade J. is there, deeply demoralized, and he lets everybody around him know it. He is also a member of the headquarters company and is a good 35 years old. He is also wounded, but not gravely, and I let him know in no uncertain terms that I do not approve of his lack of self-control which runs the risk of demoralizing the other wounded who are behaving far better than he is. At 20 years old, I do not understand how this man, 15 years older than I am, can lose it like this. Finally I go back to the other part of the *kolkhose*, where I try to get a bit of sleep. I lie down in the peas, which, all in all, make an acceptable mattress, but I do not dare take off my boots for fear of being unable to put them back on. An alarm could come at any moment, and can you see me responding in bare feet? It is not easy to fall asleep on an empty stomach that has cried famine for the last eight to 10 days! What have we eaten during these last eight days? One or two extremely incomplete meals, a few slices of bread and a bit of sausage in the last three or four days, maybe the last five days. But, during the last two days at Derenkowez, the two days at Korsun and Stieblew, the time spent on the road, we have had nothing, absolutely nothing other than the loaves of bread that I received at Korsun. To summarize, for three days I have eaten absolutely nothing, but all are in the same state! Fatigue helps, and I fall asleep on my peas, which, penetrate everywhere.

When I wake up, when I arise, I have little peas truly everywhere. My boots are full, so are my pockets, they are down my neck, in my sleeves. And there can be no question of removing my boots to empty them. Moreover, head down, feet in the air, I can get rid of a good part of them, but not all. Certainly not those that are already in the bottom of my boots. They will remain there to add to my ordeal, like a procession of expiation. Yesterday's cold persists, despite the furtive rays of sunlight between two gray clouds. No water for morning wash-up, so, primitively, a few handfuls of snow take care of the hands, and a summary rubbing of the face and torso. The towel is still my shirt tail. Hitherto I have never had more than 24 hours' beard. Now it has been at least 10 days since I have shaved, but I have other concerns! I cannot recognize myself. I go to greet Drion and his companions. Joseph's morale seems better. He no longer talks to me about his apprehensions. I then go out for a bit of air and join in the conversation of a group of comrades.

Suddenly, a few paces from the *kolkhose*, the vision of a dream, an apparition nails us to the spot! There, 20 meters from us, is a little suckling piglet, rash, for certain, frolicking and running around. Poor thing, he does not know that 20 pairs of eyes are shooting him, 20 pairs of eyes, in close rapport with 20 empty stomachs! Twenty arms extend to point out the target, to designate the next innocent victim of this war without mercy. He stands no chance against so many hollow bellies, 20 empty stomachs, desperate to survive. All these men start to turn, as if to surround this enemy that must be conquered at any price! The piglet is alarmed, and attempts to escape by wild leaps. He nearly escapes, through a weakness in the tactics of his assailants, but is again surrounded by the famished mob. Comrade Herbecq unsheathes a bayonet and throws it hard. The weapon hits the target at the base of the neck, but with the grip. A few squeals, but no more. The little pink pig also tries to survive. The circle draws tighter, with a feline bound. One of us finally dives and barely manages to grab a hind foot.

Everything now goes very quickly. The animal is stunned, more or less bled. His short existence concludes at an age where all the little piglets of the world think of nothing but play. His sacrifice will not have been in vain since it permits 20 ferocious warriors to face death without, at least, fear of starving. While some remove the animal's guts and prepare it for the sacrifice, the others go in quest of combustibles. The spitted animal soon disappears in the acrid smoke, for the flames are meager. After a quarter of an hour, 20 minutes, the men can wait no longer. The devil take recipes, fancy cooking, *adieu* to delicacies. Each of us grabs his piece! The others, curious, intrigued by our feverish activity draw near and follow our every move, their eyes riveted to the object that they covet. When it is time to divide it up, it is good that they take part in the feast, and that is why each of us ends up with such a small morsel. For my part, I receive a front foot which may well weigh 200 grams, including skin and bone. Forgetting manners, not waiting until we are at the table, I start on my piece. It is insipid, the meat is still raw, it is stringy, a piece of rubber, a little better, no doubt, than a truck tire, but that is all right! Not much to fill the stomach, but better than nothing! When there is not the least atom of meat left, when not even a nerve is left on the bone, I slip it into my pocket. One never knows.

A little later in the day I am in the lower part of Schanderovka when we receive a salvo of *Katioushkas.*[5] The "Stalin-organs" send us 36 or 72 rounds in a single firing, which arrive with a noise from hell! Everyone hits the ground where he is. Cries soon mix with detonations which succeed each other in an infernal rhythm. I do not try to count them as I have done at other times. If the number exceeds 36 or 37 I know that it will continue to 72. That is how one can tell which model has taken us for a target.

The noise of the "organs" is finally over; all those around me get back up, at least those who can. A little farther down, in the "*balka*", there was no escaping! I take the few paces that separate me from it and I find Pierre Mi., Herbecq and Lefranc with minor wounds, and several others. Quoibion is dead, Preudhomme too, but there are others. Abrassart is wounded, and the poor Everaerts is reduced to a human trunk! Horrible sight. Everaerts is perfectly lucid. We now determine that he is also blind, his eyes shredded by the bursts, burnt by the explosion. A great deal of blood flows from his legs and soaks his shredded greatcoat. We try to make tourniquets with belts, but without success. Dear God, how can we save this comrade? Pierre and Lefranc want to transport him, but one leg still hangs on by the little shred of flesh. Someone passes a pocket knife and Lefranc, I believe, cuts the flesh that still holds the limb that has been torn off. When Pierre and Lefranc lift our comrade we hear him clearly say, "My legs hurt, my feet hurt." He then asks who is carrying him, for he cannot see anything. Everything will be done in vain for him, and he dies a little later at the aid station in terrible pain, but entirely lucid. Shattered carts, dead horses, all sorts of debris are scattered on the ground.

I then go back up toward the *kolkhose*, where, too, unaccustomed activity reigns. When I arrive I learn that a shell hit the roof, right at the wall that separates the building in two, but more on the side of the infirmary. Suddenly I have a misgiving and I go to see. There are dead, others have received yet more wounds. Among the dead is my friend, Joseph. He was not wrong in his premonition! What a hecatomb of friends in these last few days, what desolation. J. is also dead. I regret having scolded him yesterday for his lack of *sang-froid*. I do not know who the other dead are. Troubled, even a bit dazed, despite all that I have experienced in the last few days, the last few weeks, I do not think of taking from him the wallet that he prepared for his mother. I will later regret that.

Searching for a bit of tranquility, of solitude, I wander for a while in the village. I meet Germans of the *Wehrmacht*, exhausted by three attacks on Novo – Buda before our arrival. They are not, as some believe, demoralized. They are simply exhausted, like us! I contemplate explanations of the sense of life and death and, calmed down again, I rejoin Deravet and the others in the *kolkhose* just as night falls. It is 16 February, and I shall remember every minute that I experienced on this day, or nearly, in any case, all of the events, the thousand details. It seems that tomorrow will be a great day, the day when we will attempt to break out. Tomorrow or never! Before that it is still necessary

5   Russian multiple rocket launchers – also called 'Stalin-organs'.

for men to go up to Novo – Buda and Deravet asks if I will go. Of course I will go! I have nothing to do here. Better to be in action while waiting.

Arthur V.E. and I set out for Novo – Buda with a dozen other volunteers. Arthur is responsible for the detachment. Novo – Buda is not far away, three or four kilometers, but the road climbs a bit, bounded by two slopes, for the village is on a little hill that commands the adjacent plain. We walk in total darkness, but the whiteness of the snow helps us in our march. When we arrive at the top of the road we find a burning *isba* on the right, lower down, and two others in a hollow that are burning. We proceed toward the left on a little footpath that wanders along the side of the hill, bordered on the left by several *isbas*. The village seems deserted, abandoned by all its residents. A light shines from one of these *isbas* and we head for that. A comfortable warmth welcomes us as we enter, and we find *Lieutenant* Darras there and several men who are finishing a meal of chickens and *sautéed* potatoes, or *kartochkas*. How the devil is there still such opulence here? There is no question of eating now; we must go into the positions. I still ask them to save us something to eat, when we return. A single *karasinka* sheds meager light in the room, especially the table loaded with all these heaps of food, which so captures my attention. We do not tarry, and go on our way. The *lieutenant* has shown us the road to follow, and we go to occupy the positions that we are to hold until midnight, or until 0100 hours in the morning at the latest. Someone will come to inform us – at least that is what they say!

Our positions are southeast of the village, facing Morency, which is held by the Russians. The foxholes are full of snow, and we lie down behind them, sheltered by the parapet, except for two or three men who prefer, regardless, to bury themselves in the snow in the holes. One of these feels a body under his feet and prefers to switch holes. Arthur and I take the trouble to scout the area, he to the left and I to the right. We can now see about 20 meters, no doubt a little less. The positions on either side of ours are deserted! There is not another living soul for at least 200 meters in every direction! Arthur and I know what to make of it but we don't say anything about it. We are here for at least four hours, maybe more, but who knows?

At first it is very cold and one of the men freeze-burns the palm of his hand by holding the barrel of his weapon without gloves. But, as time passes the temperature rises and becomes endurable, especially for such a long evening. It is hard to say, but it might be –7° to –10° [19 to 14°F]. Across from us everything seems to sleep, it is calm, but one can never trust it. Now and then, in the distance, there are fleeting flashes, but they are impossible to evaluate at that distance. Doubtless it is in the village that is about four kilometers distant. Do the Russians occupy positions around Morency, or are they closer to us, between the two villages? We know nothing of the sector where I have never been.

The minutes and hours pass slowly, interminably, and the protracted calm makes it hard for me to breathe. Hunger grips my stomach. I can well try not to think of it, but my belly cries famine. I have the impression that the tension has mounted a notch or two just now and that we are all suffering from it. To release the tension a bit and do something useful I decide to fire off a few magazines toward the enemy. At least he will know that our positions are still occupied, in case he might have thought otherwise. This will give the Russians something to think about, for they should know now that we cannot retreat further, that our positions will be defended to the end, to the last round, to the last person. Above all, they must not think that we are isolated here, that such a small number of men is facing them! It is past midnight, and there is still nothing from our rear, no sign of life, no sign of a relief or whatever. Patience and calm, that is what has saved us so often.

At 10 minutes to 0100 hours in the morning we are still there, and I know that the brigade is to be ready to move out at 0230 hours. I am sure that we have been forgotten! The advance guard of those who are to open the passage should now have left Schanderovka nearly two hours ago, with the password, "Freedom". The word is *"Freiheit"*! That is the password for this night. In order to preserve the element of surprise there has been no artillery preparation. To avoid accidental or untimely discharge, weapons cannot be loaded. It is obvious that here we have no news of the attempt. At precisely 0100 hours Arthur and I have a brief confab and, after a final inspection of the sector facing us, we decide to fall back in absolute silence.

We head back over the road that we just came on. The *karasinka* still burns in the *isba* where we found the "*Bourguignons*" when we arrived, but when we enter the house it is empty, the table still covered with hen's eggs. There is not a living soul! Are we the only ones left in Novo – Buda? Certainly there is nothing left to eat. So, in frustration, I take a few eggs to gnaw on *en route*, even though there is nothing better to eat. The other men do the same. We do not wait around, for we don't want to be surprised, and we take the road again to Schanderovka. The *isbas* that we saw burning as evening fell are still ablaze, and light our path. We take the footpath on the right, which climbs and crosses the ridge, and we descend again toward Schanderovka. It is faster than before, for the road goes downhill. It is also easier. When we reach the *kolkhose* in Schanderovka it is nearly 0230 hours in the morning, and *Adjudant* Deravet asks me where we have been, for he has been waiting for us for more than an hour. He has had to keep a small detachment here waiting for us.

We were the last and only ones to occupy the positions at Novo – Buda and no one came to tell us to fall back! What would have happened to us if we had not taken upon ourselves responsibility for the decision to fall back, if I had not convinced Arthur that we had been forgotten? The lives of these 14 men could have depended on a cruel and criminal negligence! Today we are congratulated on our initiative. It could have been that tomorrow we would be court-martialed for not waiting for confirmation of the order to fall back.

We leave the *kolkhose* to go down toward the "*balka*" from which we shall head out for liberty or some other destiny. Even though it is night, in the snow-carpeted "*balka*" we can see a multitude of men and a mass of vehicles. I do not know if the vehicles are still important, for all of the *matériel* which might encumber us, all that might interfere with our movement, anything that might hinder our progress has been destroyed so that nothing is left behind for the enemy.

While I am thinking of all this, I hear the characteristic sound of the "*petrolette*" [motorbike or moped], that is also nicknamed the "*U.v.D*" – "*Unteroffizier von Dienst*", or "non-com on duty". These are some of the names we have applied to the small Russian reconnaissance aircraft that seem propelled by two-cycle engines. They fly low and I have never seen them during the day. They are simply too vulnerable, but they have curious habits. The sound of the engine gets louder. It can't be too far away, but these machines are very slow and one hears them 15 minutes before they arrive. That is certainly the reason that we never see them during the day. Now it is probably right above us, but it does no good to scan the sky, you never see anything, even though it feels like you could catch it in your arms if you reached out. It does no good to fire at it, rather by chance, the shots are fruitless. It will not fall and continues its rounds. Suddenly the sound stops, it cuts its motor and we all know what that means! At this very moment the whistling starts, followed by the explosions. There are far more whistlings than explosions, to which yet another curious noise is mixed. The pilot of this curious machine restarts the engine and slowly moves off as he came. I go to take a look and I have not gone 30 meters when I come upon a group of "*Bourguignons*" who are gathered around a reed basket with two handles, like those that housekeepers use at home for dirty laundry. All around are a lot of big rusty bolts and screws. A few grenades have exploded, but do not seem to have done much damage.

In case you have not guessed, I shall explain this a bit. This little airplane, like its siblings, usually comes, once night has fallen, to drop one or two cases of grenades where it suspects concentrations of troops, on the front line or in the rear area, and, in addition, balances the plane with the grenades. I gather from the present circumstances that he did not have enough cases of grenades at the right moment and that, here and there, he gathered up a few grenades that he put in this basket, borrowed for this use from a housekeeper, and, to make weight, for good measure, he filled the basket to the top with the bolts and screws gathered here and there in a nearby factory. Such a bolt or screw could seriously injure a man without a helmet, especially after falling 50 meters. I am sure that this is what happened.

I hear an officer looking for some men, German-speaking if possible, and I report. A few minutes later we are *en route* toward where the breakthrough is taking place. Along with our pioneers and a few Germans we cross a little river on the deck of a collapsed bridge. We go out in the steppe where we come upon wooden poles like the ones used at home for telephone wires. Now I understand the reason for this "mission". Two by two the men of the group are to bring back as many of these poles as possible. With my comrade I approach one of these poles and, at its base, we tie two 200 gram charges of powder. We light the fuse, run back a few meters and lie down. After the explosion, we go to the next pole and do the same. In less than one hour we have carried or dragged enough poles near the destroyed bridge to make the bridge accessible for the waiting vehicles. That is how the carts will get through that are carrying the wounded from the *kolkhose*.

The departure order is for exactly 0450 hours! Now everything will take place in the hours, perhaps the minutes, that lie ahead. Yesterday evening the encircled pocket was reduced to a three by five kilometer oval, as contrasted with an area the size of Belgium on the first day of the encirclement. At that moment there remained about 52,000 men of the 100,000 or so that should have been in the 10 encircled divisions. Today we are no more than 30,000! Thirty-thousand men, exhausted by so much fighting, by so much guard duty. Thirty-thousand famished men, chilled to the bone! Thirty-thousand men, raring to go despite all their miseries and losses. All of this pent-up energy will explode, be released in one blow to make possible a miracle the like of which no one would have believed! Moscow and London have already loudly proclaimed their total annihilation! What a glorious revenge we shall take here today! We shall prove, demonstrate the duplicity of the hostile propaganda. Even if many of us will yet pay for this bold blow and will no longer be alive this evening!

It is in this spirit that the column moves out and proceeds during the night toward the west, following the path of those who, since yesterday evening, reconnoitered this same road to freedom!

The password is "*Freiheit*"! The word of the day, the password is "Liberty"!

The Ukraine in snow.

Dealing with a quagmire, as I have so often done.

15

The Breakthrough:
The Word is *"Freiheit"*!

Shortly after crossing the little river on foot at Schanderovka, a small group forms based on friendship or opportunity. It includes my comrades Paul Van Brusselen, Arthur V.I., Jean V.D.W., Charles T., four childhood friends who live in my quarters, André Bourdouxhe, Delreux, as well as two or three others whose names I no longer remember because they were not so close to me.

Right then I see comrade Vinckx, whom I knew at Wildflecken at the time when I was a pioneer. Vinckx has an impressive bandage on his head and neck. He had been wounded in earlier fighting, escaping death in curious fashion and by a miracle. His head hurt at the end of the fighting. He thought that he had hurt himself on a branch in the heat of action. Running his hand over the painful spot he found blood on his fingers. A comrade discovered a bullet hole in that precise spot and Vinckx was taken to the dressing station. There they discovered that the bullet had come out again at the base of the skull, in the nape of the neck. He remained several days at the infirmary and was then evacuated with the other wounded during the various retreats. He suffered no more since then except for a stiffness in the neck, as from a twisted neck. That is why, today, he prefers to rejoin the combatants, rather than to be transported with the other wounded. And this despite the fact that a bullet passed through his head, literally, from the temple to the base of the skull.

I shall simply narrate, as I experienced them, all the events worthy of attention, at least for those who also experienced them. But you must excuse me if, despite everything, there seems to be a certain grandiloquence in these lines what follow, but in fact it was even worse!

All of the comrades who lived through this day of 17 February and the four or five ensuing days, and there are a handful still remaining, know what it was like, and especially those who were wounded, incapable of moving on their own, at the mercy of everyone and everything. So many memories, so many reminiscences come back to me at the same time, arising from my mind and jostling around in my head, that my pen has trouble putting them on paper in the same wild rhythm! It is like being submerged in a wave that sweeps me off my feet, and I struggle to keep my head above water at all costs so as not to drown. I know, in any case, that everything is clear to me, but that I must watch out, be careful to explain myself at my own pace and in order. There are so many things to say from the hours and days that ensue. All things that are important to me, but also to those who are interested in these events that they, themselves, experienced or who want to know how a 21-year-old reacts, how one experiences such dramatic moments at that age. My memory is accurate, my recollections precise, as are my notes.

Without literary pretensions, I want to tell you how things were, exactly how I experienced them, in all humility. There are, of course, a great many anecdotes, the small events of life that are precisely those that make up everyday life and that books generally do not mention. It is these that reflect the *ambiance* more, no doubt, than the epic exploits, but they are all indissolubly bound together! Every day is not glorious. Here I close this essential little parenthetical remark and return to the story where I last left it.

I am now with eight or nine comrades and we are about to undertake the last stage, that which should lead us to freedom, at least which is supposed to so do! But at this hour of truth there is no room for doubt, at risk of losing all! It is night still, but the cold is less severe, or perhaps, it is the heat of action that warms the heart and body. From time to time there are a few flakes of snow that come in brief squalls. The ground remains uniformly white, even though others before us have trod on the snow. All around us other small groups move forward as we do, with no apparent order, no particular tactics, each improvising as the circumstances demand. When I get on the road I suddenly discover an ambulance moving along at the same rate we are and in the same direction. Our paths draw near and I discover to my astonishment that it is one of our own ambulances and that our dentist, *Lieutenant* Lejeune, follows it on foot. Since we know each other quite well, we march for a moment side by side, chatting, and he tells me that my four teeth, my false teeth, are there in the ambulance, ready to rejoin the others, their half-sisters, there in my palate, but that he will await a more propitious moment to install them there. Before we left Wildflecken he had undertaken the project of making four dental implants for me. Everything had been ready for some time, but every time, something came up that prevented completion. It is a good subject for pleasantry and we do not fail to exploit it for a moment, for we may not have much more time to laugh in a few moments. I then rejoin the group of my comrades which has not kept up the same pace.

Everything has been calm to this point, and perhaps there are some who already imagine, but falsely, that they will be able to get out thus, with a little walk for their health. Now, all of a sudden, some of the first shots that, in this case, will disillusion them. The shots come from the right, from in front of us, and the shells burst right in front of us, a few hundred meters distant. Day slowly breaks and the snow appears less white under a sky that becomes clear. As the horizon brightens, revealing the steppe in the light of day, the shots increase and shred the silence that I was accustomed to. Little by little we discover all the horror of the situation; we now know what is waiting for us!

Here the gates of a Dantesque universe open for us! The shots are increasingly violent, there are more and more of them, and the shells burst everywhere. More and more often I have to throw myself on the ground, for the explosions are closer, more menacing every instant. A tracked vehicle comes up behind us, moving a little faster than us. Four or five men are crouched or sitting on its rear, bounced around by each pothole. I tell myself that we will progress a bit faster if we follow it, so we pick up our pace and attempt to keep up with it. We place ourselves on the left of the *chenillette*,[1] for most of the gunfire is coming from the right. We do not long continue like this, for the Russian artillery target it and the shells fall thickly and ever closer. This firing comes from all sides and we think it more prudent to leave some distance between the vehicle and us. The *chenillette* speeds up to get away from the gunfire, which obviously makes it buck violently on such uneven ground, moreover, with hundreds of shell craters. One of the German comrades loses his balance and falls from the *chenillette* no more than 50 meters from us. I clearly see one of the tracks run right over one leg or a foot, and I then see the fellow get up immediately, run behind the vehicle and regain his place on the platform in the rear as if nothing had happened! Did he, then, feel nothing or how did he escape injury? I have no explanation, unless, maybe, the foot or leg happened to be in a hollow in the ground at the moment when the track ran over it.

During this incoming fire from all directions we frequently have to go our own way and hit the ground. We scatter and there are only three of us together at the moment. For all our searching, all

---

1   The French term '*chenillette*' refers to a universal carrier – a full-track cargo carrier such as the British Bren-gun carrier. In this case, it probably refers to the German *RSO* (*Raupenschlepper Ost*) – a full-tracked cargo vehicle developed by Steyr-Daimler-Puch for cargo transport in Russian conditions.

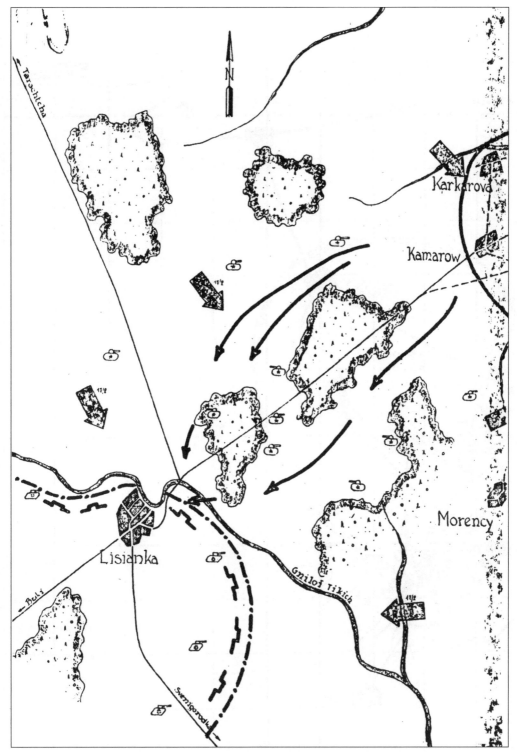

Karkarova – Kamarow – Lisjanka. Breakout from Tcherkassy
(Codeword "Freedom" – 15-18 February, 1944).

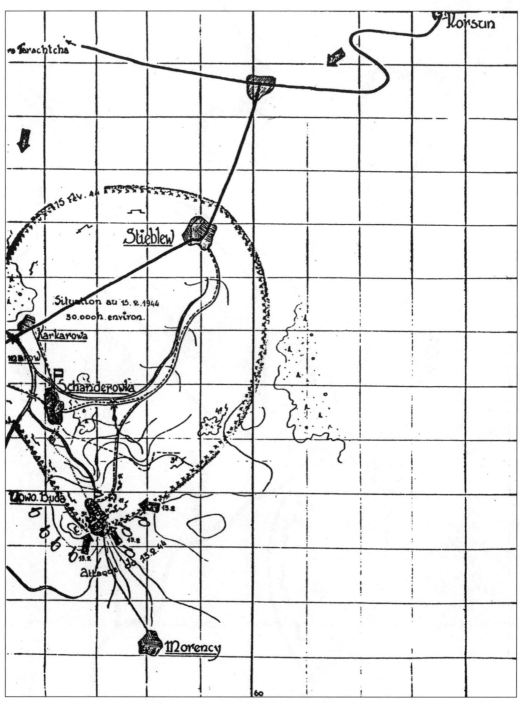

Schanderovka – Novo – Buda. Breakout from Tcherkassy
(Codeword "Freedom" – 15-18 February, 1944).

our scanning the surroundings, we no longer see our other comrades. It is snowing again, which interferes with our looking and we decide to go on without waiting longer. Regrouping takes place, due to our advance, and some silhouettes, especially the way they walk, suddenly intrigue me. When we get nearer to them I cannot believe my eyes! In the group, dressed like us, are three or four women! I was right that they did not walk like men. They wear military clothes, like ours, their hair put up under the cap. The situation seems weird to me. Intrigued, I ask one of them and learn that these women are part of a theatrical *troupe* that had just come from Germany to perform at the exact moment when the circle closed around us. What a misfortune, what destiny, would they get out? In any case, they are marching there, bravely, courageously, at the same pace as the men, with no panic. Only their greatcoats, too large, and too long for them caught my attention from the first.

As we march on, here is André Bourdouxhe, who tells me that he will not get separated from me for an instant, for he is sure that I always get through and that he will do the same, and Delreux agrees, smiling. I, myself, am not so sure, but I keep that to myself. Just like me, they wonder what has happened to the others. We keep on going and, gradually, the snow stops falling. The gunfire immediately starts up again from both sides of the corridor that we are in. At times it is incredibly heavy! I ask myself if there really is any point in going on, if there is any real chance of getting out. Yes, there must be a chance, and then willpower takes the upper hand, the doubt only lasts for a moment. I force it back deep down inside me. I stop for a moment and take advantage of the opportunity to scan this hostile horizon.

Eh bien! What I can see, now that the snow has stopped falling, is enough to freeze less resilient souls with fear. To the right and to the left I see nothing but a continuous wall of artillery pieces, flanked by mountains of ammunition! At this location the corridor is no more than 800 meters wide. That allows me to see everything, clearly and in detail, in this level steppe, covered with fresh snow. We are no more than about 400 meters from each of these walls. There must be the entire gamut of calibers there, lined up for our destruction, but mostly *"Ratsch-Boum"* anti-tank guns,[2] so named because the rounds explode among us before we even hear the sound of the gun firing.

Dozens, hundreds of artillery pieces are lined up for the entire length of this corridor of death that the Russians have had more than a month to bring to the Tcherkassy pocket! At such short range every one of these pieces is firing in direct fire, at times taking even a single man as its target. We always say that two rounds never fall in the same hole, and that, to find shelter, it is enough to lie there! *Eh bien*! I can tell you that this assertion is insane. One shell hole covers another. They straddle each other, the ground is ploughed up. Fortunately, not all the rounds arrive at the same time! We move forward under this squall of iron that has followed that of snow, but I prefer the latter, by far! One moment the gunfire lets up, the next it is stronger than ever. Sometimes it is heaviest ahead of us, sometimes behind us, sometimes more to the right, or more to the left, but always and mathematically it finishes by surrounding us closely, then giving us a few moments' respite. How is it possible to still be unharmed under such a deluge for fire and iron?

For the moment we are following a little footpath, more a track left by other feet. There, 20 or 30 meters in front of us a man is sitting on a little hillock, a haversack between his legs, which are a little apart. When we get to him I see that he is a *Major* of the *Wehrmacht*, a man of 60, but, maybe, in fact, no more than 50. He is wearing a *Jäger's* cap, a long and large *"Übermantel"*, one of those winter overcoats that one puts on over the greatcoat. I am surprised a bit as we pass him to see that he has a pistol in his hand, but we greet him with a nod of the head and continue on

---

2   A Russian 76.2 mm model 1942 field gun. Originally developed as a field gun, it became increasingly employed against armor due to its handiness and effectiveness.

our way. We have not gone 20 paces when we hear a shot behind us. I turn immediately and I see the *Major*, who does not seem to have stirred, he simply seems to be shifting his balance a little, from one side to the other. As I continue on my way I see him suddenly fall forward and slide off his improvised seat. I turn back, confused, without really thinking, and we hasten back. He lies there, lying on his stomach, his head turned on his chest, one arm folded under him and the other stretched out from his body near his haversack. His pistol is still in his hand. There is no doubt, he has killed himself! Thinking it over carefully I can understand it, but it seems truly absurd to me, after going through these months of fighting, these weeks of encirclement, after making it through all that to give it all up today, two steps from freedom! And, all the more so on the road of this renaissance. This death is futile. I would have understood it better in combat. And, now, it is not a good example.

I would not know if the artillery fire let up for a moment, I would not hear, only having eyes for our destiny, necessarily in front of us. We move on immediately. There is no reason for one of us to be impressed by this form of abdication. If it is necessary to die, let it be in combat. We think of it for a minute, then forget the vision, eliminate it, too preoccupied with our own will to live!

This day seems like an eternity to me. I have gone through so many things since morning, in the last minute! So many events in one third of a day that they would have sufficed to fill up many others, monotonous days of an entire life. And it is not yet 0800 hours in the morning!

We march on! Always onward toward the west! The firing has resumed, sometimes at greater intervals, then increasing, then letting up again. Ahead, to the right, that is, to the southeast, perhaps a thousand meters from us the ground rises like a barrier. The sort of slope that one finds in a sandpit. I think that the difference in elevation is maybe 15 or 20 meters. What catches my attention in this direction is not really this change in elevation, but rather the four dark masses profiled at the top. These silhouettes could not fool anyone, but are these tanks friendly or hostile? For we always hope to meet up with ours, which march or roll to meet us. I do not think that, in high places, they have given up all hope of saving us, since *Général* Gille, commander of the *Wiking Division*, has taken over supreme command of the encircled troops.[3] My doubt does not last long. In fact, the turrets turn for a moment and immediately spew death in our direction. They fire on the groups that are moving in the corridor of the breakout. We continue on our way, bending our line of march, however, a little to the right.

We have not gone 200 meters when we very distinctly see a little group of five or six men at the foot of the escarpment who are attempting to climb it, right below the emplacement that the tanks have chosen for firing on us! I think and fear for a moment that they have not seen the tanks and are going to throw themselves into the wolf's mouth, for they cannot see them from where they are. But there is no way that I can warn them from this distance! Very quickly I realize that they know exactly what they are doing, and then my heart beats to the rhythm of their escalades and their slips right to the foot of the hill. For the slope is steep and they slide in the snow as they attempt to reach the summit. Finally I see two of them reach the top, followed shortly by two more. But before these last two get there, I can clearly see one of the tanks as if it hiccupped at the same moment that a long yellow and red flame shoots like a flash of lightning at the level of the tank-hunters. For that is what is happening. Fortunately, men carrying *Panzerfäuste*[4] are at work!

---

3   In actual fact, on 7 February, *Generaloberst* Otto Wöhler – commanding *8. Armee* – placed *General der Artillerie* Wilhelm Stemmermann – commanding *XI. Armeekorps* – in command of all of the forces in the pocket. However, *Generalleutnant* Theo Helmut Lieb – commanding *XXXXII. Armeekorps* – commanded the final breakout force. *SS-Brigadeführer* Herbert Otto Gille remained in command of *5. SS-Panzerdivision* '*Wiking*'.
4   The *Panzerfäust* was a hand-held one-man anti-tank recoilless gun firing a large hollow-charge projectile. Later

In recent days our air force has, despite everything, still been able to drop by parachute within our lines medical supplies and ammunition, including these individual anti-tank weapons that are going to spread fear among the Russian tank men.

One or two minutes later, doubtless much sooner, two more tanks suffer the same fate, and the fourth chooses safety in flight, to the noisy acclamations of the watching comrades! Two of the tanks that were hit are now burning, giving off black smoke. The third attempts to retreat, but with only one track it doesn't get far. It turns on itself like a wounded insect. It is the only one whose turret hatch opens and a man who appears to be wounded climbs out and quickly disappears behind the hill. Nobody escapes from the other burning tanks. The death of an enemy is still the death of a man, but this short struggle presents, for us, another hope that we will get out of this, an encouragement to keep up the effort. It strengthens the heart; it reassures us that anything is still possible, so long as we believe in it, as a result of courage and tenacity.

After this interlude we resume our march with a light heart. We had stopped so as to avoid missing anything of the spectacle; it was as if we were at a news-program, at the *"Deutsche Wochenschau"*, only more realistic, from orchestra seats, at the very least. It must be about 0900 hours and we keep moving, but nothing yet on the horizon that could make us sing "Victory!" The breakout corridor widens for a time, then narrows, but the hedge consisting of Russian artillery is always there, sometimes closer, sometimes farther back, but without the least interruption! We try to keep more or less in the center, but we zig-zag due to the density of the fire. Ordinarily one would find better cover by getting closer to the guns to get into their dead space, but under direct fire that is impossible.

When pangs of hunger grip my stomach I pull from my pocket one of the eggs I picked up at Novo – Buda, or what I saved in memory of the piglet that paid the price of our starvation at Schanderovka. There is something there for every taste, for the eggs that I pull out of my pocket are covered with the remains of the brown sugar that was in my pocket, grains of tobacco, vestiges of a more abundant time, and the dust that lines the bottom of every pocket. All these residues make flour for the mill, even if the brown sugar tastes like tobacco or the morsel of pork, and even if the tobacco has a touch of sugar. What is essential is to stave off the hunger, to swallow something to line the walls of the stomach.

We do not advance very quickly, for every time the incoming fire gets near us we have to lie down, find some precarious cover, then get up and find an opening or an easier way through. It is one of these instants, the precise spot chosen by fate to stop the universe in its course, a moment of emptiness, a moment of stupefaction!

I have the impression that I am slowly emerging from a sort of absence! I see nothing but a gray sky with dark clouds shedding a few flakes of snow. Suddenly I see two comrades of my company, Lux and Dominé. They look at me curiously and they are talking. I see their lips move but I hear nothing! What a curious impression! They look at each other and talk for a moment. Then, slowly, they turn, as if in regret, and move off, disappearing from my view! Everything vanishes again. No doubt I lost consciousness again. What is it that awakens me? What sort of sleep am I leaving? I see no other horizon than the one at the level of my vision, which is the level of the grass growing on the steppe. The noise that I hear is the sound of the engine, along with the characteristic sound of tank tracks. The tank that is there, in my field of vision at 30, 40, or 50 meters distance? It is difficult to say, but I am more inclined to say 30 meters at the exact moment of which I speak. First

---

models increased the range from 30 to 100 meters – the armor penetration from 140 mm at 30° to 200 mm at 30°.

it zig-zags a bit, seeming to wander, searching for I don't know what. It approaches and presents to my view a side marked with the Soviet star, I am quite certain!

What I then see freezes me with horror and suddenly brings me wide awake. It has chosen several bodies, lying on the ground, perhaps still moving, as its target. It squashes them and pivots on them to be quite certain of achieving its goal. I see clearly the face of a man who was not dead and whose trunk disappears under the tank track. His face becomes all red, as if ready to explode, as if the blood was going to come out through the pores! When the tank pivots again, I see a sleeve torn from the uniform stuck between two links of the track and turning with them, the arm in the sleeve, and the hand at the end! I see this arm make several complete rounds with the track, hitting the armor each time, just above the track! I do not move, holding my breath for fear of attracting the attention of these modern Huns! The tank moves on and I see two more, a bit farther off, venting their fury on the wounded, lying in the snow, disarmed, defenseless, left to their mercy! I have never seen anything like this on our side. That is why I am unable to understand this bloody savagery. We have fought with all our energy against a regime that they wanted to impose on us, but never have we allowed ourselves to be possessed by hatred! We have never felt any hatred for the soldier facing us in battle!

Before long the tanks move into the distance and the noise dies away, but these images will always remain in my memory! Once more I have got away, but how many more times can I do so? I come to realize that I have been wounded. All this time I did not realize this as I regained consciousness. And this time I am both the spectator and, at the same time, the actor in my own tragedy!

I see the snow at the level of my vision and the irregularities in the ground in their smallest detail. I see the little hillocks by the hundreds and the tufts of grass of the steppe which hide the sad horizon from me and a sort of haze that hovers everywhere. It is very different in its proportions from what a man sees standing up. Incredulous about what is happening to me, I attempt, little by little, to grasp the truth, afraid of confusing my fears and the truth of the situation. Reason returns slowly, then fades and returns, more strongly. By waves, uncertain at first, things become more precise and, little by little, I am confronted by the only hypothesis that I have always feared, the worst possible case, to be wounded and conscious but nailed to the ground, at the mercy of others, at the mercy of a savage and bloody adversary from whom one cannot expect the least mercy.

When I try to get up, I immediately fall back down. The best I can do is turn myself and support myself on one knee. I then determine that my left leg is in a piteous state. Lost? I do not know, but it is, certainly, broken. Impossible for me to get up! Two timid attempts reveal that the slightest effort to move my legs result in excruciating pain. It is, indeed, the worst, for I am unable to move. A wound to one or both arms would still allow me to resume the march, maybe even body wounds, but now? My feelings return and I feel pain in my right temple. I mechanically touch it with my hand and it comes away sticky, at the level of my eyes. What horror! I seem to see skull fragments there! I don't really know very well what the skull looks like, I have never seen it, but this resembles my idea or it. I do not try this again, but can only think. A shiver runs down my back. Is it possible to have part of my brain on my fingers and, at the same time, be aware of it? This is crazy, but what else can one think of in such circumstances! For a moment I remain without daring to make the slightest movement for fear of dying!

Suddenly I realize that I was not alone! What has happened to my comrades? I look for them and, on my right, I find the lifeless body of André Bourdouxhe, his skull smashed to a pulp and his chest full of blood! I quickly realize that it is his brain that is sticking to my temple and in my hair! It is not easy to recognize him, but I know that it is him. He wears ankle boots and Delreux is shod in high boots. Furthermore, André wears the medal of the "veterans" of the movement. Since

I was marching in the center with them on both sides, obviously, I find Delreux on my left. He lies there, disjointed, his stomach, his chest, torn by shell fragments, covered with blood! Today I lose two more friends at one blow, two good comrades and, what a joke, they were keeping close to me, counting on my lucky star! They are dead. I am still here, at least for the moment. I am alone!

A multitude of thoughts assail me and churn in my head. A thick cloud of feelings, at times contradictory, but I must sort them out. First to the essentials, postpone those less urgent. I might say that it is a question of life or death, but it is not necessary to think of death, at least not in these terms. I must attempt to survive. No panic! Do not compromise the only chance of surviving. Do not hypothecate the only faculty that remains intact, that of thinking, of thinking coolly. I must take an inventory. I am wounded in my left leg by a great number of shell fragments, and the leg is broken. I have no doubt of that. It is a compound fracture and one of the fragments of the tibia protrudes from the wound. My other leg is also wounded, as is my right foot. That is certain. The holes in my boots confirm it, but I cannot determine how seriously. I do not think my body is wounded, at least not seriously. I do not feel anything, I do not see anything. As for my head, I think I have no injuries, that it is only the shreds of André's brain that are sticking in my hair.

In the state I am in I cannot make it out on my own, I cannot even stand up! Above all, I cannot wait on events. This is not courage; it is no more than lucidity. Later, if I do get out, I will always be able to say to myself that I have proven my tenacity. Today I believe that it is no more than *sang-froid*. I have a great many things that I must prove to myself! Furthermore, there are no witnesses, aside from the dazed or preoccupied shadows that are all heading for the same point, situated down there, somewhere toward the west or northwest! I must not lose my *sang-froid*. I repeat that to myself several times to imbue myself with the idea.

At first it seemed to me that I did not want to see the things immediately facing me, but, in reality, I believe that this came from losing consciousness and from not yet having fully come to my senses. In the meantime I have to reason, to assure myself, to gather my strength and to then reassure myself more easily. Left to my own devices, I am afraid that I will be weakened by seeing the misery of others, for all around me hell is always entirely present! At all costs I must clarify my thinking and find a solution. I am here, impotent, destitute, armed only with a fierce will to survive, to regain my freedom! But, on the other hand, I also think that, at any price, I must not fall, living, into Russian hands. That I have sworn, once and for all, a long time ago, after seeing so many things and I am certainly not going to change my mind today after having just seen their bestiality toward the wounded. Today there can be no other choice. I am determined on that, and the decision to avoid being taken alive is ingrained in my body and mind with a determination just as firm as that to live, but not at any price!

That idea leads me to check my armament. I still have a stick-grenade in each boot – amazing that neither of them exploded. My pistol is still in its holster, but I cannot find my submachine gun. The presence of these arms already reassures me. I suddenly remember having just seen Lux and Dominé leaning over me. Was I dreaming? I believe I remember their look, and it seems that they had anguish or something else in their eyes, the fear of two beings, intact in their physical integrity, facing a dead comrade. For they believed that I was dead. They tell me that much later, not realizing that the brains on my forehead were not mine! In a state of semi-unconsciousness my wide open eyes saw them. At first they were only vague shadows, but my vision then cleared and I distinctly saw their faces and recognized them. I must do something; I cannot remain here thinking indefinitely.

If my thoughts develop thus, it is because the ideas clarify, because my strength returns, little by little, along with the will to get out of here. I do not know how far I must go to gain freedom. That is why, doubtless, I tell myself that I must crawl, dragging my legs that cannot support me behind! And that is what I do, after one last look at my comrades that I abandon here. I have only my two elbows to move with, and every time I elbow my way ahead, it is as if someone was tearing off my left leg. The right one does not hurt, at least it is endurable. I soon realize that I will not get very far this way, but, all the same, I have crawled 50, 100, maybe even 200 meters. I have had to rest 10 times, 20 times, doubtless far more. The elbows of my coat are torn, both have holes right through, even the elbows of my tunic are worn through! The frozen ground is hard and practically everywhere it is gouged by shell fragments, pocked with thousands of craters. It gives the effect of an immense sheet of emery cloth. I stop, but enraged I go on again, each time for a shorter distance. But, all the same, I must exert all my resources to get out of this!

Always I see men marching toward the west, alone or in little groups. But how can I ask them to help me, to burden themselves with a wounded man that they must carry, when, alone and healthy they already have so little chance of getting through? I cannot persuade myself to ask for help. I do not think that it is a matter of pride on my part. Rather, I think that it is reality. The reality that we have all faced since the beginning of this campaign. How can I ask these famished, exhausted shadows to drag a wounded man along with them to God only knows where? The idea comes to me anew that, perhaps, I should put an end to my suffering and, for reassurance, I touch my grenades and my pistol. I do not know how many meters I have been able to go in this fashion, how many flea-jumps I have made, nor how long this has taken me. I think that I marched four-and-a-half hours from Schanderovka, maybe less, to the moment I was wounded. How many more hours before I reach safety?

I have not abandoned all hope, but I am making less and less progress. Doubtless I am weakening, but also my elbows are increasingly painful and raw. Sometimes the two ends of the fracture rub and grate across each other and the pain goes right to my head! Unbearable, but I must bear it, without fainting, or everything will be lost. Nevertheless, the pain often brings me right to the limit where I lose consciousness. It is during one of these short progressions that a voice behind me hails me in German. I stop immediately and the fellow is then right beside me. He is on horseback and dismounts to talk to me. He finds that I am not doing well and, doubtless, too young to die, though there are many others in my situation! He is at least 45 years old, though he might be 15 years younger for all I know, what with 15 days' beard and all that one has gone through! He has seen my "*Wallonie*" shoulder patch and compliments me on it. He knows that the brigade has done a lot and has fought valiantly.

He asks me if I can stay on a horse! That seems like salvation to me! I tell him yes, I am sure, but I cannot get up on the horse. He smiles and says that he will help me. His smile is filled with such sympathy, such assurance, too, that I tell myself that I am saved! He is big and strong and hoists me up without much trouble into the saddle on the horse, which he holds by the reins. I am in great pain, a horrible pain in my leg and I think I shall faint, but I say nothing . He holds the horse and marches beside me. He tells me he is in the *46th* or *47th Artillerie Regiment* of the *Wehrmacht*, I no longer know for sure. Now I see that a great many horses are wandering in the steppe, in one direction or another, but generally toward the west, as if they, too, know that freedom is in that direction. I mention this to the artilleryman who tells me that, in fact, all the horses that no longer had anything to pull have been turned loose. A little later several horses are within reach and my German comrade is able to catch one without difficulty. I have less scruples about riding his horse now that he is riding another.

I feel good, even though my leg gives me great pain. I may have found a better seat on the horse. But at every pothole, at every pace, it is as if a weight is pulling it downward. I can distinctly feel the fracture in the center of the tibia where the leg swings from right to left with the rhythm of the horse's gait, but I keep quiet. Since my wounding it does not seem to me that we are under fire, or is that my imagination! I cannot say. I suddenly think of it, for I hear renewed firing, at least the impacts are closer to us. But it is also true that, on horseback, I feel much more vulnerable than on foot, but what else can I do? The target is much larger and more tempting for the gunners, but I have no choice! When a shell bursts a little too close, less than 100-200 meters away, the horse shies, which, every time, I feel in my leg. We then advance in zig-zags, to make detours, to constantly change direction to complicate the life of the Russian artillerists a bit, who might think they were shooting at targets at the fairgrounds. All of a sudden I have a start and feel a violent shock through my entire body, at the moment when the horse also jumps and falls down on his right side, with me beside him. The pain in my leg passes through my entire body at the moment of the fall, but only my right leg remains wedged just under the saddle, under the horse, which thrashes about a bit but seems paralyzed. My German comrade has already jumped from the saddle, and after checking on me, puts the poor beast out of his misery. He gets me loose and pulls me aside, asking me if I have received any new wounds. It seems to me that I have not, for I didn't feel anything other than the jolt of the horse and the fall. I don't know the nature of the horse's wound. He must be lying on his wound, which seems serious, judging by the ocean of blood that expands very rapidly and reddens the snow. My comrade says to me, "'*Pech*,' bad luck, but fortunately, you didn't get farther injuries. You will make it out. Wait here a moment while I go find another horse," and he goes. I am afraid that I will not see him again! Will he return? Will something happen to him? But, in less than 15 minutes he returns. He leads a brown and white horse, larger than the other, a draft horse, no doubt. He is busy removing the saddle from the dead horse to place it on the other and secure it there, but not without difficulty, for the saddle doesn't fit on the new horse. When he has removed the saddle I see that the stomach of the other horse was torn wide open! Surely it must have been an anti-tank round, for machine gun bullets don't make such big holes. I dodged the bullet once more.

A little later we resume our journey to the west. The gunfire slows down and picks up again, only to let up again. We wind a bit as we follow the meanders of a slight depression in the terrain that offers minimal protection for a few hundred meters. There we stop a moment to catch our breath and the fellow offers me a cigarette. I have not had one for two or three days. Other men are also there, like us, but leaning against a little slope. After finishing the cigarette we continue on our way. When will we get there? How far have we yet to go? It seems quite a long time since I was wounded, the more so since we move quite slowly, but my guardian angel, no doubt, does not want to make me suffer more than I can endure.

Some flakes of snow fall on us from the sky and a cold wind picks up anew, but I bless this snow that offers a protective curtain against direct fire. So long as it falls, even if not heavily, they can only hit us by chance, and I prefer that! It must be about noon when we reach swampy ground where the horses refuse to go, and we have to head north to make another detour. There the soil is not frozen. After riding like this for 10 minutes, maybe a quarter of an hour, my comrade, who is riding in front of me, stops and listens. My horse stops behind his and I listen too. A moment later I, too, hear the cries that come from this swamp, but from far away, like they are muffled by the falling snow. We can see about 100 meters, but no more, undoubtedly less. No matter how hard we look, we can't make anything out. It may be that a man is struggling somewhere out there in this mud, in this slime, and my comrade tells me that we can do nothing for him. I see quite well that he is just as sorry as I am, but he is right. What could we do? He is alone, and I am wounded, in his care! A chill runs down my spine, all the more so, though maybe I am imagining things, because I thought I heard the cry, ""*Bour-gui-gnons*!"" With death in our souls, remorse in our hearts, we leave! Nearly 50 years later I still think of it! I have never forgotten nor tried to forget it. The remorse remains, even though I am convinced that we could not, really, have done anything, that I was in no condition to try anything, nor my comrade, either.

The snow has stopped falling. We ride on for 10 minutes, a quarter of an hour. Again we come upon several groups of five, 10 or 20 men. Suddenly gunfire breaks out! This time they are automatic weapons, machine guns, and the bursts come from the right, not too distant. I lie on the horse to blend my body with his, my head resting on his mane. To avoid swaying I slide far forward and am thus able to hang on to his mane, wrapping my arms around his neck. The smell of the horse fills my nostrils and his mane harshly caresses the skin of my cheeks. I try to keep my head in the shelter of the horse's neck, but, at the same time I try to spot where the fire is coming from. The steppe gradually rises on our right and I suppose that it must be coming from the highest point, which is, in fact, rather far from us, 400-500 meters distant, but I cannot see them.

At the very moment when I scan the horizon, new bursts of fire come and whistle over us from all around. I try to make myself very small, for it is very clear that they are aiming at us, we are the targets! This is a very disagreeable sensation to feel thus targeted, defenseless, injured and unable to take cover! It is no solution for me to get down from the horse, even if I could, and lie there, the two of us, me taking shelter behind the horse. That would only prolong the risk until they hit us all the same. So we decide to go on. But not much later, at the same moment that a new burst shreds the air and whistles by my ears, the horse rears up and I barely miss falling off. I have the sensation that all the muscles of the horse harden in an instant, are transformed into knots. My comrade suddenly realizes what is happening and he seizes my horse's bit to calm him, to hold him. He has a hard time and jumps off his horse without letting go of mine. I feel a little blow, but nothing big. A warmth on my right elbow, at the same place where my oilskin coat is torn from my progress this morning on my stomach. I immediately determine that it is the horse's blood that is flowing from his neck, in little waves, in spurts, but seriously! My artilleryman pulls me from the saddle and sets me down on the ground just the way a well-muscled medic would do. That does not prevent the shocks and the jolts, the pain. I clench my teeth so as to prevent any cry from escaping, so as not to discourage my saviour. All of this takes place as bursts of fire continue to whistle past all around us. The artilleryman also puts down this second horse with two rounds from his pistol.

I am lying there, in the snow, waiting on the course of events. Being the person I am, what troubles me the most is that I am not the master of, nor even in a position to significantly effect, my own destiny. So I make myself very small. My right arm gets numb, the cold, the lethargy, no doubt. With my left hand I massage my forearm and am amazed to find a pain! I pull up the sleeve and discover a bullet stuck in the middle of my forearm. It is buried a little in the flesh and a third of it sticks out! I ask myself which is better, to leave it there or try to pull it out? There is barely any blood, a little around the bullet, just a little circle. Perhaps I caused this bleeding when I wanted to massage it. My fingers are swollen and too weak to remove it. I raise my arm to my mouth and seize the base if the bullet with my teeth. It comes out without the slightest effort and without any pain. It stopped against the bone. I tell myself that it will be better if the wound bleeds a bit to clean it out, but hardly more than a few drops appear and dry or freeze right away. I meet the artilleryman's eyes, who is watching me with a question in his eyes. When he sees the bullet he smiles in amazement and shakes his head, as if to say, "Everything happens to you!" We study it for a minute and conclude that it is the bullet that passed right through the horse's neck, ending up in my arm, stopped by the bone. Everything seems to confirm it, the position of my arm around the animal's neck. The bullet was at the end of its course, otherwise it would have broken the bone, there is no doubt about it. I am reassured. I have no pain and, two or three days later there is nothing left but a little scab. Decidedly, I am unable to respond to the question I ask myself, am I lucky or not? Finally I believe that I am, when I think of the hell that we have passed through in the last few weeks. Even if some others got out of it without a scratch. No luck in having been wounded twice in the same day, but what luck to have found someone to get me out of it, and the insignificance of this second wound. Wounds by bullets are the "best", on the condition that they do not hit a vital organ, or that they are not explosive, such as the enemy has often used. They file the nose of the bullet a bit to make it open up when it penetrates flesh!

What are we to do now? My guardian angel has no shortage of resourcefulness nor, above all, of stubbornness. He takes advantage of a break in the firing to put me on his horse and continue on our way while holding the reins. We bear off a bit toward the left to escape the firing, at least to open the range. By so doing the road also climbs a bit. We hope that there are no Russian riflemen lying in ambush at the top. When we finally reach it my comrade stops and we are amazed at the unexpected spectacle before us! In the steppe that stretches before us, a little below us, there are hundreds and hundreds of men, standing, lying down, waiting for I don't know what, for some sort of miracle! There are also come carts and two or three tracked vehicles that have somehow escaped, I don't know how, from the deluge of iron and fire that we have gone through! Even horses are there, among the men, some also lying down, others standing, or turning around as if they might find freedom in any direction.

As we look closer we understand what is keeping all these survivors here. There is a large rift that divides this portion of the steppe stretching before us in two. It is a raging river that bars access to the far bank where the terrain undulates as it rises toward a little elevation similar to the one we are standing on. When we approach, moving between the groups, moving carefully among the men lying down, I see men throw themselves and dive into these frigid waters that seethe at our feet, a meter or a meter-and-a-half below the bank. They say that it is the "Gniloï – Tikitsch" river. It is not really big, but, all the same, between 20 and 30 meters wide. It is, on the other hand, quite deep and carries enormous blocks of ice. A little to the right there is an important portion of the river that is still covered with ice, and some men are cautiously trying to cross there. Three or four make it to the other bank, dry shod. At the very moment when I see two climb the escarpment of the bank, while slipping, I hear the sound of hooves and a cart. At this moment I am 20 meters from the river. When the cart passes a few meters in front of us I see eight or nine wounded lying pell-mell inside it and the driver looks demented. It looks to me like he is really insane and whips his horses, who are trotting, to make them gallop. Everyone watches him pass, without doubting for an instant what is going to happen. *Eh bien*! He simply keeps on going as if there was nothing there and steers his rig right toward the river, at the place where it is still covered with ice.

All of the men who are there incredulously see horses and cart and all those who are in it leave the bank and jump into the river. The ice, of course, breaks instantly and I see a large floe of this ice that tips and turns over on the rig which disappears, swallowed by the river! One or two cries, and it is all over. Already, in the distance, for the current is violent, once or twice I see the head of a horse or a body that emerges between the ice floes for an instant, only to disappear quickly and finally! Nobody had time to make the slightest gesture, to do anything, it all happened so quickly! From the looks that I meet I also see that nobody will think back to it, no one will remember what just took place before our eyes! It is all simply incredible. None of us had time to do anything. We always believe that we have seen the worst, yet the wall of horror recedes at each instant!

I see a *chenillette* start off and, for a moment, I think that other men have caught the madness. But no, the vehicle rolls very slowly toward the river, and the driver jumps out a few meters from the bank. The vehicle plunges in and disappears in an instant, nothing emerges. The river is deeper than he thought. Others then push in a cart at the same place where the *chenillette* disappeared, but the current sweeps the "*panjewagon*" away. This is not the way to salvation! I understood very quickly what was their intention in throwing these vehicles in there.

To our left there is a copse, and all the efforts of some men to cut branches, even a few young trees to attempt construction of a foot-bridge, remain in vain. The current sweeps away everything; the trees are not tall enough. Some fellows walk upstream along the bank, others downstream, hoping to find a bridge, another way to safety. Some then return, having found nothing. The others push on farther and do not return. What can we hope for? I cannot reconcile myself to leaving my skin here today, after so much work, after having made it through each of these recent days. Maybe tomorrow, if necessary, elsewhere, in any case! But not here, not now! The artilleryman whom I will call "Fritz", since I never learned his name, does not beat about the bush. He goes and returns shortly with another horse, which he mounts. For my part, I never dismounted. How, why would I have done so?

He tells me that we must go on, that we can't hope for anything if we stay here. We are going to plunge into the river, and "Fritz" explains to me the best way to hold on, that which I have just been using. But he ties the two stirrups together under the belly of the horse to allow me to at least wedge my right foot, the one on my better leg. While he is busy with that, I see an officer, whom I am told is *Général* Gille. But I am too far away to recognize him, even if it is him. He undresses as if it was nothing and makes a bundle of his clothes, which he ties up with his belt. Then, hanging onto the belt, he twirls it around and hurls it toward the other bank. The river is, perhaps, a bit narrower at that point, but I do not see whether the bundle lands on the other bank. He dives into the water, wearing his cap, which floats when he goes under. When he surfaces he grabs his cap, puts it back on and swims to the other bank. Here is a man who must be in his sixties but does not hesitate to jump into this frigid water, which also carries along big ice floes. I do not see why I cannot do the same, wounded, but on horseback. At the moment of making the big leap, my horse refuses. Doubtless he is afraid of this river, unless he is recoiling from pneumonia. "Fritz" helps with a couple of kicks with his boot while I hang on tight and clasp the horse with all that I have to clasp with, every muscle tight. At the second attempt the horse advances and suddenly plunges in. I slide to the front thinking that I am going to be engulfed in the water before my horse, but my right stirrup holds me on at the last moment. At the instant that the horse comes up I sway to the right, for my injured leg, incapable of squeezing like my right one, cannot stay in the stirrup. The pain makes me clench my teeth, but I am able to avoid falling off. I am wet to the shoulders, my face is soaked. The water now reaches my navel and I feel like my trunk has been cut off at that level. It is incredibly cold, but I am alive, at least not yet dead! I could have endured it better if it were not for the fatigue and the hunger, but that was how it was, in such conditions!

My horse hastens to reach the other bank, and, turning in the saddle I see that a fellow who jumped in the water right after me is hanging on to my horse's tail. Everyone manages as best he can! My horse struggles and fights against the current. His, at times wild, movements cause me to suffer enormously. The current presses on my wounded leg and pushes it tightly against the side of the horse. It is very painful, but I make the best of it. Futile to complain, what good would it do? And that is not my nature, anyway. The way "Fritz" looks at me is encouraging. He seems to want to say, "It's working, everything has gone well, we'll get through this." But when my horse reaches the bank there is a new problem. The bank is abrupt, like a wall a meter-and-a-half high that the horse cannot get up. I have, indeed, looked to the right and to the left, and I don't see any place that is more accessible! I suffer torture every time that the horse leaps trying to get up the bank. Each time his front hooves slip and fall heavily back into the water. I am a bit worried, for I feel that the horse is getting more and more nervous, and I am afraid that he will panic. While the animal drifts I see "Fritz", who jumps into the water without letting go of his mount. He manages to climb up the bank and, with the help of two comrades who are already there, he helps his horse to get up, too. They move toward me and do the same for my horse and me. I have clenched my teeth and bit my lips so hard that they are bleeding. The horse struggles and thrashes his hooves so suddenly and violently that at least three times I am sure I will fall in the water and be swept away by the current! It would have been absurd to perish so close to deliverance, drowned in the river. For I can no longer have any doubt, liberty is here!

When the horse gets his feet on solid ground the two other Germans help "Fritz" to get me down from the saddle and set me on the ground. The water that pours from my boots and clothing stains the snow around me. They remove my oilcloth coat and tunic, which they wring out and quickly put back on me. They then do the same for their clothes. During this time other men swim across the river and I see the officer I had seen a little early, who is also dressed again, busy helping others to tie, end to end, straps, webbing and cords that they will stretch across the river to help others to cross. The men put me back in the saddle and I discover that all my clothes are frozen, hard and brittle. I can hardly bend my elbows, the frozen clothing prevents all movement! We slowly mount the gentle slope on the right of the copse of shrubs and bushes, finally reaching the top of the hillock.

At first glance we see one, two, three tanks! A moment of fear that they are Russian, that vanishes as soon as we recognize that they are ours! They are two "*Panther*" tanks and one "*Tiger*". Now is the time for emotion! We are saved, it is done! For us, at least, for many are still at the mercy of the Russians in the encircled pocket. These three tanks are why the Russians are not firing on this horde of unarmed men at the edge of the river, but well beyond the second hillock, where they are under the protection of the German tanks. The Russians respect these three tanks with their impressive guns, but, under cover of the second hillock, the Russians can harass these phantoms who are seeking their salvation for one last time!

When we reach the level of our tanks there are greetings, accolades! These tank men of the *1st Panzer Armee* look on us with pity. Later I learn that they, too, have had their part of the hard labor. They have penetrated the Russian lines to a depth of about 80 kilometers to come to our aid, but only a few tanks made it to here. They are spread out in small groups along the "Gniloï – Tikitsch" river, forming strongpoints to link up with us. Not all of us have been able to make it to the planned location, which is why they have had to disperse to assist all of us. The condition of the terrain, the river prevented them from going farther, and the main body of the tanks has been unable to get this far, having had to battle with the difficulties of the ground more than with the Russians who wanted to stop them! These are men of the *LAH*, the men of the "Guard". The *Leibstandarte SS Adolf Hitler*. Suddenly I feel totally secure!

"Fritz" asks them where he can take me, and they point out to him a group of *isbas* 200-300 meters distant. That is where they are collecting the wounded as they arrive. When he turns me over to a medical orderly I want to say farewell to him and thanks, a thousand-fold thanks. I ask his name, his address. He looks at me, shaking his head, and says no! He says that that is unimportant! "In any case, I will be back later," he says. "We will see each other again today." I look at him without really understanding. Then he explains that he is going back down into the encirclement to find other wounded!

For a moment I look at this face, stubbled, drawn by fatigue, which seems more serious to me than recently. I only see him for an instant, for he turns away quickly and I see him depart. He mounts his horse and takes the other by the rein. I see him disappear in the direction whence we came, without looking back. I do not get over it, I am deeply moved! My throat is so choked with emotion at this moment that I cannot say a word. I clench my teeth to avoid showing my emotions, so that nothing shows. Among men, among soldiers, demonstrations of this sort are just not done! We must keep our reserve, protect our dignity! When we shook hands he pulled his back very quickly as if not to "let it go any further". I well understood. He said that I would have done the same for him, that nothing more needed to be said.

There is a man who risked his skin for me today, maybe a hundred times, who has done his duty toward himself and toward me; more than anyone could have required, more than his duty. No one could have reproached him if he had not done it! And this man is going to start all over again, to go back to zero! He is going back into that hell, this hell that everyone who is still there or who was there this morning is going to do everything, has done everything, possible to escape. And at what cost! So many are dead or are still going to die in attempting to get out, and he who knows this, he is going back there in full knowledge of the situation, knowing all that awaits him there. He has already experienced it with me, and, nevertheless, he is going back! Nothing has been able to stop him, he wants so save others! It is unbelievable, it is a Greek tragedy! "*Das ist Soldatenmut!*" as they say, that is the courage of a soldier!

I am there, lying on a litter in front of the *isba* and I think of this man whom I had never met before, whom I shall never again forget! Even if I live a hundred years. I swallow my saliva, I am all choked up. The medical orderly notices it and seeks to reassure me, saying that "Fritz" will return. He then drags my litter inside, for he is alone, and puts me in the first of the two rooms of the *isba* where two other wounded already lie, resting on the straw. My watch stopped at 1400 hours, or 1410. That must be the moment when we were in the water. It is probably about 1430 hours now. I am cold, very cold, but there is no more pain. I am also, above all, extremely tired. My clothes, which have been frozen stiff, start to thaw, very slowly, for there is no fire in this dwelling.

A little later a doctor comes in to examine me. He cuts off my boots with great care, for the water that was in them has made two gaiters of ice that surround my legs from the ankles to the calves. They are like splints that have supported the broken leg, which is why I have really had no more trouble since the water froze in my boots. In addition, the ice numbed the pain while also, perhaps, avoiding infection. The doctor has trouble breaking this coating of ice, for he does not dare strike it hard for fear of making me suffer or of aggravating the wound. When the ice is removed I can finally see the wounds. Now I can better understand the intensity of my pain throughout my journey. The doctor shows me the site of the compound fracture and points out to me the bone that protrudes from this wound, which I had not seen when I first looked because of the blood. All around it and on the leg are numerous small wounds, red in the center, blue and white from cold on the periphery. On the right foot the big toe is bloody and swollen. Other fragments are embedded in my calf, one protruding. He removes the largest fragment from my right foot without trouble and without pain, and one or two less important ones, but the extraction of the latter is very painful, for they are embedded very deep. He apologizes for causing me such pain, but he explains to me that he has no form of anesthesia. All that he has is a few instruments, a little alcohol and the bandages, for he has had to care for serious cases ever since this night. He disinfects the wounds, applies bandages and makes a sort of splint for my left leg from part of the upper shaft of a boot. He puts on another layer of bandages on top of this, consisting of broad strips of a sort of *crepe* paper, very tight, which holds very well. He leaves the medical orderly to complete the work and leaves to relieve other pains, to care for other wounds. When the medical orderly is through with me he goes off to the other room, from which I hear moans. He returns to me a little later and tells me, in a low voice, that it is one of my comrades who is there, very severely wounded with seven or eight machine gun bullets in his stomach! He asks me to talk to him, to encourage him.

I then speak the magic word, ""*Bourguignon!*"" No response. I did not want to raise my voice. After a moment of silence I call out a little louder, I ask, ""*Bourguignon?*"" A sign of life comes to me from the other room, "Who is it?" I tell him my name. "Ah! I am happy, I am Ivan." I recognized the voice, even though it is feeble. It is that of a comrade from my company's office. I know him quite well. I last saw him at Baibusy. I cannot see him but I hear him breathe with great difficulty before becoming a bit more animated. In a halting voice, broken by pauses, he tells me that he does not have much longer to live. He is very aware of the seriousness of his wounds and confides to me that he knows very well that he will not leave this *isba* alive. The medical orderly, who has, certainly, not understood a word of our conversation in French, nods his head to me as a sign of encouragement. He gets up and says to me as he leaves that he will return later. He must go and care for others.

Ivan makes no complaints, but he cannot accept that he has escaped the Russians to be brought here, wounded as he is, to die in this *isba*, outside the encirclement! And he, like me, is 21 years old! His voice has weakened. I can tell that he is tired, exhausted by the few words we have exchanged. He does not need to talk too much. I allow him to rest. We exchange only a few words in the ensuing hours. I am amazed that the two wounded who lie there in the straw along the opposite wall have not given any sign of their presence recently. The one has not stirred and I believe for a moment that I have heard the other breathe, but I am not sure. Now night falls. It is dark here, and, at times, I hear guns or gunfire in the distance. It is not yet all over in the encirclement!

The medical orderly returns a little later, nods to me and goes into the adjoining room. He carries a sort of candle that projects his wavering shadow on the ceiling and on the walls. He then returns close to me and asks how I am doing. I don't feel too bad. I am hungry and I am cold, but I do not say so. My clothes are still wet. But not frozen. The medical orderly tells me in a low voice that he is about to go and do something for my friend, but that he has no chance at all, at least not one in 10, of making it through. In any case, he tells me, if nothing is done, he has even less. The problem is the anesthesia. The doctor who just looked after me comes in a little later, followed by another man, another doctor or a medical orderly. I cannot make out the rank. They light other candles and *karasinkas*, which reminds me of a Christmas gathering, but a very sad Christmas. I can hear that they are discussing something in a low voice, not loud enough, in any case, for me to understand what is going on. Ivan has not talked to me anymore, nor manifested himself in any other fashion for a moment, but I have heard him moan several times. A moment later it seems to me from the play of the shadows that I see that they are stunning my comrade Ivan, and, what's more, at this very moment, I hear him hiccup! I may be wrong, but these certain details make me think so, especially since I know that there is not the slightest trace of anesthetic. For maybe half an hour I have been aware of feverish activity in the adjoining room. I have heard, without understanding, short phrases, monosyllables, and then silence. Total silence!

The doctor then comes back to me. He tells me that my comrade is dead! As if excusing himself, he tells me that he has tried all that he can do, but, deprived of everything as he is, he could not do very much. Perhaps my friend would have had a chance for survival if, right after he was wounded, he could have been cared for in a perfectly equipped hospital. Here, without anything, without even an electric light and electricity, it was a challenge. Knowing that, with very little time to work in, he had to take the chance and hope for a miracle! But there was no miracle! It is in this dismal place and these dramatic conditions that Ivan left us in this evening of 17 February!

The doctor places his hand on my forehead to check my temperature, or was it an impulse from his heart? I shall never know. He is exhausted, he too, that is clear, but he remains determined and endowed with an iron will. That, too, is obvious. He leaves the *isba*, followed by his assistant and, soon after, the medical orderly also leaves, saying to me, "See you later!" They leave a *karasinka*, sitting on a little board fastened to the wall. But these oil lamps give no more than a feeble light. I am alone in this dismal morgue, for I am now certain that the two German comrades are also dead. I have not observed the slightest movement or heard the least breath for a long time, and then, if that is not the case, why have the doctor and the medial orderlies not been more concerned with them? I am still hungry and cold, but these sensations fade in the face of all that is around me, before this desolate universe that is mine, reduced to four walls. I believe that this feeling of cold comes to me above all because I feel alone at present, alone among these dead, without the slightest sign of life to enliven this solitude.

I cannot stir; I know nothing that goes on beyond the threshold of this house. Alone with three dead men, lying on damp straw in this isolated hut, deprived of everything, without even a flame to warm myself. But I am alive! The minutes, the hours flow and drag slowly. It is insane how long time seems in such circumstances! I am unable to sleep, but, doubtless, I have no desire to do so.

All the same, God knows that I am tired! If I did not have a stout heart I would have been overcome by anxiety long ago. Who can say that I have not been forgotten here?

Sometimes I hear some noises outside, some sounds that are, undoubtedly, men who have come out of the encirclement and are heading southeast. But there cannot be very many of them, for, as the hours pass, the sounds become rarer, until I no longer hear any at all. It is precisely then that the calm seems to me to be long, too long, that the doubt, if not the anxiety, takes hold of me. And what if I have, indeed, been forgotten? This evening and this place seem yet more dismal this evening! I still have my pistol, but has the powder become damp since crossing the river? I do not know why, but I hesitate to take a test shot, at least for now. I no longer have my grenades. I do not know just when I lost them.

In spite of myself I must have dozed off for a moment, without really sleeping, when, all of a sudden, the sound of tracks rouses me from my torpor, followed immediately by five or six cannon shots. It is within the village, assuredly, in any case, not very far from here, for the *isba* shakes. I hear the impacts, one or two for certain. I hear the explosions, very different from the sound of the discharges! At this moment, anxiety possesses me. Not panic, which I do not know, but fear, none the less, to call it by its name. The fear of being surprised, of not having time to react. The fear that is increased by my ignorance of the situation I am in. Ten minutes later, or is it three minutes? Shortly thereafter, in any case, muffled sounds reach me from outside. When the door opens suddenly I have no time for fear. I immediately recognize the medical orderly. But I am totally amazed, pistol in my hand. The medical orderly is not surprised and tells me to put it back in its holster. It is necessary to act quickly, to leave immediately. Russian tanks have penetrated the village, but, surprised by our three tanks, they did not push. One of the Russians was hit, the other two fled, for our tanks did not fire for fear of hitting our own or destroying the *isbas* where the wounded are lying.

Out of caution, the medical orderly has blown out the *karasinka*. A sleigh, drawn by two horses, stops before the *isba* and the driver helps the medical orderly to place me alongside three other wounded. I see flames at the northern exit of the village, the Russian tank or a burning *isba*? I can't say which, but later I will learn that it was, indeed, one of the Russian tanks. After a bend in the road the sleigh slides with hardly a sound in the dark night. There are no more flames from the burning tank to light the road. Two sensations: the cold is very biting and the smell of the horse. A little later we catch up with other sleighs and carts which are attempting to take their loads of wounded to where they will be safe from incursions of the Red Army. At that moment I realize our situation. I had believed that I was safe when I got to Lisjanka, on the other bank of the "Gniloï – Tikitsch". Now I understand that it is nothing, that it will yet require much more courage and endurance to get out of it, to continue to cling to life, to not give in, not give up! At every pothole one of the wounded stifles his cries of pain as best he can, each time that the runners of the sleigh pass from one rut to the other. He tells me, when I ask, that he is wounded in the lungs and shoulder. It is a phantom convoy that stretches out in the night. Once more the thermometer is in free fall, again there is an extremely hard freeze. The snow crunches under the feet of the drivers and the horses. The straw that covers the bottom of the sleigh is packed down and no longer serves to hold in the heat. I constantly rub my feet and ankles, which are like chunks of ice, my ears and nose. Then I rub my hands and start over on my feet. Immobile in the sleigh I am afraid that one or another member will freeze. Despite my extreme fatigue I fight against dozing off. I must avoid that at any price. Stay alert, above all, do not fall asleep, even though I need it so much, if only to forget the hunger and thirst! All that I have gone through is not enough, I must still fight to avoid succumbing to the sleep that I so need and that, nevertheless, could prove fatal, or cost me a limb! Only one who has had this experience can know the effort it represents. All night this continues, to master the cold, the thirst, the hunger and sleep. This night continues like this and never ends.

The convoy stops and then moves on, at a man's walking pace, stops again, gets moving again. It is a torment for all of the wounded men, reduced to lethargy.

Dawn finally arrives and I can better judge the importance of our convoy. For as far as my eye can see I see nothing by carts and sleighs, ahead of and behind us. There are hundreds of them! Easily 200-300, I don't know. But I do not know if all who are in them are wounded. I think so, for it would be insane to remain lying down in such circumstances if one is able to march!

On 18 February, early in the morning, we arrive in a partially destroyed village whose name I do not know. Part of the convoy, the part I am in, stops and several medical orderlies go from one vehicle to another to check on our condition. One of the medical orderlies tells us that we are going to shelter for a few hours in the village so that we can warm up and get some sleep. They unload one of the wounded from our sleigh and the medical orderly determines that another died *en route*, the one who was at the rear, whom they set down elsewhere. We three who are alive are laid in an *isba* to the left of the road, whose walls are riddled with holes left by projectiles. It is already full inside. But people make room for us and I find comrade Herbecq there, who comes to join me and settles down next to me. He is not wounded.

There are at least 30 men here, if not 40. Most are wounded and lying down, all that in a 15 meter square. There is no stove burning, but the ambient heat is enough to warm us up. I have found the bones in the bottom of my pocket and suck on them, along with the tobacco and brown sugar that stick to them, for it is a long time since there was anything to chew on there, not even cartilage. That is all that I find to quench my hunger. Herbecq is downhearted about it and goes for a walk to try to find something. He returns later with a few tomatoes in brine that we share with two other wounded. My empty stomach cannot take this, and I have an attack of diarrhea. I am unable, like the others, to reconcile myself to the worst, and I ask my comrade to drag me outside to take care of my business. He does this with good grace and helps me to raise myself and then take care of all that this business implies. Like a medical orderly. I would not have believed that of him! He always seemed a bit cold to me, distant or indifferent, and today I discover another fellow! It is curious how, at times, one can be so wrong. When it is possible, he drags me back into the *isba* with a thousand precautions.

I stretch out, for I would love to sleep, at least to rest a bit. I have weeks of sleep to catch up on! I would also like to forget the gnawing pains in my stomach, desperately empty for so long! It has not received more than 500 grams of nourishment for a week! It has received no more to sustain the organism to protect against the intense cold and this long fatigue! It is little, it is meager, and yet the body resists. Even the mind remains alert and lucid. It is truly incredible, since, on top of all that I am wounded and I have lost blood, even though the bitter cold has stopped the bleeding. One never knows the limits of human resistance, especially when one has decided to live!

I am able to sleep, until the noise and activity in the *isba* wake me up. The healthy men get ready to leave and help the medical orderlies to hitch up the sleighs and carts before laying us in them. My comrade Herbecq bids me farewell before he joins the others who are going to assure the protection of the convoy, which reforms, as best they can. We are not, in fact, always safe. We always proceed in a narrow corridor, at the mercy of Soviet planes and artillery, for the cover provided by our troops is indeed thin, and extremely dispersed! The sky is clearer and, several times, large areas of clear sky allow the sun to appear. They are dangerous for us, a golden opportunity for the Russian airplanes. The column is back on the road and I am now lying on a cart with five other wounded men. It has been quite cold since morning, and this pale sun, which only appears for moments, cannot warm the atmosphere. I try to find a position that will allow me to rub my feet, to warm them up as best I can, for I have no feeling in them and I am afraid that they might freeze. The loss of sensations disturbs me, and since there is no more pain, it will be dangerous to let this go on. The problem is that I cannot bend the left leg and that I have to sit up and fold myself in two to reach the foot. There is no perfect position, but I accommodate myself to it as best I can and I change position every time that I can.

The column does not always advance quickly, and, as it did last night and this morning, it often stops and then starts again. We have been on the road at least two hours when we stop anew, but this time much longer than all the others. What is happening? I am unable to see from here, for the innumerable vehicles that are ahead of us block my view, and the road climbs a little hill whose top is several hundred meters ahead of us. It seems to me that there is an unusual disturbance on this hill, farther up the road. The stop lasts more than an hour, and there is general satisfaction when we finally start moving again. Finally we, too, make it over the little ridge before then descending the gentle slope on the other side. We get back on the road after half an hour – during which the convoy left the road on the right, in the steppe. I would not have been aware of this if the cart had not bounced around so much, causing new pain. I realize it, 10 minutes later, but without yet fully understanding the actual importance, the reason for this byway, for this curious detour.

On the road, or path, that we had left, I see in the distance, 200-300 meters distant, to the left, dark masses in the snow that cover a section of the road that is maybe 300 meters long, maybe more. At this distance I cannot distinguish the details, the more so since I have not the slightest idea of what it could be. I cannot recognize any silhouette, a familiar form, nothing that can enlighten me. An idea gradually develops, an idea that takes form, that forms in my mind, at first incredible. Soon I know that I am not dreaming, that I understand, I confirm the reality in all its horror, beyond the realm of imagination! This sort of serpent of fluid forms, with no distinct contours; is a part of our convoy reduced to the state of pulp?! What can produce something like that? Certainly it is not the effect of bombardment, we would have heard it, not strafing by Russian aircraft, which could not have produced such damage!

We hear the explanation a little later from the medical orderlies and other men of the escort who rejoin the column, returning from the site of the carnage, where they have made a final examination of the place to make sure that there are no more survivors. They explain to us that five or six Russian tanks broke through, against which there was no possible defense for lack of heavy or adequate arms. No anti-tank weapons at all, not even the shadow of a *Panzerfäust*! Very calmly the tanks advanced, took the column in enfilade and crushed pell-mell the carts, the sleighs with all the wounded, even the horses! The few rare wounded who had the strength to raise themselves and attempt to escape were pursued by the tanks, one by one, and crushed without mercy, without any chance of getting away. Thus the tanks went their way, crushing everything on 200-300 meters of road before turning 180 degrees and vanishing whence they had come, in the same direction. A few *Panzerfäuste* could have called them to account, alas there were only a few rifles, a few subma-chine guns, truly nothing to disturb the Russian tanks!

It is horrible! Now that I know what it is, this prominent mass that resembles a giant snake, I think I can make out the debris of the carts and other vehicles, doubtless mixed with the crushed, disarticulated bodies, but those I cannot make out, I cannot actually distinguish them in this shapeless mass at this distance! It is incredible! The column modified its itinerary to spare us the sight of these comrades, massacred so cruelly. What must we yet see or suffer? Have we not yet plumbed the depths of misery, attained the summit of cruelty? No one will ever be able to forget such a sight!

Our column stretches out anew and laboriously proceeds, but also inexorably! What tenacious will, what determination to live is gathered here in this convoy! The night, darkness at least, does not delay in coming. It has the effect of aiding us, for it provides us with a bit more security. This night, this intense cold and a little fog, absorbs the marching column. Only one or two vehicles ahead and behind us are visible, and they blend in with all the others. Doubtless I must have dozed off a bit, for when I open my eyes the convoy has stopped in a locality of some sort. It must be Buki. We are carried into buildings that are not dwellings. No doubt it is a former school or administrative building where I am placed, like the others, on straw mattresses on the bare ground. Not for long, in any case, for less than an hour later the medical orderlies put us back on the carts, *en route* to the airplanes that wait for us in the steppe, outside the city.

I am eager, now to get there and take wing for milder climes! I hope, but without really believing yet, that a happy outcome is near. The column moves on, but not for very long, and stops in the midst of the steppe, where I make out the silhouettes of two or three *JU52* transport aircraft, the *Junkers* maids of all work. Extremely reliable, sure and indefatigable, this type of machine truly serves all purposes. Those who are able to march head for the airplanes, and we are carried there on stretchers by the medical orderlies, who set us down beside the machines, whose side doors take the men in, one after the other. The men of the *Luftwaffe* work to speed the embarkation, for there is no time to lose. Their mission is to evacuate all those who can be evacuated as fast as possible and to make several round trips. One of them lifts me up and places me on the part of the open door that serves as the loading platform.[5] I don't understand just what happens to me at that moment, but I think that another wounded man grabs hold of me to help himself to get up on the platform. As for myself, I fall heavily on the ground, but I believe that he succeeds in hauling himself up there! I am truly surprised that I have been pulled off the plane! At that very moment one of the aviators appears, who signals that the airplane is full and closes the embarkation door. I do not think that he even saw me. Shortly thereafter the engines start and the airplane moves away to take off.

I lie there, miserably and incredibly alone on the field, and I hear, without being able to see, the airplanes taking off one by one! When the noise has died down and the field has regained its calm, everything seems to me to be hostile anew, and this calm has the effect on me of the most total desolation. Fortunately, I hear men calling out to each other and I am able to call them. They are amazed to find me there, and the same for a second wounded man a little farther on, who also failed to find a place on the airplanes. It is not despair, for the more I hear the sound of footsteps, the more I pull myself back together. But the return to the dressing station is, neverthe-less, lugubrious. The drivers bring a dozen carts there with the stretchers and the two wounded, inadvertently left behind. I want to fall asleep right away so as not to think. Fortunately the fatigue helps me.

In the morning they bring us coffee, bread and butter when we wake. After which, *en route* to the field where other aircraft wait for us, or are they the same ones as yesterday? There are a good dozen, I believe, at least three of which are painted with the colors of the red cross. This time I have a place and we are 20 wounded lying on the ground. Take-off shakes us up greatly, but we get off the ground quickly. The *JU52* that carries us is very noisy in this version, for it is the transport model, but what really matters is that it is rapidly going to take us to the receiving hospitals, at least I hope so. But hope is not certainty. I have learned that all too frequently in these recent days, each time to my cost. That is why I cherish no illusions so as to avoid subsequent disappointment. If, at times, I may have lied to others, at least I have never lied to myself. It is that, perhaps, that is still important to me in life today. Remain lucid so as not to fall from hope to despair.

In the racket that surrounds me all conversation is in vain and impossible. Also, I would like to fall asleep and wake up in Germany, in a hospital bed, alas! We have been in the air for no more than 15 minutes when we become aware of the tragedy, without really knowing the reason. Our airplane starts to zig-zag, to descend and hug the ground, then to climb with difficulty, pushing

---

5   On *JU52* cargo planes, the cargo door behind the right wing opened with the bottom half of the door extending out as a cargo platform – the top half hinged upward out of the way.

the engines to the limit. I can feel the effort of the machine in all its components, and in the corrugated sheet metal of the fuselage which creaks as it supports all the efforts and stretches to the breaking point, but the machine holds together. These faithful *JU52*s have passed every test. We are shaken up more and more, and I compare our airplane with a man who has fallen in the sea and does not know how to swim, thrashing around wildly. I do not know exactly what is going on, but there is no possible doubt. The squadron of medical airplanes is under attack and, of course, has no way to defend itself! None of our aircraft is armed. Our airplane has no windows and we can see nothing, except for two or three glimpses forward of other aircraft that appear, for an instant, through the windows of the cockpit, which is not separated from us by any wall, or, at least [if there is a door], it remains open. I thought I recognized one or two of our machines, but also one or two fighter planes, and those are certainly not ours, even if I didn't have time to see any distinctive markings – no red star! I cannot say how long this row continued, but it seemed quite long. I really think that it must have been half an hour before we returned to normal flight, but it is difficult to judge time in such circumstances.

Finally we land, after having circled to allow the planes to land properly in order. In any case, the flight did not last more than an hour and a half, perhaps two. I have no idea where we are and no one is in a position to tell me. I learn that three of our aircraft were shot down, exactly two of them with red cross markings! Where do these barbarians come from? I also learned that there were at least two *"Bourguignons"* in one of the two, but the medical orderly who told me this could not, of course, tell me the names. He had simply recognized the *"Wallonie"* shoulder patch as he loaded them into the airplane. As the wounded were unloaded from our airplane one was also found to have been killed by a bullet from the guns of a Russian fighter plane, which had passed through the cabin of our machine. One of the crew reported several hits in the cabin, but only one of these rounds hit a man, killing the wounded man, and nobody had noticed anything. I did not hear anything! Other aircraft were also hit, and their dead were also removed, two or three, I think. Other wounded received additional wounds. They were hastily treated on the spot.

The ambulances and lorries come and line up near the aircraft, and we are loaded one more time! How many more times are yet to come? An hour or two later we get to a large town, or is it a small city? A little later the vehicles stop near a railroad station of some importance. There are, all the same, several tracks where two or three trains await us. They consist of goods wagons that are longer than the standard dimensions we are used to seeing. I am placed in a bed made of wooden posts secured to the wagon, with two other beds above it. Along the entire length of the walls there are, thus, 30 beds, three high, and a stove in the center. There is wood and charcoal around it, but the stove is not burning. At the level of each bed, beside it, there is a glazed window, and my bed was ready for me, with mattress, covers and even a bed sheet!

Several medical orderlies, aided by Russian personnel, bring us hot tea and then an *Eintopf*, the traditional thick soup that one finds everywhere, which I hasten to swallow. The temperature is Siberian, the sheets and covers are not enough to warm me. Nobody in the wagon is in a condition to get up and light the stove, and I think that one of the Russians on the platform came to load it just before the train departed. In any case, it will burn for several hours and provide most-needed heat for us. It must have been at least eight days during which no stove has warmed me! God knows that it is cold, and that we need it, especially the wounded, having lost some of our blood and so poorly nourished for weeks and worn out by so much fighting, incessant battles against all the elements of the Russian winter. Despite the fatigue and emotions of these last days, I do not try to go to sleep right away. Above all I want to enjoy this comfort, rudimentary though it may be, but such as I have not known for a long time!

Every day of rest is good for me, every meter that we travel adds to my serenity. I finally feel safe, ready to relax, and slowly I release the tension. I have the feeling that finally I can let it all go, set down my arms for a while. Time to recover. I catch myself singing in a low voice, almost without realizing it. Is it to avoid disturbing my neighbors? Or from fear of making myself ridiculous in expressing my joy? Yes, I am almost ashamed of being alive, at least of expressing my joy and being unable to hide it! But it is true. I am happy to be alive. Now I really believe that I am safely out of it. As I lie there, half asleep, all the songs that emerge from my memory, one by one, and heaps of reflections assail me!

I am amazed that I got out of such carnage alive, to confirm that one can survive such hell, where all the hostile elements of nature ally with the enemy to strike us down, to annihilate us! Neither the Russians nor the exhaustion nor the cold, nor even the lack of nourishment got the best of us, of me! There is, in fact, something to marvel at when I think of it. To discover in ourselves such resources, which manifest themselves at the very moment when everything seems lost, just when they are most needed! Ten times, a hundred times, I could have given it all up, at every such crisis. I could have thought that all was lost, that there was nothing more, and how many times have I believed that I was saved, only then to have the worst come! How many times have I had to follow this road between hope and despair? How often have I also passed from insane hope, which is almost certainty, to despair that lies in wait, each time waiting for the development that precipitates us to the bottom of a new abyss, but that has not worn us down, has not broken our nerve? Our stout heart, our nervous system has held out against everything and not panicked, enabled me to keep a cool head, never to lose my *sang-froid*. It is, I believe, the only explanation for the survival of most of us. One of the principal rules of my life, from which I shall never depart, dates from this day. I know that, henceforth, nothing worse will ever happen to me, and, there-fore… nothing in the future will ever be able to beat me down. I will repeat this to myself at every such blow! I think of this at great length, then I fall asleep.

The cold then wakes me up. It is night, and I fall back asleep. The shocks also wake me up, when the train slows down or stops. But, each time, I go back to sleep. There is no noise in the wagon except for that of the wheels on the rails or the gratings of the buffers against each other. Another stop awakens me. Orders run the length of the train, the wagon doors slide, opened from the outside.

---

17 February, 1944 – 17 February, 1981!

On this 17 February, 1944 I survived solely due to the courage and selfless spirit, the cama-raderie and heroism, to call it by its proper name, of the German comrade whom I have called "Fritz".

Thirty-seven years later, on another 17 February, during the commemoration of the breakout at Bad Windsheim, in 1981, there was an encounter that I must speak of. It is, indeed, far more than an anecdote, it is better than a story. It actually happened.

We were reunited, as usual, with our German comrades and moved by a need commonly spoken of as "nature". I pushed on a door that was, from the other side, pulled open by Willi Möller. There we were, face to face. He stands six feet three inches tall, he later told me, of big build, horn-rimmed spectacles, with a big smile, though I do not think I had ever met him. He said, "You are Walloon?" neither affirmative nor interrogative. I replied, "*Ja, und Sie Wikinger?*" ["Yes, and you're of the *Wiking*?"] He immediately told me so and his beaming smile evidenced his joy. Yes, it was joy, and he then told me:

On 17 February, 1944, during the breakout, I was in a place that I could not identify and whose name I do not know. The Russians were firing on us with all the weapons they had, and, God knows, they had them at that moment. We knew that better than anyone, for it was we who were taking a beating. That day God was doing his thing too high, and the Russians were firing at ground level.

The "Stalin-organs" forced us to lie flat in the muck and prevented us from getting up. It was all we could do to breathe. And we asked ourselves how we could get away. By chance two pieces of 2 cm quad-"*Flak*" belonging to the Walloons passed by. Their crews immediately went into position despite the enemy fire, and the noise of their fireworks was far sweeter for us that day than the sound of the enemy's "organs".

These may not be the exact words of our friend Möller, but it is what I understood, for that is what we experienced. I also believe I remember that he let me know that he owed his life to these Walloons, that is what he told me, but I was not certain of anything at that moment, for I was happy and proud of my Walloon comrades, of our *Légion*! I quickly went back to my table in the first room to tell my buddies about this. What was my surprise and stupefaction when René Ladrière, sitting right at my table, and who had accompanied us on the trip, told me that he had been part of that battery! I immediately took him to the table in the other room where my friend Möller was sitting.

What joy, you may well think, to meet thus, without having known each other at the time! But all that was entirely natural at that time. Our friend René was able to identify the place for him and give detail of this action that confirmed all the memories that Möller had preserved. But neither our newspapers nor the television ever talk of such things, and we do not care, for what matters to us is what those who are dear to us, those who are close to us and those who we, ourselves, respect think of us.

I told our comrade, Möller, that it is rigorously true, that he only met me thanks to a German comrade of an artillery regiment. For without him, wounded as I was, I would never have made it out on my own. I had to tell him that he had just rendered homage to the Walloon *Légionnaires*, and I in my turn return the homage to one of his German comrades.

And are we quits for all that? Certainly not! One is never quits when we have traveled such a road together, Germans, Flemish, Walloons, French, Dutch and so many other volunteers, all nationalities mixed. It is the reason, the very essence of our friendship. It is our honor and our faith. It is our solidarity with all the comrade volunteers of Europe and even from elsewhere who had the same flag, the same emblem, but, above all, the same ideals! We are able, and we are the only ones who can write "Europe" with a capital "E". Our Europe, not theirs!

16

The Tour of the Hospitals

We learn that we are going to be transferred from the train, that the railroad tracks have been blown up. It is 0100 hours in the morning. The transfer takes part of the night and, shortly thereafter, I go back to sleep in another bed. At about 0800 hours in the morning the train finally moves on. I do not even ask myself if this will be the last stage! I believe that today is 24 February. We have rolled for two days and two nights, I believe, but the numerous stops may have put me off. We are served meals when possible. The stoves are lit, go out, and are lit again depending on the availability of the train personnel and of stops.

It is now 26 February, nine days after the breakout, when the convoy stops in sight of Lemberg or Lublin, the two names are mentioned by wounded who have already passed this way. I have passed through both these cities in the past, but the view I have from here does not allow me to recognize where we are and there are no signs to give me certainty. It is about 0700 hours in the morning. A landscape of snow under a low, gray sky. There is incredible activity around all these trains, for we are not the only ones! Lorries and ambulances arrive incessantly and depart toward the city, loaded with wounded. The road descends and goes back up toward the city, which is, perhaps, four or five kilometers distant. Like an endless chain the columns stretch in two parallel rows, one in each direction, the entire way. Hundreds of these vehicles bump along the road, forming two black lines in this white immensity. There are other dark spots in this gray and white landscape. In the distance, on the opposite slope, are towers of churches with their bell towers and the grand buildings that dominate the city.

During the nearly four hours' wait I have abundant leisure to observe this spectacle. Clouds, heavy with snow move and change shape above this hive of activity that swarms and persists in its attempt to save all that it can, in bringing these thousands of wounded to the hospitals of the city. Homage is due to all the medical and related personnel who are meeting the challenge of an unimaginable task, to unload, transport and bring nearly 30,000 wounded to the different hospitals in the city and to create entirely new structures to receive this unexpected mass of wounded who have been arriving for several days. They come from Tcherkassy, but also from Kowel, another encircled location where *Général* Gille was sent, I am told, immediately after Tcherkassy. Supreme Headquarters believes that he will succeed there, too, after having saved the main body of the troops encircled in the Tcherkassy pocket.

At about 1100 hours in the morning I finally arrive in one of the hospitals. It is the *Reserve-Lazarett Abt. IV*. The ambulance stops at the rear of the building where the personnel help the ambulance drivers to unload us. We are taken down a little outside stairway to the basement of the building, which must have three or four stories above the first floor and basements. We are placed in a corridor with white tile walls, which is soon crowded and full. Other members of the staff quickly arrive and, in teams of two or three, they undress us first and then lather us with a sort of soft soap and scrub us with stiff brushes! They then take us to a large shower room where we are washed with hot water from garden hoses! More scrubbing, then we are rinsed, after which male and female nurses place us in another room where they dry us with hot air. We are then laid upon other stretchers with covers, and, after a short wait, we are taken to rooms on the different stories. The nurses rapidly sort out the wounded and I am placed on the first story.

I have not yet had an opportunity to meet my new neighbors when they bring us our first collation, an excellent *bouillon* with biscuits. What diligence! Blessed by the German organization, everything takes place quickly, yet without any haste. I was drowsy when, at about 1500 hours, they came to take me to the operating room. There are nothing but rooms or chambers that are full of wounded. They are everywhere. There are beds and litters right in the corridors, in the smallest nooks. I am in the waiting room before one of the operation rooms, but not for long. When I am placed along a wall in the room, I am not alone. Other stretchers are already lined up there along the entire length of the wall, since the tables, and there are several, are already occupied by wounded who are being operated on while others await their turn on the table. In fact there are four or five operating tables lined up in the center of the room, which is roughly oval-shaped. Three teams of doctors pass from one table to the next. As soon as one operation is finished, they immediately start another. I thus have the opportunity to be more or less present at a whole series of interventions. From where I am I cannot see everything, but what I cannot see, I guess.

In addition to removal of projectiles or fragments, which I cannot see much of, since my stretcher is on the floor, I see the amputation of a leg, halfway up the thigh. I see much more of this, a large part of the different stages. The patient is anesthetized. It seems to me that a tourniquet is applied to the leg. I see, and partly guess, an incision entirely around the thigh, then two or three longitudinal incisions. Assistants staunch the flow of blood while others employ a multitude of hemostats to block the arteries or veins. The flaps of flesh or portions of flesh that are folded back seem to be held by rubber straps or tubing, forming an enormous roll of flesh, just below the hip. I hear, but cannot really see, the bone being scraped with a sort of spoon. Then a chrome-plated saw is passed to the surgeon, who starts to saw like one saws a tree branch, but, no doubt, with more precautions and also more precision! They then work on the bone, then pull the flesh back down and do all sorts of ligatures. In the meantime, the assistants have also passed a sort of putty to one of the surgeons, also a drain, two I think. If I have not seen everything because of the surgeons who surround the table and replace each other, I have seen a great deal. I have watched all this, coolly, without being nauseated, as an attentive spectator. Without thinking that my turn will come to take my place on one of the tables and undergo… what? I do not know!

I do not have long to wait to find out, for my turn comes and I am placed on the operating table at the extreme right of the room. I hear one of the surgeons talk to the one who seems to be the Chief Surgeon of the team, "Walloon," it is a Walloon, and he gives the details of my wounds. Apparently they have no idea that I understand German. While they remove the bandages from the leg I hear the chief of the team tell the others that it will be better to amputate my left leg to avoid farther complications. I do not immediately realize that this is about MY leg! But I react quickly, in fear of the irreparable, as in legitimate defense, for once anesthetized…! I ask them if it is absolutely necessary, if there is not some means of avoiding it, but without too much hope.

They are surprised to hear me speak German, and a few minutes later, after a brief confab they tell me that they will do their best. I understood that they were thinking of amputation because of the risk of gangrene resulting from the delayed administration of the anti-tetanus shot. "Since you are only 20 years old", they tell me, "we will take that risk." They then move on to the next table while I am given the anesthesia.

When I later wake up I am in bed in the room that I had left. It is still day, but not for much longer. Time to regain consciousness, to remember where I am. Uneasy, I immediately feel my leg, my legs. I have both of them! What a relief! The nurses later tell me that the surgeons reduced the fracture and extracted the four largest fragments.

This same day I have something like a vision. I think I am dreaming! When I open my eyes from the anesthesia I discover two comrades at the foot of my bed. They are the same two, Lux and Dominé, whom I saw when I regained consciousness after I was wounded! The two of them confirm that they found me lying, with no movements, eyes open, and that they believed I was dead.

Now, little by little, I relax, and, as the nervous tension eases, the exhaustion that has been constant throughout these recent weeks manifests all at once and entirely possesses me. I sleep for entire days and nights. I am awakened for each dinner, for care, and for being washed, but the rest of the time, I sleep! I receive another visit from Lux and Dominé, and also from the other *"Bourguignons"* who are hospitalized here, like me, but who can move about. In an adjoining room, whose open door allows me to see, is a wounded man who cannot be moved, who has been there since the first days of the war in the east. They tell me that he is wounded a bit everywhere, but what I can see is that his leg is suspended in a frame above his bed, a stirrup at the knee, another whose needle passes through his ankle. For 20 months he has been there like that!

6 March, new departure, for Germany this time. I was told of it yesterday evening. Farewell to my neighbors, to the medical personnel. I am transported on a stretcher to one of the ambulances that waits in front of the steps. Fifteen minutes *en route* and I am placed in a medical train. This time it is yet more marvelous than the last medical train I traveled in. It is a passenger train, no more goods wagons. It is perfectly set up, but, above all, we have complete and sufficient medical personnel: doctors, male and female nurses who take care of us with kindness and devotion. We shall be spoiled for the entire period of the voyage with attentive care, gentleness and cigarettes. This time there is already the characteristic *ambiance* of German *"Gemütlichkeit"* [coziness, warmth], a fragrance of *"Heimat"* [home] that surrounds us! Via Sosnowitz and Katowitz, Breslau and Glatz, always these itineraries that shift, imposed by the war, we reach the city of Bad – Kudowa.[1] Today it is called Kudow – Zdröj, thanks to the Yalta accords, on the old German-Czechoslovak frontier that is today the Polish-Czechoslovak border, for the same reasons that you already know.

The trip has gone well, three good days of rest. I slept much. It is now 9 March. The railroad station is lively in such circumstances, as you can expect with such a large train of wounded returning home! The animation is not entirely the coming and going of medical teams. The convoys of numerous ambulances that traverse the little city have caught the attention of the local residents and numerous civilians, especially the women and the youths who also come to welcome us. Leaving the station on a stretcher, I hear all sorts of comments in soft or moderate voices: *"Mein Gott ist der jung!"* ("My God, he is so young!"); "That one there seems seriously injured. Look how thin he is, his face so drawn." Nevertheless, I feel far better than a month ago! Some notice my shoulder patch on my jacket, placed on my stretcher. *"Was is den das für ein Landsman?"* ("What nationality is that one?") In any case, there are many sympathetic remarks, words of commisera-tion! So many sympathetic looks that I am almost ready to cry, myself!

Soon thereafter the ambulance deposits me before a hotel, of the family boarding house sort, which has the sign, *"Haus Franz"*. It is a large villa, with a small garden in front, big garden behind, with a driveway alongside, in the start-of-the-century style, ground floor and two stories above, sloping tiled roof. Five of us share a room, a *caporal* [*Sturmmann*] of the *Waffen-SS*, originally from the Banat, who had escaped, like me, from the Tcherkassy pocket, another *caporal* [*Gefreiter*] of the *Wehrmacht*, originally from northern Germany and a lover of great music, an *adjudant* [*Feldwebel*], also of the *Wehrmacht*, from Nordhausen, a Bavarian *soldat artilleur*, artilleryman, and myself. Two nurses, Ursula (Uschi) and Sophie, and a male nurse, all three very friendly, take

---

1 When a German town or city name starts with 'Bad', or 'Baths', it refers to the city's history as a place for curative baths in local hot springs, where people came to enjoy its healing waters.

charge of us. Uschi is very pretty, Sophie is beautiful. I ask myself why I have forgotten the name of the male nurse when I so well remember the names of the female nurses. All three of them quickly became extremely dear friends!

On 11 March, in the morning, an ambulance comes to take me to the main hospital where they operate on my right foot. The city is already covered with snow. I wake up in the afternoon in my bed at the general hospital *"Haus Franz"*. There is one unpleasant aspect of our life that we all finally get used to: Three of the five of us have frostbitten limbs, and there is a constant pestilential smell in the room. How can the nurses endure this and act as if there was nothing when they come in our room? For myself, there is nothing serious. It is only the area surrounding the wound on my foot that I was unable to massage when it was needed that was frozen. I will lose no more than a bit of my big toe. A comrade has lost all the toes on one foot; another has had both feet amputated at the level of the arch.

On 2 April, ambulance and hospital, where they operate again on my left leg. This wound is not healing and the doctors are concerned that it could get worse… On the other hand, the wound on my foot sometimes causes burning pain as it comes back to life. At the end of the month of May I am able to get up and walk, with the help of crutches, or elbow-crutches. I am getting good with them and, after two or three days, I go a bit farther, to see the city of Bad – Kudowa, at least an avenue or two. I can compare it to Spa, more from its aspect and importance than from its *ambiance*. It is more or less the same style, the same *genre*. It too is a city of the waters and of cures, with public gardens, an *orangerie*,[2] concert halls, one of them under a great glass roof, a bandstand in the gardens, and springs. My comrade, the lover of great music, takes me to two or three concerts and teaches me to love *Parsifal*. Every time I appreciate Wagner, the best musical illustrator of our epics. At one of the concerts we become acquainted with a lady who still looks young, accompanied by her daughter, a pretty blond of 20 years, whom we see with most honorable intentions several times, at concerts and in the gardens of the thermal baths. In the evening, in a state of general hilarity, we return to our clinic in a rented carriage.

One who has what I would call a less honorable *rendezvous* is the *Wehrmacht adjudant*. He makes us laugh, but at the same time disgusts us, for every evening, often in the night, when he returns he goes to the lavatory to wash off a condom! This is a matter of peasant thrift, for he has told us that he is a farmer and the son of a farmer. I don't really know whether we are more disgusted with his miserliness or his cynicism of a man of 40, in front of four young men of 18 to 25 years, for he is not friendly with any of us, nor with the nurses.

Every week we are visited by two or three women from the *NSF*, the Association of National-Socialist Women, who bring us sweets and cigarettes, and the charm of their presence, for one of them is a young woman of 24 or 25 years. This group always remains a longer time at my bedside than at those of the other wounded because I am a foreigner without family here, whereas all the others, except for the man from the Banat, receive visits from their families.

I also remember the young maid who ended up putting on long tight *culottes* [knickers] that reached below her knees under her skirt because she realized that, when she washed the panes of the windows, up on her stepladder, two pairs of eyes, those of the two of us whose beds were by the window, could easily enjoy all that the spectacle offered. My bed was just to the right of the window, and I can tell you that the girl was pretty and shapely, or at least that it was not just that my interest in life had returned, or that it was the effect of not having seen feminine charm presented so agreeably for so long.

---

2   Hothouse – or greenhouse – in the 17th to 19th centuries, usually in classical architectural form, where citrus fruit trees were grown in tubs.

I made good use of the hospital library services, since I was confined to my bed, to finish out my evenings or to get through moments of insomnia. Nearly all of the books were printed in Gothic type [*Fraktur*] and I was never able to finish a Goethe that I was stubborn enough to select. All the same, it amazed my German comrades. I had, indeed, been taught Gothic in school, but you may well believe that I remembered little! Thus my days in this delightful little provincial city went by smoothly until 8 June, when an ambulance took me to Bad – Reinertz, in the vicinity, so that I could see a specialist in bone injuries and have some x-rays of my leg. I was always afraid that they would end up with amputation, since the wound was not closing.

When I return to Bad – Kudow at the end of the afternoon, I find a letter there from one of my aunts. This letter has certainly had a hard time finding me, and I can't get over the fact that it got to me at all! It is the first letter from home since December of the previous year! Nearly six months without any news from my family! This letter arrived at my unit, which forwarded it to me, for I remember having informed the brigade of my arrival at Bad – Kudowa shortly after I got there. This is the first letter that got to me, which left me a bit perplexed. I was unable to figure out exactly what it meant; the sentences were vague and short. I was sure I was missing some link. I could feel great compassion in the lines, but without knowing what for. This aunt, whom I adored, felt sorry for my case, wounded, so far from my country, an orphan. I did not understand very well. My mother had died in 1939, but I still had my father.

The next day I receive a telegram, which explains things, but very sadly. It is from friends in Brussels and is dated earlier than yesterday's letter, brief, laconic: Your father died! I could not believe it, I never had time to tell him that, despite the divergence in our political opinions, I respected him and I loved him greatly. There was nothing wrong in saying that and forgetting about propriety. But, certainly, I was unable to go, and I had to take action in order to be able to!

Within the hour I got an interview with the Chief Surgeon, the doctor in charge. I showed him the telegram and requested my transfer to a hospital in my country, a "*Heimat-Lazarett*" [homeland hospital]. He tells me that this is impossible, it has been forbidden since the landing in France. In fact, we have just learned of the landing of the "Allies" on the continent! I must have been extremely disagreeable, for the doctor changes his tone and tells me, dryly, "*Ich kann Sie KF entlassen!*" ("I can send you back to your unit, fit for service at the front!"). I immediately agreed. "Good, you will leave tomorrow to rejoin your brigade, your papers will be ready this evening!" He then tells me that there are thousands and thousands of German soldiers in my situation, and he cannot make a difference between them and me. Every day, on all the fronts, there are thousands of German soldiers who lose their families in the bombings and they can no longer return to their families. All have to remain at their posts, where they were! The Chief Surgeon is right, that is certain, but how can a 21-year-old accept that, right after learning of the death of his father?

It is an excited young man who now hastens on his crutches, at risk of breaking something else, toward his "*Reserve-Lazarett*". Despite everything, I realize, *en route*, that my attitude and the manner in which I spoke to the Chief Surgeon could have brought me before a court martial, if he had not had more self-control than I had shown. But nothing bad came of it!

The following morning, Sister[3] Sophie came to my room, fully dressed! "Are you ready? Then let's go!" I am amazed to see her leave "*Haus Franz*" with me. "I shall go with you as far as Breslau, for you will have problems changing trains. You are still too tired from your wounds and your operations! When I have put you on the other train at Breslau, you will certainly find someone who will help you if you have another change of trains."

---

3   In Germany, it was normal to address a female nurse as '*Schwester*' or 'Sister', even though she was not in a religious order.

"Does the Chief Surgeon know?"

"No, but I arranged it with my colleagues and our doctor will say nothing about it to anyone. It is our little secret!" She has a charming little smile while she says this. She carries my belt with a bread bag that contains my *toilette* necessities, underwear and something to eat *en route*. I have no other luggage, but she does everything to spare me fatigue since our departure, for one never knows how long a trip will take under wartime conditions. We embark in the Bad – Kudowa railroad station. Shortly before noon we arrive in the Breslau station, where Sister Sophie finds out the time of departure of a connecting train toward Wildflecken. I am to take a train to Frankfurt/ Main and get off at Eisenach where I will transfer to a new train.

Since we have some time to wait, we go to the station canteen to eat a bite. When the train is announced, she takes me there and sees that I am comfortably settled in a first class compartment among the officers, who give me a place at the window. She goes so far in her solicitude as to place me in the care of the train conductor, who enters the wagon at this moment. She wishes me farewell, and, contrary to all expectations, gives me a timid kiss on the cheek! She is already on the platform, in front of my window, before I realize that she has just kissed me, and I believe that she has blushed at her boldness, she looks a little embarrassed. She waits until the train leaves, and waves goodbye to me, then disappears rapidly in the crowd as if she is fleeing! Parting under such conditions is always a bit sad, with a touch of melancholy. I am glad to be done with it in the present circumstances. This causes one of those little wrenches, one of those little wounds that I have already spoken of!

The next day, 10 June, I arrive at Wildflecken as evening begins. The male nurses help me to change trains and give me something to eat and drink, alerted, no doubt, by someone or other, but I am tired, for it is a long trip, and it is the first time since I was wounded that I have been so long out of bed. There are no longer many of us at Wildflecken. The brigade is in Poland, at Debica. I must now take a train in the opposite direction as far as Breslau, then about another 400 kilometers beyond that. All in all, about a thousand kilometers. I will rest here for a day and depart the day after tomorrow.

On the 12th I leave Wildflecken for Debica, where I arrive on 14 June. Since I arrived I have been surrounded by all the comrades who I meet here and who believed me dead. They since learned that I was still alive, when Lux and Dominé rejoined the brigade, long before me. Those who had already announced my death in the breakout from the encirclement were, by chance, the same ones who then were able to announce that I was alive, after having seen me again in the hospital! What a curious coincidence.

I must have told my story in minute detail 10 times, 20 times! I then go from office to office, where I meet all of the veterans, as happy to see me again as I am to see them, G. Bathélémi, J. Hanssen, J. Henrotay and many more! All get together to quickly find a way to get me back to Belgium, at least to allow me to be there for a sojourn. They find me a mission, or, rather, they invent one. Once in Belgium I only have to report to the military hospital and submit to an examination. They will have to hospitalize me in light of my open wounds, for the one in my left leg still has a drain.

My plan is all set and I only have to await the moment, the day of departure. That will be 18 June. While waiting, I make the rounds from one barracks to another, each time finding my buddies so that I can also listen to their stories. There is a great deal of free time here, and much freedom, also. The "*Bourguignons*" are scattered to the four corners of Germany and elsewhere, dispersed in specialist schools, which means that, dispersed, what is left of the brigade and those that have come to reinforce it have little supervision and thus, little organization of their time.

The camp is situated in a wooded, very sandy region. The weather is good, and very hot. For the first time I have occasion to see the *V1* and *V2* in flight, which I also hear about for the first time, I believe. Apparently there is a base for these missiles in the immediate vicinity of our camp.

The parade after Tcherkassy.

Another photograph of the parade after Tcherkassy.

The awarding of decorations (after the parade) at Charleroi.

L. Gillis – one of the legendary figures of the *Légion*.

17

Return on a "Mission" to Belgium

On 18 June, in the morning, an automobile takes me to the railroad station, *en route* for Brussels with a mission order in my pocket! After three nights and four days of an extremely trying journey, I arrive. I spend one night alone in the empty house, if not empty of its contents, empty of any welcoming presence. Curious impression! All of the objects that were so familiar, the furnishings that shaped my life in all my infancy, my youth, all of that today seems almost strange to me! This house, once so alive with all the family, with so many friends, is now empty and deserted. I make the rounds from the cellars to the attics without stopping anywhere, as if I am already preparing to detach, realizing, perhaps, that I shall never return here again!

The devil take sentiments, let's not get emotional! I have nothing more to do here. The next day, very early, I go to the *Kommandantur*, the throne room, and request authorizations and travel vouchers for the movements I intend. Accordingly, I, arrive at Binche on the 24th to see my *fiancée*, whom I have not seen for 14 months, since just after we had decided on the engagement! On the 24th I go to Charleroi to see my sister. On the 26th I return to Brussels and, on the 27th, I go see one of my brothers at the *camp de Bourg-Léopold*. On the 28th I am back in Brussels again and, after going to *l'Honneur Légionnaire*, which is the central administration and mutual aid center of the *Légion*, I report to *l'Hôpital* Brugmann for examination of my wounds.

They return my documents for me to present to the doctor at the *Frontleitstelle* [forward direction center for personnel in transit], which is located at the *caserne* [barracks] St. Jean on the *Boulevard Botanique*, where I report immediately. I return to my empty house for one last time to spend one night, unconsciously hoping, perhaps, to rediscover there a bit of my childhood? The next day, 30 June, I must report to the *Frontelitstelle*. There I am issued additional documents with which I am to report to the *Feldkommandantur* [military administrative headquarters in occupied countries and communications zone]. They send me to the *Institut* Bordet for a new appointment with a doctor, who directs me to *l'Hôpital* Brugmann, where I am finally admitted on 1 July, 1944. I did not expect to have to go through so much, with open wounds that called for immediate hospitalization. Sent to the *"Chirurgie-Abteilung"*, the surgical section, I meet a number of friends who are there and we form an extremely homogenous group. There is Raymond V.L., Freddy Hildesheim, Paul S., Aimé V.V., in particular, and many others, too. All are able to be up and get about, except me. I am confined to bed since my wounds are inflamed, doubtless from the fatigue caused by my recent travels and administrative diversions! They say I must undergo a new operation, which, I hope, is the last! All the same, I am happy to be able to rest for a bit, for, since my departure from Debica I have not had any rest and, for a man who needs to walk with canes, that was not easy, and was extremely exhausting.

This period is of little interest to anyone but myself, the less so in light of subsequent events. However, I think it useful to rapidly mention a couple of events that affected me, if only to evoke the atmosphere of the two ensuing months that preceded the arrival of the Allied armies in Brussels.

Our *Oberarzt* [medical first-lieutenant] is named Menzel, the *Stabsarzt* [medical captain], Waske. Our relationship with them is excellent, and our group is privileged to have extremely friendly feelings, especially with the first. He joins us several times in our evenings of fellowship, or *Kameradschaften*. One or two female nurses also participate, including one Belgian and also a rather mysterious young woman, Irène X., also Belgian. This last is under treatment here, for bullet wounds. She strikes up friendships, especially with Freddy, who livens up these evenings at the piano, with great virtuosity. A few days later I am told that Freddy has been killed on the open street by a terrorist who then fled. It was, I believe, on the *avenue de 11 Novembre*.

On 22 July I undergo the projected operation, which is supposed to be a last attempt to save my left leg, and which is successful! I am sure of it, and it is thanks to the skill of Doctors Waske and Menzel! On 2 August I receive my promotion to *Sergent*, or *Unterscharführer*, which I was not expecting, for I had never even dreamed of it. On 10 August I see one of my brothers who is going to leave for Germany to rejoin the *Légion*.

In the meantime, the hospital gradually fills with wounded, primarily coming from Normandy. Within a few days the room occupation doubles, triples, then quadruples! The corridors, the bathrooms, the storage rooms are filled, overflowing with wounded. A great number of them are burned. There are many young tankmen of the *Hitlerjugend Division* [*12. SS-Panzerdivision "Hitlerjügend"*]. It hardly needs saying that they are very young, as we, ourselves, were at the start of the campaign. They are 16, 17 or 18 years old, for the most part. In a private room there is one of them who is unrecognizable! His face is entirely swollen with only two little slits where his eyes are, another at the location of his mouth. There is no trace of nose or ears! How could one identify him? It is difficult at times to tell if he is breathing. Nurses incessantly come to coat him with a sort of salve. There are also a plethora of young paratroopers, injured in jumps. They all wear a support around the neck and thorax, like a sort of tube twisted in a figure 8 that supports the spinal column. This massive arrival of wounded has not in any way changed the care, merely everybody takes part in the activities of the hospital according to his abilities, helping each other. There are many young women of the movement *"Foi dans la Vie"* [Faith in Life] who take equal part and have come to supplement the hospital personnel. There I meet Mady J. and Jeanine R., whose father, an officer in the *Légion*, was killed in the first winter campaign, Andrée D. and others.

Toward the end of August I am able to get up, with the help of canes. The first sorties from bed are always extremely painful after an operation, and it takes a lot of resolution to avoid remaining prone, confined to bed any longer. I make even more worthy efforts because we can feel that events are coming to a head, and that, once more, I must take action, and I cannot depend on the good will of others. Each time I push myself to the extreme limit before sitting or lying down to recuperate. Thus I make rapid progress and am even able to walk, with the help of canes, by 27 or 28 August. But I know what this has cost me.

I learn from my comrades, who are able to get around and even go outside, and also from the young women who assist the medical personnel, that a large number of families of *Légionnaires* or families that belong to the movement [Rexist] are starting to leave their country's soil to expatriate in Germany. So many of ours have already fallen victim to acts of terrorism, and there is no need to add more to the list, for there is nobody here to defend them. So we know that we must leave. In addition, Brussels has been declared an "open city" and will not be defended.

Twice I report to the *Institut* St. Jean Berchmans, where the families that are departing are lodged, and there, on my second visit, I find the uncle of my future wife, who finally chooses to remain at home. A few days later he is beaten and wounded, and it is by chance that I again meet him, alive, six years later! In the court of the school and in the classrooms I find mainly families come from the province, and a few, more rare, from Brabant. The *ambiance* reminds me of May 1940, only with less agitation, and, also, less baggage.

When I get back to the hospital, accompanied by my comrade, Raymond V.L., we have to wait for a hypothetical streetcar in the *Place Simonis*. There we are, two wounded *Légionnaires*, awaiting the arrival of a streetcar in the company of seven or eight civilians. People move around on both sides of the boulevard carrying heavy burdens. They carry bags and cartons containing I don't know what, quarters of meat, typewriters. They have certainly looted warehouses and offices. That is what strikes me the most in the three days during which I wandered around in the city. We have waited about 10 minutes when a woman, coming from behind us, speaks to us in a low voice, "Be careful! Several people are watching you from the *café* just behind you!" She adds, "I know that it is a nest of the resistance."

It is now 2 September, 1944 and there are no longer many German military in the city, except for a few isolated individuals and those who are in the hospitals, none in sight, in any case. I have no intention of waiting for a bullet in the back, nor, especially, to sneak away! I do not know if I am doing the right thing, but I decide to meet events face to face, and my comrade Raymond and I cross the road toward the indicated establishment. I walk slowly to avoid showing that I limp, so as not to reveal my weak point. We enter the establishment with great confidence, apparently very relaxed, and we order two beers! We stand at the counter, where there are already four or five men, but I place myself so that I can keep an eye on a table occupied by two other customers. It seems to me that there is electricity in the air, that there is a complicity between all the people, but I may be fooling myself. In any case, I have a strong impression that we have interrupted the conversation, that they have changed the subject! Before entering the *café* we have, most discreetly and for practical reasons, shifted the holsters containing our *P 38* [pistols] to the front of our left hips. This is one of the rare occasions that I went out armed in Belgium. We were required to do so. I could feel, above all, that they mistrusted us, that they did not take us for suckers! We remain there for at least 20 minutes until a streetcar arrives. We pay our tab, cross the road and get on the streetcar, without anything happening! Only the customers whom we have just left know whether or not we were taking a risk!

Since we are young and very sure of ourselves we are afraid of nothing. Our doctors tell us that they have been designated, along with other doctors, to remain with the wounded that cannot be transported and to hand the hospital over to the "Allies" upon their arrival. We do not wish to abandon them, thinking that, once the wounded have been transferred to the hands of the "Allies" that they, the doctors, will be given a safe passage to rejoin their units in the German lines. You can see that we were extremely naive! When we tell the doctors our intentions, they ask if we have gone crazy! There is no question of waiting with them; we should already be far away. Even knowing the country well, we would never be able to leave with them, for they would not be sent back to their lines. Even the promised automobile could not change what will be! A member of the [Rexist] transport service has promised us a car, coming from one of our premises on the *Chaussée de Waterloo*. We discuss it with the doctors for several days, and, finally, we have to decide *in extremis* to leave without them.

Thus it is that, on 3 September, we are brought the promised automobile, a *Graham-Paige*. The fellows of the [Rexist] movement who bring it to us are remaining here, and my comrades are counting on me to take the wheel. As a joke, despite all, and to surprise them, I tell them that I am taking the wheel for the first time. They are convinced of that, and one or another still believe that today.

18

Exile

On 3 September I take the wheel and I go by my house to pick up a few things that I put in a suitcase. This time it really is the last time, the very last time! There is no more room in the boot and I tie this suitcase on top of the boot. We go by the school where the families waiting to depart were assembled. There is nobody there. Reassured, we depart and go through Brussels. A building is burning on *avenue Marnix*. If I remember correctly, it is the "*Galeries Marnix*". We hear several explosions. In the distance, the dome of the *Palais de Justice* is still ablaze, and the black smoke rises from it high in the sky, for it is a clear day. Earlier in the day we already saw this dome burning where the explosions came from.

As we approach the *Porte Louis* [The Louis Gate] we think we can see Allies-armored reconnaissance vehicles. We had been told this morning that several leading elements of the «Allies» are already at the city limits. We turn back 180° at top speed toward the *rue de la Loi*, which we take. A few shots are fired from here and there, without any idea where they come from or whom they are aimed at, and, above all, without troubling ourselves about them. We head for *la Place Meiser*, where we take the *Chaussée de Louvain* toward the outer suburbs. It is about 2030 hours.

Farther down the road, at the Kraainem, an automobile is stopped. It is a *Peugeot*, one of those where the headlights are behind the radiator grill, painted with the colors of German military vehicles, flat gray. The occupants are four German paratroopers. Two of them are placing an *MG 42* machine gun where the windscreen was. These models have a removable windscreen. We pull in behind them and ask if they need any help. "No, everything is going well." They are simply taking a few precautions, since they think that they have been the target of a *franc-tireur* [sniper], without, however, being hit.

We travel, together, toward Louvain. A few kilometers farther on, the road is blocked by a military lorry that is burning on the road. This vehicle is carrying ammunition, which explodes sporadically, but there are no large caliber rounds that are exploding. When we want to pass it, an officer among the German soldiers who are there at the side of the roads prevents us. It is because there are large caliber rounds in its load. We then take a detour on a little paved road to the left. It takes us to the *chaussée* at Veltem. Evening is falling as we arrive in sight of Louvain. The road descends toward the center of the city. To the left there are some houses, on the right a high slope, covered with dense thickets. Suddenly we hear a loud detonation in this thicket and a projectile strikes the front of a house to the left of the road. If it is us whom they aimed for, the shooters missed. It might have been something like a *bazooka*, but less powerful. At such a short distance it was inexcusable for them to miss us. We continue imperturbably and enter Louvain.

One fire or another forces us to make detours. There is a fire on the *Grand' Place*. We are frustrated by a *cul de sac*. It is impossible to turn, the lane, more like a footpath, is barely wider than the automobile. In front of me a great granite post, a little more than a meter high, blocks the center of the road. I always have a horror of having to back up. I go forward in low gear until we just touch the post, and, hoping that it is not very deeply set in the ground, I step on the accelerator, steadily, but strongly. The post goes down without difficulty, but scrapes the bottom of the automobile a bit. A short cinder track and then a post, identical to the first, which gives way in the same fashion.

No damage to the automobile. We get back on a main road, suitable for motor vehicles, take a few turns and there we are, on the *route d'Aarschot*.

My two comrades, Raymond and Aimé, who positioned themselves, stretched out on the large front fenders, to be prepared for any eventuality, have returned to their place inside, alongside the young ladies who are with us, whom I have not mentioned yet. They are Aimé's wife and Mady, who is going to rejoin her German *fiancée* at Bettburg or Bensburg, I cannot be more exact, and the third is Line. She, too, if I understand fully, hopes to rejoin someone in Germany. If I have not mentioned them early, it is because it hardly concerned me! All are now in the automobile and the paratrooper's *Peugeot* follows us like our shadow.

The road is semi-deserted, and only the slender beams of the blacked-out headlights make two little paths in the total blackness. The conversations have died out and the passengers are dozing. We pass through Diest, and all are sleeping there. Then Beringen, Bourg – Léopold, Hechtel and Bree. Still in the night, we reach Venlo and stop there before a *café*, where a little light filters through between the drawn blinds. For the first time since leaving Brussels we come back to life a bit, become animated. There are other German soldiers already resting here when we enter the establishment. After an improvised collation we, too, stretch out to catch a little sleep. It is already 4 September.

When we wake up, a few hours later, I discover that my suitcase that was tied on top of the boot has been stolen. Damned Dutchmen! All I have left is what I am wearing. I make a quick tour of the neighborhood, stupid, wasted energy. There are many other military vehicles parked near ours, but, alas, no guard. We get back on the road. We cross the frontier, passing through Krefeld, Düsseldorf and, from there, toward Cologne where I have to make a little visit to reassure my friends and to show them that I am still alive. Then toward Wuppertal and now we are at Unna. We have passed through numerous road blocks and controls, all the easier since we found in our vehicle an *"Ausweis"* [pass] on red-glazed paper, signed by Jungclaus.[1] This pass read something like this: 'To all authorities, civilian and military: Request that you facilitate all movements and requests for assistance from the bearers of this'. Everything went well as far as Düsseldorf, where we had to return in order to leave from Unna.

This 7 September, at 2200 hours, we reach the *"SS Polizei Stab"*, or *SS* police headquarters, and the Düsseldorf airfield. Here the wind turns! We are back on foot, but still military. We had to leave the automobile there, and, after a night of sleep, we go by train toward Paderborn, which we reach on the 9th, at about 0600 hours in the morning. Mady left us at Düsseldorf, but we have three new recruits: the sisters Renée and Simone M.A. and Betsy B., who accompany us to Paderborn. On the 10th we pass by Hildesheim to finally end up at Harsum. Harsum is a little village in the Harz, not far from Hildesheim. There we find a colony of Belgian exiles, families of *Légionnaires* or members of the [Rexist] movement who have thus escaped, at least for the moment, from the terror organized against us by the irresponsible or the gangsters, who have much to answer for, or who are looking for an excuse to appropriate the goods of their victims. For I do not believe that those who believe in unbiased justice would join in these acts of terrorism that took place on this occasion.

Among these refugees are one or two *Légionnaires* who are demobilized or kept in reserve in Belgium, including *Adjudant* Hoffmann and *Lieutenants* Gre. and Gro., from the *Gardes Wallones*. Some families are housed with local people, some in a *café* and we are similarly housed.

---

1   *SS-Brigadeführer* Richard Jungclaus – a German *SS-Gruppenführer* and *Generalleutnant der Polizei* (1943), as well as *Höherer SS und Polizeiführer* (*HSSPF*), with wide police powers, for Belgium and northern France.

Forty-eight hours later, Raymond and I report to the *Reserve-Lazarett* [general hospital], established in a convent in the village, and we take lodging there. When Sunday arrives, a nun invites us to the mass held in the convent chapel, but neither of us feels like it. At noon another nun brings us the meal. Since it seems incomplete, I remark to her that there is no dessert, unlike those served to the other wounded or sick. She retorts, without laughing, but, nevertheless, with the air of having a thin-lipped smile, without, for all that, having any visible trace of a thin-lipped smile, "No, you are punished for not having been present at the mass! You can make amends by being saved right now!"

I can't believe my ears! We laugh about it but I ask myself if I shouldn't rather cry about it. Many years later I still think about it. But, all the same, without looking there for the reason for our military defeat, I cannot help using a rather colorful vocabulary, to which, no doubt, the good sisters are not accustomed, to let her know that she can do whatever she wants with my dessert. Certainly you see what I want to say, without daring to express myself that way here in my writing? The reply is not long in coming! A few hours later the door of our room opens violently as if blown open by the wind of a tempest and there, before us, is the *adjudant-chef*, red with anger! We remain calm. That is preferable, and even without listening we know what he is speaking of! I gather that he is threatening us with serious disciplinary action, return to our unit, etc. I tell him, very calmly, that tomorrow we are going to Hildesheim, without more details. On that he leaves, not without a few other curses.

The next afternoon we report to the *Hauptlazarett*, the main hospital at Hildesheim, and we obtain an interview with the *Stabsarzt* [medical captain] to whom we explain our argument of the previous day. He listens attentively, with surprise, reassures us and asks us to come back tomorrow morning between 1000 and 1100 hours. The next day, at the hour given, Raymond and I are waiting in the hall of the hospital in front of the door of the head doctor. Shortly thereafter the Harsum *adjudant* arrives, who makes it look like he does not recognize us while he waits with us in the antechamber for a moment, after which he is asked into the office. For 10 or 15 minutes there is bellowing behind the door, which finally opens, allowing our Harsum *Spieß* to leave, white as a sheet. We suspect that things have simply been taken care of, that we will be free to go to mass or not, without infantile threats from anyone. We do not expect that things will go any farther. The *Stabsarzt* then has us enter and informs us that the problem has been taken care of. Henceforth we will be cared for here and we can go live with a local resident if we wish, for the hospital is full and my condition no longer requires hospitalization.

On 15 or 16 September I go to Bakede to visit the parents of my friend Emile, who was killed at Novo – Buda, and there I also meet Madame Matthys, whom I do not know. On the 18th I go to spend three days at Aken/Elbe near my older brother and his wife. On the 23rd we return to Harsum, where, in the meantime, we have taken lodging with a local family and, at the end of September, we change our lodging, having found private lodging in Hildesheim. There we enjoy a happy month. The late-autumn is glorious and this little city of half-timbered houses has a very particular charm. Autumn confers on it an atmosphere filled with nuances, which I remember with nostalgia. The morning frosts have appeared, delicately frosting the lawns, and every morning the sun slowly burns through the fog and then dissipates it. Dewdrops delicately pearl the last flowers in the parks and gardens. The ivy that covers every one of these marvelous houses and the "*Haus-Germania*", with the air of a cloister, lose their leaves, one by one, softly, to land on the ground in a gilded carpet.

Our noon and evening meals, in the company of friends, refugees from Belgium, are always joyous and lively in the congenial little restaurants of the city. Sometimes, when we are better off, we dine at the "*Ratskeller*", one of those typical fine restaurants that are always hiding in the basements of the city hall. We receive ration stamps from all sides, but there are always dishes that do not require ration stamps that chefs who are accustomed to accommodating all who are able excel in preparing. The Dutch waiter at the restaurant on the *Goschenstrasse*, moreover, often serves us meat dishes without collecting stamps.

In the evening fog descends on the city with the last rays of the sun on the yellow and red leaves and on the pretty colored *façades*. The sun fades into the mist and vanishes. The street lights under their blackout-globes, progressively turn on and reveal the wrought-iron arabesques that decorate them. Everything is done to preserve the ancient character and comfortable serenity of the city.

Evening promenades alternate with massages at the hospital. There are frequent air-raid alerts, but no bombs. Nevertheless, the city will be flattened after my departure. Only one street will remain, spared from the bombing. I saw it again in 1981. It is the *Kessler Strasse*.

Raymond and I stubbornly refuse to go down to the cellar during the night-time alerts, despite the urgent appeals of our hosts. We hear the fragments of the anti-aircraft shells that fall on the tile roofs and then stream down to the gutters, for our room is right under the roof. There is no doubt that I would not be telling you of this today if we had not left Hildesheim before the fatal bombing.

One morning, at about 1100 hours, the sirens sound the alert and I realize that people are being directed to the shelters with more than the usual authority. Since I do not want to go there, I take the road that leaves the city toward Moritzberg, which commands the city from a slight elevation. There is a "*Flak*" battery there and I sit in the grass nearby. Perhaps that is not the best place? The weather is uniformly beautiful, with a clear, limpid blue sky. My eye gets accustomed and I finally make out, very, very high in the air, a few, then dozens and dozens of airplanes, minuscule points, brilliant in the sun. But other objects also shine in the sky, and slowly descend. When they are low enough, I see that they are thousands of long strips of aluminum foil, intended to interfere with radar. Soon after this the airplanes become larger in my view and the "*Flak*" starts to crash and deafens me.

The first bombs then fall with the sound of locomotives driven at full speed, then the explosions, the clouds of smoke, mixed with dust, that rise over the city on my left, behind and around the railroad station. The alarm does not last very long and the bombing is of minor importance. Most of the airplanes continued on their way, only a good 20 of them, I think, attacked the city, dropping bombs. I saw two, hit by the "*Flak*", go and crash in the distance, and one or two others, also hit, get away, hedgehopping. When I return to the city I smell powder smoke and the stench of burning, and a fine powder settles in places. These are the only events that troubled this charming little city during my sojourn there. Nothing to disturb me.

On 3 November we leave Hildesheim with a touch of that melancholy that clings to you. Yet more memories to add to the others. Snapshots for every hidden recess of my memory!

Good youngsters, but they have
taken some hard knocks!

Visiting one of my brothers,
with my nephew.

Hildesheim before, during and after the first bombing.

19

Return to My Unit

Thus it is that, on this 3 November, 1944 we return to our unit at Alfeld/Leine, in Hannover, where the replacement elements are located. The *Ersatzkompanie*, the replacement company, is the unit which receives, among others, the men who return from hospitals to direct them to their respective companies or to retain them while waiting until they are fit to return to the front line, fit for service, *Dienstfähig* (*DF*), or fit for combat, *Kampffähig* (*KF*). With much joy I meet a certain number of veterans, mostly non-commissioned officers, and we form a group, united and joyful, which gets together in every free moment. There is little duty, a few hours of theory a day, which we present in turn to the new recruits, for the newcomers also pass through the "*Ersatz*". This takes place in the buildings of the "*Rote Schule*", the "Red School", which serves as barracks and central administration of the "*Ersatz*".

A little farther along this same *Kaiserstrasse* is another building where the infirmary is located, the office of Dr Marcus, our doctor, a Rumanian, and the *fourrier* [quartermaster sergeant], H. Kaison. A third building, in baroque style, the "*Gerichtsamt*", or "Justice of the Peace", obviously houses the services of our *Officier de Justice* [police officer], Adrien Godsdeel. He is a "character", and he is missing a leg and an eye that he lost in the fighting at Gromowajabalka, the well named "Valley of Thunder".

Alfeld also houses a good number of Belgian refugees, but they are scattered in all of Hannover. Among them, most of the healthy men have joined the *Légion*. There are members of the *Jeunesses*,[1] members of the [Rexist] movement and of others. They are of all ages and all conditions, quite different from preceding recruitments. There are also elements of the *Gardes Wallonnes*, which had fallen back [when the Allies invaded Belgium] to Hannover and was now sending us reinforcements.

Among all of these there are men who are good, indeed, very good and then there are others, as is true everywhere. These latter represent, in any case, no more than a weak minority and, wherever you go, you will always find these same inequalities in diverse proportions. I am very happy, speaking for myself, to have had these comrades of such a level, often outstanding and in the best sense of the word, especially among the "veterans", but also among the recent arrivals. It is true that there were also others, it would be foolish to deny it. There are always the profiteers, those who hope for the favors of the regime. But since all would have to pass through the test of being under fire, these last would disappear in the course of time to vanish into anonymity.

Among the new arrivals there are also comrades coming from the "*Charlemagne*",[2] French volunteers and others from the *Kriegsmarine*, the German Navy, the *Division Azul*,[3] consisting of Spanish volunteers that fought to the very end, the *NSKK*[4] and others that, no doubt, I forget. In

---

1 Youth movements the *Jeunesses Rexistes* and *Jeunesses Légionnaire*.
2 French recruits to the *Waffen-SS* in 1943 formed the *SS-Sturmbrigade* "*Frankreich*" which was, on 10 August 1944 reformed as *33. Waffen-Grenadier-Division der SS* "*Charlemagne*" at Greifenburg.
3 The *Blaue Division*, or *Division Azul* – the Spanish 'Blue Division' – consisted of Spanish volunteers: Spain's contribution to fight on the Eastern Front against Russia.
4 *Nationalsozialisctisches Kraftfahrkorps* (*NSKK*) – the National Socialist Motor Corps, also known as the

brief, a lot of people who came from all over the horizon and who raised the number of effectives to close to 4,500 men.

It seems that the French, Spanish and various others who joined the *Légion Wallonie* at this point came for the *esprit de corps* that reigned here and that they had heard of by word of mouth, certainly, but also for the renown that the *Légion* enjoyed. The German Army *communiquées* had mentioned the *Légion* on numerous occasions. Certain among them have also told me that they wanted to join the *Chef*, whose notoriety and *panache* had seduced them.

Here, at the "*Ersatz*", we have lots of free time, outside the regular hours of service that consisted of parades, inspections, discussions, and theories that I have already mentioned. Quite often, nearly every day, except when I am *UvD*, or non-com of the day, we gather together among friends, comrades of the *Légion* and refugees in the various establishments of the neighborhood, one or two *Bierstube* [taverns], that it is futile to translate, or in one or another *Konditorei* which one might translate as "*Salons de Thé*", [tearooms] where, paradoxically, we mostly drink *Kafee-Ersatz*. These establishments are mostly situated in the *Leinestrasse*. But we also have another rallying point in the little square near the city hall that we have christened "*Le Bouillon*", because it is there that we spend most of the time with one or another sort of meatball and some melba toast. At that time this sort of establishment was called the "*Imbiss-Stube*", [snack room] but at the present time [when the author was writing this] the sign, undoubtedly, reads "*Snack*" or "*Schnell-Imbiss*", since, today more than yesterday, everyone is in a hurry, even when there is no reason. It is also the place that our comrade R. Lenglez selected to sketch people and make their caricatures.

At the heart of our little *coterie* are Henri Ph., Raymond V.L., R. Marchal, Vroonen, J. Vandenbosch, P. Stockman and some others, civilian refugees. We profit from these blessed moments as often as is possible, for we are very aware that we may not find such an instant again. The moment will come when some will heal, others will return to the front. This time is not at all disagreeable. Compared to those that we await and those that we have already experienced, we have the impression that we are living in the delights of Capua,[5] but, believe me, with all the restrictions imposed by the war! Nevertheless, the presence here of all these refugees, in the very sector where we are billeted, is not the most suitable. Even though it provides us with numerous pleasures, it does not facilitate the difficult task of restructuring the division, for we are too close to the moral distress of certain refugees, most of whom are aged. The fear for the dear ones remaining at home, the financial problems of some of them, of clothing, too, for they have abandoned everything except a few meager suitcases. Fortunately, the German social services are going to intervene and provide relief for most, if not all.

Some of the refugees have found work, others have not. I do not know if they have looked for work or not. I do not ask questions. I prefer not to have to feel pity. It is not the moment! Egoism on my part? Doubtless, but calculated egoism, it is necessary. For the rest, as a good soldier you live one day at a time, taking advantage of each golden opportunity as it comes to distract oneself. I appreciate each day, each hour at its proper worth. My morale remains excellent and it certainly seems to me that it is the same for all of the comrades that are around me.

During this time the formation is reconstituted as a reduced infantry division. The "*Flak*" and *PAK*, anti-aircraft and anti-tank elements are reforming at Breslau, the artillery at Seltchan and the pioneers at Raditzko, two localities in Bohemia. The *TTR*, *troupes de transmission*, communications

---

National Socialist Drivers – was a uniformed paramilitary organization of the Nazi Party that existed from 1931 to 1945.

5 This is a regularly used phrase in French. In the Punic Wars, the soldiers of Hannibal became distracted by the beautiful city of Capua instead of marching on Rome and thus lost the war. It now signifies a choice made for ease at the detriment of duty.

troops, are in Italy. Here in Hannover the Division Headquarters are at Gronau, one battalion at Bruggen, another at Bensdorf and the "*Ersatz*", replacements, at Alfeld. In its entirety it is under the *Major BEM* [*Breveté d'État-Major,* General Staff corps-officer]. Franz Hellebaut, a big man, respected by all for his intellectual and moral worth, comprises the high command there.

Lucien Lippert, our so greatly missed late commander, had visited him on 12 February, 1943 in his *Oflag*[6] at Fischbeck and asked him if he would be willing to replace him in command of the *Légion* if he was killed. However, no one, especially no *Légionnaire*, had any doubt of the attachment of the commander [Lippert] to his *Légionnaires*, or his concern for them! When, much later, after the death of Lucien Lippert, in the course of the reconstitution of the *Légion* and the formation of the reduced division, our *Capitaine* J. Vermeire went to see him in his *Oflag*, Major Hellebaut, honoring his given word, rejoined us after an extremely brief leave. Thus it is that the *Légion* was able to maintain its own command.[7] We have never forgotten that!

Here, then, is this brilliant officer, *Breveté d'État-Major* who, knowing that [the war] is lost, has come to join us to attempt to save whatever can still be saved. That is what he told me in later conversations, first at the St. Gilles prison and later, after his liberation. Aware of the situation, but honoring his work, against winds and tides, he comes to us! It is that, the sense of honor, such was we conceived it then and still do today! But there are others who have not understood that and never will, for they do not have the same feeling about honor that we do! That is indeed why *Major* Hellebaut immediately gained our most profound esteem and our most sincere friendship. He was truly one of ours. *Major* Hellebaut, who died in 1984 at the age of 85, paid for his respect for his given word and his sense of honor with 16 years' imprisonment.

Life at Alfeld is calm and the days pass slowly. If I have found friends, comrades of the first hour, I have also met old acquaintances among the refugees. This leads to varied conversations, but, even with my *Légionnaire* comrades, there is in general little discussion of the war itself. Things change abruptly, however, when on 17 or 18 December we learn of the launching of a major German counter-offensive! I learned, much later – oh derision! – that on 15 December, precisely on the eve of this great operation, Marshal Montgomery declared in front of several of his associates,[8] "On all fronts, the Germans are conducting a defensive campaign. In fact, their military and strategic situation absolutely does not allow them to plan the activation of any sort of large-scale operation!"

And more, from the same source [see above footnote] "The Germans have had to assemble on the Eastern Front, and contrary to all expectations, 30 divisions, consisting of about 250,000 men, about 2,000 guns, 1,000 tanks and 1,500 airplanes."

Marshal Montgomery must have been proud of himself on this 16 December, 1944! All the more since there had already been another little "error" by the same marshal at Arnhem, where Operation "Market Garden" cost 17,000 victims among the Allied troops, not counting about 10,000 civilians, far more than the cost of the gigantic invasion of Normandy, which only cost 10,000-12,000 victims among the Allied forces.[9] Nevertheless, Montgomery had 5,000 aircraft and 2,500 gliders for this Operation "Market Garden" [see above footnote]. Happily for the "Allies", they had other generals to carry out their operations.

---

6   *Oflag, Offizierslager* – officer's prisoner of war camp.
7   The Germans insisted on German command for almost all of the other foreign formations in German service. Only the Belgian *Légion Wallonie* was able to retain Belgian command.
8   Author's footnote – Salmaggi, Cesare and Pallavisini, Alfredo, *2194 jours de guerre* [*2194 Days of War: An Illustrated Chronology of the Second World War*], *Sélection du Readers Digest*, p. 637. *1ère édition, 30 janvier, 1980.*
9   Author's footnote – Ryan, C., *Un pont trop loin* [*A Bridge Too Far*], (Robert Laffont).

The Ardennes Offensive, also called the "von Rundstedt" Offensive, was launched on 16 December, 1944 after a brief but violent artillery preparation which started at 0530 hours on a front extending from Monschau to Echternach.

It was only in later consultation of these documents that I learned the precise details on this battle, but here at Alfeld we were limited to the news reports, of necessity fragmentary, and, of course, with a 24-hour delay. Is there any need to say that this development gave rise to great hopes? It animated our conversations, causing people to talk who, generally, never opened their mouths. These commentaries in every sense, *apropos* and not *apropos*, were entirely normal. All the more so since the operation, in its initial phase, bore some resemblance to the "*Blitzkrieg*" of 1940 or the invasion of Russia in 1941. Every day, or nearly every day, we heard names of recaptured localities that had a familiar resonance in our ears!

Our troops are in a state of alert and rumors of departure circulate. And, in fact, on 21 or 22 December the *1st* and *5th Compagnies* of the *69th Regiment* embark for cantonments in the west, more precisely in the Rhineland. However, employment of our forces on the Western Front for such an eventuality was out of the question, outside the terms of our engagement. Nevertheless, so far as I am concerned – and here, as in all that I have written, I speak only for myself – I see no big difference between my enlistment for employment on the Eastern Front and a possible commitment in the west against those who have become allies of the USSR and, consequently, their accomplices in the enslavement of the west, which is what the Yalta Conferences in January and February 1945 was to confirm! But without, however, finding myself facing my compatriots.

Since the departure toward the west of a certain number of our elements, excitement mounts a notch at Alfeld and in the other locations where our elements are billeted. Undoubtedly some are already back in Belgium. Perhaps some are even dreaming of doing so? I learn that some Belgian civilians have also departed for the west in hopes of restoring, so far as possible, the administration. So much for the *ambiance*, the rumors that circulate here. True or false, it is always difficult to put things in perspective. In any case, we follow the rapid advance of some of the German armored divisions on a map pinned up on a blackboard at the "*Rote Schule*", the "Red School". After Monschau we talk of Trois – Ponts, St. Vith, Houffalize, encircled Bastogne, Hotton, Ciergnon, right by Dinant!

During this time and in order to avoid inaction for the recruits that are not yet incorporated in the units and formations, and still dependant on the arrival of replacements, P. Stockman and I, along with two other non-commissioned officers, are asked to comment in turn on the events on the Western Front. The materials we are provided with to do this are so limited that the task is extremely difficult, the more so since we are not qualified to do this properly. This is why, after the second or third session, we change the subject of these conferences in accord with *Commandant* Dengis to speak of other campaigns that we, ourselves, have experienced and that we can speak of with more assurance.

Christmas is approaching, and, in spite of the war, which manifests itself especially in numerous air-raid alerts and bombings, Germany remains her usual self, calm, serene, immutable in its traditions. On every street corner, here and elsewhere, we meet city dwellers and villagers carrying enormous platters loaded with pastries shaped like figurines of all sorts that they are taking to their baker who will bake these for them. This same custom is equally practiced as Easter approaches. Our hosts offer these to us during the entire period of the celebration! I feel that it is interesting, that it is, in any case, useful to present all of these little details which help immerse one in the *ambiance* in which we were living and that others, who have not had this experience, could not otherwise understand.

One can never sufficiently praise the courage of these civilian populations subjected to the imperatives of the war! It is not the same for us, even if many of us are still adolescents, for we chose action and exposed ourselves voluntarily.

One morning, a few days before Christmas, I wake up with an acute pain in my left index finger. It is swollen and purplish. The shooting pains are such that I must immediately go the house of Dr Marcus. He cuts into the finger, applies a green ointment and bandages it. I am relieved. Nevertheless, I have to return to see him on Christmas Day, for the pain has returned even more intensely. The doctor is on leave for a few days and the medical orderly, von Zachnovski, a White Russian, as his name shows, cares for me, but poorly, putting a wound-healing ointment on the suppurating finger! I am sorry for him, for he is an extremely kind young man whom I appreciate, but my finger goes from bad to worse.

I must wait until the morning of 3 January to see Dr Marcus, who sends me for emergency care to the Gronau hospital. I talk of this because I want to speak a bit about everything that has more or less left its mark on me, in my spirit or in my flesh, but I summarize. At the hospital they amputate my finger to the last phalange, under local anesthetic, since I refuse the mask, which I cannot put up with. After an hour of rest in an armchair, a doctor asks me if I want transportation back. No, I think I am able to make it back to the "*Ersatz*" on my own. I then return to Alfeld on foot, a dozen kilometers! But that is what I wanted. In any case, I am quite content to see the finest homes of Alfeld.

When I see Dr Marcus the following afternoon he has me take private lodging with a local resident with an orderly! What luxury! My orderly will be R. Loos, a boy of 16 years, a member of the *Jeunesses*, the youth movements, who arrived in Germany in September with his mother. I find lodging with an engineer, five minutes from the "*Rote Schule*". A villa in an adjoining street. My hosts are a couple in their sixties, simple and charming, who invite me to share the meals any time that I desire.

What is the situation in this end of December? Between Christmas and New Year's Day the fighting continues in the west, and, in the east, the Battle of Budapest rages. The winter is severe, and it freezes hard here at Alfeld. West of Trier or Trèves the German troops have achieved a breakthrough that is more than 100 kilometers deep in nine days. The ground captured is more or less triangular, the base being a line that extends from Trier to five kilometers from Dinant. The altitude of the triangle is 75 kilometers, measured from the base, a little north of Martelange to Monschau.

New Year's Eve: Joseph Dupont and I are invited to the home of comrade Williame. Dinner and chess until 0200 hours in the morning.

In the first days of the month of January the Battle of the Ardennes continues, and the German forces seem to progress further. On the other hand, the *Luftwaffe* violently bombs Allied airports in Belgium, Holland and France, destroying or damaging more than 500 enemy aircraft, to the great surprise of the "Allies".

By mid-January we learn of the retreat of the German divisions engaged in the Battle of the Ardennes, and also that a group of German troops encircled at Warsaw have succeeded in breaking through the encirclement and getting out. By the end of January or the start of February hope dies when we learn of the end of the so-called "von Rundstedt" Offensive. The troops fall back to their lines of departure from which they had attacked on 16 December, 1944. The Battle of the Ardennes will have lasted one month!

Between the end of January and the end of March several developments take place that we learn of a few hours, a few days or even a few months after they took place. Some are comic to the highest degree, the others dramatic. Among the latter is the torpedoing by Russian submarine *S 13* of the passenger liner "*Wilhelm Gustloff*", transporting more than 6,000 wounded and refugees.

More than 5,000 of them perish in the waters of the Baltic Sea, at a temperature of –20° [–4° F]. But there was also the ship *"Goya"*, sunk by another Russian submarine, with the loss of 6,000 men, without counting the other hospital ships sunk by the Russians or the "Allies".[10]

Among the "diverse actions", it must be assuredly noted, the most comical are these: On 2 February, 1945 Ecuador declares war on Germany and Japan, and Paraguay does the same on the 8th of the same month! (contagion). On 12 February it is Peru's turn to also declare war on Germany and Japan on the same occasion. Egypt and Syria then do so on 26 February, Lebanon on the 27th, Saudi Arabia on the 28th and, in March, Turkey on the 1st, Finland on the 3rd, but, by way of additional refinement, this last was made retroactive to 15 September, 1944! Will this retroactivity become contagious? All the same, so long as it is far from our country. And, while we're at it, why not make it retroactive to 3 September, 1939? Finally, pity for this poor Finland, which has already seen so much of it.

When, on 27 March, 1945 Argentina, in turn, declares war on Germany, 53 countries have done so by then! What a blow to our morale, to learn at this point that all these banana republics and others are soon going to fall on us! But, doubtless, these countries have said, "Let us do this more for the humor than for the war", for they were certain that they would not have to fight! The mad scramble is developing and each one is looking to be in a good place for the kill!

In the meantime, on the 13th, the bombing of Dresden took place in two waves, among others, but in Dresden there were between 200,000 and 300,000 killed.[11] Then, there were "only" 70,000 victims at Hiroshima on 6 August, 1945! The carnage at Dresden was so appalling that, by the time they got to about 70,000 victims, they could no longer count them! It is tragic for Japan, but it has been much discussed and there has even been a movie. But Dresden was of little significance for the media, for German cadavers come cheap. Nevertheless, it is truly closer to us!

At this same time the Battle of Budapest ended. Several hundred German combatants managed to escape from Buda after desperate fighting and to make it to the positions of the German *8. Armee*. In the last eight days of February I am summoned to Grünenplan in order to spend my days in the company of several officers of the *Gardes Wallones*, but I do not know the reason. These are officers who have decided not to join the ranks of the *Légion*. One of them, *Lieutenant* Hlb, changes his mind and does enlist. But one who does not change his mind is *Capitaine* Hb, the one who, at Namur, vehemently exhorted his men to join the ranks of the *Légion*. I feel that he is very embarrassed every time that I run into him, for he knows what I am thinking, I had occasion to tell him. And myself, I feel better about myself because I did not wait for his diatribes to do so. Several times I shall be lodged with them in a barracks placed at our disposal and which is located under a big linden tree. I do not remain there, for my amputation has already healed well and I want to rejoin my comrades who are on the Oder. I make my request to *Commandant* Dengis, and, on 2 or 3 March I depart for Sack, a little village four kilometers northeast of Alfeld.

I am to join *Sergent* Fontigny there and join with him in training a platoon that is there. Comrade Fontigny comes from the *NSKK*, or *Nationalsozialisctisches Kraftfahrkorps*, the National Socialist Motor Corps, and the 30 men arrived from Belgium in September. Three or four of them have also left German factories to join us. Fontigny and I are lodged in the house of a local resident, the men in a room in the village. An old *café* serves as our office. Several times notables of the village, or of others, come to pass a moment in our company. Among them is the director of the local brewery, who, I think, is also a *burgermeister*. They come to talk, to discuss the situation with us and ask what we think of it, as if were privy to the secrets of the gods!

10 Author's footnote – De Launay, J., *La grande Débacle* (Albin Michel).
11 Author's footnote – According to *le Petit Robert,* 250,000 dead; according to German authorities, 300,000 dead.

I think that they want to be reassured. We can do nothing but encourage them. They have read articles in the press that eulogize us. They have heard *communiquées* on the radio that cite our *Légion* as mentioned in the army order of the day. They have seen the *Führer* decorate Léon Degrelle in the newsreels. They hold us in extremely high esteem.

I think that the daughter of the brewer and one of her friends also think highly of us, for they come quite regularly to see us to talk and spend the afternoon or the evening at our office. The first is a tall brunette, very pretty. Her friend, blond and plump, is not bad at all. The two of them are charming and brighten up our sojourn in this totally rural little village.

Fifteen days go by thus, pleasantly, on 19 March we are notified that our departure for the east is planned for tomorrow.

20

Departure for the Oder: The Final Endeavors

On 20 March, once again, we are on the platform of the railroad station, about to depart. I know full well, before embarking, that another segment of my life is beginning, and that nothing will remain the same. All things considered, this is the spice of life, not knowing in advance what tomorrow will bring, and it is not so bad this way. It agrees perfectly with my temperament.

My lodging housekeeper and her daughter have come on foot from Sack and are there on the platform, which I was not expecting. They are not the only ones. Other villagers have also come to say farewell. What do we have that is so special that these people become so attached to us? Or is it German romanticism? A touch of the exotic? Each time I am surprised, and always confused, even though it has become habitual! Must I regret that I have not sought to become intimate with all of the people who have shown kindness toward us? I have done so before, and each time there has been the heartbreaks that wound and leave scars. After all those that we have already left with the deaths and disappearances of so many comrades, it is not necessary to provoke yet more! The separation on the platform of the railroad station has something very sad for those who are left behind and, it seems to me, marks even more those who leave, when these farewells are made on the doorstep.

Before I continue this account, I must call attention to an important point. Although I have kept numerous notes on events up to this point, and although I have numerous points of reference up to this point, it is not the same for the period that follows. Circumstances did not give me leisure, except in a few, rare instances and I had to get rid of these few notes before my captivity. This is entirely understandable in such circumstances, in the torment of the last weeks of the war, on constant alert, always on the move. Nevertheless, I have talked with a certain number of comrades who survived about events that they went through with me. I have had access to notes of several friends, in particular those of my comrade Raymond V.L., who had more luck than I did with his notes, which I copied during our captivity. Nevertheless, there are bound to be some small errors in the chronological order or geographic errors, but that do not significantly alter the reality of the events.

This is why some dates are missing, at least the ones that I could not confirm with one or more of my comrades who were my companions at the time. The same is true for certain place names, either because I have forgotten them or because, even at that time, I never knew them. Nor do I know the names of all the villages that we simply passed through with, at the most, an occasional stop for a few hours.

For the period that describes my itinerary during the final days of the war and my semi-clandestine return home, I have been able to compare the notes and memories of the two comrades who were my companions every day on this long road back to Belgium, Charles T. and Pierre Moreau, both of whom were still alive at the time I started to write down this account. I thank them warmly.

So here I am, on the platform of the Alfeld railroad station with my comrade, R. Fontigny and 30 recruits for whom we are responsible. The *"Bourguignons"* of the *"Ersatz"* are already there. Others are still coming to join us, coming from the entire Hannover region to fill the gaps left in the ranks of the division as a result of the intense fighting it has undergone in Pomerania. The atmosphere on the railroad platforms is always the same on such occasions, the calls, the embraces of the little girlfriends, the tears of the various women, the emotional farewells from several veterans of the 1914–18 war, invalids or too old to go with us, often converted to service with the German railroad services.

The train slowly moves out, the faces bathed in tears fade away and then the silhouettes, them-selves, shrink and disappear. The steam and smoke of the train is frayed by the movement of the train. Now we are on our way, but the images stay with us, and we also remember the living memory of the farewells.

I do not know how much time the trip will take, but we have provisions for two or three days. The train heads south before turning off to the east, finally to head back north again. Bad – Gandersheim, Salzgitter, Braunschweig. Many of the railroad lines have been damaged by the bombing and we are delayed by numerous detours, even though, once the aerial attacks end, all the services go into action to restore the lines to service. In these conditions all the usable tracks are in great demand, so there are many stops and delays. When night comes we are somewhere between Braunschweig and Magdeburg. I do not know what time it is when, one more time, the train stops. We were, for the most part, dozing. The night is pitch-black and we see innumerable bursts of anti-aircraft fire in the sky. It is probably an attack on Magdeburg and undoubtedly the reason that the train has stopped.

Some of us get out and get down on the tracks, as much to stretch our legs as to look at the sky. Soon afterwards we see the glow of fires that rapidly grow, but the anti-aircraft gunners do not let up! The sky is streaked with the rounds, which increase, and then diminish in intensity, only to then intensify even more, and the bursts light the sky with an insane rhythm, ending up with a multitude of little white clouds. Then, very high in the sky, a red and white glow that rapidly grows and comes toward us, toward the west. Surely it is an "Allied" bomber that has been hit, and that is attempting to make it back to their lines. It flies parallel to our train, but at a distance, and then disappears. A few minutes later we see a second, then yet another catch fire and crash in the distance, exploding spectacularly.

We get back in the wagons to sleep. When we wake up it is day and we are rolling on. I don't know where we are. A new stop in open country. We receive good hot coffee. The train moves on, we eat our bread. Scanning the horizon to our right, toward the south, we see thick clouds of smoke that climb and join with others that adorn the sky. No doubt these are the ruins of Magdeburg that are burning up. We have, certainly, bypassed the city and, once more, the train heads north.

All day long we roll in the same direction, with numerous halts and two or three air-raid alarms, but our train is not targeted. If I remember correctly, our itinerary went by Stendal, Wittenberge, Pritzwalke and, in one of these stations the *DRK*, the German Red Cross, serves us good soup. These angels of devotion are always at their post! Day and night, in any weather, always in service and always, too, with a smile, even in the worst of circumstances! A new night, and again with numerous stops. The train heads eastward this time, toward Neustreliz, then Neubrandenburg, and we finally disembark a little farther on. This train will not go farther!

It is now 22 March, I believe, when we move on, now on foot – and on 23 or 24 March we arrive at Plöwen. *En route* I have dysentery again. Because I have not been imprudent, I have not had an attack since my time in the hospital, after the Caucasus. Was it the food? The water? I do not know. On the 29th we leave Plöwen to report to Bergholz, west of Stettin, where we arrive this same day. There I find one of my brothers, completely unexpected! I haven't seen him since July 1944. A moment of emotion!

After a night spent with our platoon in a barn, my brother becomes concerned for my state of health. Blessed with private lodging as an officer, he invites me to sleep there and spend the night with him. It is true that an attack of dysentery has caused me to rapidly lose several kilos, and that it has left its mark on my face. It is also true that I already feel greatly weakened. I also meet the medical orderly, Pierre V.D.G., but, after two or three days of care, nothing has improved and the doctor, Dr Buy, has me evacuated to the hospital in Neubrandenburg.

Not only is the hospital overcrowded, but numerous fine homes serve as annexes to it. Everything is full, packed with wounded, sick and the German hospital personnel, aided by foreign medical orderlies, Polish and Russian, who have preferred to leave their countries and follow the German troops. Many wounded or sick sleep, like me, on straw mattresses or with the ground, itself, as their mattress, eight or 10 to a room, with no furniture whatsoever except for one or two stools. After four or five days of care I feel better and ask to return to my unit. The doctor agrees, but the chief medical orderly proves less willing.

On 7 April, however, I go back to Bergholz and, the next day, I ask to rejoin my comrades who are going into the front line, to the great dissatisfaction of my brother, who does not believe that I am well. We move out toward Wolschow and go into position before a lake, in the dunes. It does not rain, but the night is cold and damp, and I do not have a greatcoat. This lake is more like a river, which extends in front of us. The next afternoon a dispatch rider comes to tell me to report to Bergholz and take a group of recruits in order to prepare positions in the sector of the lakes, near Prenzlau. I get on the Prenzlau – Löcknitz road near Brüssow, where, almost immediately, I come upon a group of 30 "Bourguignons", accompanied by another non-commissioned officer. It is the very group that I was to pick up. The road from Prenzlau, and the two others that run farther to the south, are filled with columns and convoys heading north. Alone, like us, are a few groups of soldiers heading south. I stop a convoy of several lorries that, like us, is heading south, and we are able to climb aboard and sit on boxes of ammunition. If we come under fire, we will be catapulted, very quickly and very high into the open sky.

The route is not long, and shortly thereafter we disembark at the exit of the city. The lorries continue toward the west and we set out on foot toward Angermünde, marching along the railroad, which should save us time. The march is not easy. We have to march on the tracks, since the verges are not practicable and, in the meantime, night has fallen. Already, we can make out a first lake on our right. We have, perhaps, marched a good hour when the tracks diverge from the lake. When the tracks again come back to the lake we have marched two hours. It is, perhaps, another lake, but there is not a sign of life. Absolute calm prevails, except for, at times, a very soft lapping of the water in the lake or, in the distance, the sound of the cannon as background noise. That is a constant ever since I came to Pomerania and, up to the last day of the war, the sound of the guns will be omnipresent, sometimes very close, sometimes in the distance, on our right, on our left and in front of us, but also, sometimes, behind us. That makes us think we are encircled. In actual fact, more than once we have had no withdrawal route, for the pressure of the Red Army has been strong all around the horizon. There can no longer be any doubt, the Russians are now seeking to finish it up rapidly, and they are convinced that it was only a question of hours, perhaps even less.

The night is black and moonless and we can't see much. We don't really know where we are. During a halt, we agree, the other sergent and I, that it is not really necessary to jump into the wolf's mouth, or, more apt to the present moment, the bear's mouth! Prenzlau already seems really far off to us, as if it has been a day-and-a-half since we left it. We must find a habitation, a village! We decide to go on, but with more precautions, hoping to find, if nothing more, a level crossing with a crossing-guard's hut. The name of the other sergent escapes me. I have searched for it desperately. He belonged to the *Gardes-Wallones* and the *NSKK*. He has also already been in Russia. I think it might have been Behets or Behagel, or something like that. If it is really him, he is a fellow who, after the war, entered the communal administration of St. Josse, before it was known that he had been one of us, and that he was then condemned, like all of us, after being dismissed, in spite of his good services, of course.

We continue on our way. I will march at the point, with a volunteer on the left, myself on the right of the track to look for the lakes, and the group will follow 30 meters behind, the other *sergent* at the rear, with another man, as file closers, to avoid losing men. We march like this for more than an hour, maybe two, without seeing or hearing anything. There are no more lakes, at least none close to or visible from the tracks. I have just acknowledged this when I hear someone call me. It is my companion who is on the left of the tracks. I climb up on the ballast and he points something out that I do not see. When I get to him I can distinguish, like him, a dark mass without being able to identify it or tell how far away it is. While he remains there, I head toward this mass. The soil is spongy and uneven. After about 30 meters I suddenly find that I am in front of a fairly tall building, but without visible stories, a blank wall. No sound. I go around the building and find a large old wooden door, barely ajar. I enter but I only have a lighter with which to check it out. It is an old barn which has, doubtless, sheltered horses.

I go back to the railroad tracks where I meet the group which has joined my scout, and we decide to spend the night here. We go to the barn and summarily settle down there. We also decide to place two guards: one toward the railroad, the other near the door. It is better to take precautions. Our insouciance has, at times, already cost us very dear! Since I do not know the men who are with me, there are no veterans, I do not know if I can have full confidence in all of them. A double-guard seems much better. The men are relieved every hour. We are sufficient in number and all of us are tired. I will take the first hour with a man. By setting the example the new men will be reassured, and I will thus gain their confidence. It must be about 2300 hours in the evening.

When I wake up those who are supposed to provide the relief, I lend my watch to one of them, since nobody else has one. I do not have total confidence in mine, but it is better than none. When I wake up in the morning it is nearly 0700 hours. Those who were on guard when day broke spotted a village a few hundred meters distant! Those who still had some bread ate it or are eating it while marching toward the village. I settle for a little coffee, black and cold, of course. Before arriving at the hamlet we pass under a bridge of an auto-route. We had not seen it and, undoubtedly, the confused and distant noises that we heard sometimes came from there, and not only from artillery. In the village we find several other "*Bourguignons*", mostly from the "*Ersatz*" at Alfeld, but who had left it before I did. They point out to us the vacant lodging in the farms and I take three men with me. The farmer's wife prepares coffee for us and gives us something to eat, without our actually having to ask. It has been a long time since we have eaten bread like this. I have not had anything at all to eat since yesterday afternoon. It is only now that I realize that. And these two big slabs of cured ham, what a godsend, what a delicacy!

One of our officers comes by and quickly explains our mission. I think it was the *Premier Lieutenant* Closset. We must prepare positions and dig foxholes and trenches behind the road and between the lakes, for the lakes are spread out everywhere, along the length of the road and also to the rear. As I reflect and analyze the instructions, I realize that these defenses will protect as well against attacks coming from the northeast as from the east, the south and even the southeast! It is true that frequently we have already experienced such situations, in the Caucasus and at Tcherkassy, where the front was not a continuous line, more or less precise, but a series of rather isolated strongpoints which the enemy could bypass easily enough as he pleased if we were not careful.

What is the date today? The 10th, maybe the 11th of April. This afternoon, after the soup, my intestinal problems return! I have no medication. The tea does not help. I dig along with the men, frantically. It is worse! I thought I was doing the right thing, numbing the pain by avoiding hanging around in the wind, the cold, the humidity. I have hung on, not heroically, but stoically for two days, but, finally, I have to get sent back to the hospital at Neubrandenburg, deeply humiliated. At the hospital there are always as many wounded, but now there are also many who are sick. One of the medical assistants is a female doctor, a Russian, 30 years old, very beautiful, from the south or the Caucasus, with black hair. She manages quite well in German. I'd rather be dealing with a pretty girl than an ugly one. She recognized me, the doctor did not. Perhaps it is another [doctor]. I don't remember him either.

Draconian regime, diet, then tea and melba toast and a fistful of pills to take every day, 20. Not an hour goes by without the arrival of wounded. Others leave, evacuated farther to the rear. The coming and going is constant. Doctors, nurses, and health aides are exhausted, going full tilt day and night, for activity is just as intense at night as in the day. No difference, to a degree where it is difficult to sleep. But I do not complain when I see the others! That would be the last straw, I do not forget that.

After a week I feel really better, better than at my departure from the hospital 12 days ago. Steadier on my feet and more ashamed to be there among all these wounded. Since I cannot leave the hospital yet, despite my requests, I ask to be useful and help the nurses, the personnel and the wounded who need care. Among the latter I find several *"Bourguignons"* who talk to me of the hecatomb, of the enormous losses our units have suffered at all points on the front. They tell me of combat groups that have gone into the line up to three times in 48 hours, each time returning from the front with losses of up to two thirds of their effectives. And I learn of the death of so many comrades, that Madame Neuteleers, one of our nurses serving at the dressing station at New Rosow, had to be informed of the death of her fourth and last son! In actual fact, she had three, and has lost them all on the Russian Front. This last one she had adopted, cared for him as if he had been one of her own, and now lost him too! Certainly it is the mothers that have paid the heaviest price in this campaign in Russia. What a tragedy! What an appalling drama! And to say that, next, the "justice" of her country is going to hound this poor woman, condemning and locking her up! Where, then, was God at this moment?

How can I remain here after all that I have just learned? I demand to see the doctor, whom I finally see the next day in the corridor. He advises me to be patient for two more days in light of my relapse after my previous too brief a stay in the hospital.

When I am discharged from the hospital on 23 April, I believe, I discover far greater activity in the city and on the roads. Since I am not certain where our unit is located, I report to the military authorities of the city who tell me that the situation evolves from one hour to the next, that they no longer know, but advise me to go toward Woldegk and Prenzlau. I do not find a vehicle to take me there so I set out on foot. It is a counter-current that directs me to the east, passing interminable columns of refugees, fleeing the deluge of iron and fire, but, especially, fleeing the Red Army.

I also meet units of the army that are falling back in more or less good order. But, all the same, there are also several companies and platoons, all arms mixed, that, apparently, are seeking to get to the front and are marching in the same direction as I am. I also meet many wounded, sometimes with field dressings, covered with blood, who march toward the hospitals in the rear. On the other hand I am astonished to see an entire battalion, completely equipped with entirely new heavy weapons, the *"Überschwere Granatwerfer"*, or super-heavy mortars. These pieces are painted the color of sand, clearly pieces that were intended for the *Afrika Korps*. Obviously they were never in use! The carts that transport the ammunition boxes seem to me to be far too heavy for the boxes, which are empty! The men of this unit are all clearly older than we are, but they are also much older than those at the front. A German *Feldwebel* who is marching right beside me, seeing my evident astonishment, tells me, "It is certainly a *"Magen-Bataillon"* [stomach battalion]." Battalions of sick men who only are put in the front line in cases of absolute necessity and are, somewhat ironically, given this name.[1] We then met ambulances and lorries full of wounded, many of whom still had open wounds for lack of bandages, or, perhaps, lack of time in the heat of the fighting. I have the impression that I have become a part of a *tableau* representing the Apocalypse. The German *Feldwebel* and I walk together for a stretch of road, chatting, before separating a little farther. He heads toward Prenzlau, I go toward Trebenow, where I have just been told are the *"Bourguignons"*. I do, indeed, find them there shortly before nightfall.

The guns thunder constantly, as much to the northeast as to the east and south. But it is certainly Russian artillery, for there is an extreme shortage of ammunition on our side. It is at such a point that the German guns in the sector and the few tanks that are there, in support, are only permitted, most of the time, to fire three rounds per day! And that is the situation today, 27 April.

Since yesterday we have been rear guard on the river Ucker, and today, the *Bataillon* Bonniver occupies Schönwerder, south of Pasewalk, with a battalion of the *Wehrmacht*. I left Trebenow this morning heading toward Bandelow to rejoin the *"Kampfgruppe"*, with the other comrades. I met the young R. Loos, who came from the youth movements and who has become my orderly. He follows me like my shadow.

At the end of the morning, at the start of the afternoon, we regroup a platoon under *Lieutenant* A. Delannoy at Bandelow, or very close to it, and we start out southward. At this moment, as I learn a little later, Russian tanks move out of Prenzlau on the road from Neubrandenburg and are only just stopped by our men's *Panzerfäuste*. These individual anti-tank weapons have done good service by us. Prenzlau has now fallen and we have barely avoided encirclement. Decidedly this makes itself clear. We have Russians in front of us, but also behind us. The front is everywhere now, and there is firing on all sides. The firing to the south, toward Prenzlau, has not yet particularly hit us, and it is no more than seven or eight kilometers from here. We have been told that we are more than 20 kilometers south of Prenzlau and that we still have several days in which to dig defenses. They will not have served very long!

En route, near a crossroad, is *Lieutenant* A. Nortier, who hands out ammunition from one or two of the little ammunition cars, or *"Muiwagen"*. Each *Grenadier* receives a clip with five cartridges! Yes, five cartridges, you read it well! And the men who carry submachine guns also get one magazine! That gives me two clips, since I already have one, but one clip is emptied in a few seconds, less than one second per round, for certain, and, in addition, the target must be closer than 50 meters to be effective! The *lieutenant* tells us that we must deliver a counter-attack on Schönwerder from west to east, since half of the village is held by the Russians; the other is still in the hands of *Bataillon* Bonniver, or what is left of it! Since, they tell us, there are already many casualties, they promise us a supply of ammunition, very quickly, before we start the actual assault. Even if some of the men still have one or another round in the bottom of their cartridge pouches or their pockets, for few still have cartridge pouches, that is less than 10 rounds per man! I do not see how to conduct a counter-attack in these conditions. And there are only the two or three pistols that *Lieutenant* Delannoy, myself and, possibly, a third man carry, as a supplement. There are even one or two men that have no weapon, one of which has been issued a *Panzerfaust* as his entire armament, but he does not know how to use it. Of the 20 men that form this group, at least 12 have never seen the front and, certainly, they have not had the slightest practical instruction in using weapons! This is a suicide mission, but I consider it thus without any pessimism.

It is about three hours later when we are ready to go to work, if I may put it thus. We are indeed on the road, turning 90 degrees to the left. Now we are facing the village, with its bell tower

---

1   Such *'Magen-Bataillone'* – composed of men with stomach problems – were given special diets and care.

roughly in the center. Between us and it there is a big field, about 200 meters, and then the back walls of several farms, with few windows. Above the roofs of the farms is the bell tower. We know that this is held by the Russians, but that is all that we know, other than that our [superiors] have requested the German artillery, positioned some distance north of the village, to fire a few rounds at this bell tower, since the Russian snipers who are there hinder all movement in the village. Their response, sad but clear, "No." As I have said, they can only fire three rounds per day and they have already exhausted their ammunition for this 27 April.

Now it will be necessary for us to go there and we fan out before advancing. I scrutinize every detail of this bit of meadow where we are going to venture. Quite flat, without the slightest irregularity, a dozen plum trees with trunks no bigger than my wrist, two or three apple trees a bit larger, but not much, and not a leaf to provide any protective screen. In brief, absolutely no cover, like a billiard table! Undoubtedly we are the best targets that the "Popovs" have ever dreamed of!

Of course, the additional ammunition that we had just been promised has not arrived and will not reach us! I talk about it with my comrade Abel, who tells me to go get it. How are we to conduct this diversionary attack to relieve our comrades who are in the place without ammunition, especially since it is precisely the intensity of our fire that is supposed to distract them from our companions by obliging them to concentrate on us, or even force them to take cover to avoid our fire? Indeed, a single man in the bell tower would be sufficient to calmly pick us off, one by one, leaving all the others free to concentrate on *Bataillon* Bonniver.

At the moment when I am about to go in quest of resupply with ammunition, the little *Sergent* D.W., who is right behind me, cries out, "Don't stir, I go there." I allow him to go and he takes off running. We will never see him again! We wait no longer and we begin our advance, but we do not know where the Russians are, other than those in the bell tower. We advance, standing up, fanned out and in a saw-tooth formation. Twenty meters, 30, 50. Then, all of a sudden, the first bursts of fire. Of course they spotted us from the first step, but waited for us to draw near. Everybody, including me, hits the dirt. The firing definitely comes from the bell tower which is, at present, less than 200 meters from us and commands our positions with its 30 or so meters. Hardly surprising that the bullets whiz by us so close when they are fired at such short range. Rather surprising that we have not yet had any killed in our ranks. At least that there have not yet been, since it is not possible to assure ourselves of it with even a single glance. But, at 200 meters, with a maladroit marksman, one does have a small chance. On the other hand, for him to miss us at 150 meters he would really have to be trying to miss us. I have the sensation, for a moment, that I am at my last action, that this will be the end. At this instant? In a few minutes? What impotence, without ammunition in such circumstances! There is no possible doubt that most of us will be cut down before we reach those walls, dead or wounded, and those that escape death or wounding will probably have no chance to enter the village. One or two shells in the bell tower, a few more clips of ammunition for our men would change everything, not the outcome of the war, for sure, but possibly postpone the fall of Schönwerder and maybe other strongpoints, as well.

Nevertheless, we resume our advance, but this time by bounds, then lying down, no more standing up. The bounds become shorter and shorter as we advance and as a result of increasing accuracy and volume of the opposing fire. Moreover, I can feel more and more menacing and sustained bursts of fire barely missing my face and body. I immediately think that my peaked cap makes them think that I am the platoon leader! The shiny visor must have caught their attention. Immediately I turn it around, with the visor on the nape of my neck. I bought this cap at Hildesheim, a few weeks ago.

We continue our advance, but the intensity and accuracy of the enemy fire is such that our bounds are now measured in seconds. No more than two or three paces. The bullets whistle and throw up dirt all around us. We have no means to reply, or we will not have a single cartridge or bullet left at the moment we finally make contact. I feel like a rabbit facing a hunter, but with no hope of a hole to shelter me after the final bound. This sensation is most disagreeable. I would rather be in a hole, awaiting the assailant and the first five clients with my last five bullets! But I have no choice, especially now.

I make another four or five bounds, like my comrades, but these last ones are worth no more than a flea's jumps. At present we are about 60 meters from the walls before us, which means from the bell tower, and the bursts now come at us from an angle that approaches the vertical, and I tell myself that, for the gunners up there, a man lying down where we are becomes a better target than a man standing up. He offers a larger surface. Are there also shooters behind the few windows above us, in the walls? It is hard to say. That is why I do not take the risk of remaining standing. The platoon leader must have made the same observation as me, I suppose. He must realize the inanity of this attempt with no means and with no benefit to be derived from it. He now orders the retreat, by echelons, to be accomplished without turning our back to the enemy. The fire diminishes as we fall back and we soon regain the road; then cover behind a building.

We bypass the village to the west in order to penetrate from the north. We thereby link up with our comrades who still hold this part of the village. We advance toward the center of the village, more or less under cover of the houses, but it quickly turns out that they offer no real cover. We are under fire from every direction and we advance a little by chance, guided by the fire and the smell of the powder more than by precise orders. The Russians in the bell tower are always well concealed, and our last bullets, our last cartridges are not going to dislodge them, the more so since they are firing down on us without exposing themselves.

Among our survivors there are also some German soldiers, no more spared by the bullets and shells than the "*Bourguignons*", judging by the dead scattered here and there on the road. We make a little forward progress and I search desperately for an opportunity to make good use of my last magazine. But the Russian silhouettes that I glimpse are truly furtive behind the fragments of walls, and they disappear before I can take proper aim. Mind you that I know very well where they are… and then, with my submachine gun, which is by no means a rifle with a telescopic sight or an assault rifle, I have little chance of hitting them! Ah, if, at this moment, we only had the super-heavy mortars that I met up with not so long ago with their ammunition! But there is no need to dream. It is not the time for that. Reality is entirely different, seeing our wounded comrades, covered with blood, their uniforms ripped or pierced by the fragments of bullets, who move toward the rear, hoping to find a medical orderly or to get to a dressing station!

The last combatants also slowly fall back, out of ammunition, but the order to retreat has arrived. I still have my last magazine, since I have not been able to find a sure shot, but also because I would feel totally naked and disarmed if I did not have a bullet when facing an adversary. Then, in the last few meters, before leaving the village, I turn around and fire my last bullets toward the bell tower that has caused us so much concern, with no illusions about hitting a target, but to make a noise and, above all, so that I do not leave the field of battle without having fired my last cartridge!

Now we go back up to the northwest, part way by the road, then keeping near the woods. There are none of our troops here. The Russians are behind us, to the right and to the left. There is just a narrow corridor before us, almost like Tcherkassy, the breakout, the cold, the snow, but, at least, without the "Gniloï – Tikitsch". I find young Loos beside me. Amazing that I have just turned 22 and that he is only 16! Considering all that we have gone through in these last four years, I feel that I am at least 40! Loos tells me that he has never left my side since this morning. I cannot really confirm this, but it is true that I have found him beside me once or twice. I remember that now.

We talk little or none. I think each of us is lost in his own thoughts. As for me, I am angry. I am angry that I could do so little or nothing. But I think that my comrades must feel the same way. I am angry that I have had to be fired on from above without being able to reply, impotent and destitute of all, especially the essential, ammunition. At least we would have had the feeling of being able to defend ourselves and not die if we had a few cartridges! And the arms and ammunition of the *"Magen-Bataillon"* that I had seen pass by me, retreating, but armed to the teeth, still sticks in my gullet, even today!

Now that the tension has subsided I hear again the sound of artillery and it is always Russian artillery, rather than ours, which is no more able today than yesterday, or this afternoon, to fire more than their three rounds! These muffled sounds come from all points of the horizon. Are we encircled yet again? When night falls we billet ourselves in a barn in a village southeast of Woldegk. Then yet more *"Bourguignons"* arrive, also coming from Schönwerder. Among other deaths they tell me of the death of *Lieutenant Comte* de Backer de Réville. We also learn that we are temporarily, placed in reserve. It is true that everything now is only temporary, except death, when it arrives. The cannonade continues all night, but the only ones that hear it are those with insomnia, for it has become a background noise due to its familiarity. It is only when the impacts get nearer, or when the salvoes increase that one raises his head.

On the 28th the order arrives to move out toward the northwest, toward Neubrandenburg. What is striking on this march is the increase in the number of civilians on the roads, on foot, with carts loaded with their most precious belongings, not necessarily the most costly, but the most indispensable to continue their lives. Brave mothers, alone with young children since their husbands are at war, the poor old folks for whom this is not their first war. All these poor people have waited for the extreme limit, the last moment to take the road, hoping, no doubt, until the ultimate second that the Red Army would be stopped. For the first time I also see, with great astonishment, uniforms of the Belgian Army of 1940![2]

While *en route* I suddenly come face to face with one of my very best old comrades, Raymond P., and I discover that he is in bad shape with an ugly wound. With a haggard face, exhausted, he marches courageously, saying nothing. I can see full well that he will not get far like this, that he will have a hard time getting through like this. I lend a shoulder and my authority and take him to a field hospital where I leave him in the care of a doctor. Unfortunately, I cannot wait. I must follow the others, but confident and reassured to know that he is in good hands, I resume my journey in all haste to catch up with my comrades.

The rumor runs through the marching columns that the Russians are very near, yet, nevertheless, there is no nervousness, not the least panic manifests, though this disorder is not customary in the German people. At about 1600 or 1700 hours a noise in the sky makes us look up. It is one of those little reconnaissance airplanes, a *Fieseler-Storch*, which flies at no more than 50 meters' altitude. It makes a few arabesques in the sky, descending even lower. Everyone moves aside, for it becomes obvious that it is trying to land. Indeed, it lands and stops a few meters away. Along with the others I approach it, thinking that it needs help, but I see that it hails two nurses who were marching among us. The pilot throws some things from its cabin and unloads one or two cases that he leaves at the side of the road. I understand that they must be lightened, since this machine was not intended to transport three people, for he is going to embark these young women. At the moment of take-off I can see that he is having a difficult time and requires a long distance to get off the ground. For a moment I thought that he would not make it. Did he see from on high the approach of the Russians and fear for these two young nurses? Or was their presence otherwise required?

---

2   When the 'Last *Levée*' or the '*Volkssturm*' was called out, there was a desperate shortage of uniforms – as well as weapons and equipment. All sorts of uniforms were issued, including Nazi Party uniforms and captured Belgian Army uniforms.

On the evening of this 28 April, or, at least, it was not the 29th, we are in one of these immense agricultural properties – a *"Gut"*, as they say here. Aside from the immense building with wings disposed in a square, with a monumental columned entrance, there are no other structures nearby. No village or hamlet, not a single house. Nothing but fields, tilled and sowed fields, for nothing, even the war, has troubled this rhythm and this bucolic peace. Fields and pastures stretch as far as the eye can see!

To the right of the entrance is the main building, then the equipment storage, the stable, the cowshed, the pigsty and, to complete the square, the sheep pen. I quickly make acquaintance with the master of the place, tall, thin, with a stern air, but that is only an air, for, in fact, he is very simple and extremely friendly. He immediately reminds me of *Capitaine* Lambricht, whom we had at Brasschaat. I stayed here no more than 48 hours, maybe a little less, I don't know why, but I have such memories of the place that it has always stayed with me. The proprietor explains to me that all of the family left yesterday, and the farm workers also, with all of the horses, cows and sheep. He is leaving the bred cows, two or three sick animals, and the pigs and the poultry.

He tells me to inform my comrades that they can slaughter and eat all the animals that remain here, and to kill all of the others before leaving. There are a good hundred to 150 soldiers in the enormous court and in all these buildings, especially *"Bourguignons"*, but also Germans and, possibly, other nationalities. Among the *"Bourguignons"* I am particularly happy to find an excellent childhood friend who joined the *Légion* at the same time I did, Arthur V.E. We eat lots of chickens, we slaughter the pigs, and Arthur will cut them up, since he understands butchery, so that we can stock up on pork. Something to make up for all these days and recent weeks of fasting! When I say that Arthur understands something about butchery, of course, I mean in the proper sense of the term.

In the evening, with two buddies, including Charles T., we are invited to have a glass with the proprietor. We cannot remember ever finding such luxury and such good taste in furnishing a place, nothing flashy, but exemplary comfort. Carpets that one would love to have for a mattress, they are so thick, and a good assortment of antique furniture, everything good, even the hangings. The carpets and fabrics are very light colors, contrasting marvelously and with great harmony with the dark wood of the period furniture. The books of the library, where we are, entirely cover two large walls. There are somewhere between 2,000-3,000 volumes, including numerous editions with precious bindings. If it were not for our dusty wrinkled uniforms one would never believe there is a war, nor, especially, a retreat, in the hushed calm of this library!

Our host explains that he employs more than 200 agricultural workers and that all lived at the farm, in dormitories set up in the attics of the different buildings. They included French, Polish and other prisoners of war, but also civilians of six or seven different nationalities. We have seen these dormitories. They are dormitories, naturally, but with all sanitary and other comforts and conveniences, showers, washbasins, toilets and cupboards. Far different from what we would find, after the war, in our jails.

This *"Gutsherr"* is going to abandon all his goods this night, after a few hours of sleep. He is going to leave with these three last and faithful servants kept close to him, with two carts and several horses, also kept for this final departure. He is leaving without any hope of returning, with no illusions. Without being able to completely hide his emotion, he asks us to set fire to the entire property before leaving, and not to forget to slaughter the last animals. He wants nothing to remain, nothing of what was certainly his entire life, but also that of his parents, grandparents and other generations before them. This sort of patrimony was created by the labor of numerous generations over innumerable decades. And all this work, the labor of so many who have gone before over so many generations will disappear in a few hours, prey to flames!

It is close to midnight when we take our leave, as moved as he. He leaves before dawn to avoid the Russian airplanes. We can sleep here, on the wall-to-wall carpet or in the bedrooms. I am the one who was thinking of the carpet. He suggested the bedrooms. Curiously, however, I don't know why, maybe from some sort of humility, we prefer to rejoin our comrades in the hayloft above the sheep pen. Others go to sleep in the dormitories. We spend the one night there, but it seems like more to me, and, when we leave, nobody has the heart to set fire to what represented maybe three or four centuries of rural civilization and the fruit of so much labor! Decidedly we remain sentimental.

In the morning we take to the road again, always toward the northwest. Beside me is Charles T., a long-time comrade, a childhood friend. In the Tcherkassy pocket, more precisely at Mochny, when his company, the infantry gun company, had to fall back like the others and abandon their heavy guns, he retraced his steps and blew up the 150 mm guns that were going to fall, intact, into Russian hands when the latter were already too close and attempted to kill him. Do I need to point out that we are not alone on the road that we have just taken? There are groups of soldiers, civilians too, but much less than yesterday, on foot and with carts. There are also ambulances, overloaded, stuffed with misery. The lightly wounded also march like those who are uninjured. The ones who limp are aided by their comrades. Bandaged heads, the bandages spotted with blood, are visible from afar!

We head toward Neubrandenburg. As we walk we converse with those whom we overtake, or those who overtake us. There are many questions in these conversations about a redoubt that will be formed in the most inaccessible parts of Norway for an ultimate last stand in the event that there is no reversal of alliances. For there is also the question in these discussions of whether we will be able to hurl ourselves again toward the east, this time with other allies. At least an American general is supposed to have raised the possibility, even to have the resolute will to realize this project. I have no idea where these rumors come from, but they are very present, and well after the end of the war we will learn that it was actually true, that General Patton really would have loved to be able to act like this. This was, indeed, the opposite of his state of mind and his declarations at the start of the Italian campaign. However, he died in a curious traffic accident before he was able to put his ideas into effect. Very convenient for those who did not conceive of things in the same manner.

The rallying point of going to create the redoubt that I am talking about is at Flensburg, where ships will be waiting for us – always conditional – to take us to the fjords of the north. This *leitmotif* will often return! We also again meet prisoners of war, Belgian officers coming from Prenzlau. I have already met a few of them. Among them several pull little carts, as the Germans often do. They are filled with the most varied bundles of clothing, but also with food. I am amazed at the variety and also the quality of foodstuffs that they have, but I do not envy any of what they have. One or two of them very amiably offer us a bit of chocolate or some cigarettes! Unfortunately we have nothing to offer them in exchange. We are truly destitute. We would have loved not to be outdone. Perhaps we would have raised the question, but without any ulterior motives, for the officer in question explained to us that the idea of heading toward the east never crossed his mind, that, on the contrary, he was "fleeing" toward the west! Even though the road might be much too long, even though they could have simply awaited the arrival of the Russians in their camp, he and his companions had not taken the risk. I understand them. Had they heard talk of Katyn? On the other hand, we learned much later that the advancing Russians made no difference in their treatment between captured German soldiers and "Allied" prisoners of war who awaited their "liberation". If, later on, different arrangements were made for some of them, others never returned! In 1988 I had the opportunity to talk on a number of occasions with the sister of one of the latter. A little later we continued our journey, all of our party, always heading toward Neubrandenburg. Except for the marching troops, the city seems deserted, abandoned by its inhabitants. Not by everyone, however, A few homes are still inhabited, and their occupants watch us pass by from their doorstep or from a few windows, with an absent air, as if they had already resigned themselves. It is awful, but what can we do! What use now are our submachine guns, our rifles without cartridges, the guns without shells?

Shortly before we leave the city, two *"Feldgendarmes"*[3] advise us to head toward Neustrelitz. Thus it is that we change course, this time due south! We proceed along the length of a lake on our right for three hours, only coming upon one or two villages on our route. Then, going around the lake, we march northwest again, cross country and through woods, threading our way through an infinite number of lakes, sometimes on footpaths, sometimes straight ahead over open moor. This, I believe, was the site of the following story: We have just seen a village a few hundred meters ahead of us and we decide to go there, for it is time to sleep. We have marched a good eight hours. When we arrive there, a feeling of oppression comes over us, total silence, a sinister atmosphere surrounds us. There is not a soul, the village is absolutely deserted! Yet there, a few paces from us, lies a corpse, a little doubled up. Blond hair, medium long, a young girl, maybe 17 or 18 years old. And pretty! She is dead, but with no apparent wounds. Charles and I are loathe to touch the body, as if we are afraid to profane it. We do not even try to learn how she died. Maybe that would be even worse. At her feet is a handbag, its contents scattered. There are a few photos, which we pick up. We look at them without dwelling on them, but here is her picture of herself. It really is her, the young girl lying there who seems asleep.

Less than 100 meters distant, on a grassy hillock, is the village church, deserted, like the village. What can have happened here? The entire village could have retreated to the west, but no village would have abandoned this adolescent corpse, alone and with no grave! What a distressing mystery! We do not understand this at all, and it is only at this moment that we realize, Charles and I, that we are absolutely alone in this village, that nobody has followed in our footsteps. A painful situation, extremely sad moments never to be forgotten! Mechanically I put the photo in my pocket, I don't know why, but I still have it and I take it out regularly. Each time that I open the notebook into which I slipped it. On the back is a date: 1924. Is it, no doubt, her date of birth? Would she, then, be 21 years old? It is plausible, but she did not look it. Nevertheless, we cannot stay there. We look at each other for a moment, both shaking our heads at the same time, thus tacitly deciding to go on our way without trying to find shelter for the night in this sinister village, deserted but not destroyed.

We leave the place without a word, without even looking back, as if we want to quickly forget what happened there, quickly forget what we have just seen. We march more than an hour before finding another village. Halfway there we got back on a big road and also see other living beings. It is true that in the other village we did not even see an animal nor hear a bird's song, but we have not heard birdsong for a long time.

Here there are other soldiers, looking like us for shelter to sleep in. I do not know if there are civilians still here, but we do not see them. The two or three houses that we try to enter are closed, but not the barns. We go into one of them with five or six German soldiers. We take some jute bags from a pile and use them for bedclothes, stretched right on the straw. We have not eaten since morning and the chicken thighs, like the pork liver in our mess tins, are inedible. There had been no way to roast them, and that would have taken too much time. Fortunately our German comrades have bread and butter which they willingly share with us. Ah! This camaraderie! Since none of us have any coffee, we drink water from the well. We tell these comrades what we saw this afternoon in the deserted village. They are just as disconcerted as we are. Then we do not delay in

---

3 German military police.

going to sleep, after the fatigue of the march and of the emotions. We all sleep like logs, as if the war did not exist!

On 30 April we resume our journey and go past Waren toward Malchow. This road passes between two lakes, one of which is very big. A baker in Waren gives us some bread, before he leaves his shop, also to embark on the road to exile. In a little village before Malchow a peasant welcomes us for the night and serves us food. Soup and an omelet! It has been a long time since we have had such a feast! He is alone with an old servant, but plans to leave tomorrow to rejoin his wife, his daughter and the small children who were sent as a family farther west a few days earlier. We sleep in the beds! That, too, we have not done for a long time.

Today is 1 May, and, once more, we are back on the road toward Malchow. The peasant filled our bread bags with bread, bacon and canned meat, made at home. We have already experienced much kindness. This changes the horrors of war.

If the nights are cool, the days, on the other hand, are still spring-like. Up till now we have covered an average of 30 to 40 kilometers each day, but we are still far from reaching Flensburg. We cannot let up on the pace, we must, indeed, pick it up! After Malchow we skirt a lake, a big lake, it is the Plauersee, then others, smaller, three or four. Then we leave the big road to take another on to the left, smaller, which leads to Crivitz and, farther on, toward Schwerin. We have another good 10 to 12 days' marching to Flensburg! At least we want to find a vehicle to take us there, but they are all loaded with wounded, if not with *matériel*. We spend this night in a farm near a small river.

The next day, 2 May, the afternoon is already well advanced when we arrive in a village whose name I do not know, but which is situated in the Crivitz region. In the center, in a square, we find a group of soldiers belonging to different units. It is most evident that they are exclusively older men. Some of them surround a quad-20 mm anti-aircraft gun (*Flak Vierling*). It is a very effective weapon, as effective against vehicles on the ground and in direct fire against infantry as against aircraft.

While we talk with another group of German soldiers, two motorcycles with side-cars arrive. Their riders are men in khaki uniforms!!! Stupefaction, but short-lived. We have already seen such! They are English or New Zealanders, I do not remember more exactly. We are two paces from a well in the center of the square. One of the motorcyclists points to our submachine guns, pistols and the binoculars that Charles has slung on his chest. In a flash we throw the desired items over the coping and into the well, after having let go of the submachine guns with both hands. The men in khaki look at us for a moment, right in the eyes, without turning a hair! It is logical, they are five; we are maybe 40. Do they realize that they are the first "Allies" that we have yet seen? Did they lose their way? In any case, it is a totally fortuitous meeting. I wait for the others to appear! No more, absolutely none. The road remains deserted as far as we can see. Besides, and I understand them, they suddenly seem in a hurry to go. They make a half-turn and go back whence they came, quite simply.

Obviously no one had any desire to fire on them when they came to us, their arms slung over their shoulders. Moreover, when they first arrived we did not realize that they were not some of ours! But nobody thought it useful to keep them as prisoners!

Are we really that close to the end? I cannot believe it! I really think that I do not want to believe it. Nevertheless, we have just thrown away our weapons. But what use would they have been since we have no more ammunition, not a single cartridge...

We scan the horizon to make sure that no one is going to fall on us after the departure of these motorcycle scouts and, to the northeast, we see tanks advancing on a tree-lined road a few hundred meters from here and others to the southwest! A detail strikes and intrigues us! A second glance at first one, then the other, reveals that the identifying marks are different! To the northeast they are

Russian, the others are the "Allies"!!! A new surprise! Are we going to allow ourselves to be crushed between the two jaws of these pincers? On one side as on the other, these are not isolated tanks. They are entire columns of considerable armored forces!

Then Charles heads toward the quadruple anti-aircraft gun mounted on the bed of a lorry. I follow him. He talks to the artilleryman, himself being an artilleryman, but in the infantry guns, and suggests that they put the piece in position to fire on the Russians. To start, in any case! We do not have to wait for the reaction of these "oldsters". They are close to 40 years old. The older ones, in any case, are sick of it all and are ready to tear us to pieces! It is evident that we do not need to antagonize them. It is necessary, unwillingly, to give up the idea of a gallant last stand, to do something so that we do not later regret having been unable to do it. Disappointed, truly disappointed, we leave the place. A young German follows us and addresses us. He wears the paratroopers' jumpsuit and is, probably, 20 to 22 years old. He is a hefty person. Together we head for a small wood southeast of the village. Why there rather than elsewhere? I do not know, nor have my comrades any better idea.

Suddenly we discover an ambulance there in the open field right by the edge of the woods, less than 100 meters away. Some copses have prevented us from seeing it sooner. We head for the vehicle and determine that it has been abandoned, the double rear door is open and heaps of objects are scattered at the foot of the steps.

We find a bit of everything there. Several pairs of mountain boots, new socks and shoes. I also find a black training jacket with a white leather badge, ornamented with black *SS* runes, which I slip on over my shirt before putting my jacket back on. We do not know what tomorrow may bring, so plan ahead! We fill our bread bags with all they can hold. Bread, jam and several cans of meat that we find. Then the three of us enter the woods, taking a footpath rather than the road, which descends toward the south. A little later, in a clearing, we discover a crossing-guard's house at the side of a small railroad track and decide to spend the night there. It is occupied, and already a good half-dozen other soldiers have also taken refuge there.

The occupant of the place is an old man, employed to guard the tracks. An old veteran of 1914–18, he has lost a leg. We take our place among the other soldiers and have a bite to eat, sitting on the ground, waiting for night. While we are there, our host talks with us about the war, of this one but also of the other one, when the radio announces a *communiqué*.

It is the announcement of the death of Hitler, the surrender of Berlin and, if I remember correctly, also the very dignified message from *Grand Amiral* Dönitz, successor to Hitler. The tears that run gently down the wrinkled face of our host and the contents of the message overwhelm us, the one as much as the other! The man has turned off the radio and is sitting among us. He forces himself to discreetly suppress the sobs that shake him. Nobody says anything. No one feels like speaking. The silence is heavy.

The paratrooper who was just with us gets up and leaves. I follow him to the threshold of the door but he asks me to remain there, not to follow him. He descends the two or three steps and disappears into the night. I go back in and take my place among the other comrades, lying down in the two rooms of the ground floor. Charles is there, close by, but no one feels the need to talk. Everybody tries to sleep, to get a little rest or to be alone. What can all these men think of, exhausted by so much fatigue, by so much fighting? The only consolation for so much suffering will, doubtless, be having contained the torrents of the Red Army until the final exhaustion and collapse. Will the western adversary, at least, make good use of it and draw the necessary conclusions?

During the night I am awakened. It is the paratrooper who has just returned. One lightbulb is still lit. The paratrooper shows me an English helmet and a khaki military jacket! He has a curious look but does not want to say any more than that he could not deal with the tears of the old veteran of 1914–18, nor his distress, nor all that he heard on the radio, so he had to do something. But we know no more of it.

The next morning he takes the old man in his arms. These developments have certainly affected him deeply, more than we can realize. Then we leave. Shortly thereafter he leaves us after shaking our hands very intensely. We have known each other for no more than a single day's march, no more. And, nevertheless, Charles and I will never forget him. We immediately fraternized and it was as if we had always known each other. It is still, today, as if we had always been old friends, after so many years and without ever having seen each other again! Perhaps it is also because those few hours of absence that night will always remain enigmatic. I can find no other explanation than an individual *coup de main* on his part. To find relief from all the deception, the tears of the old man. But can one really know?

After the years of effort, of pain, of blood. There can be no possible balance, for it is not simply an assemblage of columns of numbers, of statistics with so many dead, missing, wounded and crippled! One cannot put numbers to the individual suffering, day after day and hour by hour. I think of the many wounded who could not be aided, who died all alone. There is all this suffering and distress often experienced in solitude that must be multiplied by so many millions. There are those who were wounded two times, three times or more, which implies that, each time, they returned to the front. It is necessary to add up all the sufferings of each individual in particular, to comprehend the magnitude of the sacrifices of all the young people, but also of the older ones in the final months of the war, for all were called upon at that moment, there. And this is true for both sides, for it is just as true on the other side that those who fight the wars are not those who declared them. And I do not say this for myself, for those of us who were volunteers and who took responsibility for our actions in full knowledge of the cause, not for the pleasure of making war, which disgusts me, as it does everyone, but because we felt that, in the position we were in, that it was not possible to peacefully await the end, in more or less safety, without having the courage to go and defend the values that were ours and were precious to us there where it was taking place.

But, all the same, I must say that it is true that, for the German soldier and those who fought at his side, the war was assuredly the longest and hardest. The Russian soldier and the "Allied" soldiers had the consolation of their place among the victors. I have no desire to complain, for that is not my nature, nor is it glorious to do so, but, all the same, it is permitted to present this evidence. We are now marching on the road that leads from Crivitz to Lübeck, and which passes via Schwerin and Gadebusch. Will we now be able to reach Flensburg? This prospect becomes increasingly uncertain since our encounter yesterday with the English and the Russian motorized columns at rifle range, or, at least, artillery range. But, all the same, it will be amusing if we get there, after all! We are foot-soldiers and, what is more, exhausted foot-soldiers who are retreating. Exhausted, but, for all that, not demoralized! It is true that tenacity, acquired dearly over the course of these years of war without mercy, will save the great majority of us, at least the survivors.

At present we see no more civilians fleeing before the armies, only soldiers, isolated or in small groups. Thus it is that, while marching, we suddenly recognize Pierre Moreau, whom we were about to overtake. We shall, out of necessity, overtake him, because he marches with difficulty, but with determination and a great deal of courage. His ankle is wounded, and has received no care, a wound received in recent days, in the final hours of fighting. Pierre is a good and, already, very long-time comrade of Charles and myself, and we are happy to meet him and to be able to help him a bit, if by no more than our presence beside him.

Proceeding at present with great difficulty, Pierre tells us that he is counting on returning to Belgium. He hopes for nothing more than to see his mother again. His mother is, at present, all alone, for his father has been the victim of a cowardly murder, while he, himself, was at the front. War is not gentle, but that was not war. If it was hard for all, it was a hundred times harder for some! Charles and I have thought of staying in Germany and losing ourselves in the population. That was not really difficult; there were opportunities and we were simply waiting for the best. There were so many dead and so many still missing that there was a desperate shortage of men to rebuild the German homeland. One such possibility had already been presented to us. Charles and I had already talked about this possibility as an aside, but after meeting up with Pierre we immediately decided, without the least hesitation, to stay with him. We could not abandon him; that was clear.

I no longer remember, nor do my friends, where it was that we spent this night. On the other hand, it is certain that, the next day, we were taken prisoner, for better or worse, by the Canadians near Gadebusch.

A photograph of the young girl who was found dead during the retreat in May 1945.

Deployment of the four Walloon companies during the Altdamm fighting – 17-19 March, 1945. (Arch. E. de Bruyne, via R. Devresse)

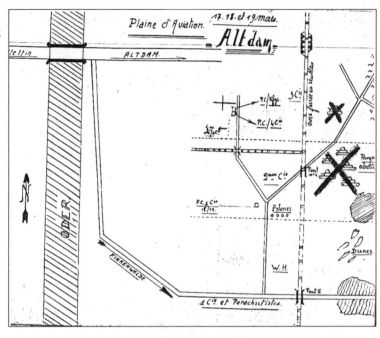

A post-war hand-drawn chart by F. Hellebaut; the Walloon and Flemish contingents withdrew across this terrain to the west and northwest. (Arch. E. de Bruyne)

21

Ephemeral Prisoners

Surprised, all the same, for, despite everything, we always preserved the hope and desire to reach Flensburg and, perhaps, there rejoin the formations that were still well organized. We were unable to completely give up this idea. Suddenly, at a bend in the road, we were face to face with a group of soldiers, their submachine guns pointed at us. What could we do? We no longer had any weapons, other than the miserable pistol that Charles had concealed and hung on to. If we had only remained on guard, if we had only been wary and taken more precautions, what could we have done? Would resistance have been worth the cost? And what would have happened to the other soldiers, mostly without weapons and scattered along this portion of the road? The next day, 5 May, moreover, we will learn that *Großadmiral* Dönitz has ordered the cessation of all fighting in the west!

The soldiers who have us at their mercy direct us to a meadow where thousands of other prisoners of all arms are assembled. On this occasion we learn that, among other exactions, the "Allied" soldiers are generous, without the least restraint, with blows of their rifle butts on all the prisoners that pass within their reach, including several [female] German nurses! As we approach the meadow we meet columns, already in formation, which are marching off. We immediately slip in among the ranks. I think that it will be better not to surrender at the meadow and not to stick around here!

In this column there are no more blows, at least I don't see any. On the other hand, just like the vulgar *moujiks* of times past, our guards take watches, wedding rings and decorations worn by their prisoners! I would not have believed this ahead of time, for the German authorities never used this sort of propaganda. I still preserved my illusions, you see! We escape this, for we slipped into the start of the column, at least in the first part where the plunder had already ended. Already, however, the column moves out headed south.

We are the only "youngsters" among our immediate neighbors, except for one young Dutchman, tall and blond as he should be, who quickly drew near us and struck up an acquaintance. In a few minutes we decided to escape on the first opportunity. We then spent half an hour continuously observing the column and the behavior of the guards, in order to determine how best to escape. That is all it took to determine that this would not be difficult and there would be minimal risk. The road winds through the woods and the armed guards who are distributed along the column are approximately 100 meters apart, which is to say that, every hundred meters there is a guard, one time on the right, one time on the left of the column. We need only wait for a bend in the road and that, precisely, the guard behind us turns around or looks in some other direction.

Within the hour the opportunity arrives and we do not wait for another occasion. The woods border the road, below it. We have already warned those near us of our intentions so as to avoid surprising our neighbors and any inopportune reaction on their part. One or two of these "oldsters" did protest a bit and attempted to dissuade us. But others entirely approved and made the reticent ones keep quiet. With one leap we are in the ditch and, in a few strides we disappear in the woods. Hardly a few minutes later we are in a little farm from which we watch the endless column that we just left, which proceeds along the road. The man who has taken us in takes risks, but without the slightest hesitation. He has given us work clothes. From now on we should melt into the crowd in these clothes. We can no longer be soldiers; at least we must lose the appearance. It is hard to resign myself to this, very hard. I feel humiliated as I have never been before. Not that I ever had the ambition to make a career of the army, but it is disappointing to leave the uniform in this fashion. There is nothing dishonorable about being a soldier in a defeated army, especially when this army has fought like no other, overwhelmed primarily by the inexhaustible reserves and armament of its adversaries. That does not in any way suggest that they were not well beaten, at least many of them. The cause of this defeat was neither cowardice or the lack of combativity. It is having to go into hiding that is most humiliating! It is necessary if we do not want to molder in captivity and want to attempt, by every possible means, to get back to our homeland as fast as possible.

It is necessary to act this way because the organization that will certainly be put in place without delay, now that the fighting has ceased, will make all evasion more difficult or impossible. We have confirmation of this immediately in the comrades who remain penned up for months, like beasts under the open sky on the meadows, without the least shelter, not even tents, at Neungamme, Fallingbostel and in others until autumn. One of my brothers experienced that in all kinds of weather and with miserable food, when there was food. More often than was reasonable they went for several days without any food at all, even for several months after the end of the war, when the victors no longer had the excuse of difficulties caused by military operations. What might have been understandable then, could not be justified now! The Canadian historian, James Bacque, has confirmed this brilliantly.[1]

It is well that we decided to escape. We had the right reaction at the right moment! After donning our work clothes and quenching our thirsts we leave our host who was so friendly with us. It is better to avoid delay. After expressing our gratitude and shaking hands warmly we turn our backs on the farm and disappear in the woods. It is obviously out of the question to go back on the road where our comrades, prisoners in the column we just left, are marching.

So we now march in woods and on moors to the east of the road that goes from Lützow to Wittenburg toward the south. Thus it is farewell to Flensburg. That is over with! As we are following a little road in the woods, a bicyclist suddenly emerges from a side road. It is Graff! *Lieutenant* Graff, in civilian clothes like us! A friendly wave and he goes on his way. What an unexpected encounter, in the middle of nowhere. We saw him a day or two earlier, still in uniform. He will finish his days in Argentina, but we will learn later that, before surrendering, on two or three occasions, he escorted trains of French prisoners from Germany to France, returning to Germany to look for others whom he also brought back to France before experiencing the adventure of exile!

It is true that Graff was one of the elite of our officers and that he inspires respect. Nor is he the only one of us to have such comic adventures, but all of us did our best to make our own way in a variety of circumstances – and now it became a sort of game for us.

In the evening we knock on a door to find shelter for the night. It is a little old lady who opens the door. She is all alone and does not dare put us up. We understand all the more so now that we are in civilian clothes. We knock on another door and spend the night there without the least hesitation on the part of the residents.

On the 5th we resume our march once more. A little later we take the risk of again using a more important road so as to avoid major detours. As we approach an intersection where the road forks there is a GI there who appears to be collecting bicycles. Near him there is a pile of bicycles, and each bicyclist that passes him has to leave his bicycle there. It is the first American that we have

1   Author's footnote – Bacque, James, *Other Losses* (Stoddart Publishing); in French: *Mort pour raisons diverses, chez* SAND.

seen since our escape. I feel a twinge of anxiety, but after an imperceptible hesitation we continue on our way and pass by him. When he is 20 or 30 meters behind us he blows his whistle and calls us back! Has our escapade come to an end?

When we draw near him, he points to the heap of bicycles and gestures that Pierre should take one. He has seen that Pierre has trouble walking. On the same occasion it seems that he gives us two other bicycles. I say that it seems so, because Pierre's and my memories are confused; they are not entirely clear on this subject. In any case, a little later we found another bicycle, abandoned with a flat tire behind a hedge. This bicycle was not equipped with a pump, and all that we need to do is to inflate the tire with the pump from one of our bicycles to restore it to service. That was why it had been abandoned by another soldier. Within a short time we end up with all four of us riding bicycles after the little excitement of our encounter with the GI who hailed us, but, by good fortune, to do us a real service, not to arrest us! Thus we could, henceforth, greatly increase our daily journeys.

In the evening we find lodging with a peasant who allows us to spend the night in his hayloft. In the morning, as we are eating a crust of bread before getting back on the road, the sound of voices outside catches our attention and makes us listen! Someone, at the foot of the ladder that leads to our retreat, is talking with another person who is farther away in the courtyard of the farm. Then the ladder starts to move and we hear footsteps climbing the ladder. Suddenly, framed in the opening of the access to the hayloft, is a silhouette. There can be no doubt: a beret, a battle-dress! He stops at the top of the ladder, leaning on the ladder and attempts to scrutinize the darkness of the loft, while addressing us in German!

"Who are you? What are you doing here?"

"We are Belgian workers in Germany, on our way back to our own country."

He then talks to us in Dutch and I talk a moment with him. Only for a few moments, but enough to make it clear that he must be a Dutch Jew, he cannot hide it. The face and the accent. He is a lieutenant. He does not seem at ease, for he is always looking into the darkness, but without getting too near, since he cannot know how many of us are in this dark loft with recesses that he cannot see into.

He asks us if we are planning to remain here for long. The idea immediately comes to me that he is going to return with reinforcements! I tell him that we are tired and that we are definitely going to spend another night here before going on. With that he goes back down the ladder and requisitions a couple of hens from the farmer. Our Dutch comrade avoided opening his mouth, with good reason.

We discreetly observe the "Allied" soldier and, after he has left the courtyard of the farm, we hastily gather our things and leave the place in the opposite direction from the way he went. It is only after we have pedaled far enough on little footpaths to but a good distance between him and us that we are able to relax. We have consciously changed our direction frequently to better confuse our track. This is no great problem for us now that we have the bicycles.

He will certainly look the fool when he returns with his men to find the barn deserted, for I am certain that he returned, it was entirely too clear from what he said.

Since we are on wheels, we are much less tired and we move much faster. At the start of the afternoon we already reach the Elbe near Boitzenburg. The bridges are certainly watched, and I would like to find another way of crossing the river, but there is no boat in sight. Finally we cross it without trouble on a pontoon bridge established by the "Allies". Then, before we turn toward Lüneburg, our Dutch comrade leaves us. One more friend from whom we must part, and it is always hard, particularly in the situations in which we now live. For this comrade here is worthy of real friendship! A friend found on the road a few days ago, our paratrooper. But we have already become attached to him, and he to us. He was one of us. He had, like us, attempted to make a

"Europe", a Europe of the nations, like all these comrades from so many other countries, well before others tried with such difficulty to make the "European Economic Community".

He is going to continue alone toward the west, toward his Holland. Did he get there? Is he still alive today? What happened to him? I talk about that for several days at least with my comrade Pierre, and we imagine the joy that we would have, indeed, in seeing him again, the one-time paratrooper!

Then, three of us now, and always by little roads or footpaths, we arrive in a village named Ebstorf, a little north of Lüneburg. The second house we knock at takes us in. There we are welcomed with the same warmth that we have already met, indeed, even more intimately. We are served a meal while they prepare beds for us upstairs. What kindness, what gentleness in the words of welcome! It is the Voss family. The husband, Wilhelm, died a few years ago; his wife, Dora, is still alive, 86 years old.[2] I have seen them two times since, in 1981 and 1984, and we also spent a weekend with one of their daughters.

And this family, with all of 12 children, feed us and quench our thirst even though they, themselves, have so little! One must realize the absolute uncertainty about the coming day at that time, and they have 12 children to feed and clothe! The children did not tell me until later that their mother raised four more children who were not theirs! Where can we now find such devotion, such self-sacrifice?

I entrust these people with my decorations and my "*Soldbuch*", or military paybook, but the Polish workers stole them a few days later. One of the daughters unsews the *SS* badge that was on the jacket I wore under my overalls. She remembered it in 1981 when I saw them again for the first time in more than 36 years!

Here I must again express my admiration, my gratitude and that of my comrades for the few hours of grace at a moment when everything was collapsing around us, both literally and figuratively. That came at the moment when we most needed it, or, in any case, at the instant where we most appreciated it and certainly at its true worth. For, in fact, we did not lose our morale at any point, we never lost the pedals, literally or figuratively, as one might also say since we were on bicycles.

For us it was a bit as if the war was continuing, but in another form. To survive and to attain our goal, whatever happens, while remaining on guard every moment, using ruses each time to get out of tight situations. We slept like logs, knowing that someone was looking out for us and devoured the breakfast that *Madame* Voss served us in the morning. We were able to wash ourselves up properly and, finally, shave after several days when it was impossible because I no longer had a razor. They gave me one.

Our farewells are moving, even more than the preceding ones. But these people have done so much for us, in the circumstances of the end of the world! Like us, they have lost the war and the victor will make them pay dearly and in cash. "*Vae victis!*"[3] Concerned for our safety, they advise us to avoid the center of the village, the roads and the nearby town of Lüneburg. They point us toward the woods behind their home. Emotions are strong and show on their faces, parents and children, and before we turn away to take the direction they indicated, I see the tears that flow, that flow down the face of this mother who would have gladly added us to her brood, as if caring for her own children was not enough.

As we enter the woods I take a last look back toward these silhouettes and hands that wave farewell! After a detour to the east to avoid the proscribed places we return to our southwest axis

---

2   Written in 1991.
3   Latin for 'Woe to the vanquished!'

of march. It is now 6 May. As much as possible we take nothing but little tracks or roads through woods and moors, but, at times, also roads that are not the main roads. It is precisely on one of these roads, roughly halfway between Lüneburg and Celle, that two lorries of the American Army pass us and stop 50 meters ahead of us.

Two men, armed with submachine guns, get out and order us to stop as soon as we reach them! We did not have time to hide and it would be insane for us to turn around to escape. The lorries are full of prisoners, and we have to join them. But our bicycles go with us. The lorries are not covered with canvas and we place our bicycles against the right slatted side, right, that is, facing forward. The soldiers get back in the cab, there are none in the rear, and the lorries move on.

We strike up conversations with our neighbors in misfortune, but especially with three nurses. They are prisoners, like the soldiers! And they are not alone. We have already seen others, and we will see more, captives of the "Liberators"! Doesn't the Geneva Convention apply to the victors? It is an observation and I have never heard even one voice that denounced these acts. If it is true that for the military personnel of the medical services the detainer can delay one to three months in freeing them, these women cannot even be considered to be soldiers and, moreover, we are no longer in a period of war once the arms have been laid down.

A few minutes later these nurses and several people nearby know who we are. There is no need that they should take us for foreign workers. Not that I have anything against these workers, but we must rapidly gain the confidence of our companions, and they must not confuse us with those foreigners who pillage and hold to ransom the German population, profiting in the defeat. Not all, fortunately, act like that. We rapidly win the sympathy of the nurses and several people near us. That is why we do not hide from them our intention to escape as soon as an occasion presents itself.

We do not have long to wait, for after half an hour on the road, at the top of a hill, the lorries stop in front of an inn. The American soldiers leave their cabs, cross the road and vanish into the establishment. Absolutely all of them! Not a single one remains near the lorries or on the threshold of the inn! No one to guard us! There are six or seven of them. Such an opportunity is too good to miss! We could even have left with the lorries. That would not have been impossible, but one should not tempt fate, and that would be a bit conspicuous. Perhaps we would not have gotten that far, though… if all the American soldiers act like this, as casual as these…? But no, be modest, cautious, above all!

Instinctively I trust the nurses more. They go to watch the door of the inn to see if the GI s get up. We can have confidence in them, and they will prove it. It is our misfortune that, again, we are surrounded by "oldsters", and one or two of them fear retaliation if we escape. Again it is the nurses that make them keep quiet and help us in our flight.

We have little time for expressing gratitude. Very quickly we lower our bicycles over the side of the truck. Once they are on the ground, we only have to slide down onto the bicycle seats and, without even putting our feet on the ground, make a fast start and take off as if we were in a *grand prix*. The road that descends in front of us favors setting records. Happily, the lorries hide us from the inn for our first pedaling. We are far off in no time at all. We take the first crossroad to disappear once more into the woods, once we are certain that nobody is following us. Each time the woods is our ultimate refuge. Under cover of the trees we finally breathe freely. I smile as I envision what our guards will do when they discover our disappearance! This is not the first time.

That will, undoubtedly, only be when they arrive at their destination, for the other prisoners will be careful not to say anything, and I think that, with their customary insouciance, our ex-guardians will not think of counting their prisoners when they return to the lorries. We have one more debt, a debt of gratitude toward the three nurses, and God only knows how many soldiers owe them gratitude for their courage and their devotion in all circumstances. I certainly cannot say. We harbor no resentment toward those reluctant prisoners. It was certainly fear of reprisals in case they were suspected of complicity in our escape. But I have come to know their type well in these last three years. I think I can say that it is, above all, a certain sense of discipline that prevents them from getting out of the ruts. They find it difficult to conceive that a prisoner can escape that state without being officially freed, with a "*Schein*", a certificate in due and proper form in his pocket! I do not think I am wrong in this analysis, but all are not the same, that is certain.

This evening we stay in the suburbs of Celle, and, if I remember well, it was in the house of a former official of the *SA*, the *Sturmabteilung*, of the party. We are spoiled, and the next day, 7 May, we depart, heading always to the south. I want to pass by way of Sack, from where I was sent back to the line at the Oder about two months earlier. I know that we will be very well received there. In order to get there we bypass Hannover toward Hildesheim, where I enjoyed several happy weeks. I have a marvelous memory of this charming medieval city, a memory filled with fondness for its architectural treasures, its old half-timbered houses, where the peak of the roof of one of them, right near the *grand' place*, the main square, has leaned, over the centuries, toward another that faces it on the other side of the alley as if from a long intimacy.

I also have memories of the tranquility of the little provincial city, even in the midst of the war, and of the welcome that we found there. This day it is all in ruins! Only one street remains intact, as I think I already said, the *Kesslerstrasse*. I can only wonder by what quirk of fate it has escaped when I see all the rest, absolutely all the city leveled except for a few houses or sections of walls. Ninety-five percent destroyed, those are the official statistics. Near the railroad station is a railroad wagon overturned on the roof of a ruined house! There was nothing at Hildesheim but hospitals and refugees, no military troops, and the bombardments took place in the last weeks of the war, when all the German war effort was on the Eastern Front, against the Soviets. This was nothing but pure terrorist logic, to petrify the civilian population, as Churchill said, and to destroy these artistic treasures. They were, however, the patrimony of all of Europe!

From Hildesheim we head for Alfeld. Sack, where I have also recently sojourned, is five or six kilometers northeast of Alfeld. It is the end of the afternoon when we enter Sack, after a roughly 150 kilometer stage of our journey, with detours. It is a curious sensation to return to this little village, clean and calm, far calmer, now, than when we were there before. It is as if part of the population deserted it after our departure. Hardly anyone in the street, except for one or two furtive silhouettes that quickly vanish. Not a child playing there.

The enormous oak tree in front of the brewery seems even more impressive today, but nothing seems to have changed, except the weight of the atmosphere. Then, two or more months ago, still in the midst of the war, when I was attempting to return to the front, this village was alive, everything seemed natural to me and the air was light, despite the threats on all the fronts. Today the air is heavy. How subjective everything is! It is evident that it is our state as hunted men that creates this sensation. Though our hope of winning the war was extinguished this 7 May, our morale remains intact! We are disappointed, but not desperate.

There is the door of the house where I lived two months ago, and, 30 seconds after I knock, the door opens and the face of my landlady goes from extreme astonishment to exceeding joy! What joy for us also. There seem to be no lodgers, the house is empty. In the desolation of defeat, the joy of meeting still surpasses everything. Although I already know my landlady, my companions never knew her. They have never been here. The intimacy is immediately revived and the lady, whose daughter quickly joins us, talks with me of our parting, last March, when they came to the Alfeld railroad station to bid us farewell. They shed tears over it again, but the pleasure of our reunion quickly dries their tears. Our animated conversations continue late into the night.

The next day, 8 May, the radio announces the signature of the act of surrender at Reims, the preceding day. This announcement provokes another round of tears for our hostesses and triggers a fit of rage against destiny in the daughter despite the sacrifices, the acts of courage of all the German people supporting their army. Her rage redoubles when, at the end of the announcements, the radio plays "God Save the King" and then, the "Stars and Stripes". And there we are, impotent, helpless in the face of this distress!

I returned to Sack in 1981, but, based on information from the neighbors, I went to the cemetery. The lady was dead and I went to her grave. The monument is there, where I was told it would be, with her name, Senk. The daughter no longer lived in the village nor even the region. She had moved to Bavaria, or somewhere near Lake Constance. No one could give me more precise details.

On 10 May, 1945 we arrive at the right bank of the Weser. A young girl who just passed by on a bicycle turns around. She realizes that we are former soldiers. She comes toward us and tells us to avoid the nearest bridge. It is guarded by the "Belgium" she tells us. She could not know that we are Belgian, but there is no connection of cause and effect; it is pure chance. "They are much worse than the Americans," she adds! And I can only repeat what she told us: "Go farther south, but first stop at my uncle and aunt's house. They will help you." She gives us the address and her recommendation. When we tell her that we are Belgian volunteers in the *Waffen-SS* she does not react negatively but redoubles her friendliness.

This is the second or third time that young people have helped us like this. I have later heard that these young folk undoubtedly "worked" for the "*Wehrwolf*" – a clandestine organization that helped German soldiers or friends in difficulty. Every time that we have gone through this network the lodging and food were provided and, when we left the next day each of us received provisions for at least a day. It was truly awesome that, despite all the difficulties born in defeat and the dangers arising from foreign occupation, good Samaritans thought of and took care of things like that!

We spend the night with this uncle and aunt, spoiled like children of the house, even though they did not know us that morning, did not even know of our existence. We would have had to feel remorse if all this had not been done with such simplicity and kindness. The next day, hoping to avoid difficulties, we go to another bridge over the Weser. It is also guarded by the Belgians! Nevertheless, we do have to cross this river. Is it sensible? But we take the risk.

When we approach the bridge a Belgian officer hails us and tells us to report to their "*Kommandantur*", that is the word he used, on the other bank, one street to the right and then to the left. We make a pretense of going there, but it will be no more than a pretense. Charles, from some sort of bravado, actually wants to see it a little closer. Nevertheless, he rejoins us in haste. He just recognized someone he knows standing guard in front of the building.

Once past the city of Höxter we abandon the main road leading south for one leading west, toward Paderborn. It seems better to pass through regions that I am familiar with. Happily the weather is very good, like that in May 1940. We spend this night at Paderborn. Then we go on via Soest and Unna in order to reach Dortmund, leveled like all the Ruhr basin. The locals use piles of rubble as best they can to construct precarious shelters. Where the cellars remain, they make their homes there. Millions of people have thus lived in their basements or in the ruins where they have excavated a nest with their hands. Throughout the years they have thus cleaned things up, by hand, brick by brick, stone by stone. The men that have survived are prisoners and will not return soon. It is the women, the children and the old men that engage in this rude and interminable labor and who, moreover, clear the streets and the roads, meter by meter, [The Allies] did not seek to terrorize them. Judging by these ruins it is evident that they also deliberately attempted to exterminate them, to destroy all the German people, or at any rate, to break them, once and for all. Contrary to what Churchill hoped, the civilians, the German people, did not break, did not give up. On the contrary, the disaster has released their energy, and this industrious people has regained its place in Europe, despite numerous politicians, thanks to their inner courage!

At Essen it is the same desolation! One could say that by climbing up onto a garbage can one could see the entire city, all that is left of it from north to south and from east to west. There is no longer anything left! Today go and see it. All of the rubble has been piled up and covered with dirt, cleverly forming green wooded hills that separate the residential areas from the industrial ones, hiding the latter from the view of the dwellings.

I no longer remember, nor does Pierre nor Charles, where we found lodging between Paderborn and Düsseldorf, but it was 14 May when we arrived in this last city. Here we faced the biggest problem: how to cross the Rhine. We cannot swim across it, and the people we ask assure us that there are no rowboats available anywhere! The occupying forces destroyed those that they did not confiscate. We discuss the matter among ourselves and have to decide to report ourselves to a center for assisting foreign workers. Local people point it out to us. However, before we report there I want to take advantage a bit of our semi-freedom while we still have it. I also want to exchange my bicycle, if possible, for a bit of food and some cigarettes. My comrades abandon theirs with no compensation. We wander around a bit in the suburbs, which are less destroyed than the centers of the other cities we have passed through in the last few days. We finally meet a student whom providence placed in our path. He is interested in my bicycle and he lives in the house of a baker, which definitely facilitates the transaction. I accompany him to his home and, 15 minutes later, I leave the bakery with three loaves of bread and several packages of cigarettes.

Now on foot we head for the reception center that I mentioned, but in no hurry. It is a two story housing scheme in red brick and blue stone. In front is a large courtyard enclosed by a high wall bordering the street. In the center of the wall is a large wrought-iron double gate. His chair tipped back against the wall, a "sentinel", a white GI, an opera hat on his head and a submachine gun on his knees, is standing guard, sitting! Beside him is a black GI, in proper uniform. What a meeting! But, we must enter. It is the black GI who accompanies us to show us to the reception office. There must be at least 200 people there in this courtyard. Men, women and children, pell-mell. There is even an entire orchestra, complete with its instruments!

We report to the office where we conceal our true identities and claim to be voluntary workers in Germany. Behind a table several military types consult lists; some are Belgian, the others Americans. Apparently our names are not there. Since we have no identification, we are given a little cardboard "D.P. INDEX-CARD" with the first and last names we gave them. Obviously it was easy to invent false names. We are then told to find a little space in the buildings while waiting for the next departure.

Because it is beautiful weather, we settle, for the time being, in the courtyard. Several members of the orchestra that we just saw are singing, accompanied by a guitar. They are Dutch. It is a variety orchestra that worked for one or another German organization. We exchange a few words with them but, discreetly ask no questions to avoid embarrassing them. But I am convinced that they have just as many doubts about us as we have about them. It is best to be prudent and we will maintain these precautions as may be necessary. In this crowd there are certainly others who are in our situation, but how are we to know them, and for what good purpose? We do not come across any acquaintances. We spend two nights here, and the following morning lorries line up in the courtyard waiting for us. We are invited to get in them and the column moves out.

22

Our Return to Belgium

Thus it is that, early in the afternoon of 16 May, we reach Verviers, where the lorries soon left us at *l'école* St-Claire, if I remember correctly. There we are directed to the classrooms or other rooms on the first story. Imagine my amazement at meeting Ach. M. and his wife there. He is the brother of one of my best friends who was killed at Novo – Buda in February 1944. What is more, I was, by pure chance, present at his marriage in 1943 during my convalescence at Spa.

He was not in the *Légion*. Doubtless they later went to Germany, perhaps to work there. We talked discreetly for a moment, without being conspicuous, for if one of us is arrested, someone might connect us and arrest all of us. It seems better to pretend that we do not know each other. A little later we meet another of our comrades, B. He was in the *Légion*, and in the same contingent that I was. By joint accord, after a brief conversation, we will also pretend not to know each other. Nevertheless, he does take time to confide to me that he is going to attempt to join his family, which lives in Brittany and, in case I meet his father, he asks me to tell him and to reassure him. However, I do not know his father. They are from the Charleroi area, I from the Brussels region. And yet!

In the heart of the school, at the very back there is a group of huts, transformed, doubtless, for the occasion into a *bureau de change*, a foreign exchange office. There one exchanges the mark for one franc, even though last September one got 12.5 francs for a mark. A windfall for the bankers and for the state. While I am there exchanging my money I determine that the wall behind this group of huts is damaged and might, in an emergency, serve as an escape route. In the present circumstances and in the situation in which we are living all the senses are on the alert in the spirit of self-preservation, and no detail escapes observation – the more so since we are going to have to take action. When we first entered the school we were told that we must report to the *Bureau de la Sûreté*, the Security Office, for security clearance. This is the first time that I hear this word, at least, in this sense of the term.

This office is on the ground floor, to the right on entering by the *porte cochère*, the carriage entrance. We go back up to "our room" for a moment to make plans. We are alone there, the others are already below in the lines, waiting to leave, or still in the Security Office. I tell myself that it is better to divide the risk and wait for the last possible moment to go there. That is why I suggest that I go first and that the others wait to see if I pass the test without difficulty. If I do not, they will know that flight will be the better choice.

Since the groups are already gathering in the courtyard and in the corridor, we can wait no longer. I go down and report to the office, presenting my index-card, the only document that I possess, to the official. I answer the few questions I am asked while another consults the registers. He points to a name with his index finger. It is that of one of my brothers, four years older than me. I tell him that this is, doubtless, a homonym, maybe a cousin, since I am certain that I do not have one with that name. They discuss it for a moment, but finally I am cleared, since they can see that I am certainly not 26 years old. But, all the same, I felt the heat for a brief moment. I had to keep my calm and preserve an innocent air.

I am just leaving the office when I see my comrade Pierre enter. He did not wait for my exit as we had agreed, but evidently that would have made no difference in the course of events. Very quickly he is spotted, beaten up and arrested! The blows rain down on him and there is absolutely nothing that I can do to help. It is true that an intervention on my part would have accomplished nothing, the more so since there were at least 20 people present in the office. I would simply have been arrested, too, without being able to do anything. It was hard for me, especially since Pierre had only recently been wounded. I was filled with a feeling of impotence, but also of shame, for it had never been our custom to leave a comrade in a tight spot.

The outcome was thus: the one who passes through the meshes of the net can do nothing for the one who is caught! It is now necessary, very quickly, to take advantage of the excitement caused by Pierre's arrest to vanish discreetly. I hastily rejoin Charles, who is waiting in the room upstairs, to fill him in. We decide to escape as rapidly as possible by the wall behind the group of huts. Behind that we are out of sight. Already, as we go down the rumor is running through the corridors, "They have arrested an *SS*, they have arrested an *SS*!"

The porch of the entry is already full of repatriates waiting for the exit inspection, but most have already exited and are marching in a column toward the railroad station. We quickly pass into the courtyard and then to the wall. After going round the block we rejoin the column that is heading toward the station, walking, at first, alongside it but on the sidewalk. Imperceptibly we draw near to the column to slip discreetly into it with no problems.

When we arrive on the platforms of the railroad station the Red Cross is there, distributing food to those departing. We await our turn to be served. Among the uniformed nurses is a matron who is, at least, 40 years old. I do not know what was bugging her, but suddenly she begins to bellow, to bawl at a young repatriated woman who carries a baby in her arms who is less than two years old. When I draw near, I note that the young woman speaks Flemish. Is that what has made the nurse see red? She then strikes the woman carrying the baby, who is upset by all this and starts to cry. The nurse shouts at the top of her voice that it is not necessary to give food to this woman, who, she claims, is certainly a collaborator. Obviously, she knows nothing to this effect, for if it was proven, the young woman would not have been here. But, in fact, under this pressure, no other nurse dares to defy her and the woman receives nothing, nor does the baby!

Two or three people who are close to the epicenter of this earthquake and who timidly object to the conduct of this unworthy representative of the Red Cross are also deprived of food and insulted! Sad image of the Red Cross that this virago has just given! In all fairness, I must say that there must have been other representatives more worthy of this organization. Nevertheless, it is with this bad impression that the train moves out, about an hour later.

Night has fallen when the train stops in the railroad station north of Brussels. On the platforms are people who have doubtless come in hopes of seeing a member of their family or a friend. There are tables on trestles, marked with the Red Cross, where soup and a bit of bread are distributed, but without blows, this time. Charles and I go to get food with the others. Since Charles did not go through security at Verviers, he has no train ticket, nor have I. And there is a checkpoint at the exit. We have to find a way to exit, but while we wait, and to gain time, we stroll along the platforms, hoping that after all these repatriates have departed, the attendant at the gate will leave for a moment.

I do not know how long we wander on these platforms, and I really fear that our behavior will attract attention, for there are not that many people on the platforms, but the attendant remains at his post. In the event we have to go there. Finally we take advantage of a moment of inattention of the inspector to run past, right under his nose! Everything happens quickly, but I think that he shouted something, gesturing that we should be stopped, but we are already long gone and there are not that many people in the vicinity at this time. When we get to the *Place Rogier*, after crossing the boulevard, we stop running and go at a normal pace, while assuming the air of altar boys. It must be nearly 0100 hours in the morning! What are we going to do now?

In fact, we have already made our decisions. Charles knows a hideout where he goes. As for me, I improvise from day to day, hour by hour if necessary, but I am going to try to see my *fiancée*, who lives in Binche, and my sister, who is a in a convent at Namur. Then, I will decide what comes next. I do not know if I will be able to see my brothers, or how to find them. Have they been or will they be arrested?

When businesses open I will go and get something so that I can write to my *fiancée* to set up some sort of *rendezvous* with her, since it is obviously out of the question to go there. Her house will certainly be under surveillance. From all that I have seen so far, there can be no doubt of that. The appeals for violence broadcast on the waves of Radio London have found sympathetic ears, and, today, even though the war has ended, the hatred sown so lightly remains alive. In order to allow time for my *fiancée* to get my letter, I will go see my sister first.

While waiting for morning, Charles and I spend the night on a boulevard bench. There still were such at that time. There was no other solution, but the weather was good. All the same, the night is cool and we are but lightly dressed. Happily, our preoccupations prevent us from suffering too much from the cold. Above all, we cannot sleep on this bench, for the first policeman to pass would certainly take us to the station and, in that case, *adieu* to all our plans. For the rest of the night we talk about the past, the future, of our tribulations in recent days and of Pierre, who is no longer with us. Always on the alert, but not at all at bay. In actual fact, we are very calm, our *sang-froid* can stand any test. I ponder our curious situation. The two of us returned to Belgium so as not to abandon Pierre, to leave him alone to face all these traps. Except for that we would have remained in Germany, and now we are in Brussels, the two of us, but without our friend. Where is he at this moment?

When day breaks the hour of farewell comes, the instant of separation! When will we see each other again? We are a bit emotional, the two of us, no doubt, but that does not necessarily have to show. Without turning back, each of us goes off in an opposite direction, but at random. I walk a bit waiting for the shops to open. Then, not far from the *Gare du Midi* I buy some writing materials at a stationers. I scribble a few hasty words that I slip into an envelope. Since I am sending my letter very early, she will have it tomorrow morning. So I set up a *rendezvous* for tomorrow afternoon, 18 May, at 1400 or 1500 hours on the bridge that crosses the railroad tracks at Charleroi.

After paying for my ticket to Namur, I have only a few Belgian francs, but also several marks. I must not spend them for food. On the other hand, I ate a bowl of soup and a bit of bread yesterday evening, so I can easily wait to be at my sister's house where I shall certainly get something to eat. As I leave the railroad station at Namur, I wonder how I shall get to my sister's house, since she lives far from the city. I am afraid to spend my last francs for food, for taking a bus or any other way to get there, that costs money. I leave the city in the desired direction but without really knowing the road, for I have never gone there.

A little farther on I accost a gentleman who is getting behind the wheel of his automobile. I tell him that I am returning from Germany and want to see my sister who is in this convent, having no other relatives to go to. It is the most logical explanation, but it is also the strict truth. What else could I say? I ask myself what good it would do for me to invent some fantastic story, to lie in order to misrepresent a perfectly credible reality? Perhaps the man is touched. In any case, he offers to drive me there. What a blessing! How can I refuse?

En route he tells me that his name is M., and that he is an officer of the judicial police! That takes the cake! Has he guessed who or what I am? Does he want to trap me, to see my face? For a moment I think that I have been discovered and that my adventure will end here. That would be sad, for I am starting to find this very exciting! I must play the game to the fullest. Above all, he must not see my astonishment, my perplexity! I must compose a mask of imperturbability and never let it slip! But is he going to take me to my sister's or to the local police station? Is he going to interrogate or question me? I remain on my guard and maintain my *sang-froid*. But every time that the conversation lags, I wonder what subject he will bring up. I am not completely reassured when he drops me off 20 or 30 meters from the entrance of my sister's place. Obviously, in such a situation, all sorts of ideas come to mind, whether justified or not! So I ask myself if he is going to return, later, in force. Should I disappear before he can return, as soon as he turns the corner, without going to the convent? In any case, I take the risk and I go up the alley that leads to the building.

Do I need to say how astonished my sister is when she sees me before her, thinned down by all the exhaustion and adventures of recent weeks and the sleepless night on the bench in the chill of last night? Moreover, one of my most recent wounds on my leg is festering with all this fatigue. I was told to keep myself clean and to eat well. Soon, after a bit of rest, it will not be visible there. My sister seems considerably more frightened than I am about what will happen to me! But she should know what happens to people like us. It is true that I have not really had time to think of it, since the improvisations required by my situation takes my full attention hour by hour. And then, I am not of an anxious nature.

As she asks me about my plans, I tell her that the first one is to attempt to see my *fiancée*, then to go to Anvers, where one of my uncles lives, a sea-going captain. I do not think that, if there is any possibility, he will refuse to provide me with passage abroad. My preference is for Paraguay or Uruguay. Why one of these two countries? Perhaps because little is said about them and that I ought to be able to make a place for myself there. Maybe in forestry development, since I have taken courses of study to prepare for that. It is, above all, an intuition.

I do not want to stay with my sister for fear of causing her problems. I am going to leave her right away. At the moment of farewell she slips some money into my hand. I have neither the courage nor the means to refuse. Otherwise, and it starts to preoccupy my thoughts, how will I be able to pursue my immediate projects with the few francs I have left? When I see tears gather in my sister's eyes I hasten to conclude our farewells and turn away to disappear as quickly as possible. It is not the moment to delay.

Since it is not yet noon I have time to get back to the station on foot. I must save money. The train takes me back to Brussels, where I go to the railroad station at noon. Why return to Brussels to then go to Charleroi? Because I believe that there is no train to Charleroi, at least not at this hour.

While I wait for the train to depart I go for a walk in front of the station on *avenue Fonsny*. A man approaches me and asks if he can help me! What a preposterous idea, what a curious encounter, one more time. The man is dressed in a suit, dark or black, with a bowler hat, like certain middle-class men wore at the time. All I see of him at first is his shoes, then his watch chain. Truly one of the Dupont-Dupond[1] of the illustrator, Hergé, less the walking stick! He speaks to me in a very friendly fashion, almost as if it was he who was asking me to help him. But, since he looks so much like a policeman and I must be suspicious of all, I politely decline, still totally surprised that someone talked to me thus without knowing me. He then goes, as if regretfully. He seems sad. I ask myself what I should think of it, if I should have accepted his help. Perhaps he was a sympathizer, the parent of one of ours who is truly trying to help those that he can and who has guessed, or believes he has guessed my precarious condition from seeing my outfit.

---

1   Dupont and Dupond were two detectives in Hergé's *Tintin* cartoon series. In the English version they were named Thompson and Thomson. They are often dressed in a black suit with a black bowler hat and carry walking sticks – and appear absolutely identical except for a slight difference in their moustaches.

I must say that, at this time I am still wearing my old German Army boots, but many people can have those, stolen from German depots last September. I am also wearing my *"Feldgrau"* pants, moreover! But I wear them openly, telling myself that no one would imagine that an actual veteran would walk around like this, that it is, rather, a young man who has nothing else to wear and who wears it as a trophy after having stolen it from the Germans. Other than that, I have only a light black cloth jacket that I found in the ambulance a few days ago.

But, it is time for the train, between 1400 and 1500 hours, if I remember. Thus it is a little later in the afternoon that I get off the train in the Charleroi station. Now I must prepare for tomorrow's meeting and I first go to scout out the area. After studying the geography of the approaches to the bridge, I decide that the best place for a good view is located at the start of the main road that leads from Mont sur Marchienne, the *avenue Paul Pastur*. There I am a little higher than the bridge and will be able to see my *fiancée* arrive, since she will have to come from the other side. I will then have time to meet her after assuring myself that she is not being followed, one can never be sure.

This decided, I have to find a place to spend the night. That is not so simple! But, just now, I have seen the goods wagons on the tracks below and that gives me an idea. I go back down toward the railroad and walk along the tracks until I find a stretch of wire fencing that runs along the tracks, but this time at the same level as them. And there, on the rails, are cars that are waiting. It is still light and I am not about to take the chance of scrambling over the fence at the risk of being spotted, the more so since workers are moving about on the tracks.

I would happily go and buy something to eat, but it is not prudent to invade my little nest egg. I must now pass the time until night. I have no other prospect than to stroll and I move to another quarter for now to avoid making myself conspicuous by too many comings and goings. I head for the central city and, from there, toward the upper city where I wander around until night falls. Ten times I am tempted to enter a pastry shop to buy a bit of bread. Ten times I resist the temptation. When I reach the spot I have chosen to get to a wagon where I can sleep. I must be patient for a while and let the passersby move away before climbing over the wire mesh. When I am on the tracks I wonder which wagon to choose. I don't want to be hitched onto a train while I am asleep and wake up tomorrow in some other part of the country or, who knows, even in Germany! I must choose at random, and I climb into one of the five or six that form part of a string of wagons. I choose one where the door is half open, to avoid making noise. I sit down for a bit, my back leaning against the wall. The darkness is total, but, all the same, I am able to confirm that the wagon is empty. It is amazing how much noise there is near a railroad station, even when no train is passing through! But I soon get used to it and finally conclude that it is calm. Then, without knowing where I am lying down, since it is dark, I stretch out. I will forget my hunger better while sleeping. And I do finally fall asleep, but with one eye or one ear open, for throughout the night I hear sounds.

What with the coolness of the place, and having nothing to cover myself up with, I am definitely awake well before dawn. I take advantage of the darkness that still reigns to go looking for some water so I can wash up before leaving the place, for the workers will arrive soon and I must leave before they come. I find some water in a barrel along the wall, near the bridge. It is certainly rain-water, but that is better for the skin. It is only after I am wet that I remember that I have no towel. I have to put my jacket back on like this. I am colder now. I return to my wagon to sit there a little longer. But my wet body does not warm up. I have to walk around a bit, the more so since my stomach is crying famine. So I leave the wagon and head for the wire mesh fence, which I scramble over without problems, in spite of a few morning passersby who are already going to their work. But nobody pays any attention to me.

I wander around a bit in the lower city while waiting for the stores to open. I am in a hurry to buy something to eat. When I see an open bakery I hasten in and buy two little loaves of brown bread. I slip one of them inside my jacket and eat the other while I walk, but as discreetly as possible. Now I have to await the hour of our meeting, and I am impatient. The time drags and all this walking is tiring. I think that it would be good to freshen up the *façade* a bit in light of meeting my *fiancée*. Accordingly, I enter the first hairdresser's I come to, which allows me to sit down for a moment and let the time go by. After a shave and a haircut I feel more presentable and a bit rested, but I do not know what people will think of the *coiffeur* of this vagabond in quest of elegance.

It is not yet noon when I am already at the place where I decided to wait. Finally, to make the time pass, I eat the second little loaf of bread. At 1300 hours I already start to glance at the bridge, and starting at 1330 hours I watch it constantly. I scan its length and breadth and often look back over the same places for fear of having missed something. It must be about 1400 hours when a silhouette catches my attention. She is about to go onto the bridge. My heart is racing! The silhouette, the gait seem familiar. Others before have also caught my attention, but, very quickly I determined that they were not her.

I start toward the bridge, to meet her, after assuring myself that she is not being followed. After a few more steps I stop, disappointed. It is not her! I return to my lookout post where I remain for nearly two more hours, certainly an hour-and-a-half, passing from hope to despair every time that I think I see her before, finally, determining that it is not her. Finally I have to accept the evidence and admit that she is not coming, that she will not come! What has happened? Did she receive my letter? So many things might have intervened! At a moment like this and in the present circumstances the mind is subject to so many thoughts, to questions with no answers!

I later learned that she did, indeed, receive my letter and that, while she was coming to the *rendezvous*, she was followed. She did not lose her presence of mind and commit the error of coming there and leading those who were following her to me. She then went to a friend's house in Charleroi and the police that were following her entered her friend's house to interrogate her on her reasons for being there. Moreover, her friends told her that they heard tell that I had been arrested. My letter had been intercepted and read before being sent on to her to simplify catching me!

As for me, for the first time I was a bit distraught. It is true, I was totally counting on our *rendezvous* and everything had just fallen apart! A little, also, because I had not yet definitively worked out my program, thinking that I would organize the future in accord with her. While waiting, while strolling, I determined that it was still beautiful weather. Now I notice nothing else! Good, now I have to take action, I must go forward and not feel sorry for myself. I think that the first thing to do is to cash in the few marks I still have. I will need money, even if only pocket money. One-hundred or 150 marks, as well as the few Belgian francs that I have.

I remember that, yesterday, I saw a bank in the upper city, the *Banque Nationale*, I believe. I shall go there, on the *rue Léopold*. I am weary of standing since before the dawn, except for the few moments in the barber's chair, and I decide to take the streetcar. On the street, near the streetcar stop, I pause a few moments to look with desire in the window of a pastry shop. I look at the display with an air of false detachment, Then a woman comes out of the shop. I stay there without paying particular attention to her. After a moment I am surprised to see that she is still there, beside me. When I raise my eyes I meet her gaze and realize that she is watching me! She makes a sort of grimace at me which might pass for a smile and offers me a chocolate éclair! I take it, without thinking, and thank her. While the two of us eat, she opens a conversation. While she speaks I look her over. She is a woman without age, though she certainly must have one! I would say between 30 and 50 years, thin, platinum-blond hair, coarse and poorly dressed, no better than myself, in any case. Sort of a harpy.

She asks me if she can do anything for me, even suggesting that I come stay with her. I decline her offers as politely as possible, forcing myself to avoid hurting her feelings. Then she wants to slip money into my hands, which I keep firmly closed so that she can't slip into them the one or more bank notes and refuse anew. Only the arrival of the streetcar allows me to escape from her! Decidedly everybody is trying to help me! There are, assuredly, people who are on the lookout for stray people. They must be drawn to discover those who are made vulnerable by an uncomfortable situation like mine! At the very least, my appearance leaves no doubt as to my condition, at least for those who are not too preoccupied with other problems. In any case, I am well out of it, for the moment.

When I am standing on the rear platform of the streetcar, another surprise awaits me! Pressed against the rear wall I suddenly discover, opposite me, one of the old cooks of my company, handcuffed to two *gendarmes*! Our gazes suddenly meet and I know, right away, that he has recognized me and that he must have seen that I recognized him! What a moment! We each turn away so as not to arouse suspicion. But a momentary glance can say a lot. I then put on the most detached air that I can. All this is becoming unhealthy. Too many disturbing events in too little time. One might think that the entire population is on the lookout.

I thought for a moment of passing a second night in "my" wagon and trying again, the next day, for the *rendezvous*, in case my letter did not arrive on time or that some other chance hazard prevented the meeting, and that she will show up, a day late, at the *rendezvous*. But that is unlikely. At the moment, because of these last two encounters, I think the risk is too great for an improbable outcome. I must leave Charleroi as soon as possible. After the bank I will go to the station and take the first train arriving for Brussels and, from there, to Anvers.

In order to avoid attracting attention I should not get off right away. I have to control myself to pass by four or five stops, even if it then means retracing my own steps. A last discreet and friendly glance at my comrade and I get off the streetcar as casually as possible. After turning the first corner and making sure that I am not followed I can finally breathe! At last I enter the bank, a sort of vast and ancient patrician house. There are a dozen people there, in front of two or three tellers' windows and I go to the end of one of these lines. I wait 10 minutes, a quarter of an hour, without thinking of anything. My attention is relaxed for a few minutes, no doubt, a few minutes too many… my suspicion is relaxed, long enough to smoke a cigarette. And it should not have been!

23

Arrested and a Captive in My Own Land

Doubtless, thinking myself safe among these people who are more attentive to their financial concerns than with myself, I have not noticed anything. Suddenly I feel two hands nimbly placed on me at the level of my waist, and they rapidly slide down along my hips to my knees! By natural reflex I quickly turn around and strike with my fist, without seeing where nor whom I aim it at. The moment before I was not, strictly, paying attention to anything, doubtless lost in elaborating a plan for the hours to come. And, in an instant, I am plunged into reality, to my immense astonishment and to my total detriment! But it is my own fault.

Facing me is a man who seems as surprised as I am, but more excited. In his forties, *petit bourgeois*. At the same time I discover five or six men armed with submachine guns and red armbands a few meters behind him. They are against the wall and bar the exit. I realize that it is a police officer with civil reinforcements.

As a result of my reaction, at least I think so, the policeman starts to shout, "Attention! He is an *SS*, he is armed. Disarm him." Even though he has just confirmed the opposite in patting me down. Is he trying to get me shot down? But none of those accompanying him stirs. All the bank customers are suddenly grouped near the wall, in the corner to my right and I am alone, driven into the other corner. The policeman and his men have not made a move. Nobody has actually tried to apprehend me, as if they are afraid to do so. Yet I am alone, truly alone and unarmed facing all these armed men! What have people been saying about us?

I then ask the policeman what he wants with me. I tell him that I am not armed. He seems very nervous and repeats, "He is an *SS*!" I attempt to disabuse him of this notion, but in vain. He then asks if I will go with him voluntarily. I promise that I will, on the condition that he and his men behave correctly. I see a young man who is with the armed men, but who does not appear to be a part of the group. Upon reflection this face is not entirely strange to me. But whence comes this vague memory? A little later I will identify him when an image suddenly comes to mind. It was at Bergholz, in Pomerania, when I was coming to rejoin my unit. He was there, in a barn, with the other recruits of the final hour that had only just arrived. He did not smoke and asked me if I had some bread for him in exchange for cigarettes. Now, all of a sudden, I remember well, but I do not remember ever seeing him again. I suppose that he enlisted to get away from his status as a worker in Germany.

We leave the bank. I am surrounded by these men, their submachine guns and pistols always pointed at me, on our way to a police station. Do they really need so much? Surely they must have seen this in the movies. The promise to behave correctly toward me does not, however, prevent one or two of the "resistance men" from giving me a few good blows with their gun butts, in the back, of course! I call this to the policeman's attention and tell him that the threats to shoot me will not prevent me from defending myself if they keep this up. The blows stop and soon we enter a police station.

Before and after interrogation I see the young man again and understand that he is the one who denounced me! Doubtless to gain a pardon, or to hide his enlistment at the final hour? I later identify him in my dossier that I consult at the *Auditorat Militaire*,[1] *rue de la Lois*, in Brussels. His name is Cuvelier. This name is common enough so that this is not a denunciation, since I am not giving his first name, nor his address, which I have. This sort of baseness is incompatible with the spirit of our enlistment, to say nothing of hatred. He can be reassured. I have never felt the desire for vengeance, despite his declarations that are in my dossier, and if that had been the case, I would have done it when I was released, in 1950.

The "resistance" who "support" the forces of law and order – and these men told me that they were members of the resistance – are certainly, for the most part, those who joined its ranks in September 1944 and waited until the end of all the danger to enter and take part in the kill with the most ostentation!

After the interrogation and some time spent waiting, we leave the police station. Before the door, on the sidewalk, there are several onlookers. And who is there, among these onlookers? Quite simply, the good woman from whom I had so recently inopportunely accepted the chocolate éclair! Decidedly, the inopportune encounters succeeded one another! She recognizes me. Did she follow me? It makes you wonder! All of a sudden she starts to shout, "B*****d! You must arrest him! And I am the one who gave him money!" I immediately stop her and tell her that this is not true, that she is lying. And I say that only two hours ago she would have taken me in her bed without first demanding my *certificat de civisme*![2] She follows the group consisting of my jailors and myself and her vociferations redouble. It is evident that she wants to take revenge and make me pay for my refusal. It is only at the threshold of the *auditorat* that the raging shrew is forced to abandon her pursuit and the harassment ceases.

No more than in the rest of this account, nothing, not a one of these last encounters, is invented. Everything truly happened as I have just stated.

At the *auditorat* comes a new interrogation, confirming the preceding one. What good would it do to stall? They have my identity and a denunciation. Moreover, even a great many people that were absolute strangers to the events of the war were arrested and interned on the basis of a simple denunciation by anyone, without the slightest proof. It was enough that one or another neighbor did not like his looks for him to rot away for months and months in the worst conditions, then to regain his liberty without having seen a judge or having a hearing, without even being interrogated a single time!

My adventure ends here. I think about it while waiting to be taken to one or another detention center. I took advantage of this delay to hide the arrest warrant that the deputy clerk of the court had just given me in my socks. I did this on the spur of the moment, almost by reflex, but without any real purpose, without the least reason. As a result, I have it today, as well as the manuscript copy of the essentials of my dossier. Much later I found it very amusing to confirm that, at that time in any case, there was no cohesion at all between the different services of justice. Much later I discovered, in consulting my dossier before my appearance, that they were still looking for me on 13 January, 1946 as confirmed by a document that I now have a copy of.

For the present moment, this is by no means fun and games. I ask to go to the toilet, with no great hopes of escaping, but you never know… Of course, there is wire-mesh and bars on the little skylight. We then depart, one policeman chained to me and a second policeman as backup, but without chains.

---

1 Military Prosecutor.

2 During the French Revolution, the *certificat de civisme* – issued in Paris by *le Conseil général de la Commune de Paris* – attested that the possessor had fulfilled his civic duties (certifying his good conduct and political orthodoxy). During the time of the Terror, as a result of *la Lois des suspects* – enacted on 17 September, 1793 – those lacking this certificate were subject to arrest.

24

From Dampremy to St. Gilles

We have arrived at Dampremy, before the iron double door of the Fourcauld glassworks. We enter a great rectangular court and the heavy door closes noisily. I have an immediate sensation that my chains tighten and that a leaden cope settles on my shoulders. I really feel that the atmosphere could be cut with a knife! The policemen who accompany me complete the formalities of my commitment and leave.

A guard leads me to a building that is to the right of the entrance, without ceasing to harass me, to insult me and to heap a pile of rubbish on me. Real hooligan language! He may be trying to provoke me, he may be feeling very brave, knowing that I cannot reply. I must keep my self-control to avoid responding to this sort of provocation, for, doubtless, this is only the beginning. I would be ill-advised to react a bit too vigorously. This guard brings me into a little room that serves as the office. A guard is seated behind the table and, standing near him, are two other fellows. One is a big, sturdy man, a bit on the stupid side, the other small and black, a bit nervous, D.B. and C. Apparently two prisoners, but with sneaky faces. That is a first impression, but very strong and soon confirmed. I also quickly learn that they are two *Kapos*.[1]

The guard asks me for my arrest warrant! I tell him that I did not have it. He is hardly disturbed by that and talks to me of discipline. He tells me that the good life is over!!! He says a bunch of stupid things and one or the other two seems to want to join into what seems like a new interrogation. At this moment I receive a blow of the fist from behind, at the base of my skull. I turn around immediately and put my back to the wall, determined not to permit this with impunity! I did not see who struck me! I ask myself for a moment whether the other two are not also guards, auxiliaries, perhaps, dressed in American Army surplus clothes. The third wears a guards uniform, black or very dark blue with a matching *képi*. This last then asks me what I am doing, where I come from. I answer that I come from Germany and that I was in the *Division SS Wallonie*. "Ah!" he says. "Finally we have one! One who admits it." According to them, no one was ever there, or, at least, they were all cooks or drivers of horses. "*Eh bien*, nobody is to touch this one, nobody is to beat him anymore," turning to the others, who immediately acquiesce. As for me, I thought that the blows would be redoubled, and now they have stopped, at least for the moment! It is true that certain *Légionnaires* thought that they would thus minimize the rigors of justice.

The smaller of the other two, who now has in his hands a cardboard box with barbers' instruments, turns to the guard and says, "Chief, he has a good haircut, quite short. Is it really necessary to shave him?"

"No, it's OK," he responds. And thus I escape the triple-zero shearing! It is true that I just went to the barbers this very afternoon. Is it because the "Chief" has mellowed toward me that the other feels obliged to prove his benevolence toward me? I do not know, but during my sojourn here I will never have to undergo any abuse. That embarrasses me at times, not that I am masochistic,

---

1 In the Nazi concentration camps, *Kapos* were prisoners empowered to command the other prisoners.

but with regard to certain companions in detention who are regularly beaten. It is curious, all the same, to be embarrassed at not being beaten like the others! What sort of name is given to this syndrome?

I am then taken through the second door of this little office into a place where there are already 30 other prisoners. They are there, standing, sitting or squatting on the floor. One of them is sitting, immobile, on a filthy straw mattress. The floor is made of cement paving stones, the walls whitewashed with two small windows very high up and without glass, which let in a very parsimonious amount of light. One cannot see outside, except for a scrap of sky between the bars. The place is always dim! It is an old warehouse of the glassworks, a bit elevated above the courtyard. There is a smell of creoline.[2] I regularly remember odors, and the odor of creoline will be omnipresent for five years!

After a moment, one, then two, then several other prisoners came to me. A new arrival is always an event in prison! He always carries a little whiff of liberty, of the last hours of his liberty. Among those whom I know there is G. Leclerq, whom I knew in the *Gardes Wallonnes* in 1941, and Servais, a former prisoner of war who came to the *Légion* directly from a *Stalag*,[3] in 1943. There is also an older man whom I do not know but who knows me, a friend of the family of my *fiancée*, a certain P. Not that many acquaintances, but that is normal, I am not from here. I am happy to meet these comrades with whom I get along perfectly. They fill me in on life here, on its pitfalls, of all that might be useful for me to know, but also of all that has happened here, that they have experienced, endured!

Those who have some possessions have lined up their meager rags along the wall, but most are like me, they have absolutely nothing. Visits are rare or non-existent; few of the prisoners receive any. There are a dozen straw mattresses for the 30 men, which means that most who are there sleep right on the damp concrete slab. There is only one place available for me to stretch out on, beside the man sitting on a straw mattress whom I've just noticed. Absolutely immobile, he always seems to sleep. I ask my comrades what he is doing there. Leclerq tells me that he is the father of B.! Precisely the father of the comrade I ran into at Verviers who asked me to tell his father of his departure for Bretagne, if, by chance, I ran into him. What a chain of coincidences! At that moment I was a hundred leagues from thinking of going to Charleroi, and furthermore, I did not know the father of B. from Adam or Eve!

However, the event is a far less happy coincidence. Leclerq and the others tell me that this poor man, who must be nearly 60 years old, maybe more, has been beaten and tortured for weeks on end. By day or by night the guards come and take him to beat him and torture him. They have heard this unfortunate scream for hours, until he no longer had the strength to cry out or until he lost consciousness. They wanted to make him tell where his son is, but he did not know. And me, I do know it, to my misfortune! The man is covered with purulent abscesses and the straw mattress soaked up the pus, soiling the concrete right through the mattress! The stench is unbearable, and I sleep with this miasma in my nostrils right beside the man, right on the concrete slab, as I said, with no covers. B.'s father regains consciousness two or three days later, but not for very long. And there were only two or maybe three times during the time that I was there that the poor man had a few moments of lucidity. Enough for me to talk softly with him for maybe five or 10 minutes in all. I told him that I had seen his son alive, but never where he was planning to go, for fear that he might be forced to tell under torture. Knowing that he was in his final hours, I did not want to burden him with the secret. During these days he was no longer being beaten, but they did not

---

2   Creoline is a concentrated black disinfecting solution distilled from coal. It is used for industrial, institutional and domestic disinfection.

3   German prisoner of war camp.

care for him either. Others took over for him and were beaten, by day or by night according to the mood or the nature of the guards.

I remained at Dampremy until 12 June, 1945. I later learned that the unhappy father of my comrade died shortly after my departure in circumstances one can well imagine. I do not know if there were any decent guards at Dampremy, but the four or five that I had to deal with were no more than pathetic little rogues or downright villains. In order to avoid trouble, I withdrew into myself, only talking with the few comrades I knew, and having simple friendly relationships or being a good neighbor with those who were less close.

Through my comrades I thus learn all that was going on here, but also in the other concentration camps in the vicinity. Some have members of their family in the other camps in the region.

We never learned much of the reason that the two *Kapos* I mentioned were incarcerated. They were neither *légionnaires* nor members of the new order; that much we knew. According to one or another, they were deserters from the *NSKK*. In any case, they amounted to guards. Paradoxically, the bigger of the two was afraid of the smaller one. That we determined, for the latter did not refrain from playing dirty tricks on his bigger friend – at least at times.

As for food, in the morning we have a bit of bread and a tepid black beverage that one could not name. In the afternoon we are given a sort of clear water, also tepid, with a few unidentifiable dried legumes floating in it. Aside from that, in the 25 days I spend there, twice we received a dozen morsels of sugar, one spoonful of jam. Absolutely nothing more!

My comrades described a scenario to me that had taken place several times before my arrival. The guards came to get a prisoner, made him go out in the courtyard, then the prisoners heard several shots and a cry, as if their comrade had just been executed! They then came to get another, at random, and the same macabre performance was enacted. Then, to make the others believe that they really had killed these men, they placed these victims in another room to prevent their companions in the room from seeing them again. The imagination of the guards was inexhaustible when it came to finding a means to distract themselves, to invent tortures. It is evident that the effect on the nerves of the "victims "was the same as if they really had been executed. There could be no doubt that they were already dead one time. Two of my comrades who had family interned at the Trezignie barracks told me that the tortures there were even worse than here. During the night the guards disposed of the bodies of prisoners who had died of beatings and tortures to eliminate the evidence of their infamy.

During my entire time here I was never given a chance to walk, not the slightest minute of yard time. In 25 days I knew only the four walls of this room. Nothing to read, of course, no mail, not a single letter, no writing materials, no visit, not even a change of underwear nor any way to wash what I was wearing. No news of anyone at all. Enough to make one envy the prisoners of Cayenne. It required a strong and resolute heart, to be hardened as we were, to survive such a regime and not to sink into depression, allow oneself to be destroyed, and perish!

Happily, on 12 June, 1945 I am transferred to Brussels, where I arrive in the evening at the prison of St. Gilles by way of the Forest prison.

I shall not recount my five long years of detention, but only a few diverse events, relate a few of many varied memories that left their mark on me for one reason or another and not necessarily because of their dramatic aspects. Thus I hope to impart an idea of the atmosphere that surrounded us. It is true, on the other hand, one most willingly remembers the best moments, if, indeed, there were some that were good, when one is 20 years old and is in prison.

When a prison van, coming from Dampremy, deposits me at the entrance of the Forest prison, it is the end of the afternoon. Nevertheless, I could believe that it is already night since it is dark in these corridors.

After the formalities of commitment at the office, I arrive at the "center" in a great racket of keys and barred doors that open and then close behind me. The "center" is a sort of rotunda where the different wings of the prison meet, also closed with heavy bars. When I have passed through one more set of bars I find myself before the office of B Wing.

If the sounds of the keys and of bars opening and closing takes on such a dimension, it is because the silence that reigns could be cut with a knife, and the feeble glow of the little lightbulbs that hang high under the vaults are not capable of dissipating this impression. Everything here is gray or black, without nuances, and the silence is that of the pyramids!

A man, dressed in gray canvas, approaches me. I immediately recognize him and he me. It is Pierre O., a firm friend from way back, about 35 years old, tall and hefty, even-tempered and always calm. He is of White Russian origin and lived in a commune adjoining mine. That is why we were in the same section of the *Formations de Combat*[4] before enlisting in the *Légion*. We had known each other since the start of the *Formations de Combat* and we were in the same contingent at the time of our departure for the Eastern Front, but he had to be evacuated for reasons of health during the "*Vormarsch*" (the march during the advance in 1942).

We exchange a few words in a low voice, for total silence is always required. He gives me a mess tin and then, with a ladle, he fills the mess tin to the rim with a very thick soup from a great can that is there, in front of the office. He advises me to empty it rapidly so that he can refill it. He waits and watches me while I eat. My stomach cannot believe its ears! It has been such a long time since I have had such satisfaction.

I then empty a second mess tin. Then Pierre fills it again before a guard conducts me to my cell, 198B, on the first level, where I enter with this mess tin, nearly cold but full. I immediately share it with two famished young men and another, older, but no less famished. I have been lucky, they tell me, to have received the bottom of the can, for, when mixed, it is no more than a shadow of what I received!

With my entry in this cell we are eight in all! It is an individual cell measuring about 3.50 meters by 2/2.2 meters!!! 7.70 square meters, let's say eight square meters. That gives each of us 0.96 square meters.

My companions in misery are extremely varied. Walter D. is a political prisoner from the ranks of *AGRA* (*Amis du Grand Reich Allemand*).[5] A veteran of the troops that occupied the Rhineland, he married a German woman at that time. Like the others, during this period he very quickly fraternized upon contact with the German people. He has been closely tied for a long time with another Belgian, Max W., married like him in the same circumstances and who occupies a cell quite close to ours. This makes me think that, in the future, it will be necessary to avoid having the Belgian Army occupy countries other than their own! It is, in any case, already too late, for after the Second World War a not-negligible number of the soldiers of the occupation troops recently declared on two or three occasions over Belgian television (*RTBf*) that, upon the return to Belgium of our occupation troops, they will remain there [in Germany]. Having married a German girl, their children have sometimes been going to German schools. Having already married German citizens, they have no more attachments to Belgium.

Another companion in the cell, Piet P., is an economic collaborator of Dutch origin. Like most of the other economic collaborators, who only co-operated in the spirit of making a profit, he

4   Rexist boys were expected to join the paramilitary *Formations de Combat* at age 18.
5   *AGRA* (*Amis du Grand Reich Allemand*) was founded on 13 March, 1941 by a group of *Liégois* militants who defected from Rex and considered Degrelle's espousal of the German cause to have been too cautious. They advocated dismantling the unitary Belgian state and integration of the Walloon race into an expanded Germanic confederation.

will be liberated and exonerated very quickly. He will regain his honor at the same time as his funds, after a small deduction of an economic amends, or, in plain language, a commission for the Belgian state. Certain economic collaborators collaborated for political convictions and they will, in general, remain in prison much longer. Piet, himself, never had any political convictions, and has never supported anyone, except for professional politicians.

S., a one-time seminarian, a decorated veteran of the 1914–18 war, vows a ferocious hatred toward anything that touches the church, from near or far. He has found other words of his own devising for all the liturgical airs and sings them to us, in their new version, on every occasion! He is also a political prisoner.

G., a factory guard, a "pauper", is also a 1914–18 veteran on the verge of illiteracy. Another, whose name escapes me, is past 40, from Braine – l'Alleud. I will never learn what he has done that brought him here.

Marcel W., who must be my age, was a member of the *Jeunesses* [Rexist youth] and the older brother of a *légionnaire* whom I knew, who died on the Russian Front.

M.S., another young man, is very young. He is not yet 18. *NSKK*, if I remember correctly. He belongs to a large family. His mother, father, brothers and sisters are all in prison. Eight or nine, in all. He lived near Tervuren.

We are all companions, but Walter, Marcel and M.S. are my friends.

The day after my arrival, in the morning, the door opens and the chaplain presents himself. He is small and potbellied. He asks if anyone wants to talk with him. But nobody responds. He goes on, "Surely there must be someone?" Out of politeness I get up and go toward him, in the doorway. I tell him that I have no desire to talk to anyone other than my comrades. His face darkens, turns Bordeaux red. He shouts, "They are *boche*[6] here!"

After more than a month of captivity I control my emotions, but today I let go. I violently push the door with him behind it. I hear the heavy door, which hits him, and he, who screams, leaves – and without taking the trouble to shut the door! Shortly thereafter someone pushes open the door. It is the guard, a man named Rutten. I give his name for he is, certainly, no longer of this world and that will not harm anyone. I have learned that he is a communist. I do not say that out of prejudice. There are good people everywhere, especially among the rank and file. I say it to describe him. He must not have been far away and had to come and see what has happened.

With an air that is quietly mocking and unusually friendly he asks if there is a problem. He asks what has just happened and one of my companions explains it to him. He then offers me a packet of cigarettes so that I can take one! With an extremely wide smile! I decline his offer, though I have a furious desire to smoke. His smile vanishes, but he says nothing and leaves, but he does close the door again. I did not think of it in time to shout at the chaplain, "Close the door because of drafts!" The chaplain will never set foot again in our cell at any moment during my stay here. We nickname him "*Canard*" [duck] because of his gait.

Ten or 15 days later a new companion arrives, Maurice V.D.K., head chef in one of the grand hotels of Brussels. He was a member of the *Algemein SS*.[7] He is Flemish, a sporting type, tall and blond. Arrested in 1944 and then released, he has just been arrested for a second time. He already has prison experience. That is why, in addition to a change of clothes, he has a suitcase full of slices of bread with jam! He gives them all to us, distributes them all. It is for us, whom he does not yet know, that he brought all this! What a beautiful gesture of solidarity! What a considerate fellow! This friendship will never die. We will remain close until his death, in 1987. One of his neighbors

---

6 French equivalent to 'Kraut' – an insulting word for a German.
7 The *Algemein SS* (or General *SS*) was the general body of the *SS* as distinct from the *Waffen-SS*, or armed *SS* and the *SS-Totenkopfverbände*, or concentration camp guards.

told me, when I dropped in at his house on the spur of the moment, that he committed suicide after the death of his wife. And, another coincidence, in the course of our conversations, it will turn out that I knew his sister, a nurse at Brugmann, during the war!

Now there are nine of us in the cell! Nevertheless, it is no larger than it was, it is still the same cell, approximately seven or eight meters square. This reduces our living space to approximately 0.85 square meters per prisoner! Despite all this, nobody is ever disturbed in this situation! Rights of Man, Red Cross, where were you at this time? And the journalists searching for injustices or little scandals? Out of all honesty I must say that, at times, that one or another journalist, two or three in all, had the courage to denounce the scandal of the bad treatment, or certain absolutely unjustified executions, of excesses of purification in some articles.

A little later we will be 11 in the cell! Always the same cell, without a centimeter more! The personal space is thus reduced to 0.70 square meters! Happily, after a few weeks, we will be back to nine again, with a few exceptions. But it was not the same for all of the cells. In some others, there will be up to 12 occupants for eight to 10 months!

Since the summer of 1945 is very hot, we live in a suffocating atmosphere! We decide to break a window pane and immediately do so. When winter comes, a severe winter, by chance, to punish us the window pane will not be replaced!

I must mention these things, since nobody has spoken of these details, which are, no doubt, trivial, but which take on unsuspected proportions in such a small confined space, where we were confined, nine, 10 or 11 months; for nine months that concern me, but far longer for the others! It takes an uncommon constitution, steel morale and perfect equanimity to survive such a regime without going mad, I can assure you.

For 11 men, as for eight or nine, we have only two waste buckets, or latrines, totally rusty, their rims chipped, each containing about four liters. These buckets are only emptied once a day! They serve for all of our needs, strictly for all, including water used for our washing! That allows 0.73 liters per man per day. You read it correctly: 7.3 deciliters.[8] Since they were full to the brim, one had to hold it in until the next emptying, regardless of intestinal problems! It is true that we did not have much to eat, but all the same! We all try to preserve a certain minimal dignity, despite it all, in spite of all the deprivations imposed on us by the administration. For our ablutions we have no alternative but to use the water in the basin to the very bottom, barely more than enough to brush our teeth! There can be no rinsing the basin for the next user!

Since, regardless, it is sometimes necessary to let off steam, one morning I let all my comrades wash themselves, do their *toilette*, and tell them not to worry about me. I can feel their looks, which wonder what I am cooking up! Every morning there is a guard whom we nickname "the Mexican", because of his physique, who goes along the outside to strike the bars of each cell to make sure that nobody has taken advantage of the night to saw through them in preparation for an escape. We hear him coming from afar. When my companions have finished their *toilette*, I ask M. Waroquiers to watch for the arrival of "the Mexican". Perched on the stool, pressed against the bars, he watches. When, from the noise, he reports the arrival of "the Mexican's" beater on the bars, two cells from ours, but on the ground floor, for sure, for the man is not an acrobat, Waroquiers jumps off the stool to give me his place. When I estimate that the right moment has come, with a sudden, rapid movement I hurl the waste bucket, or, at least, its contents, through the window. Immediately the oaths, loud and profuse, confirm that I have hit my target!

8   To assist the American reader to form a picture of how much volume the author is speaking of, wine and liquor is now sold primarily in 750 ml bottles – roughly the size of the old 'fifth'. That is slightly larger than the volume provided for each prisoner's total daily 'waste'.

Everyone bursts into laughter and our cell fills with our loud and irrepressible mirth. That is very good, now and again! I estimate that it will take "the Mexican" five to 10 minutes to get to us. He has to go all the way around the wing, enter at the center, then into our wing to get to us on the second story. Yet I estimate that three minutes have hardly passed when a nervous key opens the lock of our cell and the door flies open violently! In the opening stands "the Mexican", his skin red, this time, downright scarlet. He is furious, his eyes bulging. But none of us can control our mirth! He is still dripping with the contents of the waste bucket! He shouts and has to try three times over before we can understand what he is saying, but there is no need for that. We have already guessed! He demands to know who threw the contents of a waste bucket on his head. We all look at each other as innocently as possible, without, in any case, being able to hide our laughs. Beyond himself, he says that if the perpetrator of the deed does not confess, he will put all the occupants of the cell in solitary. Not wanting all my comrades to be punished,, of course, I approach him and say that it was me, because there was too much in the waste bucket, but that we could never have guessed that he was below, especially since we were strictly forbidden to look out the window and, all the more so, because we could not lean out to see what is below! My remark does not calm him, for he well knows the impertinence that it conceals, which I have made no effort to hide. He indicates that he will take me to the dungeon and, in his rage, he does not even allow me to take my bedclothes.

After a long journey in a series of darker and darker corridors, I find myself in the promised dungeon. It is about 1000 hours in the morning and it is full sunshine outdoors, though here it is like night! A tiny window, way up in the wall, allows only a faint ray of light to penetrate. The height of the dungeon may well be one-and-a-half times that of the cell I just left, its area is about the same, but it seems much larger to me because I am alone. At the very back, on a masonry base, is a plank; it is my pallet! The plank is varnished, and proves even harder to sleep on than an ordinary plank. It is also slightly inclined, which means that, all night, I have to move back up the slope every time I slide down, about every 30 minutes! The night seems to last forever, without even granting me any sleep. Is it by refinement or stupidity that this pallet is disposed like this?

The walls ooze moisture, they are saturated with it and, without the slightest covers, the cold and moisture are my only companions! It is hard to make it through the nights in these conditions. I am wearing only pants and a very light jacket, the same as always. The days are no less long, without reading, without being able to write, with nothing at all to do, nothing to see, and nothing to study, no furniture. If I had something with which to write, or to read, that would not, indeed, be possible in this semi-darkness. And the silence! It is so great that it seems deafening to me! Since there is a double door to this dungeon, with a vestibule, no sound at all comes to me from the corridor, especially since this corridor is deserted and is separated from the wings by yet another corridor and another door. Not a sound penetrates from outside, either. Ordinarily I love silence, but here it is hard to endure.

I have to find some way to pass the time here, so I inspect my dungeon, centimeter by centimeter. The red brick walls are tarred and whitewashed where they are not flaking. And there I discover inscriptions on the walls, hundreds of graffiti reaching up to the limit of a man's reach. How have they been able to do them? I find all sorts there: "*Mort au vaches!*" ["Down with the cops!"]; or, of course, it is classic – the ABC of the prisoner: "*Toi qui entres ici, abandonne tout espoir!*" ["Abandon all hope, ye who enter here!"]; "If you confess you are lost"; "They have unleashed the terror, like Danton. Like Robespierre, they shall perish by the terror." They range from the most smutty to the highest philosophy. Intellectuals have sojourned here!

I have spent three days and three nights here. Seventy-two hours and each hour seems to last for an entire day. Alone, absolutely alone, for the morning guard leaves a pitcher of water and a crust of bread and, in the evening, a bowl of watery soup, nothing to open one's mouth for. They give me nothing more to eat. Without any contact, without the slightest sound, I might as well be deaf.

It is like a tomb where I can walk on a space of six or seven meters square, less the surface of the pallet. Only reflection allows me to assure myself that I am still in this world, that I am a living, thinking being! Even if I thought bad thoughts, in the eyes of some people. As the days pass by a feeling arises in me of interminable incarceration. Contrary to the horror, to the bitterness, then to the panic which seizes all innocent people who are incarcerated or condemned, such as I have read at times, for me the certainty of the injustice, the awareness of having nothing to reproach myself with helps me to endure it all, but not always without reacting.

After the incredulity comes disgust, and my scorn for the present regime is reinforced. Then comes a feeling of superiority, yes, even though that may seem presumptuous! Until then, such an idea had never come to me, but as my detention continues, day after day, seeing the actions of those who sought our destruction, their hate, a feeling of superiority over them comes to me, along with the willpower to let all the storms go by without allowing them to touch my spirit, to do my best to take nothing seriously, to armor myself in some way. This state of mind will enable me to surmount everything and to endure with minimal harm.

To know that, outdoors, it is springtime or summer, without seeing a flower, a leaf or the least blade of grass! To see snow fall in winter through the bars! That is hard.

After three days in the dungeon I am led to report to the prison governor. He seems smaller than before, and I feel that I am stronger than when I entered the dungeon. I am then back with my companions in my cell. I feel as if I left them weeks ago. They treat me like a hero. Every day my friends have saved a little part of their rations for me! This solidarity quickly makes me forget the long days of isolation. I tell them of my experience until evening. What particularly strikes me on returning to the cell is the difference in temperature. It is at least 30° here [86°F], no doubt more, while in the dungeon it must have been no more than 14 or 15° [57–59°F]. The crowding. Down there I never had a straw mattress. Here there are five or six for nine men! And what straw mattresses! One third straw, one third of little fragments of straw, and one third dust! For sleeping we arrange the straw mattresses so that each of us has a part to rest his head and loins on. By day, we place them, part against the wall, part on the floor, and thus we have a seat with a back.

Obviously there is little room to move, just a narrow passage between the straw mattresses, the waste buckets and the single stool. One foot of this stool cunningly serves as the hiding place for a flint, for, of course, smoking is forbidden and possession of any way at all to make a fire is also prohibited. Hence the hiding place for the flint and another for the fragment of razor blade to strike the flint. A throat-lozenge tin contains a bit of handkerchief transformed into tinder. My companions have already found the means to organize this, some of them having been here since September 1944! The flints arrived in the cell wrapped in sliver paper in the bottom of the tooth-paste tubes that were brought in by the families of those who had visiting privileges. The razor blades, more precisely the fragments thereof, come from the blades that we receive on a given day for a few minutes, time to shave ourselves. For fear of suicides! That, however, does not prevent those who have decided to end it all from accomplishing their goal.

By way of a promenade, we are given half an hour a day! Ten minutes of that go for going and returning. Thirty minutes for us to stretch our legs that have been immobilized for 23 hours and 30 minutes in the cell, our legs folded for most of the time, and 20 minutes to fill our lungs with fresh air, to escape the suffocating atmosphere of this overcrowded cage and the overheating like a steam room. Every morning, while waiting for the hour of our yard time, Piet – the "economic" prisoner – paces up and down the little space in the cell, dragging his worn-out shoes. During this time we hear nothing but him, we see nothing but him. Until the day when, exasperated by his behavior, which irritates everyone, I threaten to strangle him unless he sits down immediately, like everyone else. It is not possible for each of us to do this, so there is no reason why he should be the only one able to do so, obliging all the others to fold their legs. It was not even possible to read at this moment, even to form a thought with his coming and going and the noise of his worn-out shoes! Piet does as he is told and my comrades thank me for my intervention.

But how could I desire to strangle a companion in prison, even if he is an economic prisoner? The crowding of so many men in such a small space without the least opportunity for privacy, even for an instant, for whatever, for nature's needs or for personal hygiene! Everything, absolutely everything, is done jointly! My *fiancée*, arrested in September 1944, was released six months later. By letter I learn that she has just been arrested again! I have had no visitors. My parents are dead, my two brothers are also prisoners, my sister is in a convent and cannot go out in the world. She is voluntarily cloistered. Did they release my *fiancée* to serve as bait so that they could catch me more easily? High morals! What charges could they have had to incarcerate her? Membership in the *Jeunesses Féminines* [Rexist girls' movement] at the age of 17 or 18 years? Not all of these youths have been arrested, but many, yes, and based on what criteria? Impossible to discover, and justice herself will have a hard time explaining it to us. Chance. A fine example of dispassionate justice, as two former "*auditeurs militaires*" [military prosecutors] dared to assert during a television appearance and also a number of "historians" solicited more than is reasonable by the producers of this show that purported to retrace history and re-establish the truth! Why was my *fiancée* arrested for the second time? Was it because she was engaged to a *légionnaire*? What crime could be more horrible than that?! In the event, one could have decreed that it was, apparently, a war crime!

My *fiancée* was condemned to a year of imprisonment, without parole, and she did, indeed, serve 365 days in prison, in two periods! She had no benefit of the slightest measure of "clemency", nor of the "*La Loi Lejeune*,"[9] nor of reduction of sentence for good time! I will not describe her experience, for she does not wish me to do so! Behold the greatness of soul of the victor, without even having to make war. And for that I shall never forgive them, at least, so long as they do not admit having committed these barbarities. I do not say that they excuse themselves for it or that they justify it, and I am not talking about myself.

How many spouses, parents, *fiancées*, even children have been arrested, to say nothing of the tortures, and have thus served as hostages of the "justice", even though the war is over? There has been more or less legal process against the "civilians" or military responsible for the atrocities against our people, and those who were, in spite of everything, actually tried and condemned in the extremely rare trials, only served a part of the sentences pronounced. At any rate, this was not the case with the Belgian soldiers who coldly and in a cowardly fashion murdered four parents of *légionnaires* at Lauenau in 1945 – including a journalist and a disabled young person!

How many imprisoned parents have had their minor children taken from them and committed to houses of correction? As if it was also necessary to punish these kids and to mark them for life? This shame of the "repression" is not yet ready to be blurred over. I have two friends who were in the *NSKK*, simple drivers, who drove vehicles for this organization, whose aged parents were arrested by the chaplain of the scouts of the troop that they were in or had belonged to! These parents said that he wore the red armband of the resistance movement of communist origin and that he was accompanied by five or six other "resistance" people armed to the teeth. All this to arrest two old people who had committed the crime of having given birth to two sons who had enlisted without, of course, even asking their parents' permission. But I am not writing a black or white book to denounce all these excesses, all these crimes. These documents exist. All the same, it is necessary for me to recall these, for we had to suffer these too; it was our universe.

---

9   *La Loi Lejeune*, passed in 1888, allowed conditional restoration of a condemned individual to society before completion of their original sentence under certain conditions – essentially based on the changes in the individual's comportment during incarceration and the fact that it is difficult for a judge, at the time of sentencing, to know what effect the sentence will have on the comportment of the individual.

But now I return to St. Gilles, where, under cover of the yard time, I find it possible to slip into the yard time of the adjoining cell. I only have to be the last of my cell to go out, to lag a bit and allow the first of those going out of the other cell to pass in front of me. Thus that person goes into my cell's yard time and I into his. All it requires is a moment of inattention from the guard in the tower. That allows me to see my other buddies, including Guy W. and *Major* Hellebaut, who wanted to meet with me for several pieces of information that I am in a position to provide him, since he is preparing documentation on the *Légion*.

This is also an occasion to learn a few anecdotes of life in the adjoining cell. I present two of them which, though they may not have changed the face of the world, all the same, gave me a good laugh at the time and in the circumstances of that epoch. They both concern the same prisoner, Félix L. He decided to learn English and he obtained authorization from the authorities to have a book sent in by means of a method that was common at the time. Since he found that this method [of learning English] was too simple for his intellectual level, he copied the entire book onto index-cards, with one lesson per card. Then, every day, he drew two or three cards at random, and thus learned English in no particular order. The same Félix could never control his appetite, so, upon receiving his daily ration of bread, he devoured the whole ration at once, without leaving a crumb and without thinking of the 24 hours that he would have to wait for his next morsel of bread. Then, every time one of his companions in the cell would eat a bit of bread, Félix would be so frustrated that he would grab his toothbrush and toothpaste and brush his teeth fervently! He used two or three tubes of toothpaste a week and wore out a toothbrush in 15 days!

After a few weeks I obtain authorization to receive a visit from one of my sisters-in-law. In that way I have a sort of thread, a thin one, that links me with the outside world, but it is the only one. It is very little, and yet very great at the time, when I have no other. And the news that thus comes to me from outside seems to come from another world, from out there! In all truth, it is little enough, but it gives me great pleasure. To my great astonishment, several times I receive visits from some old acquaintances, also prisoners, who work in the prison for the administration and, thereby, have some freedom to circulate. This is the case with W., our former coal dealer, who lived in the *avenue de la Couronne*, as with Raoul C. and V.E., the father of my comrade Arthur, and with one or another in addition.

These may seem pretty meager distractions when you read them like this, but believe me, in the conditions that I experienced, they were events, as is proven by the fact that I have not forgotten them 45 years later!

At times, as you may well imagine, we talked about women, and one of my companions in the cell, whose spouse had left him to his fate, tells us that, without any outside relations, he could not always wait for the conclusion of an idyllic romance, nor follow all the approaches that men of good company do and that, as soon as he could save the necessary money, he would go to a brothel, provided that, at that moment, they were not closed. That is what he told us, for we talked of such things.

There were servants in prison. They were the prisoners who came to bring food to the cells and who also emptied the waste buckets. But it was also prisoners who maintained the buildings, who did the cooking and took care of a vast number of other tasks. Sometimes we received news from them when the guards were distracted by other things.

There was also another means of communication that functioned very well, by day or night. We called it the "internal telephone". We used Morse code to send our messages to the other cells, knocking on the heating pipes with a metal spoon. That is how, in particular, we were informed every time one of our people was to be executed. In this instance everything started during the night. The "internal telephone" suddenly rattled and we would awake with a start! We immediately guessed the reason for a communication at such an hour! One of our own was about to be sacrificed!

Sometimes this was for political motives, sometimes to satisfy the bloodlust of a populace excited by certain newspapers or other pressure groups that it is futile to be more specific about, and, more rarely, for reasons of pure justice! But, in this case, can one speak of reason? The deciphered message confirmed our fears! We were all up and already wide awake! Then, immediately and well before dawn, the thousands of prisoners would begin to hammer on the bars and the doors of the cells with their mess tins or other objects and, from all the skylights of the prison, would come the vengeful cries, "Murderers! Murderers!" The bedlam, the externalization of our revolt, was noisily manifested for a half-hour or more. Enough to deafen our guards, who would come to bang on our doors and yell, but these noises were drowned out in the enormous racket that we raised and which woke up all the residents of the adjoining streets.

It was the neighbors of the cell who were also condemned to death, for they were all grouped in the same section, who sounded the alert, for they heard the arrival of the procession of the birds of bad omen who came to inform the victim that his hour had come! This was the only circumstance in which a cell door was opened before the morning *Reveille*. On those days, there was no joking of any sort.

During my sojourn here this was the case, in particular, for V. Meulenyzer, K. De Feyter, J. Streel and A. Borms, for we were also informed like this of executions that took place at places other than at the St. Gilles prison. I did not know them all, but all of them were my comrades, whatever language they spoke. We all felt profound solidarity, with the possible exception of those who were not one of ours and who had acted out of self-interest or who had betrayed our ideals.

My companions, who had been here since September 1944, told me many things from that epoch, all that happened before my arrival here. They explained to me how, during the "von Rundstedt" Offensive,[10] certain guards came to the cells to collect testimonials of their good conduct, sort of a certificate of "lack of civic virtue" in expectation of the return of German troops to Brussels. Those who had been the worst "*vache*"[11] were transformed into trembling, bleating sheep. "We were not really that bad, were we?" they said. Will you say that? Will you bear witness to that? All sorts of things like that when they had beaten the crap out of all these prisoners! And they were precisely the same ones who redoubled the fury and cruelty against these same prisoners as soon as the fear of the return of German troops to Brussels vanished! One can understand their shame and humiliation after such cowardice, but it was yet more cowardly to then take vengeance on those whom they had so basely solicited! The bad treatment, the blows and humiliations redoubled and became the daily fare. But the daily fare, I mean to say the food, was not increased. It was vile, and was distributed sparingly. Certain guards, as was also true in other places of detention or concentration, did not hesitate to urinate in the cans of food before they were distributed!

For amounts ranging from 200 to 500 francs of the time, certain guards were willing to pass letters for the prisoner's family to the outside. The better-off prisoners even managed to have packages of food "parachuted" in this way. Alas, the fees charged by the guards for this sort of "service" were beyond the means of 99.99 percent of us. Most of the time it was only, or principally, the economic collaborators who could engage in this. Fortunately, and I must say this out of all honesty, not all of the guards behaved this way, even if most of them did. There were a few guards, especially the professionals, who behaved correctly.

---

10 The Ardennes Offensive, or Battle of the Bulge.
11 French slang equivalent to 'pigs', with reference to police – or 'screws' – in relation to prison guards.

Today [when the author was a prisoner there] prisoners are not beaten, at least not here. In any case, I do not know of it. That is not necessarily the case for other concentration camps of the realm where they vigorously beat up prisoners – especially in Wallonia. But courtesy, the most elementary politeness or simple respect for man, are not yet standard. Shouts from most of the guards haunt the corridors and echo from the bare walls and the tiles of the high vaults.

"*Zwijgen!*"

"*Smoel toe!*"

"Silence!"

"Shut up!"

"*Smoel ou bakkes tegen de muur!*"

"Faces to the wall!" That was the mildest language.

One day our guard, Rutten, told us that, henceforth, we must salute him in military fashion when we passed by him. But, obviously, not in our fashion. We saluted with the outstretched arm, and it is obvious that that is not done here. In the *Wehrmacht* one salutes with the hand to the cap, at least until the day of the attempt to assassinate Hitler. When one was not wearing a cap, they would turn their head energetically to the right or to the left, toward the one they were saluting. It was esthetically ridiculous, in effect, to salute with the hand level with a cap if one wasn't wearing one. In brief, we had to salute the guard as if we were wearing a cap. As I may have already said, this guardian was at least a head shorter than the shortest of us. *Alors*, like a single man we all pass in front of him while saluting him, but doing so in a fashion that is half-angelic, half-sarcastic, while conspicuously bowing to him. We all do this with such irony in looking at him that, on the third day, he asks us not to salute him anymore.

Another time M. Waroquiers was able to hide in a seam of a garment his parents brought him a few little cones that looked like they were made of silver paper, like one would otherwise find on the fairgrounds and which burst into flame when they contact a drop of water. One could put one of these cones in the tobacco of a cigarette and light with a simple drop of water. I quickly envisaged a comic scenario that I wanted to try out that same day. I put five or six cigarettes in a case, where only one contained one of these little cones, and that one was on the edge so that I could keep it in place with a finger.

At the moment that we knew that the guard would pass and glance into the cell through the peephole in the door, for he always passed by at about the same time, I lit a cigarette and smoked very conspicuously. Do I need to say that it was forbidden to smoke in the cell? The only time smoking was allowed was during yard time, for about 20 minutes. As a rule, one only smoked in the cell in turn, while hiding and while doing one's best to dissipate the smoke or to waft it toward the broken window with a towel.

That which is to happen happens, and, upon glancing through the peephole the guard vigorously opens the door and, with a gloating smile, asks us where our matches are. I answer in all innocence, "But, chief, we do not have any. We have never had any!" His smile changes and becomes skeptical, as if to say, "Do you take me for an idiot?" I repeat the same thing, and he the same, then asking how I lit my cigarette. "With water, chief," I tell him. At that he becomes a bit paler! Only then do I appear to realize that he does not believe me and I offer to prove it to him. This he accepts, curious!

Then I take the only cigarette in the case that has the cone and I light it with a drop of water. I can see in his face that he thinks he has gone crazy! Still, he has just seen what I did. Nothing in my hands, nothing in my pockets. I offer him a cigarette so that he can try it for himself. To my great, but delighted, astonishment, he immediately accepts it.

He wets his finger, as he saw me do, and holds it to the end of the cigarette, at the same time that he sucks at the other end. But all in vain! We all force back the laughs that arise in us, all clenching our teeth to avoid exploding. All the more so because he wets the end of the cigarette a second time and, he sucks so hard on the end in his mouth that the cigarette starts to swell from his saliva. Now all that he has in his hand is a shapeless cigarette. The paper that has come unglued is sticking to his fingers. From the green that he was becoming, he goes to red.

He then departs quickly, slamming the door without thinking anymore of searching for our matches or where they might be, nor even of punishing us! I tell myself that punishment will wait for tomorrow and, in advance, I accept it voluntarily, for we had a good laugh, and really needed it! But no, the next day he acts as if nothing happened, except that when our eyes meet, he drops his, ashamed, it seems to me. In any case, we had a good laugh!

I could write a book devoted entirely to all the jokes we played, but I shall stop here. Do not, however, think that it was a pleasure party. Not every day was humorous, and, for us, it was the only way to endure, for better or worse, those years there!

The vermin, the bugs especially, made our life hard. To a degree where even the administration, which, in general, concerned itself with so little, decided to take action, for fear of succumbing itself.

One beautiful day they had us evacuate the cells by sections and lodged us in the forge area, if I remember correctly. We were smoked there for three days. There we were very numerous, 60 or 70, perhaps, or maybe a few more. It was an occasion to see other friends, to make new acquaintances. I met, among others, *Major* Hellebaut, from the adjoining cell, Guy W. and their other companions – journalists of the printed press and of the radio. If, at that time, there had been television we would have been even more numerous! I found myself part of a table of bridge; indeed, the administration, possibly fearing an uprising from such a large assembly, relaxed discipline. My partner was Raymond De Becker, of the *"Le Soir"*, and Ch. René and another, from the radio, as our adversaries. The conversations were animated and ran over a most varied range of subjects, and even the guards joined in as if nothing separated us. By day they remained shut in with us, doubtless for the same reasons that I mentioned above. Three days in a very different atmosphere! The cell will seem very somber when we have to return to it. The treatment that it received was no more than a glance, if one can put it that way. If we counted them, we would have found the same number of bugs as before, perhaps even recognizing some of them.

On 18 February, 1946 after nine months of imprisonment, I am called for the first time to appear before a deputy military prosecutor. The first and only time, I think, for I have no recollection of a second confrontation.

25

The *"Petit Château"*

Shortly thereafter I am transferred to the *"Petit Château"*, but it is no promotion, even if it is better, a bit better. I am in *Pavillon H* (a grandiose name for such rooms), in Room 352 on the first story [*premier étage*, literally 'first story', but, actually, the story above the ground floor]. The window panes are whitewashed and I can only see a bit of sky and a few windows through the windows far above that are not whitewashed. Someone has managed to scrape off a little corner of the paint on the exterior of the window pane, which allows us to make out a few *façades* and the sign of the *café* *"Au chien vert"* ["the Green Dog"] which is on the corner of the street and where, it seems, several families fraternize after visiting their family members that are here. We are a little more than 30 in a room, but there are beds. Bunk beds, but beds. Two fairly large tables and some benches. This does not leave much room, but, all the same, the large volume of the room allows us to breathe better than in the cell. The comfort is very relative, but it is a hundred times better than where I have been.

The prison governor, P., is also far better than the old fossil of St. Gilles! We pass our days reading, writing, or playing cards, after the morning session of exercises that we do as a group, led by the room chief, P. V.D.V. We also get half an hour of walking, daily, in the courtyard of this ancient barracks and larger than the triangular cage, only a few square meters, at St. Gilles.

One day, while I am sitting at the table playing cards, the door opens and one of our guards (who sold balloons in the vicinity of the Bourse after the war) calls me. "Visiting room," he tells me.

"Visiting room? I am not expecting a visit!"

"Yes, visiting room, it is your lawyer."

"But I do not have a lawyer!"

"Yet it is good for you and it really is your lawyer."

"That is not possible! How can he call himself that?"

"I will go and ask him." When the guard returns he is still more insistent, gives me the name, Me P., and tells me that he has been sent by my sister. Suddenly everything is clear! Our families were friends and we lived in the same quarter of Anvers until 1935. My sister remained close to one of the daughters and one of the brothers. The two of them, I believe, attended the Jesuit *collège* [secondary school] on the *avenue de France*.

I was a bit taken aback, surprised. My embarrassment did not, however, last long and I tell the guard that I am not receiving today, that this is my day for bridge and I am unable to dismiss my guests. He smiles and waits, doubtless not believing me. "Come on, hurry, don't keep the people waiting!" I again tell him that I am not receiving. The guard still does not take me seriously; he has never seen anything like this. I have to turn my back on him and return to my place at the table with my partners for him to comprehend my determination. The good man – on the whole he was not really nasty with us – seemed truly sorry and said no more about it, no more than my comrades did in the room. But the bridge party resumed, not without some laughter over it much later.

In the course of the good dozen months of detention which had just begun, I had plenty of opportunities to realize that we were already condemned, without even being judged and that it made no difference whether or not one had a lawyer. I also already knew that if one did not have

293

one of one's own, the judge, on his own initiative, would assign us one. We did not have the right to defend ourselves. I had neither the desire nor the means to choose a lawyer, especially since, at that time, it was not uncommon for a lawyer to do more harm than good for his client, without neglecting to solicit a generous fee and cash on the nail. That is not to say that there were not lawyers who were devoted and perfectly honest. They did what they could in the context of the times. Some *"Pro Deo"*[1] lawyers, despite the *"Pro Deo"*, still managed to extract payment from the ruined families under the pretext that it would allow them to better defend the son or beloved spouse.

Perhaps the one that my sister had sent would have done the best he could for me, indeed, I am nearly certain that he would have, but the defense, at that time, could not accomplish much. In this case why involve him, and create obligations? I never want to owe anything to anyone. But it is true that I was lacking in courtesy toward Me P., and also in the most elementary politeness when he had taken the trouble to come to see me! If it had only occurred to me to respond politely, to explain my regrets and ask his forgiveness! Doubtless my reaction was not courteous, but it was logical. What's more, our nerves were on edge from all that we had seen and undergone. That is not an excuse, but an explanation. I do not regret my actions, no more today than at the time. I simply regret that I may have humiliated Me P. and put my sister in a very awkward situation.

I also remember two escapes from the *"Petit Chateau."* There may well have been more, but I knew both of these escapees. They did not, in any case, escape together. There was Franz L., a veteran *légionnaire* who escaped while requesting to be alone during transport to the *Palais de Justice* [court building]. He shoved aside a guard and the *gendarmes* and was not recaptured until much later. The other, Willy V., was a lawyer or editor at the newspaper *le Soir*. Tall, elegant, personable, he had class. He, too, managed to escape during transport to the *Palais de Justice*. He was truly calm and reserved, almost timid, so that his escape surprised us all. But, as you will see, there have been other similar cases. We later learned that Willy had planned it all. His wife and his five or six children had already left, a few weeks earlier, for Argentina and he arrived there a little later without difficulties.

Some escapees even had the amiable intention of sending postcards of their new *Eldorado* to their former companions in prison. And, the height of refinement, even to one or another of the ill-disposed guards, and a prison governor received one or another card from Venezuela or somewhere else! Absolutely true! There was also a card from Ireland. I have strong memories of another highly characteristic anecdote that well illustrates the mentality of the time. It was during a transport to the *Palais de Justice* and, if my memory is correct, it was on 9 May, 1946 when I had just learned that my trial had been postponed to a later date. Like the others, I had waited for hours in a narrow cell in the court building, only to be told that my *"affaire"* had been postponed. At the moment when I took my place in a police vehicle, a prison van, among all the "political" prisoners, there was also a "common law" prisoner. If my memory is correct, he had been sentenced to two to three years in prison for killing his mother! Offended at being mixed with the collaborators, he stubbornly refused to get into the vehicle with us. He did not want to associate with b******s like us! *Eh bien*! You can believe me or not, but he returned to prison in a taxi! Put yourself in our place for a moment, with we who always thought that killing one's mother was assuredly the worst of crimes. We were dumbfounded. Apparently our morals were obsolete; things had certainly changed since the "Liberation"! Did we now have to get used to living in another world?

---

1   *'Pro Deo'* ('for God') – equivalent to *'pro bono publico'*, or *'pro bono'* ('for the public good') – professional work done at no charge or at a reduced fee.

But I am speaking to you here of the palace, of the *"Petit Château"*, and it was indeed so, but do not believe that we lived the life of a *château*, and, if you came to see us, that we would only be rubbing shoulders with the good folk! Nevertheless, when walking in the court, every day I would see or rub shoulders with a prince. A genuine prince of the blood, not a lost prince or an operetta prince. Extremely distinguished, tall and handsome, he regularly wore an "Eden" hat[2] and he could be recognized from afar.

I also got to know two 15-year-old German kids. One of them came to Belgium in hopes of finding his Belgian father, a certain Van K., living at Anvers. His mother had been killed in the bombing during the last years of the war, in Germany. Left alone, he hoped to find his father, his only remaining possible family tie, his last hope. But he was arrested as suspicious before he found him! What were this child and his buddy doing in prison? Doubtless they posed a serious danger for the security of the state! What drama, confronted there with human bestiality! At that age! He and his buddy, who simply came along with him so that he would not be alone, were sent back to Germany after months of captivity and without having been able to find his father. What opinion will they have of the "adults" and "responsible authorities" someday when they are grown up?

Another day, going down to the courtyard for the promenade, I had another problem with a guard. The courtyard of the barracks where the promenade took place was bounded by the peristyle that ran along the buildings on three of the four sides of the court, and between the columns of the peristyle, the administration had stretched a barbed wire entanglement. I was descending the stairs leading to the ground floor with the other prisoners on our way to the promenade. As usual, and like many other prisoners, I had an unlit cigarette in my mouth. I emphasize that it was not lit! I saw a guard, at the bottom of the steps, staring at me. I immediately got the idea that he was looking at my cigarette, but I had no reason to put it away. When I got down to him he could not fail to see that this cigarette was not lit, nor had it ever been, for we were no more than half a meter apart. Nevertheless, he knocked it out of my mouth with the back of his hand, touching my face! My blood rose and I vigorously pushed him back, without actually striking him. Thus he found himself with the back of his jacket caught in the barbed wire behind him, without being able to free himself. He immediately shouted that I attacked him and called his colleagues and two *gendarmes* who happened to be passing to help him. They grabbed hold of me without ceremony and, two minutes later, I was in the dungeon below the wing on the right, on the ground floor.

Apparently this ill-tempered idiot was only intending to be nasty for the fun of it, or to provoke a scuffle. The internal rules stipulated that smoking was forbidden except on the promenade, and this guard, no doubt, considered that the promenade started when one's feet were actually in the courtyard itself, and that I was a dozen steps, or five meters, from this courtyard. But it was no less true that nothing forbad one having a cigarette in the mouth, especially since it was not lit.

Here is another story of a cigarette, in brief. One of my brothers, held in the same room as me, was caught smoking in the room. It was custom, in such a case, for the prisoner to be deprived of visitors for a month. Since he had a wife and children, and since my *fiancée* had gone back to prison, as I said above, I went to see the prison governor in his place. I had a little idea I wanted to talk about with him. I would thus keep my brother from being deprived of visits and I would give myself some pleasure at the same time, especially since I wasn't running any great risk, only of a day or two in the dungeon.

I employed my usual shrewdness to get to his office. I then freely admitted to the prison governor that I had been smoking in the room, but that I did not really understand why one could buy 250

---

2 An 'Anthony Eden' hat, or simply an 'Anthony Eden', was a silk-brimmed, black felt Homburg of the kind favored in the 1930's by Anthony Eden.

grams of tobacco a week at the canteen when the daily half-hour of promenade only gave time to smoke one cigarette per day, amounting to 10 or 15 grams of tobacco a week, or 14 cigarettes. The prison governor seemed perplexed by my remarks and my boldness and, *grand seigneur*,[3] allowed me to return to my room with no punishment! Nobody in the room expected to see me again for a day or two. And, for all that, the authorized tobacco ration was not reduced! It is true that the administration's canteen did not lose anything there!

It is now 45 years later and, as I sift through my memories, I find that I have mentioned nearly 20 names among the 30 or so of those in my room. Every one, or nearly everyone is linked to stories, and I remember many. I will not tell them, for they would fill a library! Nevertheless, I will say that there were people in my room of all nationalities, and that they were there for all sorts of varied reasons, I presume. I do, indeed, say I presume, for I did not ask questions of those whom I did not know to avoid embarrassing them. It is evident that there were people who were in prison for less respectable reasons; that those would, in any case, have told some sort of story. As for our own, I knew why they had been arrested.

Among us, in our room, there was a Luxembourg industrialist, an incomparable Danish gymnast, an Italian, a French hairdresser from Lyon, and an Austrian Jew from Vienna, 50 years old, who perfumed himself like a tart and wore a hairnet while sleeping. There was also a priest, a chaplain in the German Army who came from Saint Vith. He was a marvelous man who would have been able to reconcile all of us with the church. But there was also one of our veterans who served the mass and who, himself, once and for all, definitively spoiled relationships with that church for all of us. In actual fact, all of this influenced nobody. Every one of us had seen enough to come to our own opinion about such things! I also remember a fairground person, a sort of gypsy who was a good 20 years old. I wondered what he was doing here, but I did not ask him. One day, when he returned from a visit with one of his people, he said that his wife told him that the Americans kiss like bags! (Those are his own words) And he never understood why. At that moment we all burst out laughing! But I shall cease writing about this sort of details, for I will never finish, so many memories come back, and I shall go on with my story.

When the prosecutor asks me the name of my lawyer I tell him that I do not want one. A good day, if I can put it thus, for are there good days when one is in prison? One day, then, I receive a letter from a lawyer who advises me that he has been appointed by the office [of the prosecutor] to defend me. What irony! Those who are going to judge me and do everything possible to sentence me to the maximum, who have, in fact, already condemned me, are sending me an attorney to defend me! A crowning hypocrisy! What equivocation! When he comes to see me, a few days later, I find that he is a man of 50, with one arm amputated. Mr Paul Berton presented himself. I knew immediately that he was an invalid of the 1914–18 war, where he lost his right arm, but the decorations in his buttonhole already let me guess that. He was very friendly, and I believe, the sympathy was mutual. Even so, I did not change my mind and explained to him that his presence at my trial would be sufficient, if it was forced on me, but that there was no need for him to plead nor to intervene; that I already knew full well that the outcome for me was already decided and that I intended in this manner to bring it to the court's attention. I asked him to take no offense; that I had confidence in him but not in the court. He attempted, by other means, to persuade me that he needed arguments to refute those of the prosecutor and, thereby, to obtain a less severe sentence. [He asked] me to provide him with the arguments. I could not make up my mind to do that. [I felt] that it would be naive to believe in that and that I felt angry that I was not condemned to death like so many of my friends. I would not go so far as to say that I desired

---

3   With the air of a 'great lord'.

to be executed, but that I wanted to, at least, be sentenced to death! Nevertheless, there were one or two times, in certain circumstances, in certain moments of exaltation, when I was in such a mood that execution would not make me change my mind. He did not return to that subject and, to attempt other things, he told me that he too had been Rexist, like practically everyone at some time or other. I replied to him that, as for me, I had been so for a long time, to the very bottom of my convictions, and that I was all the more so today than in the past. I was confident that I had behaved as I should have. That was not because of the treatment that we had received, certainly myself, but because of the tortures inflicted on so many of my comrades and, especially, also on their families!

I also told him that I did not despise those who did not agree with me. That, on the other hand, nobody had ever proved to me that I was wrong, and that I would not necessarily be wrong because they were going to condemn me. That had already taken place, one could see it today; one would see it again tomorrow. We spoke thus for a long time, but I gave him no argument for I told him I did not seek any extenuating circumstances. I would, to the contrary, take full responsibility for my enlistment. We parted with a very friendly handshake. He would write to me, he would come back to see me, he said. And it is true. He often wrote to me and came to see me again. I had, in truth, come upon a good man who took his profession to heart, and I could not have done better by hiring a defender of my choice!

As *"mon Cher Maître"* [my Dear Master] – I now call him that – told me that he was going to look at my dossier, the idea came to me that I should do the same, and I so requested. This was less out of curiosity to see what I was accused of, which the dossier contained, than for a change of air, to stir a bit and to visit the *Bureaux de l'Audotorat* [office of the prosecutor] – there where the administration was cobbling up its case to put us away. Early in the morning a prison van deposits me, with other prisoners, in a building in the *rue de la Loi*. After a wait in the basement we are brought to the first story. Another prisoner tells me that innumerable prisoners have gone through very bad moments in these basements during the last months of 1945 and the first of 1946. After we take our places at these tables we are brought our dossiers. My neighbor at the table is the Flemish poet, Bert P., and I remember it well for we laughed a lot! It is true that I decided to laugh at everything. And could I not laugh at all that was in my dossier, all that I was accused of? It might have been the dossier of the Dalton Brothers or of Al Capone. That might have made sense, but my dossier made no sense at all. If my name had not appeared on each page I would have believed I had the wrong dossier. I copied only a part of it, for it was so thick; they were so thick, for there were two folders. I would have needed two or three weeks to read them, and I only had one day, or, at the most, two.

I do not remember finding anonymous letters there, but the denunciations all came from people who were totally anonymous to me. The only one I knew was my stepmother! But you must understand that there was a history of separation here! My father died in 1944! You already know that I have had nothing at all to do with religion since 1941, nor had my brothers, nor even my sister. Religion was always foreign to our political inclinations, but not to my heart. Like my father, it was always poles apart from our political convictions!

No acquaintance, no neighbor, near or distant, not even the person who swiped my shirts in 1940, during the exodus! No one bore witness against us, not the slightest unfavorable declaration. These people may have had different political orientations than mine, but we never argued. It had to be unknowns who accused me. You can imagine who solicited them! And, to cap it all, they accused my father and my sister at the same time. All this was truly unreal. I had the impression that I was reading the dossier of a stranger. It belonged to a novel, and I had this impression since my arrest. I constantly asked myself if I was dreaming, but the reality of all of the days could not help but prove that wrong every instant!

Another memory comes back to me of which I must speak, for it was rare, even non-existent at this time, to run into the sentiment of compassion regarding us. But we did not ask anyone for the slightest compassion! It would have been unworthy of us. I did not want it at any price. We demanded impartial justice and humane treatment. We found neither – though, in the course of years, the regime moderated its imprisonment; "liberalized" a bit. But this was not uniform in all the camps, as you will see later. I offer you this memory. It was a Christmas Eve and suddenly, the harmony of a musical ensemble reached us from outside! What seemed confusing to us at first, for we were a hundred leagues from expecting such a serenade, quickly proved to be the hymns and music of Christmas that a band and choir of the Salvation Army had come to perform for us outside our prison! One of them, equipped with a megaphone, even addressed a few words to us: "For the benefit of our prisoners, of ALL the prisoners," he or she insisted. I no longer know all the details, but it had to do with peace, with love, with solidarity, with understanding, and with the hope for a prompt liberation. I really think that we were all moved, for all of us fell silent. In any case, I was touched. They were the only ones who made such a gesture toward us in public and in an epoch where everyone submitted to the terror, and nobody dared evince such a sentiment regarding us. This attention, which might seem derisory today, was of such importance for us at that moment that I have never forgotten it. Aside from our families and a few friends, rare in such circumstances, there was, indeed, a group of people who thought of us and proved it publicly. They had to have courage so to do, especially at that epoch. These lines must be considered a witness of gratitude, for, though it may be late, it is no less sincere.

In reality, one or two journalists, and also one or two personalities came to our defense several times, more or less timidly, alas, without great echoes, and without resulting in the slightest amelioration of our conditions of imprisonment. I believe that I have already spoken of this, but I am afraid that I might forget, and that one might believe that I was forgetful!

> And for peace, it would have been necessary that to have been right, repentant and confused, we ask forgiveness.
>
> André Chénier

The Rights of Man

Article 10. Everyone has the right, in complete equality, that his case be heard fairly and publicly by an independent and impartial tribunal, that will decide in accord with his rights and obligations whether there are fit grounds for all accusations in criminal matters of which he is accused.

Article 11. All persons accused of criminal acts are presumed innocent until their guilt has been established in the course of a public trial where all guarantees necessary for his defense have been provided for him. No-one will be condemned for actions or omissions which, at the time they were committed, did not constitute a criminal act according to national or international law. Likewise, no punishment will be inflicted that is more severe than that which was applicable at the time when the criminal act was committed.

Article 12. No-one will be the object of arbitrary interference with his private life, his family or his correspondence, nor of infringements on his honor and reputation. Everyone has the right to the protection of the law against such interference or such infringements.

Article 19. Each individual has the right and the freedom of opinion and of expression, which implies the right not to be persecuted for his opinions and to be able to search for, to receive and to disseminate, without concern for frontiers, the information and the ideas by every method of expression that there is.

Article 20. Everyone has the right to the liberty of peaceful meeting and association. – Nobody is obliged to join an association.

26

The Tribunal

The day comes for me to go to the *Palas de Justice* to appear before my judges. I am invited to appear before them on 6 July, 1946 at precisely 0900 hours. If the appointed hour is punctual, the tribunal is much less so, for it is just before or just after the noon break when I am brought in. I cannot be more precise about this detail. I told my lawyer, whom I have again seen, to say nothing, to make no plea, but he told me that he is obliged to do so. In that case, I told him, say as little as possible and, above all, no regrets! I really do think that my lawyer respects me, precisely because I renounce nothing; that I wish to keep intact the sense of dignity. But let us avoid grandiloquence. I am there, sitting on the "bench of infamy" and I look at the spectacle, this court martial and all of the ceremony that surrounds it. This grand chamber with its paneling that is worthy of better things. The great crucifix, the paintings with truly stupid allegorical figures. Despite all this pomp, these golds and these purples, I simply cannot take all this seriously. So many things seem derisory to me! And all these old gentlemen, with sad faces when they should appear serious. But I see little enough of them, only their finery attracts my attention. In front of me are the lawyers. For the work is like an assembly line. In the room the journalists are on the lookout for victims. They are more numerous than the sparse audience. And there, in the audience, is one of my brothers, free. And also two friends, two sisters. And, suddenly, I also discover one of my old secondary school teachers. Believing, in my naivety, that he has come out of sympathy I nod slightly to him, as I do to those who are dear to me. But his eyes shoot sparks at me, wanting to strike me down! He holds his hand at his throat as if to say, "Someone should cut your throat!" But then I think that he is a "math" teacher, something I was never good at, nor even took seriously. He was a Christian, but never showed it. He showed up at the kill without having taken part in the chase. Bilious, he always had been and never stood for my word-plays in class. But that was his right. I could not, however, suppress a smile, indeed, I laughed openly, for he seemed so ridiculous to me, and he seemed well aware of it.

As for the rest, I was there as a spectator but I looked at the spectacle with detachment, without ostentation, but without hiding my feelings, as if all this was of no concern to me. When my turn came I stood up when I was told to and sat down when I was invited to. The president of the tribunal spoke two or three minutes, the prosecutor 10 minutes, then my lawyer also spoke for two or three minutes. I wanted to speak but I was told to hold my tongue. In less than 20 minutes I was condemned to 20 years of extraordinary imprisonment, though there was nothing extraordinary about it. We were hundreds, several thousand, no doubt, in this case. The terms of this sentence did not move me, no more than all the rest, for I believe that it did not move most of us. I do not say this out of boastfulness. It really was that way for most of my comrades and there are still enough of them living to bear witness. Perhaps I was a little humiliated, I told my lawyer, that I was not condemned to death, but nothing more. That is, in fact, how it went. In a quarter of an hour, 20 minutes, they condemned us, on an assembly line, to 10 years, 20 years. It took hardly more time to condemn for life, or to death, for the duration of the trial or the judgment had no necessary connection to the gravity of the sentence pronounced, except in a few special cases. In one region or another, sometimes even in one chamber or another, in the same judicial district, the same case might result in five years here and 20 years there, in 10 years before one chamber and to life before another!

The judicial system opened more than 500,000 dossiers concerning the "collaboration", and it is no exaggeration to think that, with the families, this concerned no less than a million people! Nevertheless, except for a few timid and sporadic attempts in the past, no more than a few Flemish journalists, bolder than the rest, have recently opened this dossier and revealed what the "purging" was like; that people were condemned in so little time to such severe sentences without the accused even having the right to speak at all, or, in some occasions, so little. Doubtless I shall take the "medias" more seriously when their investigations become less selective and not uniquely aimed at stirring up trouble. They must take a balanced approach. They have, though, fortunately, not all, attempted to consolidate the idea that they had of us, nosing around more in one direction than the other, seeking more for the comfort of a good conscience than to uncover the naked truth. But it takes courage to tell the truth, a great deal, and perseverance, for those who try will find pitfalls on their road, and pressure groups, as for certain television productions which were, at first, purely and simply forbidden, before they could finally be diffused, after being expurgated.

In the matter of justice, the commonly used expression is that a tribunal "renders" justice, but there, we all had the feeling that it "took" it; that the special tribunals [*les tribuneaux d'exception*] confiscated justice! Could one seriously talk of impartial justice? What could this have to do with the allegorical image, there on the wall of the *Palais* that represented justice with her eyes blindfolded? In effect, justice was blind, afflicted with total blindness. In 1946 one did not yet talk of "impaired vision"! In any case, my morale remained the same as it was before my conviction, because I had already come to that decision, well in advance, but also, because I never was able to take this comedy seriously, in spite of my conviction and the whole procession of bitter frustrations that it would yet engender!

I believe that it is useful to comment, at times, on certain developments without simply relating them. Those who will read my account will also know in this manner of the state of mind in which we experienced these adventures, the atmosphere that bathed us and not merely the events.

As I left the room of the *Deuxième Chamber* [Second Chamber] which had just sentenced me, I again saw my friends and my brother for a moment. They had received permission to give me some sandwiches, which I then ate in a cell of the *Palais*, where I was locked up. My conviction had not, in the least, reduced my appetite! At the end of the afternoon the *gendarmes* returned me to the "*Petit Château*" and, when I returned to my room, I was welcomed with the habitual curiosity of my comrades. "*Alors*, how much?"

"*A mort, a mort, a mort!*" ["To death, to death, to death!"] I tell them, humming for fun a tune that was popular on the radio at the time, *Amor, amor, amor*! They laugh heartily, saying to me, "That is what you really wanted." I disabuse them and tell them that I have received 20 years.

Then everyday life resumes and we talk of other things. I am not going to file an appeal, despite the advice of my lawyer. That would be pointless and I want to go to the Beverloo concentration camp as soon as possible where, at least, one is not locked up 24 hours a day between four walls and where one has the benefit of open air, even if behind barbed wire. Once the delay of the appeal is done, one would, in effect, go to a permanent camp at the first opportunity. Faced with the aberrations of our "justice", you will see that I here present together those in particular that perplex me. Even though, "in principle", we were only suspects, we were all confined behind thick walls and the most secure bars of the realm, and as soon as we were sentenced, we were entitled to the open air of the country! Explain this inconsistency to me! We should have benefited from this regime as long as we were or might have been supposed to be innocent!

I remember saying to my comrades at that time that, if we are not freed in a year to 18 months, we would not be freed for at least five years. They must remember it. I must say that there was no basis for this belief, no more than simple intuition. It turned out that most served an average of five years. My brother, the one who was with me, served seven years, a friend did nine, *Major* Hellebaut served 16!

For a moment I thought of escaping from Beverloo, but my brother made me promise not to leave without him. It turned out that his conviction was delayed and he left Beverloo to work in the mine almost immediately after rejoining me there. There was no time for an escape at that point and the project went on the back burner and petered out. That is why neither the prison governor nor any of the guards ever received a "picture postcard" from me.

27

Beverloo

I go to Beverloo in a *gendarmerie* lorry in the first half of September 1946. The camp is located east of the Leopoldsburg commune (Bourg Léopold), as everyone knows. But this presented a problem for our families who came to visit, once a month. It turned out to be beneficial, for this resulted in tightening the bonds, if that was needed, between the families of the prisoners, whether Flemish or French-speaking. These families formed groups to hire taxis together, for the road is long from the railroad station to the camp and, after all, some of the parents are aged. That gave birth to friendships that crossed all community boundaries.

The solidarity and comraderie of the *Waffen-SS*, the solidarity and comraderie of the front and those of adversity succeeded in uniting us fraternally there where the State of Belgium had failed. It was a victory over mediocrity. Since my arrival at Camp E, where all the newcomers went, I feel truly light. Not because the regime there was "liberal", but because there was a world of difference from where I had been. Already there is the air! Nothing but the air. To be able to take a deep breath! What happiness, what pleasure! To see the ground again, the grass, the trees, the forest! I finally see the sun, I will also see the snow, when it comes, and I will again feel the breath of the wind on my face!

I want to present an accurate picture of what life was like at Beverloo. There was also, and it is very important, the opportunity to walk, to move about and to meet so many comrades while moving from one room to another, and also from one block to another. I walked hundreds of kilometers in the camp, talking with one or another, for the entire time of the roughly three years I spent there.

There was the Camp E, where all those who were sentenced for life were grouped, and, among them, a comrade who was actually named Perpète (which is the name that was used to designate those who were sentenced for life) [in perpetuity]. Did his judges want to be ironic? It was also, as I said, the camp that all the new arrivals passed through. Camp F sheltered, if one can put it that way, those who were unable to work, at least in theory. It turned out, as if by chance, that it is there that I go after my sojourn in Camp E.

Camp G was for the workers. Every morning "*commandos*" [working parties] left there, but also a certain number from Camp F, who joined them. They went to demolish other disused buildings of the camp, to clean the bricks, to work at the Schaffen airfield and for yet other tasks. At Camp H was the infirmary, the social service and all the other services of the camp. The entire facility was enclosed by a double barbed-wire fence, four or five meters high and by a collection of watchtowers to command this enclosure, not to forget the searchlights, to better watch over the camp when night fell. When on two or three occasions these searchlights failed for one reason or another, which at least provided the pleasure of causing trouble for the guards, it was found that some prisoners had caused a short-circuit by throwing a chain over the aerial wires which, by its weight, brought the wires together, thus plunging the entire camp into total darkness. Then there was panic in the watchtowers, at least once or twice, and people had to take cover, for the bursts of fire from the watchtowers struck rather at random in the camp. As always, there were, among the guards, some that were thoroughly decent, others who were less so, and one or two that were hooligans, but, in general, they were far superior to the ones I had met hitherto. The chiefs, especially Scheveneels and another whose name I forget, were thoroughly correct and humane, as were some of the guards, too. Were they always like that? I do not know. Obviously I talk of what I saw during the time that I was there.

Those who were the first to return from Germany told me that, at the beginning, it was hell. There were many blows and innumerable cases of mistreatment! Some of the comrades were killed by Belgian soldiers on the road from the railroad station to the camp. If I remember correctly, it was while passing through the artillery camp, and those soldiers threw paving stones that were intended for rebuilding the road at the column of prisoners. Several prisoners were killed and many wounded. However, so far as we know, there were no proceedings, not the slightest sanction against the assailants! It was definitely not done by the guards, and the guards at that time were, possibly, not the same guards as today.

I myself knew a guard, more stupid than nasty. He did not beat people, but tried to pick a quarrel about nothing. We nicknamed him "*Spitsmuis*" (shrew) because his face had that aspect and because he was always sniffing around trying to catch us at fault, whereas the other guards did not waste their time in such infantile behavior. He lived only for that and that was his only function. He was that insignificant.

In 1947 the summer was terribly hot and the nights were suffocating in the overcrowded rooms. We preferred to sleep right on the ground, outside, between the blocks. "*Spitsmuis*" claimed that he would force us to go back into the rooms, while the other guards closed their eyes and let us sleep there. So, one night that "*Spitsmuis*" was on duty, we stretched cords between the blocks, a few centimeters above the ground. Drawn there by the noise, he fell flat, swearing, of course, and got out of there as if he had fire in his ass. That problem, at least, was taken care of! He never again ventured between the blocks at night.

One final little anecdote about "*Spitsmuis*": when the regime of our prison began to loosen up a bit, it became possible to create football and handball teams. The guards were present at the matches and, among them, "*Spitsmuis*". When we saw him arrive at the edge of the field we immediately gathered on both sides of him and began to shout encouragement to the two teams as loudly as we could. To avoid hearing trouble, "*Spitsmuis*" moved, but we followed him around the entire perimeter of the field, always beside him. Finally he left in disgust, but I am not sure that he reported our behavior.

One day, when one of these groups of newcomers arrived, there was some swirling at first, then a real act of violence. Among the "newcomers" was a certain Py., a Fleming, immediately recognized by some of the comrades. He had denounced some of them at the end of the war and those he denounced were immediately arrested. When he was recognized there was a free-for-all and a fight started. Others also recognized him and, in a few minutes, a mob formed. The guards that were present tried to intervene, to protect him. They were soon assisted by others, but in vain. It took a while before they were able to isolate him and protect him from the revenge of his victims. Py. was there, against a wall of the block where the guards' office was located, protected by a cordon of guards. Not only had he been beaten, he was missing a big handful of hair that had been torn out. I saw a window open, right behind the denouncer, and before the guards realized it, a stool, brandished by another prisoner who was inside, crashed down on Py.'s head. It took a squad of *gendarmes* to come and take the man and get him out of range. He left the camp that same day for another destination where, perhaps, he would not be recognized.

There were three or four other informers who suffered the same fate among us: P., B., and C. are the names I recall, and I suppose that about the same thing happened with our Flemish friends. Did those people hope to soften the rigors of justice by their behavior? Isolated somewhere we never saw them again, even after our liberation. In 1990 I learned in the newspaper of the death of one of them, C., at Braine – l'Alleud.

I alternate the memories a bit, as they come to mind, and not necessarily in chronological order. The doctors, dentists, medical orderlies, all the medical personnel were our people – and the prison administration must have got something and made some sort of profit from it. All in all, there were about a dozen doctors and dentists and, I believe, only two were civilian. Actually, 95 percent of the prisoners here were "uniformed personnel" and the remaining 5 percent were former collaborators on the radio, the *INR*. Some of them had only been *légionnaires* and there were also some others who were here for reasons I do not know.

Obviously, there was total agreement between the two linguistic communities, and I believe there were about 60 percent Flemish and 40 percent French-speaking. At Camp E, however, this proportion was reversed among those sentenced for life. I believe that I can say that 70 percent of those sentenced for life were French-speaking and 30 percent Flemish. Apparently pure chance! Did the tribunals in the north of the country and those in the south have a different *"Argus"* [market value guide for used automobiles]? Or did one or the other use the *"Argus"* for an obsolete year? For it is quite evident that all the "Belgians" were, are and always will be equal before the law!

Among my companions were a notary, lawyers, at least one stockbroker, teachers, primary school teachers, comedians, writers, journalists… in brief, all the professions were represented.

To avoid leading a sterile life, courses were soon organized in all the principal branches, but also in other domains, like photography, sketching, and anatomy. All the teachers were prisoners, but not all of the students. Soon our teachers were also teaching guards, at least some of them, no doubt the most talented, and also some of the administrative personnel of the camp!

Do you know of other examples of this sort? At the Nivelles prison the "un-civic" prisoners drew up a charter, with the support of the administration, and this charter is still in effect, and honored, one may say, today. A newspaper has recently spoken of it. And this charter governs the relations between the administration and the prisoners. A charter of good behavior, as it were!

If we had to suffer from hot summers, especially that of 1947, the harsh winters were even worse! During the winter of 1947–48, in this flat land, open to all the winds, we had temperatures of -15 and –20° C [+4 to –4°F]. The doors and windows of the room did not close tightly and, under the door, a space of at least five centimeters allowed the north wind, and the dust too, to enter. The wind left through the space between the roof tiles, our canopy, but the dust remained on our straw mattresses and on our meager possessions.

The water that some of us, with foresight, brought in the evening to wash ourselves froze by morning in the pitchers and buckets, at times to its full depth. We had few clothes and, for the night, only a single, very light cotton cover. We were thus chilled to the bone when, in the morning, we stood at roll call in front of the blocks, where the wait in the glacial wind sometimes took forever, since some of the guards had trouble counting. What with the shortage of food and its increasingly bad quality, we were not prepared to face such a climate!

To heat these rooms, open to all the winds, we had, all in all, one bucket per day and per room of *"schlamm"* – a sort of peat mixed with earth and dust, and a sort of fossil wood! We burned anything that was good to burn: a few old pieces of cardboard found here and there, a few bits of wood brought in by a worker on the *"commandos"* and, indeed, the joists supporting our roof! We really had to. First a morsel here, then there; then a slat, then another; then a rafter, then another… finally one out of two rafters and so on, so that in spring we had a sagging roof!

In Camp F, as in the other camps, we had a medical block. Oh! Totally basic, you can be sure, but a medical block, all the same. There were only a few window panes left in the windows, at the top of the walls, just a reminder as if to indicate where they should have been – which is to say that the wind could gallop through this building of brick and concrete. There were long zinc washbasins with faucets above them. Showers, hot at times, that we could use once a week or once every fortnight. But the number using these showers diminished as the outside temperature dropped, if one can say so, because without window panes there was no great difference [between inside and out]. When it started to freeze, there were only three of us using these showers, and for good reason. The water froze under our feet, on the ground. And, nevertheless, these showers were constantly supplied with water, except, perhaps, for a short period during the greatest cold. But, of these three, out of self-respect and also, a bit, for sanitary concern, nobody wanted to be the first to quit. That is why Pierre V.D.B., 20 years older than me, Marcel H. and I made it to spring without having missed a single glacial shower in the entire winter, except the few days that the showers were closed. We did it to harden ourselves, even if we were only two or three minutes under the water, enough time to moisten ourselves before soaping and then to rinse off.

During this same winter of 1947 when it was so cold, according to rumor some of the comrades of Camp H had to stand for two hours, outside, in front of the barbed wire, their arms in the air! This included invalids, one of whom had a leg amputated. Was that Jules D.V.? The reason? It was Sunday and thus there was no need to go work. The morning roll call was prolonged. They were frozen! Therefore, to warm themselves up as quickly as possible, they got back into bed, under their covers, when they returned from roll call. Nothing more, nothing less.

In 1945, in July, our comrade Van Steenbruggen, *Légionnaire* of 8 August, 1941 – veteran combatant of 1914–18, an old man, arrived at the Beverloo camp, coming from Germany, suffering from acute dysentery. He was placed in isolation in a small room and left in agony for three days, without the slightest care, without being seen by a doctor. At this point our doctors could not yet practice and were not authorized to approach their comrade, nor given any equipment. The sad outcome was death under the eyes of the indifferent prison administration.

In 1945 the administration also separated the "young men", born in 1924 or later, in Camp H. Their families could have ration stamps sent to them for bread. Their families saved these stamps from their own meager rations. The administration noted these stamps to the credit of the benefi-ciary in a ledger. Every now and then, always in the evening, a truck arrived at the camp and distributed old loaves of vile, stale, moldy bread in exchange for these stamps, saved with so much love by the parents who were already so sorely tried.

Aside from what I have seen or experienced myself, I relate only a few facts that have been reported to me by absolutely credible friends, things that they experienced. For, thank God, I have been spared many horrors, but since nobody has spoken of these things aside from programs of the BRT, Flemish television – transmissions interrupted, moreover, doubtless under pressure for reasons of state – I decided that I would include a few, but it is truly very little in light of what actu-ally took place. That was not the purpose of this book; it is why I have not sought out testimony on this subject and why I do not go into this aspect in great detail. As for the rest, it is only the narration of what I, myself, experienced, as I have already said.

And yet! Despite all that we have had to undergo, others more than myself, despite all that I have already said or that I shall yet say, all that has happened and what has not yet been said, all that the television programs that I have just mentioned have shown or been unable to show, there has not, to my knowledge, been any act of vengeance on the part of our people! Is that not admirable? Can our adversaries of yesterday say the same? At least, certain circles!

I must also speak a moment of the visit of a delegation from the Red Cross to this same Beverloo camp where I "resided" at that time. We were informed the evening before, I believe, that a delega-tion of this organization was going to come and "inspect" the camp on that date. And, of course, if we knew it, the prison administration also knew it. And the best proof is that our "buildings and grounds services" had been told to clean the place from top to bottom. It is rather as if the "underworld" was notified by an official circular of an "Operation Blitz" in their quarter!

We knew that this delegation had just arrived and was at Camp H, and it lingered there, doubtless because that camp had been turned into the "shop window" of Beverloo. Since we had wanted to attract the attention of this delegation and, if possible, talk to them since the morning, one or another of us had taken the precaution of throwing a few kilos of yeast into the latrines. Our cooks had it in their stocks. And the reaction was not slow in coming, you can be sure. These latrines "*á la Turque*"[1] were located on a little headland about one meter above the surrounding ground. It was a little round building, like a circus carrousel, but less gay, with a round roof, also. Five or six sort of triangular niches surrounded a central column, without any sort of door, exposed to all the winds.

Then, under the influence of the yeast, the contents of these trenches at first started to simmer, then to bubble and expand. A little later the basins overflowed and the magma, like that of a volcano, spilled over in flows that slowly descended all around the little hillock. I apologize to you for the smell, but it was in a good cause. After maybe an hour the cast-iron covers of the sewage system, weighing 50 kilos and at least 30 meters from the latrines, lifted up like wisps of straw and moved several meters on their own! By their amplitude and, above all, by their odor, nobody anywhere around could fail to note this phenomenon! We were only spared the shaking of the ground. It was at the height of this equally natural "eruption" that we saw the procession of the Red Cross delegation approach in the distance. These ladies and gentlemen, in dashing uniforms, some of them decorated as if with a constellation of stars, passed well clear of (at least 50 meters from) the "crater" and from us, without seeing us, without a glance! But were they unable to see these flows, ignore these odors when, at Camp H, at least 300 meters away, everyone was holding their noses? Yet they ignored it, to go to Camp E, then return and pass by again to go back whence they had come! Nevertheless, there was never a report on this subject, in any case, we never knew of one, and nothing ever changed in the matter of hygiene! For I cannot imagine that, if there had been a report, that the prison administration would have simply ignored it. Like justice, they seemed to be blind, and, moreover, they all also suffered from a total lack of the most elementary sense of smell.

Two words, also, regarding the visits of our families, to which we were entitled once a month. After strenuous efforts, and not without difficulty, I was able to obtain permission for my *fiancée*, after her liberation, to come see me several times at the "*Petit Château*" in Brussels. But here, I had to start all over again. Fortunately, my efforts were successful! The visits lasted for one hour, and we were separated from the visitor by a wire mesh like those that were used for the "tarmacs" at airfields and also by the tables between us. Later, in 1949, or maybe at the end of 1948, there were only the tables. Finally, after three years or three-and-a-half years, we were able to embrace our families, those that were dear to us. It was a revolution, an immeasurable happiness! I believe that I had not embraced my family or others who were dear to my heart since August 1944. Others had been deprived far longer, not having returned home since 1943!

You must imagine, for example, that at St. Gilles or other places, when visited we were separated from our visitors by panes of glass much thicker than a finger and that, moreover, these panes of glass were backed by rows of thick iron bars! And to speak, we had to shout! But here, as well as there, we had to shout to be understood, for there were so many people gathered in the visiting room, and each one hastened to say all that they could, since they would have to wait a month for the next visit. But, at last, we could embrace, even if the time of the embraces was limited and timed!

---

1   Squat toilet.

I believe that I have spoken of the rooms, but not at all of the bugs. Here is a word in their memory. Each room had 10 or 12 beds, wooden bunk beds. And the essence of this wood was, doubtless, the special favorite of the bugs and all the vermin! There were so many! I think that if you listened closely you could hear them march. There were hundreds, maybe thousands in each bed! They came from all of Belgium and, doubtless, from central Europe, with the exception of those at St. Gilles that one had not been able to take along. We did our best, we tried everything, for the prison administration did nothing, attempted nothing. We even took all the beds apart, not without difficulty, with makeshift tools, since we had no others. We passed all the wood, the uprights and the slats, through flame. There were not many slats left, for they had also served as wood for heating in the depths of winter. Two or three had gone that way. Most of the beds had no more than eight or nine boards, spread apart to support the straw mattress.

When all of the wood had been seared in the flame and no bugs or eggs could be found there, we reassembled the beds. But, by the next morning, those that were in the straw mattress had already left their lodgings to "squat" in the lodgings left vacant by our intervention. And others, coming from the ceiling, came to take the place of those that had left our mattresses for the more comfortable lodgings on the beds. In any case, that is how it looked to me. It was evident that there was no way that we could get rid of them, so we better get used to them! Disgusted and tired, I could not even scratch myself more.

When, finally, the regime "liberalized" and the camp authorities allowed a bit more varied packages, we had pudding, *crêpes* or soup in tins or small bags. We invented what we called the *"Gazogène"*. We made these of metal jam tins of various sizes that we got from the kitchen which we fitted together after having punched holes in their sides. These "furnaces" were very well conceived to be fueled by pellets of paper or a few twigs, and to consume these very sparingly, since we had nothing else to burn. In summer we did not receive combustibles for the stoves, and in winter there was far too little *"schlamm"*. Furthermore, how could all 20 to 24 of us cook on the minuscule official heating stove?

While we are at it, I shall explain, a bit, why I was here in Camp F rather than in another. It is also a way to see other facets of life in camp, to enter our privacy. A few days after my arrival at Beverloo, at Camp E, we were visited by an administration doctor, perhaps a doctor of the mines? He came to certify the health and aptitude of the "new arrivals" to work in the coal mines, as needed, or in the *"commandos"*, the work parties doing the camp work. I showed him my wounds and my remarks left him in no doubt as to my desire to work in the present conditions. I was declared unfit for work, for work in the mine.

When a few days later the chief of the Camp E guards asked me what work I was able to do I answered quite frankly, none. And that no matter what work, I was not going to help support the prison administration and thus permit them to keep me indefinitely while pocketing my "wages", which were for them a source of income. He did not take it badly and the chief, Scheveneels, sent me to Camp F. There, knowing my state of mind, I was made *"chef de chambre"* [room chief] at the room of the *"Blokchef"*, the chief of the block, as you will understand.

He, Jef C., a former local primary school teacher, took me in as room chief. The assistant *"Blokchef"*, Fons, from Merksem, also lived there. My role here was to clean and maintain the room, and also to go to the kitchen and bring the meals back for all the prisoners in the block, with the help of two other prisoners. Since the *"Blokchef"* and his assistant were perfectly willing to clean the room, I let them do it, especially since they were used to so doing before my arrival. But I made it my business to feed my block, and I never failed to do so. Thus it is that all those who knew me at Camp F can confirm exactly what I am going to say. As a reminder, here is my identification: registration number 35525 – Camp F – Block 52 – Room 1, *CIB*, Beverloo.

A social service, composed of prisoners, was set up. Acting timidly at first, increasing in importance as time passed, it became extremely active, and also very effective, finally disposing of ample means through the good will and work of the prisoners. These, of all professions, worked there and constructed all sorts of things. There were tailors, and I had them make a suit, and also a pair of shoes, sewn by hand.

People worked in wood, and I had them make a casket. They also worked with aluminum and plexiglass for all sorts of finery, necklaces and chain bracelets. And the plexiglass was worked with inlays of flowers or other motifs. This plexiglass and aluminum were taken from the wrecked airplanes by our work parties that left the camp. There was everything; we even made furniture. Everything was sold for the benefit of the social service, which helped the poorest. The prison governor, the guards, and many other people outside thus bought these things, usually for a bit of bread, which they would not otherwise have been able to allow without our social service.

There was also our printing press, which was in Camp H. The administration increasingly trusted the prisoners, and benefited by so doing. It never had any sort of problem with the prisoners, who were better treated and extremely busy with their activities. We were able to create our own newspaper, Le Patrimoine [The Heritage] at first, then Le Journal sans titre [The Newspaper with no name]. The whole thing was written and printed by our comrades. But members of the administration and guards also came there. And all the "menus", visiting cards and other things that were printed there were at the expense of the princess and were destined entirely for her personal use. There were also those who wanted "favors", outside their official capacities. We did not mind doing this, since it also helped us.

We also had our "Journal mural" [Wall inscriptions], before knowing that the Chinese had or would have theirs. And, finally, we also had our theatrical troupe and our orchestra. Everything, absolutely everything, was paid for by proceeds from our social service or furnished by the families of the prisoners. The costumes and sets were created here, the musical instruments, donated by the families. Our orchestra, like the theatrical troupe, could well compete with other orchestras or other theaters. Besides, we had professionals among us. Moreover, I remember that one day, at Merksplas, a great comedian of a Brussels theater, cousin of an uncle of a prisoner, came to present and to play "Cyrano", in collaboration (one more time) with our own troupe. He was not disappointed and did not fail to congratulate the comedians for their presentation.

But, to get to this point it took years of rotting away and suffering indignities – and in our flesh! It required certain men or certain women, more open than others, to finally comprehend and admit that they were dealing with prisoners who, for the most part, were worthy people of quality, and not the criminals or the delinquents such as they had tried to depict us. It will suffice to remember in what inhumane conditions we were forced to live for years and to know that, today, the prisoners like us were teaching courses, to say nothing of lessons, to our guards and to others of the prison administration! What a road we had traversed!

I shall now recount in a few lines certain escapes of which I know a few details. I think of a comrade Légionnaire C., who disappeared one day from a "commando" where he was working. He went to Spain and later returned to us here, after long months of vacations, and also a stay at the Miranda camp,[2] where, among others, he met our comrade, Franz Ch. There was our dentist, R. Leheune, who got out one night through the sewers, and had made himself a mask for so doing. He preferred to arrange his escape himself and later wrote me from Venezuela. I also remember a nice big man, very placid, a bit older than myself. He had been a math teacher as a civilian. His name

2   From 1940 to 1947 the Miranda de Ebro Camp was the central camp in Spain for foreign prisoners – including prisoners from the time of the Spanish Civil Car, illegal male border-crossers and German military personnel and German collaborators interned in the so-called 'Campo Aleman'.

escapes me. I was amazed, and we were all amazed, at his escape, for he seemed resigned, maybe even timid. Which shows that we should never judge by appearances, but you already know that. One day he mingled with a "*commando*", which he joined. He disappeared and never returned. There was also Luyckx, a Flemish comrade whom I may have already mentioned. He shared the same name as the prison governor. He worked in the camp wood shop. He went to deliver furniture in Brussels with a camp lorry. He left the guard who went with him and the lorry standing there. He later wrote from Ireland, where he had established a factory producing furniture or toys.

And I shall relate one last case that amused us greatly. Kennis was a violinist and played in our orchestra. He was especially small, nearly stunted, with curly blond hair. I give these details to remind those who knew him. He had slender hands, the hands of a violinist. Timid, unassuming, but above all apparently timid! He too mingled one day with a "*commando*" from Camp G and disappeared without leaving a trace. And he too was never seen again. Right after his absence was discovered at roll call, we saw the guards disperse through the camp and ask everywhere, "*Hebt U Kennis niet gezien?*" ["Have you seen Kennis?"] For, doubtless, they could not imagine that Kennis had actually escaped! Nevertheless, Kennis had well and truly escaped and I must say that each of us rejoiced in each escape. For at least two days, all around the camp, we heard the guards ask the same pointed question, "Have you seen Kennis?" We ended up by moaning along with them. For the next two or three days, every time we met a guard, especially "*Spitsmuis*", each of us in our turn would ask him, "*Hebt U Kennis niet gezien?*" I do not need to describe the guard's face at that moment!

The governor of the Beverloo camp left us one day, with neither he nor we asking or expecting it. He died, drowned while swimming. All, or most of us, regretted the loss, despite his initial misguided ways before he learned to know us. I think that he must have been the only governor of a prison or camp who received the respect of his prisoners. There was a wreath of flowers at his funeral, and a delegation of prisoners was present!

Since the beginning of 1949 rumors circulated regarding the abandonment of Camp Beverloo. The camp would be closed. It seemed that it was to be demolished. But we had already commenced that to keep warm, as you will recall. Just between us, it would be neither long nor difficult, for the barracks only remained standing out of habit. For us that would be a hard blow, for where would we rot away now? Here, in the open air, we no longer felt that we were "imprisoned"! Moreover, the prisoners had, on their own, even if with the approval of the governor, accomplished excellent things. I shall tell you of it for a moment, so that you will know it all, if you were not there. The social service, by its action, had gathered substantial means and had also convinced the governor and the administration of the utility of its action and of the soundness of all the proposals that it had submitted. Thus it was that the construction of a swimming pool was proposed, developed and accomplished – entirely by the efforts and means of the prisoners! It was not a heated pool, nor was it Olympic, but, all the same, it was approximately 20 meters long and six meters wide. It could not be heated, for our very rooms were practically unheated during the winter. It was built at Camp E and each camp could go there in turn.

The men of Camp G worked on it, as did those of Camp H. There was room at the pool in the afternoon. I told myself that it was better to swim than to stroll in my corner, and, furthermore, I love swimming. Even before that I had developed the habit of circulating from one camp to another for some time to go see my friends. At first I had to make use of a variety of tricks, but the guards soon became accustomed to seeing me go from one camp to another. In order to do that, one had to have a permit, which I did not have. A number of my comrades were constantly amazed at the facility with which I went here and there without any special authorization other than habit. That made it possible for me to go nearly every day in the afternoon to the swimming pool, at least when it was open, for in winter it was obviously out of the question.

I must also make a last report concerning our comrades who worked in the mines, which was told to me by an excellent friend, wholly worthy of confidence, for the good things that happened here do nothing to deny the fact that there were also the worst! My comrade, Robert H., worked in the coal mines at Eisden. In accord with the time of the shift changes where he worked, by day or by night, he got up at 0400 hours in the morning for the morning shift and left with his comrades on a little train for the mine pits. These men who lacked the most elementary nutrition, especially for such hard labor in the depths of the mine, thus found themselves already in the depths of the mine before the civilians, who received hard-labor rations. In addition, and this was current usage, the miners, whether voluntary or forced, were beaten, struck with the copper miners' lamps. Once the work was ended, it is obvious that the civilians were the first to go back to the surface, leaving ours to wait in the galleries. Thus it was that they often spent up to 10 consecutive hours every day, or even a bit more, in the depths of the mine!

When our comrades finally returned to the light of day they then had to wait upon the good will of the Belgian soldiers to take them back to their camp. And, to get back to camp they then had to walk the dozen kilometers on foot! After such hard labor to then have to walk 10 kilometers on foot! It was often 16 hours or even more before they finally got back to their barracks! They were truly so tired that they no longer had the strength nor desire to fix something to eat! Fortunately, there were sympathetic comrades who looked after feeding them.

These hundreds of young prisoners and the German prisoners, who were also forced to work in our mines, definitely contributed more than a little to the economic restoration of the country. One or another "personality" should well remember that! And, despite all that, those responsible closed their eyes, having no right to do so, when, in the mine, for no rhyme or reason, these workers were struck at times with lamps or pickaxe handles! Moreover, though they were not needed, the guards were accompanied with sheepdogs to keep these exploited, famished and weakened boys on the right road. What right road?

There were also, always, I am told, though I was not there myself, other "civilian" or non-prisoner miners who were humane with the prisoners and, in the same way, friendly.

Several volumes could be written on all these bad treatments and also on the crimes. But that is not relevant for me and I end the subject here.

28

The Merksplas Colony

What was meant to happen happened! On 5 July, 1949 I am transferred to Merksplas. Immediately I find myself nearly plunged into the middle ages! We arrive in the evening and we are lodged in the attics, in dormitories. The next day we report in turn to the prison governor. He is right out of a Dickens novel, or some other pessimistic novel! He is the sort of governor one ought to meet in the prisons of 150 years ago! One could judge him by the style of his clothes or by his mentality. He wants me to promise and even sign a document, if I remember correctly, saying that I will not escape! Curious! Do they trust our word or signature? I am already sick of Merksplas and reply to him that I cannot promise anything; that today, I do not think of escaping, but that I cannot promise anything for tomorrow. He immediately sends me to reflect in the dungeon. Decidedly, I am no longer at Beverloo! As if my day was not already bad enough, I arrive at the dungeon and I see a crucifix. I take it off the wall and hand it to the guard, telling him that I want to be alone. At first he gets angry, but I do not back off. He wants to put it back, but I prevent him by standing in front of the nail. After several attempts he calms down, telling me that he is going to have problems with me, after first saying that I would be the one having problems with him. Me, I told him that I was used to them. He becomes almost kind, to the point where I nearly give in. But I get a hold of myself and tell him to put it away until I leave the cell. That is what he finally does. He has to say to himself that the people from Beverloo were revolutionaries!

The next day I am brought back to the prison governor and since I have not changed my attitude, I return to my cell, my dungeon, where they have already replaced the crucifix. The guard must have thought that I would not return to it. He takes it down on his own and I remain there three more days and three nights. Three days of dry bread, water and a foul gruel. The fourth day, where would they take me? Why, to the prison governor, of course! I already know the way. He tells me that I will go to "*l'herstel*" [repair]! For a moment I think this is a joke, but only for a moment, for the prison governor does not really have the air of one who makes jokes. But perhaps I did not really understand. But no, I understood perfectly, and half an hour later I find myself in a sewing room – the "repair"! The prison governor had told me that I would not escape from there. There I find Paul R. and Gérard D., along with other comrades. Happily the "chief" who guards us has a sense of humor, at least with us, for silence is the rule, as at St. Gilles four years ago and the prison governor here resembles the one there like a Siamese twin, at least in his appearance and in his ideas on running a concentration camp. But Gérard and I chat throughout the day as good neighbors. And the chief is amused by it because we make him laugh. That was not the case with my comrade Paul, who changes place, perhaps to avoid punishment? But I follow him on the other bench.

I arrive in this workshop on 9 July, 1949. I am given a jacket of unbleached canvas, like the ones we are supposed to wear when we move around here or to go on a visit. It has a tear and is missing two or three buttons. I work very conscientiously, then, just as conscientiously, I cut off the buttons and tear apart the rip I have just repaired. Then I start over again and do the work again, just as conscientiously, only to undo it again. The chief sees nothing or acts as if he doesn't… Gérard and I openly have a good laugh. Paul tries to hide his laughter. Thus it is that, on 24 August, 1949 after 47 days in the sewing workshop, I return to the guard the same jacket, a bit crumpled, it is true, without buttons but with the tear! And he says, very kindly, *"Au revoir – tot genoegen, Au plaisir."* ["Farewell, See you again."] But I would not return there, though I wasn't really sure of it on 24 August, 1949.

When I left my dungeon cell I rejoined my comrades and adopted, if one may say so, the life and the routine of the concentration camp in the Campine, near Turnhout. When I leave the dormitory in the morning I go into the wash room with the others to do my ablutions. The showers are only available once every week, or every fortnight, I do not remember more exactly. I find myself before an enameled cast-iron basin and I start to take my clothes off. I have not yet placed my briefs on my other clothes when two guards jump on me, shouting and gesticulating, making me cover my nudity! I learn that here, aside from the showers, we are not allowed to wash more than the hands, the face, the feet, if necessary the torso, but nothing more! At Beverloo, to say nothing of our customary showers under cold water, we took hot showers in common and, when I say in common, that is to say that we took them in groups of 40 or 50 men, and stark naked! None of that hanky-panky here, it is out of the question, at least there was no such question until the arrival of a group as important as ours, coming from Beverloo.

The next day we are already five or six doing as I did the day before. The guards intervene, but there are not enough of them to be effective. The next day there are more than 20 of us washing entirely, and the guards can yell all they want, but nothing changes and their recriminations die down! After that they can only acquiesce. The arrival of such a great number of determined prisoners, coming from Beverloo, where they have benefited from a certain "freedom", has contributed to changing the customs and outmoded regulations here, doubtless dating from the past century, from the creation of the center. Faced with the risk of provoking revolts, the administration has indeed been forced and constrained to put some wine in its holy water!

It is true that, on arriving here, we all felt the weight of the prudishness and influence of an old-fashioned clergy like a burdensome screed. We learned in confidence from one or another guard that it was not good for them to miss mass or to put their children in lay schools. They are well watched over and chaperoned, the more so since, for the most part, they live in what we call "the colony" – and it could not be better named! It is, in effect, the colony of Merksplas, as it has always been known by that designation.

Aside from the time that we spend in our "sewing workshop" (we are the little hands there), we have, for our amusement, reading, ping-pong and a bit of basketball. It is always that. With one or two exceptions the guards are correct, sometimes even understanding, but they have not always been that way, the "old-timers" tell me. These "old-timers" also tell me that, in the few weeks since our arrival, everything has gotten better for them!

I was going to forget it, but I must say it to be objective, that I and my comrades too have had the right to go to two, maybe even three cinema performances during my stay here. And on the same occasion, I remember that at Beverloo too we had cinema shows, but there it was not surprising, and it took time to get there. At Merksplas I was also entitled to two or three visits from my *fiancée*, though not without several humiliating appeals to the prison governor. There was no other way for all of the convicts that we were to "redeem" ourselves other than in the sewing shop. That was the term that we heard *ad nauseam*. We were supposed to "redeem" ourselves! That is also a term used by "the media". For economic reasons the condemned have to do it, for their fortune, and that suffices for the state, which has taken such good care of them without asking anything in return. And we, we have the sewing! But those who have, probably, promised not to escape from Merksplas have the additional choice between making bricks, working in the field, the cardboard factory and no doubt one or two additional occupations, but each one assuredly more worthwhile, more enriching than the other.

In our free time the sports or other distractions take place within the four walls of the courtyard of Pavilion B – in any case, for those of that pavilion. As I reread my correspondence from that period I find my "identity": Prisoner No. 45, Cell 50. That was, if I may say, during my "isolation". Then, always the same: No. 45, but Room 283 of Pavilion B. On 5 July, 1949 – the day of my arrival here – I was already writing that everything was quite satisfactorily clean there. It is true that with the censor, we could not write anything we pleased. Our letter would not pass [the censor] and we had to reassure our families. But whatever I wrote was how it was, always compared with all that I had known since I was first arrested. But I was not quibbling about that subject. It was clean. I also wrote that I greatly missed the open air and the swimming pool. What more could we say in letters that we knew would be censored?

I was entitled to write one 25-line letter on special paper every week and I was also entitled to a "medical" package. I could also receive a visit every fortnight. It was still a problem for the families to travel so far, for Merksplas was not just around the corner from the far points in Wallonia and Flanders, for our Flemish comrades. Few people, at this time, had automobiles, and our families less than others. It took hours of travel by train, bus and streetcar to get one small hour of visit and then as much to return. As I reread these old yellowed letters I also discovered, to my astonishment, that at Beverloo we were only entitled to write one letter a month, but that on the other hand, we had many ways to get letters out illegally there. My first authorized letter is dated 7 August, 1946 from the "*Petit Château*". I had to wait 15 months! Fifteen long months from the date of my incarceration to send her a single word – and that was also the day after her first visit. With time, everything becomes blurred, even the worst miseries! In rereading all these old letters the details come back!

As I leaf through these letters, even I have to admit that things that seemed so important at the time seem laughable today, and especially to me. But I am the one who lived through them and I remember that even though I wrote them, even with a bit of humor, that our distress was truly profound, even though we did not want to admit it to ourselves, especially not to ourselves, and that, in addition, we did not want our families to lose confidence! Indeed, at times, we had to encourage them! But happily our families had courage and in my case my betrothed had to wait eight years after our engagement for me to be with her again! I maintained a discreet but eloquent homage for the well-being of my *fiancée* for fear of offending her modesty.

Happily I found other good comrades at Merksplas and, to my great astonishment, a very good friend of my parents, a former neighbor from the time when we still lived in Antwerp, a stockbroker.

The Merksplas episode comes to an end, for I have obtained my transfer to the "*Petit Château*", both to escape this depressing atmosphere at Merksplas, and also to spare my *fiancée* the long and costly trips. It must be kept in mind that I depended entirely on her and also to a certain degree on my older brother, who was freed at this moment. I have not forgotten him! I must say so. Neither have I forgotten that whenever he could, my other brother sent me food from the mine where he worked! This, too, I must say.

Finally, on 25 August, 1949 I leave the "colony" to go back to Brussels, but it is not as far as Kinshasa[1] is from Brussels.

---

1   Kinshasa is the capital and largest city of what was, at that time, the Belgian Congo.

Shadow, Freedom, Rebirth

So I return to the *"Petit Château"* – Registration No. 1003. I have had numbers, and I have also known them. I live in Pavilion C, Room 331 and not in a blue room or pink room, as is the custom for the guests in these *châteaux*, whether they are small or grand. Two or three days later I am transferred to Room 86 in the *"CROP"*. I no longer remember the origin of the acronym, but it is the school pavilion. In fact, I requested to come here, to the decoration section. In addition to this branch it is also possible to take courses in watchmaking, sketching, painting, sculpture, music and several other areas. We also have here several masters in these areas, renowned orchestra conductors, musicians, painters, sculptors, and also teachers and elementary school teachers.

There are our rooms, the shops and the classrooms, where we circulate freely, but we only get to be out in the air, on the promenade, one half-hour a day. That is the hardest thing, we are again behind bars! In one of my letters, dated 11 November, 1949 I say that my brother has left the mine where he was working and has just arrived here too at the *"Petit Château"*. However, since he had been sentenced to life, he is not permitted to come and take the courses at *"CROP"*. Prisoners with long sentences have to continue to rot away, despite three years working in the depths of the mine! Of the 15 letters from this period, nine carry the censor's stamp and six got out by other routes, at the price of a thousand tricks.

As I leaf through them I come across so many other memories in these old and touching archives. I have to consult them to retrieve certain details and precise dates. And also I have a little oak casket, unfinished, because my friend, K. Snel [similar to the German word *'schnell'*, or 'fast'], was the slowest workman in all Beverloo; but also, above all, an excellent comrade as well as an excellent cabinet-maker. May he forgive me for saying so today, but I have waited 45 years to say it! It is true that if I had told him so at the time, he would not have undertaken the work. To reassure him, he has always held my highest esteem.

The days, weeks and months thus pass by in monotonous fashion but, all the same, there is a day, two days to be precise, that there is "open house" at *"CROP"*. But, do not misunderstand me: the "open house" is not for everyone. It is only to allow our families to come, admire, and also buy the works or creations of the school. This is the occasion for us to walk here, hand in hand with a cherished being, even to take her by the shoulders, since most of the time the cherished being is above all and, obviously, of the opposite sex. It is possible for an instant, discreetly, to hold her waist, but stop there! No farther. It is however tremendous, after four-and-a-half years of captivity and nearly six years since our last kiss! And yet, she held up and I too, but how could I have done otherwise? It is she who deserves all of the credit. Regarding these days of "open house", I remember one painful scene where I was and wish to remain a discreet witness. That is why I am not even giving the initials of this companion of misfortune, simply to avoid confusing him with another. I can say that he was a *fourrier* [quartermaster sergeant]. Like us, he received a visit. It was his mother. It is true that she was not a fashion model, nor a winner of the *"Prix d'élégance"*, but she was his mother. She was no more than 20 years old when she brought him into the world! And he, apparently ashamed of his mother, doubtless compared with the others, he walked some distance from his mother, though no one would have prevented him from taking her arm, or even of taking her in his arms! As for me, I was ashamed of him and could not forget the thing, even so many years later and also his conduct was an outrage against his mother. I said it. But I must say it, because it shocked me terribly, I could not keep silent. Doubtless in such a closed society these things affect one more than elsewhere, but for him, he still had his mother and she came to see him!

Another day a poster announces an upcoming lecture, "Léopold II and the Belgian Congo", by G. Rhodius, a former member of the resistance. I was thrilled. G. Rhodius had in fact been an excellent friend of my parents, of the entire family. A long-time friend, also. They were known "in the colonies", but not in that of Merksplas! And he had never lost touch, nor had I ever forgot him. He was a member of the resistance, but not one of those of "the final hour". He gathered "intelligence", but not murders. He had as much right to his ideas as I did to mine, and that did not prevent us from respecting each other. He had never said anything that was even slightly negative about me to my father. He was not one of those who killed our people, the women, the children, the parents of the *légionnaires* or the old people, nor those who glorified themselves by going 10 at a time, armed to the teeth, but after the departure of the last German soldier, to arrest a child because he had been a member of the *Jeunesse* [the Rexist youth movement]!

I was happy to find an occasion to see him again, an unhoped for occasion. Without that, I would never have thought of speaking to him, not knowing where to find him, but also from a sort of pride. As it was, I was meeting him by chance and thus had no reason not to present myself to him. I knew that I would not embarrass him. On the day of the lecture I succeeded in finding a place on a bench directly adjoining the central aisle of the room. When the lecture ended, accompanied by the prison governor and his suite, the lecturer walked down the aisle toward the exit. To avoid being nabbed by a zealous guard I waited until G. Rhodius was only five or six paces away from me. Then I got up and took a step or two in his direction. He and his companions stopped then, a bit astonished, doubtless asking himself what I wanted of them. I immediately presented myself to G. Rhodius. A moment of stupefaction and he took me in his arms, by the shoulders! Now it was the turn for his companions to be stupefied and incredulous! The first gesture of the prison governor, when he saw me advance, was to push me aside. In addition to the governor and the assistant governor of our "establishment" there was Councilor Hanssen and other members of the *SRRT*, of *Service de rééducation, de reclassement et de tutelle* [Service of re-education, reclassification and supervision]. Behind me was another prisoner who had also known the lecturer in Africa and who also hoped to talk to him.

Monsieur Rhodius recognized me, but not at first sight. As for myself, I had not seen him since 1939! He was surprised to meet me by such a random chance, but he knew of my political orientation and my enlistment. Modesty prevents me from repeating all the good things that he said to the prison governor about my family and myself, but all his entourage heard that. He then told me that he was going to write to me, that he would take responsibility for all that, that he would be my legal guardian [*tuteur*], if I so desired, for in order to get out we had to have a *tuteur*, just as aged people needed a walking stick, or young tomato plants required a support.! As a result, the governors and their entourage showed me a certain deference, they even addressed me as "*Monsieur*"! It had been years since anyone had given me this title, for here, "*Monsieur*" was a title!

About five weeks later the governor informed me that I would be liberated in the afternoon! It was 11 March, 1950 after five years of captivity – 1,758 days of detention, as stated in my *livret de liberation conditionelle* [conditional release booklet], which I was supposed to turn in, but which I kept as a souvenir. It was the "*CROP*" secretary, Gevaert, another prisoner, who came to tell me. It was indeed the first time that a "liberation" gave me such pleasure! Other, obviously, than that of my comrades.

You can believe me or not, once the first moments of joy passed, I was taken by remorse and told the secretary that I would not leave without my brother, and that he should say this to the prison governor! I do believe that Freddy J. was with me at that moment. I went to hide in my room. Then, certain that they would come to get me there, I went into the toilets. They called for me a bit in the corridors; then they came there where they could easily see my feet under the door. I realized the futility of this behavior and asked to see my brother, whom they brought. He was in another pavilion, but I was able to see him for a moment. Then I was taken willy-nilly to the door. I do not believe that I really thought I could succeed, but it was, indeed, the only moment where I volunteered to remain here. The administration remained opposed right to the end!

I have no doubt at all that it was only thanks to my encounter with G. Rhodius that I was freed that day, but I cannot ignore nor keep silent regarding the efforts that my lawyer, Paul Berton, made for me and that also contributed to my liberation. All that he did for me he did *"Pro Deo"*, and I found in him a noble-hearted man, a truly fine man, quite simply. My readers must know that there was no moral in my liberation. You may well say that I am difficult! I can expect no more, nor less. Oh, if only justice had, for my spiritual tranquility, to "restore" my confidence in her, if only justice had freed me on the basis of other criteria than those of my relations, as honest, as well known, as respectable or eminent as they might have been! Other comrades, luckier, but neither more nor less guilty than I, had been free for a year, for two years, and others, no different, would still remain there for a long time!

My sentence was to have been reviewed for the first time at 15 years. A few months prior to my release G. Rhodius first had it reduced to 12 years but then had me liberated immediately! At the start of the afternoon I find myself, in less than a minute, on the other side of the last grill and heavy door of the *"Petit Château"*! The doors of prisons are always heavy. I am there, on the sidewalk of the prison and I suddenly feel as if I am breathing a different air than on the other side of this door. I have not had the slightest sip of alcohol in five years or more, and I am intoxicated simply by breathing!

Many of my comrades, who still remain behind bars, have charged me with a great many "commissions", with so many messages that I will have a hard time seeing all these families in fulfilling all these requests! I have to immediately and before all else set to work without delay, after so many sterile years of inactivity. To prove to the others, but especially to ourselves, that we are men of quality, for the administration did not let us go so quickly, under the pressure of certain circles. It is true that I am at liberty, and that is what is essential, but it is liberty under surveillance, and that will not be over for some time!

My definitive liberation does not take place until 1966! 18 May, to be precise. Sixteen years and two months later. Some have told me, but I have no way of proving it, that this was yet another of those perfidies regarding us. When I was freed two months before fulfilling five years of the 12 that remained for me to do, this trick allowed them to thereby prolong the time of my probation by several more years. But I have no concern with all that, for I do not envision myself becoming a terrorist, vandalizing benches, or even violating the laws, let alone women and children, as doubt-less those hope who remain on the lookout for the least of our escapades.

But the most perfidious invention to contribute to our loss was the creation of the *"certificat de civisme"* [certificate of good citizenship]![1] For to find employment, one had to show one's credentials, which is to say, one had to be able to present a *"certificat de civisme"* in addition to a certificate of good living and morals. Some businesses voluntarily dispensed with the latter, but not the first. By preventing former prisoners from finding work, and the administration could not be ignorant

---

1   See previous footnote on *'Certificat de Civism'* instituted during the French Revolution.

of the fact, it forced them into crime! What would certain associations say today if one did the same for murderers, thieves and rapists? What would these good souls say? But I doubt if they would raise the slightest protest for people like us! Do you know that tens of thousands of us were confronted with this problem of the *"certificat de civisme"*? Nevertheless, do you know how many sank into a life of crime? Even though everything had been done to produce this result! In fact, there were not many.

Don't tell me that this was necessary to prevent us from entering public administration? The prospective employers would have every means of knowing our past without the necessity of our presenting them with this certificate. And don't tell me either, that after a certain point in time, the certificates that were meant to serve in search of a job no longer stated all the details. It was only much later that this measure took effect, after we had already been at work for a long time. But an employer only had to telephone one or another service for an obliging soul to provide information. Some had to buy false documents for a high price, but they had to do this in self-defense!

Some, when applying for a job, immediately informed the employer of their situation, as I did. Or else they happened upon a dishonest man, a profiteer, quite happy at the windfall, and they earned only half the salary that another would be paid for the same work, but often worked with more zeal and efficiency. I have experienced that, but that employer did not profit from me for long. And there were also those who happened, quite simply, upon an employer who was, above all, concerned with hiring capable people who were efficient and courageous. And those employers never had to regret what they did. It is indeed true that there were firms that asked these new employees to bring in their comrades and gave priority in hiring to our people! And I am not speaking of just one isolated firm.

It is necessary to tell these truths that nobody seems to know of except those who suffered from them. Nobody has ever told this. If others remember, they are silent about it, not out of modesty or shame, but for want of opportunity. And thus people continue to say the worst lies and rubbish about us. If we do not speak of it, who else will do so in our place? There is so much yet to say on this subject, but I shall not go on in order to avoid tiring my readers.

Epilogue

Obviously it would be presumptuous of me to assert that everything would have been perfect if the outcome of the war had been in our favor, if we had won the war. But we are not necessarily wrong because we lost the war!

If nobody could say, today, that it would have been "Eden", neither can anyone claim that it would have been hell or worse than it is today if we had won the victory. And I deny anyone the right to assert that our good faith was not total for the majority of us. And nobody ought to deny our good intentions and claim, as some have done, though rarely, it is true, that the *légionnaires* left for the Eastern Front for love of money. That is truly stupid, evidence of such bad faith that it can safely be ignored. Who would believe it? As if there were 16-, 18- or 20-year-olds, or even older, who were crazy enough to go to get themselves killed on the Eastern Front for one DM per day (at the time, 12 F 50), if they were not motivated by higher sentiments. Those who make such assertions must, themselves, be stirred by sentiments equally base, must have such a vile conscience!

Neither did we dream of establishing a new order as quickly as possible, a better order, more socially responsible. We all did everything we could, and "paid very dearly" with our sweat, with our blood and, many, with their lives, to succeed. And then, I absolutely contest the right of all those who did nothing, those who were not born or who did not experience it and, today, want to hold forth. I contest their right to judge us. In any case, I consider that they count for nothing. For they have often, and with great complacency, demonstrated their bias in looking no farther than or publishing nothing but documents that support their theses *a priori* and in painstakingly and systematically suppressing all that might largely re-establish the truth and, in so doing, deny their lying affirmations! This, one knows, is disinformation!

But I may also affirm another thing, and for the men of action that we were, these are not empty words. If the order that would have been established after the victory of our arms did not conform to what we had wished, if it did not measure up to the agreed sacrifices, we would have been resolute enough to make it known and to react with just as much determination as we had put into fighting. And, quite simply, in this eventuality the struggle would have continued! The possibility cannot be excluded that, in this eventuality, we would also have ended up in prison, this time for refusing to collaborate with the new regime that we found to be no more suitable than the one we had tried to change. And then, for certain, we would have been shouted down by the same populace as we were in 1944 and 1945, condemned perhaps by the same "historians" and politicians who judged and condemned us after the "liberation". And, possibly, it would have been the same judges who would have pronounced the same sentences. Why not? Based on these same laws, all also retroactive, tampered with for the needs of the cause as the laws had been "modified" (shameful words) in London in 1943. Perhaps we would also have had the same guards to mistreat us.

For it is true that the multitude always runs after the victory! And the true members of the resistance will not contradict me in this, having themselves been submerged by this emergence in 1944 and 1945 of this multitude that waited to jump to the winning side and profit, no matter who won the victory! And if we had won the victory ourselves, there is no doubt that we would have had a hard time avoiding being surpassed by the zeal of this same mob, avid, this time to "collaborate," to prove their fervid loyalty to the new regime that we would have established!

Behold the unchained masses, since the regimes of the countries of central Europe – and not of the East, as some journalistic ignoramuses abusively say – have been liquidated and that these people have been liberated from the communist yoke! From reading the press and watching television one would think, if one was not well informed, that the West, that our "media", had been the artisans; that this was their victory! Whereas it was these populations themselves that achieved the victory with their bare hands. Because the West had ignored them until then! It was normal for us to rejoice. We never wanted anything else. We had wanted to preserve Europe from communism. But it is astounding that our democracies of the West also rejoice! For our memory is not short, and we have not forgotten that even though all the countries of the West were not consulted, nor invited by their "big brother" the USSR, nor for that matter by their other "great allies" to give their opinion or to sign the Yalta Accords in 1945 or the subsequent ones at Potsdam; all of them at that time rejoiced in the partition of Germany and applauded the accords as they then later applauded the collapse of those same accords and of their former ally! Did they really, then, need 45 or even 50 years to see clearly? There is, indeed, flagrant proof of their inconsistency.

Logic would have required that they react to the contrary with the greatest firmness to maintain these accords and demand their application. Or, then, they should have, at the very least, rehabilitated our thesis!

Apropos, have you noticed, as I have, and is it not curious that the more events have proven us right, the more difficulty our detractors have in proving that we were wrong? As for myself, in any case I feel very comfortable in my skin, but I understand that the others are afflicted with an imperious need to scratch!…

Appendix I

Additional Illustrations

vieux moujick – race tatar. 13 août 42

A sketch of John Hagemans less than 15 days prior to his death.

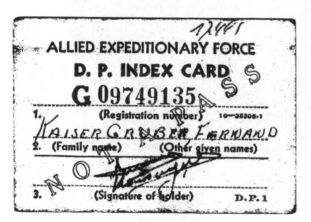

CONSEIL DE GUERRE DE CHARLEROI

AUDIENCE DU 8 JANVIER
(matin)

Une jeune rexiste

━━━━ Marie, 22 ans, employée domiciliée avenue ━━━━ 14, à Binche, a fait partie, durant l'occupation, de la jeunesse rexiste et ensuite de la Jeunesse légionnaire. Tenant compte de son jeune âge, le tribunal la condamne à un an d'emprisonnement correctionnel.

Tentative de dénonciation

━━━━ Berthe, 58 ans, épouse de ━━━━ ━━━━, domiciliée chaussée de Philippeville, 8 à Beaumont, est la mère d'un N. S. K. K. Elle est accusée de tentative de dénonciation. Le tribunal lui inflige 5 ans de prison.

ALLIED EXPEDITIONARY FORCE

D. P. INDEX CARD

G 09749135

1. _____ (Registration number) 16—38305-1
2. KAISERGRUBER FERNAND
   (Family name)   (Other given names)
3. _____ (Signature of holder)   D.P. 1

WELFARE - BEVERLOO

Zwembad - Toegangskaart

Naam KAISERGRUBE   Voornaam Fernand
Sectie F   Blok 52   Kamer
Groep of Kommando Kameroverste

Baddagen en uren :

Zondag. 18.~ – 18.30
Dinsdag: 14,15 – 15.~

The first item in this illustration is an extract from a newspaper showing two brief news pieces: one providing details of being sentenced to one year for having belonged to *la Jeunesse* [the Rexist youth movement]; the other detailing a sentence to five years for 'attempted' denunciation. The remaining two items in this illustration are an index-card and an admission card for the swimming pool at Camp Beverloo.

A medical evacuation card.

Kaisengruber	Ferdinand	4-Strm.	W-1275
Geb. :	Art der Verwundung	Wann Verwundet	Heimat-Anschrift
18.1.23	Gran.Spl.11. U'Schenkel u.re. grosse Zehe I. u.2.Grades	17.2.44 Kessel/ Tscherkassy	Boitsfort Rue Behrens- Heide 256
Laz.-Anschrift	Letzte Einheit	Ersatz-Einheit	Entlassen
Res.Laz.Kudowa /Schles. Teillaz. Haus Franz 6.3.44		1 4 DÉC. 1944	*in Brüssel, am 20.6. in Urlaub. Nr. 4-6-45 /31*

Am 12.6.44 als Schw.vers. nach Prag eingereicht

MANDAT D'ARRÊT

L'Auditeur Militaire :

Vu les articles 35 - - 76 et 133 de la loi du 15 juin 1899 ; 56 du Code de procédure pénale militaire du 20 juillet 1814 ;

Attendu que ~~KAIZENGRUBER~~ Fernand
né à Anvers le 19-1-23
dé à Bruxelles

est inculpé d ~~avoir porté les armes contre la Belgique~~

infraction........ prévue .... par les articles....113 et 117 CP.

Attendu qu'il existe des circonstances qui exigent la détention de l'inculpé, résultant

de la gravité des faits

Ordonne que le dit inculpé sera arrêté et détenu en la prison........Dampremy..........

Approuvé........ ....mots rayés nuls.

Fait et scellé, à ....Charleroi.... le ..18 mai 1945..

SCEAU   Le Substitut de l'Auditeur Militaire.

NOTIFICATION

L'an mil neuf cent ..quarante cinq.. le ..18 mai..

notification du présent mandat d'arrêt a été faite par Nous, Greffier adjoint au Conseil de

guerre ...Charleroi...

à l'inculpé désigné ci-dessus, qui déclare bien comprendre et a signé avec Nous.

L'inculpé,   Le Greffier adjoint,

An arrest warrant.

Appendix II

"Impressions of Beverloo"

(**Tune**: *C'est des choses qu'on dit...*)
By Pierre Châtelain-Tailhade

Presentation

Dear Comrades,
Everything always finishes by changing, even the atmosphere of an internment camp.
  For those of us who knew Beverloo in its most gloomy times, I have written this little song that I shall now present to you:

I

We have been told: It is a model camp,
Such as can be seen nowhere else in the world;
That is true of the fashionable beach and the grand boulevards.
Two or three thousand men live in this domain
And, every day, more arrive,
Even though the administration (it is still a stroke of luck)
Does not advertise the establishment...

II

The first impression is rather nice;
There is barbed wire all around the camp,
There is greenery, air and sand,
A great deal of brick and plenty of wind.

III

A quartermaster, concerned but skillful,
Issues you seven boards, which he counts three times.
That seems like nothing, but it is difficult
To stop at seven when one has ten fingers...
You will find one or another use for these boards,
For, at Beverloo, take it as given,
Where one makes one bed on firewood
One provides heat with one's bed-wood.

IV

Otherwise, the beds are extremely practical,
They will sleep two men with no difficulty.
One on the ground floor (it's nicer)
And the other above (it's more airy).
At rest during the night, things happen
Such that there is no jealousy:
Under the sleeper on high, the mess collapses,
And *Monsieur* wakes up with his buddy below.

V

Wearing a badge is required
And it is the triangle that we know.
Some are large and ostentatious,
Others are shy and almost unobtrusive.
Some, elegant souls, compete with each other
And I know a type, a bit of a braggart,
Who made one of Venetian lace
Decorated with a salmon-pink ribbon.

VI

In this model camp there are artists,
Mechanics, cobblers,
Bricklayers, scribes, painters, dentists.
All skills and all trades.
To the sound of hammers, saws and picks,
When, perchance, a man does nothing
And when he stands to windward, his hands in his pockets
With a tired air… fine, it is a guard.

VII

Messieurs, let us bless the charitable hearts
That formerly looked out for our comfort,
And had these remarkable showers installed
Where, from time to time, we bathe our bodies.
One thing, however, is paradoxical
Regarding these showers – I almost forgot.
It is that when one enters, one is not too dirty,
But when one leaves, one must wash his feet.

VIII

Filled with these memories that one talks of in the evening,
An old-timer told me: "This charming sojourn,
These bugle calls remind me of the time
When I came here to serve my twenty-eight days."
Then, scratching his ear, the poor fellow
Added, "See, what is annoying
Is that, this time here, by all that is holy,
Instead of twenty-eight days, I have to serve twenty-eight years…"

"*Certificat de bonne vie et moeurs*" ("Certificate of good living and morals and of public spiritedness") dated July 1963!

"Blazon"

Those first have the floor who ventured forth,
And not those who are satisfied to sit and judge,
To place their black cap or *Képi* on their calm forehead
And pay with little blood for their career and their food.
                    (Robert Brasillach – 13 January 1945)

"Blazon" by Robert Brasillach.

"Tree"

"An endless march was our life, and, as the wind blows, far from home, we traversed the ground, covered with war."
Schiller (Wallenstein)

"Tree" by Schiller (Wallenstein).